Kurdish Awakening

Kurdish Awakening

Nation Building in
a Fragmented Homeland

EDITED BY OFRA BENGIO

University of Texas Press ◆ *Austin*

First edition, 2014
First paperback edition, 2015

Requests for permission to reproduce material from this work should be sent to:
    Permissions
    University of Texas Press
    P.O. Box 7819
    Austin, TX 78713-7819
    http://utpress.utexas.edu/index.php/rp-form

♾ The paper used in this book meets the minimum requirements of ANSI/NISO
Z39.48-1992 (R1997) (Permanence of Paper).

Library of Congress Cataloging-in-Publication Data
    The Kurds : nation building in a fragmented homeland / edited by Ofra Bengio.
— First edition.
        pages   cm
    Includes bibliographical references and index.
    ISBN 978-0-292-75813-1 (cloth : alk. paper)
    1. Kurds—Politics and government—21st century.   2. Kurds—History—
Autonomy and independence movements.   I. Bengio, Ofra.
    DS59.K86K864   2014
    956.6′7041—dc23   2014019431

ISBN 978-1-4773-0989-6 (paperback)
doi: 10.7560/758131

Contents

Acronyms

AKP	Adalet ve Kalkınma Partisi (Justice and Development Party)
ANAP	Anavatan Partisi (Motherland Party)
BDP	Barış ve Demokrasi Partisi (Peace and Democracy Party)
DDKO	Devrimci Doğu Kültür Ocakları (Eastern Revolutionary Cultural Hearths)
DEHAP	Demokratik Halk Partisi (Democratic People's Party)
DEP	Demokrasi Partisi (Democracy Party)
DTH	Demokratik Toplum Hareketi (Democratic Society Movement)
DTK	Demokratik Toplum Kongresi (Democratic Society Congress)
DTP	Demokratik Toplum Partisi (Democratic Society Party)
GAP	Güneydoğu Anadolu Projesi (Southeastern Anatolia Project)
HADEP	Halkın Demokrasi Partisi (People's Democracy Party)
HEP	Halkın Emek Partisi (People's Labor Party)
ICP	Iraqi Communist Party
JİTEM	Jandarma İstihbarat ve Terörle Mücadele (Gendarmerie Intelligence and Fight against Terrorism)
KCK	Koma Civakên Kurdistan (Union of Communities in Kurdistan)
KDP	Kurdistan Democratic Party
KDPI	Kurdistan Democratic Party of Iran
KDPS	Kurdistan Democratic Party of Syria
KIPI	Kurdistan Institute for Political Issues
KRG	Kurdistan Regional Government

KRG-ME	Kurdistan Regional Government—Ministry of Education
KRM	Kurdish Referendum Movement
LHR	Linguistic Human Rights
MHP	Milliyetçi Hareket Partisi (Nationalist Movement Party)
MİT	Milli İstihbarat Teşkilatı (Turkish National Intelligence Organization)
NSF	National Salvation Front
PJAK	Partiya Jiyana Azad a Kurdistan (Free Life Party of Kurdistan)
PKK	Partiya Karkerên Kurdistan (Kurdistan Workers' Party)
PUK	Patriotic Union of Kurdistan
PYD	Partiya Yekîtiya Demokrat (Democratic Union Party)
RI-ME	Republic of Iraq—Ministry of Education
SCP	Syrian Communist Party
SHP	Sosyal Demokrat Halkçı Parti (Social Democratic Populist Party)
TBMM	Türkiye Büyük Millet Meclisi (Turkish Grand National Assembly)
TİP	Türkiye İşçi Partisi (Turkish Labor Party)
TKDP	Türkiye Kürdistan Demokrat Partisi (Kurdistan Democratic Party in Turkey)
TSK	Türk Silahlı Kuvvetleri (Turkish Armed Forces)
TÜSİAD	Türk Sanayicileri ve İşadamları Derneği (Turkish Industrialists' and Businessmen's Association)
UAR	United Arab Republic
YÖK	Yükseköğretim Kurulu (Turkish Board of Higher Education)
YSK	Yüksek Seçim Kurulu (Turkish High Election Authority)

Foreword

UZI RABI, DIRECTOR, THE MOSHE DAYAN CENTER
FOR MIDDLE EASTERN AND AFRICAN STUDIES,
TEL AVIV UNIVERSITY

Divided among several nation-states and situated at the heart of a complex geopolitical landscape, Kurds constitute the world's largest stateless ethnic group. In recent decades, and especially in the aftermath of the "Arab Spring," they have steadily grown in importance as a political power to be reckoned with in the Middle East. As a result, a wide range of Kurdish issues—political, cultural, and historical alike—now draw intense scholarly interest.

The Moshe Dayan Center for Middle Eastern and African Studies at Tel Aviv University has, therefore, launched the Kurdish Studies Program, which aims to foster in-depth understanding of Kurdish-related issues through scholarly research and debate. The program operates under the supervision of Professor Ofra Bengio, Senior Research Fellow at the Moshe Dayan Center and the author of *The Kurds of Iraq: Building a State within a State?* (Lynne Rienner Publishers, 2012). Open to all researchers and students who wish to take part in this academic endeavor, the Kurdish Studies Program includes, among other activities, lectures, Kurdish language classes, and film screenings. A key aspect is the Forum on Kurdish Society, History and Culture, which brings academicians and students together to discuss central issues in the discourse on modern Kurdish history, society, and culture, for the purpose of stimulating further research. This volume is in the main the product of the academic gatherings that were held in the framework of the Kurdish Forum between 2010 and 2012. The essays collected here are the contributions of well-known experts in the field from around the globe.

Kurdish Awakening: Nation Building in a Fragmented Homeland copes with key questions related to Kurdish nationalism and identity formation in Syria, Iraq, Iran, and Turkey. It includes voices from Kurdish academia, which approach the subject from different angles, and is based on a variety of sources in various languages. As such, I am convinced that it will contribute significantly to the scholarly literature in Kurdish studies.

This collection would not have come to fruition without the concerted efforts of a number of key individuals. I would like to thank my colleagues of the Moshe Dayan Center and the other authors who contributed to this volume. Thanks go especially to Ofra Bengio, who organized the Kurdish Forum and skillfully edited this highly needed and timely volume. I would like to express my appreciation to Dr. Belina Neuberger, who copyedited the entire volume with great accuracy and professionalism. Thanks also go to Duygu Atlas, Dotan Halevy, Assaf Biron, and Hay Eytan Cohen Yanarocak for their invaluable assistance in bringing this project to completion. Special thanks go to Ceng Sagnic for indexing the book and other assistance.

Acknowledgments

An edited volume is a collective endeavor, and I am fortunate to have worked with an impressive group of people who were willing to lend their time and intellect to its success. The Moshe Dayan Center and its researchers headed by Professor Uzi Rabi provided support and intellectual energy. Belina Neuberger labored long and hard with the English and the style. Ibrahim Halil Baran contributed the maps that reflect Kurdish nationalists' outlook. Ceng Sagnic was my right hand in the final and most difficult stage of the book. Jim Burr and Molly Frisinger at the University of Texas Press and freelance editor John Brenner did a great job in editing the book and seeing to its precision and consistency. I am grateful to everyone who has been involved in this project as well as to the many Kurdish friends who are both the silent heroes of this book and the sources for it.

Kurdish Awakening

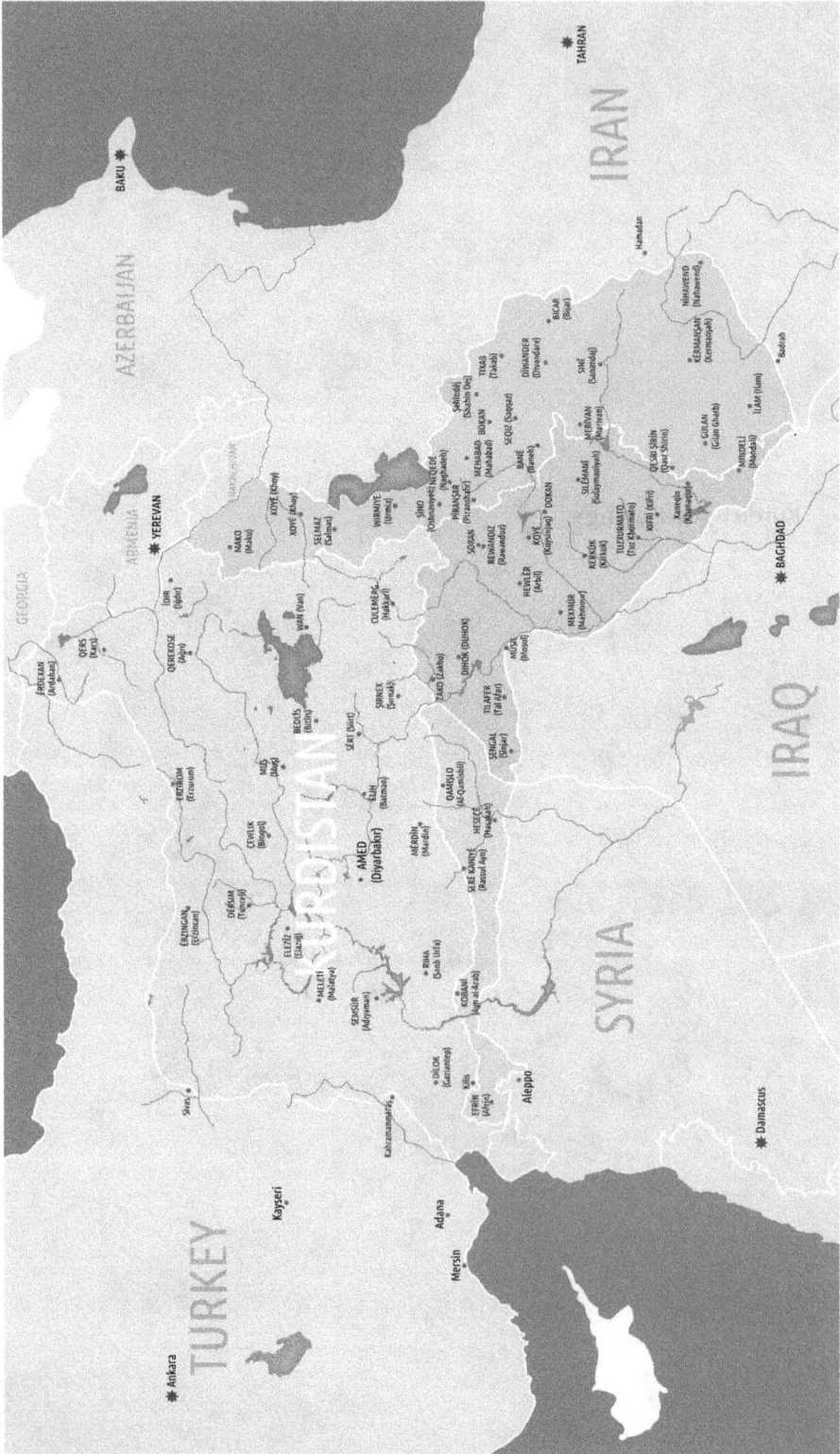

© İbrahim Halil Baran - 2013

Introduction

OFRA BENGIO

This book addresses a crucial issue in a dramatically changing Middle East: the emerging Kurdish challenge to the current state system. While most of the world's attention since December 2010 has been directed to the Arab Spring, the sweeping developments in Greater Kurdistan, which encompasses about thirty million Kurds living in parts of Iraq, Turkey, Syria, and Iran, suggest another geopolitical shift is under way that will shape the Middle East for years to come. This shift provides fresh ways of understanding the historical and sociopolitical underpinnings of the ongoing Kurdish Spring and its impact on the region.

Filling a gap in the literature on the Kurds in many respects, this book provides a panoramic view of all four parts of the fragmented Kurdish homeland and brings to the fore the Kurdish voices that were subsumed for the greater part of the twentieth century by hegemonic, state-centered narratives. The book focuses on the various Kurdish communities and their interactions with host states, delineating the gradual metamorphosis of these community efforts into a coherent national movement with different constituent parts. The volume discusses important aspects of Kurdish nationalism and identity formation not addressed elsewhere — in such realms as literature, gender studies, and constitution making.[1] It also contains broad thematic essays, including comparisons of Kurdish nationalism in Iraq, Turkey, Iran, and Syria with nationalisms of other peoples in Europe, Asia, and Africa; up-to-date research on the historical experiences of the Kurds from the time of their Islamization more than a millennium ago to the modern era; and discussions of the role played by tribalism in modern nation building. The authors use original sources in various languages, including Kurdish, Turkish, and Arabic. The result is an analytically rich portrayal that sheds new light on the Kurds' prospects for autonomy or independence as well as on the challenges they confront in a region that is currently undergoing sweeping upheavals.

This collection of studies focuses on nation building and identity formation among the Kurds in the four parts of Kurdistan. According to the terminology applied in the four host states, these regions are northern Iraq, eastern Turkey, northern Syria, and Kordistan [in Iran]. But Kurdish nationalists employ a different terminology, one that portrays Kurdistan as one unit, Greater Kurdistan, divided among four countries. Hence the terms: *rojhalat* (east, Iran), *bashur* (south, Iraq) *bakur* (north, Turkey) and *rojava* (west, Syria). Similarly, when using names and titles, they prefer the term "Kurdistan" to "Kurdish" in order to emphasize their entitlement to the homeland of Kurdistan. One example is the use of the term "Kurdistan," not "Kurdish," in the names of almost all Kurdish parties, for instance, the Kurdistan Democratic Party (KDP). Another example is the name of the Kurdish entity in Iraq, namely the Kurdistan Regional Government (KRG).

Each of the regions experiences distinct dynamics, in accordance with the sociopolitical developments in the respective countries. Although Kurdistan is fragmented, its parts are nonetheless connected by thin threads, which had grown steadily stronger by the turn of the twenty-first century. At times these parts function as complementary, interconnected vessels, and at other times as rivals and competitors.[2] Recognizing this duality is crucial for understanding the complex relationship between the four parts. This volume sheds light on the complexity of the Kurdish scene, while also bringing to light the mosaic of voices and views it represents.

The term "nation building," which was coined in 1963, refers to a range of different ideas and concepts.[3] For the purpose of this discussion I would like to choose a simple, yet lucid, definition of the term, namely "a wide and diverse range of policies: from state consolidation to identity policies, to democratization efforts."[4] If we take this definition as a basis for evaluating the "degree" of nation building among the Kurds, the conclusion reached will be that the picture is diversified, as the Kurds in each part of Kurdistan have achieved a different degree of nation building. Thus, as demonstrated in this volume, Kurdistan in Iraq is the most advanced, having progressed in all three arenas mentioned above. The Kurds in Turkey are focused mainly on identity policies, while those of Syria are in the initial stages of state consolidation, and in Iran the Kurds are lagging behind in all three categories. Still, it must be stressed that as a strategy all the Kurds have consistently called for democratizing the political system of the state as a sine qua non to guarantee their rights and have refrained from secession.

Indeed, the terms "democracy," "democratic," or "democratization" have become part and parcel of the Kurdish national discourse in all four regions. For example, the major Kurdish parties have names such as the Kurdistan Democratic Party of Iran (KDPI), which was established in 1945, and the Kurdistan Democratic Party of Iraq (KDP), which was established shortly afterward. One party in Syria and one in Turkey actually carry the same name. Similarly, a key slogan in all areas has long been "autonomy for the Kurds, democracy for the state." The chapters included in this volume illustrate, each in its own way, the Kurds' insistence on democracy, since their basic rights were always trampled upon by totalitarian, authoritarian, or military regimes.

Every nation has to cope with the question of collective identity in the process of nation building. But for the Kurds this task was especially challenging and agonizing in the twentieth century. This was so because all the host states attempted—periodically, and with different levels of forcefulness and various rates of success—to divest them from their identity as individuals and as a group.[5] The states employed a number of strategies to achieve this goal. Considering language as a most important symbol of identity and a tool for identity formation, all of them at some point banned the use of the Kurdish language.[6] Concurrently, they implemented policies of Arabization, Turkification, or Persianization, depending on the case in question. In Syria, the government even divested a great number of Kurds of their citizenship. As shown by Duygu Atlas, the most extreme case is that of Turkey. Not only was the written and spoken language forbidden for a long period of time, but the Turkish policy reached a point of absurdity in which the letters Q, W, and X employed in Kurdish were banned and their use could result in criminal prosecution.[7] Kurdish names were forbidden, as was all Kurdish political expression and organization.

If one were to compare Kurdish identity formation in premodern times with that in the twentieth century, one would most probably conclude that, ironically enough, the process was much easier and more natural in earlier times. As Michael Eppel shows in his chapter, "Historical Setting: The Roots of Modern Kurdish Nationalism," even though the Kurds were Islamized early on, they managed to keep other markers of identity intact. Moreover, under Ottoman rule they managed to establish principalities that were autonomous despite falling short of being independent states. By contrast, in the twentieth century the nation-states that were established on the ruins of the Ottoman and Persian empires perceived themselves as extremely vulnerable and therefore felt a need to safeguard their own identity, cohesion, and unity by suppressing the identity of the Kurds. Moreover, they saw it as the right of a nation-state to impose the nationality of the dominant group, be it Turks, Arabs, or Persians, on the ethnic and national minorities. Accordingly, in equating identity with loyalty, the new nation-state rationalized that a person or a group that insists on keeping its identity is disloyal to the state and should be treated accordingly. In other words, the multiculturalism of the pre-modern period was seen as a threat to the modern state. Thus, throughout modern times the struggle was between nation-states and a nonstate nation, the Kurds.

These policies impeded the development of a natural and spontaneous Kurdish identity. As a result, the twentieth century witnessed recurrent attempts to suppress Kurdish identity on both the cultural and the socio-political level, because this very identity seemed to endanger the unity and the integrity of each of the four states ruling the Kurdish homeland.

Like nation building, identity formation also can vary in form and intensity. In the course of modern history, the Kurds have grappled with problems of split identity, dual identity, or crisis of identity. All of them at some point have been forced to choose between their identification with the state or with the nation, which in turn caused an identity crisis. As Nader Entessar and Hussein Tahiri suggest in Part V of this book, the dual identity of the Kurds in Iran, for example, has been a major obstacle for Kurdish nation building there. What is certain, however, is that at the turn of the twenty-first century the Kurds in all four regions were struggling to reclaim the identity that had been denied them over the greater part of the twentieth century.

The Kurds' endeavor to reclaim their identity was bound to meet with strong reactions from the four host states, which feared that any concession in this regard would jeopardize their very existence and lead to Kurdish separatism. In fact, Turkey, the state where Kurdish identity was most repressed, was the state in which reclaiming it was the most agonizing and traumatic. In Turkey, the Kurds were labeled "mountain Turks" until quite recently and all the markers of their unique identity were effaced. It was hence there that the Kurdish backlash was most violent, including terrorist activities by the Kurdistan Workers' Party (Partiya Karkerěn Kurdistan, or PKK), whereas such actions were quite rare in the other Kurdish areas. As Hay Eytan Cohen Yanarocak illustrates in his chapter, even when political parties were formed openly in Turkey in the early 1990s, they continued to have symbiotic relations with the PKK, the military arm, which posed as the champion of the Kurdish national movement as a whole.

At the other pole stand the Kurds of Iraq, whose special identity was recognized by the state and backed by international law in the form of "local languages law" as early as the beginning of the 1930s. Even if it was not always honored, this law accorded Kurds in Iraq the right to use their language as well as some degree of autonomy, all of which conferred upon them important advantages over their brethren in the other countries. Sherko Kirmanj's study proves that the Kurdish identity in Iraq is indeed far more crystallized than in other areas. The Kurdish case in Iraq, where the Kurds have accomplished their greatest achievement, a quasi-Kurdish state, may also suggest a strong correlation between identity formation and state building.

For most of the twentieth century, the Kurds of Syria were a silenced minority. This is not to say that significant changes were not brewing underneath the surface. Theirs was a double struggle, against the Syrian government as well as within the Kurdish community itself. On one level, the Kurds fought to reclaim their Kurdish identity and also, as Eyal Zisser emphasizes in his chapter, to gain the very right to citizenship that had been denied some of them earlier on. On another level, the Kurdish youth initiated an internal revolution against the older generation because they considered it too passive. Jordi Tejel concludes that this could have caused a generational rupture within the community. However, the events of summer 2012, during which the Kurds took control of the Kurdish area evacuated by the Syrian army and declared Kurdish autonomy, put to rest the generational split, at least for the time being.

Reclaiming Kurdish identity in Iran has been more complicated because of the dual identity that has accompanied Kurds there from time immemorial. The Kurds of the Ottoman Empire had engaged in a fight to regain autonomous privileges that they had lost in the mid-nineteenth century, but no such process took place in Iran until the early twentieth century. As Entessar makes clear, the Ottoman-Persian dichotomy thus had a strong impact on the Kurds in the twentieth century. One can indeed argue that the Kurds of Iran are in a dormant situation, but this is not likely to continue forever, as earlier experiences have shown that cross-border influences are almost axiomatic and Iran might not be an exception to the rule.

The Kurdish struggle over matters of identity and nationhood was not just against the four host states, but also within the Kurdish societies themselves. A crucial issue is that of tribalism and its impact on nation building. The received wisdom is that tribalism competes with the evolution of a national movement and more often than not impedes it. However, Eli Amarilyo presents a much more nuanced and complex picture of this phenomenon in Kurdish society, which is quite unique and differs greatly from that of tribalism among Arab societies. In the Kurdish case, tribes and heads of tribes did at times contribute to the process of nation building.

Although this volume has no specific chapter on religion, it is important to emphasize certain religious points raised in different chapters that reflect on Kurdish identity. Like tribalism, religion has played a dual role in Kurdish societies. On the one hand, religious leaders have assumed an important role in galvanizing Kurdish movements. On the other hand, the multitude of religious sects was divisive. Thus, for example, Muslim Kurds persecuted Yezidis to the point where some Yezidi groups disavowed the Kurdish national movement and are now attempting to develop a separate identity of their own. The Kurdish Sunni and Shi'i sects in Iran do not see eye to eye on the issue of Kurdish identity and the Kurdish national project,[8] and there is rivalry and animosity between the Naqshbandiyya and Qadiriryya Sufi Tariqas, whose modern embodiments are the Barzanis and Talabanis.[9]

On another level, it is also important to investigate the role of women in Kurdish society and their contributions to the national project. Here, too, the level of engagement and politicization is not identical in all regions—the most active without question are the Kurdish women in Turkey, who, as Heidi Basch-Harod demonstrates, had to battle for both their place in society and their role in the Kurdish national project. Both of these battles are at the heart of identity issues. The Turkish women's achievements have been quite impressive in comparison not only to other Kurdish societies but also to Middle Eastern ones as a whole.

In the realm of culture and literature, the main problem for writers and artists has been restrictions on their use of the Kurdish language to express their identity and worldview. Kurdish-language writers have faced a threefold challenge: bans by the state on the use of Kurdish, the fact that Kurdish itself has not yet been standardized, and the targeted public's lack of mastery of the language. Yet, even when Kurdish writers chose to write their novels in the language of the state, in Arabic for instance, they could not refrain from identifying with the Kurdish cause. The complexity of dual identity is illustrated clearly in the novels analyzed by Ronen Zeidel.

If Kurdish identity formation and nation building were severely obstructed in the twentieth century, this is all the more true of state building. Though nearly all the wars in the last century held the promise of a Kurdish independent or autonomous state, all of them ended in a catastrophe with regard to the Kurdish national project. The end of World War I, with its 1920 Treaty of Sèvres, aroused the expectations of a possible Kurdish state but ended with the Kurds being divided among five states.[10] The end of World War II brought about the establishment in Iran of the first Kurdish republic in history, the Republic of Mahabad, but this too turned into an ephemeral dream within months. Nor was the outcome of the 1980–1988 Iraqi-Iranian war any better for the Kurds of Iraq, who became the cannon fodder of that war.

This pattern of wars turning into Kurdish catastrophes suddenly changed in the aftermath of the 1991 Gulf War. Initially, the end of this war seemed to follow the old pattern, but by 1992 a Kurdish entity had been created—with all the ups and downs of state building. The Iraqi war of 2003 turned out to be even more crucial for the project of Kurdish state building. The Kurdistan Regional Government (KRG) assumed all the trappings of a quasi-state. In addition to national emblems and state institutions, it drafted a constitution of its own, which is one of the symbols of statehood. As Rachel Kantz Feder explains, this constitution illustrates the complexity of Kurdish-Iraqi relations, while also indicating the big strides the Kurds made on the way to a separate Kurdish state.

Developments in Iraqi Kurdistan began to have synergic effects on all the other parts of the Kurdish homeland as early as the 1990s, but the turning point came at the beginning of the twenty-first century, when transborder influences and even signs of pan-Kurdism became more salient. Thus, in contrast to a more passive stance and fragmented vision throughout most of the twentieth century, the Kurds seem to have become much more assertive, dynamic, and more unified in their vision, including their view of a Greater Kurdistan, at the beginning of the twenty-first century.

A combination of internal and external sociopolitical factors may explain this transformation. The new mass media boosted the use of common language and accelerated communication among Kurds all over the world.[11] Kurdish Internet sites became a tool for circumventing the physical borders separating the four Kurdish regions, spreading Kurdish among the younger generation and in countries where it was banned.[12] The Kurdish discourse was also revolutionized. Old Kurdish names of places, like Hewler (Erbil) or Amed (Diyarbakır), were retrieved as part of an identity revivalism. Rewriting history also became part of the new national undertaking. The Treaty of Sèvres, the Republic of Mahabad, and the chemical attacks on Halabja in 1988 were all added to the arsenal of collective memory and became engraved in Kurdish identity, contributing to the advocacy of Kurdish statehood.

The role of the Kurdish diaspora has also become crucial, especially with the influx to the KRG of intellectuals and businessmen who were willing to contribute their experience and vision.[13] The KRG itself has become the epicenter of Kurdish nationalism, with Masʿud Barzani taking on the pan-Kurdish mantle and the entity becoming the hub of Kurdish politicians, activists, students, entrepreneurs, and fighters from all over Kurdistan.

Concurrently, geopolitical changes also had an impact. The rise of ethnonationalism in various parts of the world contributed significantly to Kurdish self-assertion and to Kurds' demand for self-determination. The American invasion of Iraq in 2003 and withdrawal in 2011 gave another boost to the Kurds, though this may not have been the American intention. The weakening of the host states as a result of regional and international dynamics, including the American withdrawal from Iraq, has changed the balance of power between the state and its minorities, especially the Kurds. The formation of new states, South Sudan and Azawad in 2011 and 2012 respectively, brought home the message that the borders that separated the Kurds in the aftermath of World War I were no longer sacred.[14] The culmination came in the so-called Arab Spring, which helped galvanize the Kurdish Spring in Syria as well as Turkey.

Comparing the experience of the Kurdish national movements with other national movements, Benyamin Neuberger finds great similarities between them. True, the Kurds lagged significantly behind ethnonational groups that managed to establish a state of their own. Still, with the important transformations that are taking place both among the Kurds themselves and throughout the world that surrounds them, one cannot exclude the possibility that one part of this fragmented homeland will eventually manage to proclaim its independence. The most likely candidate is, of course, the KRG.

This volume comprises five parts, each reflecting one aspect or one part of Kurdistan. The first part comprises three general chapters.

In his chapter "Kurdish Nationalism in Comparative Perspective," Benyamin Neuberger presents a comparative analysis of Kurdish nationalism in Iraq, Turkey, Iran, and Syria, relating it to the nationalisms of other peoples in Europe, Asia, and Africa. He analyzes Kurdish national identity, addressing a wide range of topics such as geopolitics, the colonial legacy, the variety of "imagined communities," and the roles of ethnic origin, language, religion, history, territory, and topography. He also expands on the connection of Kurdish nationalism with socioeconomic modernization, "tribalism," conflict and war, autonomism, and secession. Finally, the chapter considers the role of international relations in nationalist struggles.

Michael Eppel's "Historical Setting: The Roots of Modern Kurdish Nationalism" delves into the distant past. Eppel points to the emergence of the Kurds as a collective group, tracing the appearance of Kurdish tribes and emirates throughout Islamic history. He argues that Kurdish nation building and the creation of a national narrative by the modern Kurdish national movement require a closer examination of the collective memory, of the historical developments that affected the development of the Kurdish identity, of language, and of the sociopolitical conditions that preceded the rise of modern nationalism.

Eli Amarilyo discusses "The Dual Relationship between Kurdish Tribalism and Nationalism." On the one hand, he suggests that as a military system, tribalism constituted the primary framework by which the Kurds conducted their national revolts. On the other hand, tribalism as a cultural system, with its proneness to divisiveness, rivalry, retribution, and short-lived alliances, has created an ongoing obstacle to Kurdish national unity. He concludes that Kurdish tribalism is a multifaceted phenomenon, with some characteristics which serve as a basis for the development of national movements and others which constitute a barrier to national unity.

The second part of the book deals with the Kurds of Iraq. In his chapter "Kurdish Integration in Iraq: The Paradoxes of Nation Formation and Nation Building," Sherko Kirmanj claims that despite promising security and economic developments, Iraq remains fragile, primarily because the underlying sources of instability have yet to be resolved. His study examines a number of documents and sources in an attempt to identify the main obstacles to the integration of Kurds into Iraqi society. Kirmanj concludes that the absence of core national values, myths of descent, common memories, shared beliefs and culture, and belief in a common destiny are major impediments to creating a unified Iraqi national identity. Kurdish identity has hence become stronger in the KRG.

In "The Evolution of National Identity and the Constitution-Drafting Process in the Kurdistan-Iraq Region," Rachel Kantz Feder analyzes the various official and nonofficial Kurdistan Regional Government draft constitutions (none of which have been ratified) in an attempt to explore issues of national identity in the Kurdistan-Iraq region after 1991. The chapter investigates how both internal and external political dynamics have impacted the ruling elite's representation of national identity and core issues such as communal membership, ideological orientation, and self-determination. A comparative analysis of the drafts reveals the political elite's deemphasis of the Kurdish right to independence, a development that has widened the gap between the leaders and the many constituents in the Kurdistan-Iraq region.

Ronen Zeidel highlights another aspect of Kurdish collective imagining. Zeidel's chapter, "Forging an Iraqi-Kurdish Identity: A Case Study of Kurdish Novelists Writing in Arabic," is based on four novels by Kurdish writers from Iraq who write in Arabic rather than in Kurdish. For Kurdish writers, writing in Arabic should have been a loaded issue. Yet in looking at the biographies of these and other such prominent writers, their choice of Arabic seems logical. Zeidel uncovers a genuine Kurdish-Iraqi or Iraqi-Kurdish identity, one that is often overshadowed by the more dominant ethnic identities: Kurdish and Iraqi Arab. On the whole, the essay reflects the complexities of multiple identities in a region that is undergoing sweeping changes of identity formation.

The third part of the volume addresses the Kurds of Turkey. In his chapter "A Tale of Political Consciousness: The Rise of the Nonviolent Kurdish Political Movement in Turkey," Hay Eytan Cohen Yanarocak analyzes the history of the nonviolent Kurdish political movement and its symbiotic relationship with the insurgent PKK. While tracing the roots of this movement to the establishment of Kemalist Turkey, the essay focuses on political activism from the 1960s onward. Portraying the Kurdish political parties' struggle for existence in the face of a debilitating electoral system, Yanarocak concludes that this activity has had a positive impact on the Turkish political system. Indeed, it has contributed to the democratization process in Turkey.

In her chapter "The Role of Language in the Evolution of Kurdish National Identity in Turkey," Duygu Atlas examines the centrality of the Kurdish language to the development of Kurdish identity and political movement in Turkey. Following a brief theoretical discussion on the relationship between nationalism and language, Atlas analyzes the changing state policies toward the Kurdish language—from the early Republican period to the 2009 "Democratic Opening" initiative—and the Kurdish responses, in particular the intensification of political activism that the initiative generated. This chapter also deals with the social and political obstacles to language rights.

Heidi Basch-Harod addresses the subject of "The Kurdish Women in Turkey: Nation Building and the Struggle for Gender Parity." She argues that while Arab and Iranian women of the Middle East have for many generations used the state apparatus to negotiate and gradually gain some measure of civil and political rights, Kurdish women cannot claim the same legacy. But paradoxically, she maintains that over the past three decades, tens of thousands of Kurdish women in Turkey have played an increasingly active and essential role in the Kurdish nation-building movement that is taking place within the Turkish state. Parallel to this activism is an ongoing campaign, led by Kurdish women, to promote women's rights in Turkish society as a whole.

The fourth part of the book addresses the situation of the Kurds in Syria. Eyal Zisser provides a panoramic view of this community in his chapter "The Kurds in Syria: Caught between the Struggle for Civil Equality and the Search for National Identity." Analyzing the fluctuations in the relationship between the state and its minority, Zisser maintains that the Syrian state moved from an initial policy of tolerance and patience to one of cultural, ethnic, and national repression under the Ba'th Party. He concludes, however, that the outbreak of the Arab Spring in Syria presented Kurds with a window of opportunity, while at the same time posing new challenges and dilemmas.

Jordi Tejel's study focuses on Kurdish youth. His chapter "Toward a Generational Rupture within the Kurdish Movement in Syria?" posits that in the aftermath of the Syrian uprising of 2011, growing numbers of Kurdish youth felt alienated from the traditional Kurdish parties, either because they wished to establish bridges with their Syrian counterparts, or because they sought a more radical solution to the Kurdish issue in Syria, namely autonomy. Consequently, Tejel claims, the danger of a generational rupture affected all parties, without exception. He maintains that the PKK's successful buildup of the party in the 1980s and 1990s, the Qamishli revolt of 2004, and the 2011 "Syrian revolution" were behind the increasing alienation of Kurdish youth from the traditional political arena.

The fifth part of the book deals with the Kurds of Iran. In his chapter "The Kurds in Iran: The Quest for Identity," Nader Entessar emphasizes that the Kurds have been an integral part of the Iranian sociopolitical mosaic since the time of the ancient Medes. The advent of modern nationalism, however, prompted them to demand recognition of their national identity from the central government in Iran. This drive for self-determination led to the establishment of the short-lived Kurdish Republic of Mahabad in the 1940s. Nonetheless, the Kurds of Iran continued to push for autonomy during the Pahlavi monarchy as well as in the Islamic Republic.

Hussein Tahiri examines the role of the short-lived Mahabad Republic in Kurdish memory in his essay "The Nostalgic Republic: The Kurdish Republic of 1946 and Its Effect on Kurdish Identity and Nation Building in Iran." Tahiri maintains that though it survived for only eleven months, the republic has continued to inspire Kurdish nationalists. At the same time, Tahiri points out that the perceived historical affiliation between the Kurds and Persians and the Iranian state's assimilation policies have contributed to the development of a dual identity among the Kurds of Iran: Kurdish and Iranian. This dual identity has prevented the emergence of a distinct Kurdish identity and the development of pan-Kurdism.

In her conclusion Ofra Bengio analyzes the changing paradigms in the Middle East among the nation-states as well as among the Kurds. She argues that the upheavals in the Arab countries which started at the end of 2010, the withdrawal of the American forces from Iraq at the end of 2011, and the rising hostilities among Turkey, Syria, Iraq, and Iran worked together to weaken the nation-states and strengthen the Kurdish identity and the Kurds' drive for nation building and state building. Thus, the changing geopolitical system in the Middle East together with the strengthening of the Kurdish subsystem might end up altering the geopolitical map of the region that had been enshrined by the Sykes-Picot agreement of 1916.

PART I

Kurdish Nationalism in Comparative Perspective

BENYAMIN NEUBERGER

The Kurdish people still exist and their flag will never fall.
KURDISH NATIONAL ANTHEM

The Kurds . . . had scarcely anything in common with the [Arab]
Sunni Moslems save for the religious bond. Their deep attachment
to their own language and customs made it more natural for them
to look for reunion with their fellow Kurds in Turkey and Persia
than to be a minority in an Arab state.
PALESTINIAN-ARAB NATIONALIST GEORGE ANTONIUS,
THE ARAB AWAKENING

It's time to correct the injustices of the post-World War One settlement.
We are not Arabs, Turks or Iranians. Why shouldn't we have the same
rights as a string of Gulf tribes who declared themselves state?
SAIDI BARZINIGI, PRESIDENT OF IRBIL UNIVERSITY
IN IRAQI KURDISTAN

The Kurdish national question—that of a large ethnonational people divided as minorities within Turkey, Iran, Iraq, Syria, and Armenia—has
haunted the Middle East for nearly a century. In this sense the Kurds are
similar to other divided peoples, like the Berbers in Algeria, Morocco,
and five other African states; the Druze in Syria, Lebanon, and Israel; the
Baluchis in Iran, Pakistan, and Afghanistan; the Bakongo in the Democratic Republic of Congo, the Republic of Congo, and Angola; and the
Basques in Spain and France.

In the Kurdish case the partition of the people between different
states has deep imperial roots. For hundreds of years, they were a "fron-

tier ethnie,"[1] divided between the Persian and Ottoman Empires. Like other peoples they suffered from being crushed by strong neighbors. A comparison that comes to mind is nineteenth-century Poland, which was divided between Tsarist Russia, Prussia-Germany, and the Habsburg Empire, states that were all fiercely opposed to Polish unification and independence.

The colonial and anticolonial context is also important for understanding the nature of the Kurdish plight. Throughout Asia, Africa, and the Middle East, colonialism has created new colonies and protectorates, which eventually became states with "new" boundaries that often split up ethnonational groups. The present partition of the Kurds resulted from the creation of the post-Ottoman new order and its new states, namely Turkey, Iraq, and Syria. Only the Kurds of Iran were not affected by the post-World War I partition of the Ottoman Empire. Nor were they scheduled to be part of an independent Kurdistan, which was promised to the Kurds in the 1920 Treaty of Sèvres.

In many of the postcolonial states of Asia and Africa, the colonial heritage of "artificial," non-nation-based states has brought about violent conflicts between the newly sovereign territorial states and ethnonational groups within these states.[2] In such cases, territorial-statist nationalism opposed ethnic nationalism. Examples abound: The Indian state fought Sikh, Naga, and Tamili ethnonationalism; Nigeria fought Ibo separatism; and the newly independent Congo suppressed Bakongo, Lunda, and Baluba ethnic movements. The Kurdish case is somewhat different because the Kurds did not face a territorial nationalism that was "neutral" in the ethnic sense, but rather a state nationalism dominated by a clearly defined ethnonation—Arabs in Iraq and Syria, Turks in Turkey, and Persians in Iran. The Kurdish conflict with these states was hence bitter and violent, and could be compared with the Tamili struggle against Sinhala-dominated Sri Lanka, or the bloody war of the Africans in Southern Sudan against Arab-ruled Sudan. These cases resemble the Kurdish situation because—contrary to the cases of India, Nigeria, and Congo—the conflict is between two ethnonational groups: one dominates the state, while the other is oppressed by the state. We also have to differentiate divided nations that are dominant in more than one state, like the Koreans in North and South Korea, from partitioned nations that have no nation-state, like the Kurds, Berbers, or Basques. The Somali case makes for an interesting comparison: In colonial times the Somalis were divided between Ethiopia, British Kenya, Italian Somalia, British Somaliland, and Côte Française des Somalis, today's Djibouti. The difference between the

Somalis and the Kurds is that the former are a minority only in Ethiopia and Kenya, while the latter are a minority in all the states they inhabit. One scholar, Walker Connor, draws distinctions among nations that overlap with a state (the Swedes), are part of a state (the Welsh), are dominant in one state but not in others (the Hungarians in Hungary but not in Romania, Slovakia, or Serbia), or are not dominant in any state (the Kurds).[3]

In his seminal *Ethnic Politics*, Milton Esman stated,

> Where the state has been created or captured by a particular ethnic community and operates as an agent of that community, that state becomes a party to ethnic conflicts.[4]

In Iran, Turkey, Syria, and Iraq, the Kurds are involved in a conflict with both the territorial nationalism of the state and the nationalism of the ruling ethnonational groups—Turks, Arabs, and Persians. Ever since World War I an aggressive nationalism has ruled supreme in all four states, making any peaceful accommodation with the Kurds impossible. It will suffice to recall the harsh nationalist regimes of Kemal Atatürk in Turkey, Saddam Husayn in Iraq, Hafez al-Assad in Syria, and Ayatollah Khomeini in Iran.

The failure of Kurdish nationalism to achieve a state has to be seen in historical perspective. In his 1971 classic, *Theories of Nationalism*, Anthony Smith defined both Lithuanian and Croat nationalism as failures because they did not succeed in breaking away from the former Soviet Union and Yugoslavia to create separate nation-states. Peter Alter did the same with Armenian and Ukrainian nationalism in his 1989 *Nationalism*,[5] as did Donald Horowitz with regard to Slovenia, Macedonia, and Azerbaijan in his 1985 *Ethnic Groups in Conflict*.[6] Meanwhile, more than twenty ethnonations have established independent nation-states—including Croatia, Lithuania, Ukraine, Armenia, Slovenia, Macedonia, and Azerbaijan. A comparative historical analysis of Kurdish nationalism thus demands caution as to predicting its future.

Any discussion of national identity raises the following questions: What is a nation? What are its roots? How does it relate to ethnicity? How recent is it? Is it homogeneous? Is there agreement on its boundaries? And, indeed, the Kurds grapple with all of these issues, as did the Germans, Italians, Irish, and Arabs. The nation, says Anderson, is an "imagined community," but not all Kurds thought of the nation in the same way. Some emphasized more objective characteristics like race, language, geography, and culture, while others stressed subjective components of nationhood like feelings, solidarity, consciousness, and aspirations for autonomy and statehood.

Before 1920 there was hardly a sense of Kurdish nationhood in Turkey, Iraq, Iran, and Syria. Loyalties were basically tribal, local, or religious. The Kurds as Kurds were a "non-imagined community,"[7] a divided community—not only between states, but also within states. Nevertheless, their modern sense of nationhood is steeped in deep historical roots, like the Jews, Armenians, Arabs, Japanese, and English, whose sense of nationhood is based on ethnic continuity, ancient history, popular myths of a common origin, and ethnic symbols as well as on language and culture. The Kurdish case closely fits the perennialist and ethnosymbolic theories of nationalism.[8] Although "thinking the nation" is also based on the objective components of language, religion, culture, and race, it includes subjective elements too, so that different Kurds imagined different nations. Some assimilated Kurds saw themselves mainly as Turks, Iranians, or Arabs (such as former leaders of modern Syria, Husni al Zaʿim, Adib bin Hasan al-Shishakli, and the leader of the Syrian Communist Party Khalid Bakdash), just as some nineteenth-century Poles saw themselves as Russians or Austrians.[9] Others saw themselves as part of a pan-Islamist *umma*. Still others, with a strong ethnic identity, thought of themselves as ethnic Kurds within a civic Turkish, Iraqi, Iranian, or Syrian nation. Where ethnicity became highly politicized, they viewed themselves as one pan-Kurdish nation aspiring to a pan-Kurdish state.[10]

Pan-Kurdish nationalism comes to the fore again and again in literature and poetry; in the cooperation between the Kurdish nationalist parties of Iran, Turkey, Syria, and Iraq; in the ties between Kurds from different states in the European diaspora; or in the pan-Kurdish emotional identification with Kurdish achievements (e.g., the creation of the Kurdish Mahabad Republic after World War II) and tragedies (the genocidal campaign against the Iraqi Kurds in the late 1980s).

Two further observations are in place. Kurds with a strong sense of nationhood and ethnicity objected to a pan-Turkish or pan-Arab nationalism because the Kurdish minorities in Turkey, Iraq, or Syria would then no longer exert any influence in a pan-Turanian or pan-Arab state. Indeed, the Iraqi Kurds opposed all schemes that would lead to unification with other Arab countries, and the Syrian Kurds opposed the short-lived United Arab Republic (1958–1961). The opposition of major ethnonational groups to state expansion, which would dilute their role as a dominant force or a meaningful minority, is well known. For the very same reasons, the Kikuyu in Kenya opposed a strong East African

Federation,[11] the Southern Sudanese Africans opposed the idea of pan-Arab unity, and the Chinese in Singapore seceded from the Malaysian Federation.

In addition, Kurdish identification with Iraq or Syria is more complex than with Iran and Turkey. Kurdish participation goes back a long way in the historical empires that preceded the Iranian and Ottoman Turkish states, although Kurds did not participate on an equal basis. The Iraqi state, on the other hand, is a recent, "artificial" colonial creation. Before 1918, it consisted of three Ottoman provinces, which hardly constituted a sensible geographical unit.[12] In this respect, the Iraqi Kurdish situation resembles that of ethnonational minorities in African and Asian states that are also colonial legacies, such as Indonesia, Sri Lanka, Nigeria, and Angola. The same is true for the Kurds of Syria.

Many nations have attempted to base their nationhood on objective characteristics—race, history, language, religion, and geography. In this, too, Kurdish nationalism is no different. The myth of common biological origins (i.e., race) goes as far back as the idea of nationalism. The root of the word "nation" is the Latin *natio* (from *nasci*, to be born, or by implication "of common biological origin.") The conviction that the French are of common Frankish stock—"only a 'true' Frenchman can speak real French," said the nationalist anti-Semite Charles Maurras—or that the English are of Anglo-Saxon and the Germans of Aryan-Teutonic stock represents a mythological, racial-biological nationalism. Turks and Iranians, too, nurtured myths about belonging to a Turanian or Aryan race. We find similar notions about the Kurds being an "Aryan nation," and thus very different from the Semitic Arabs of Iraq and Syria.[13]

History is a basic ingredient of nationalism. While modern nations are based on historical narratives, they also create their own national history. Ernest Renan claimed that the essence of a nation is that all the individuals should have many things in common and also that they should have forgotten a good many of their differences ("l'essence d'une nation est que tous les individus aient beaucoup de choses en commun, et aussi que tous aient oubliés bien des choses").[14] In other words, "forgetting is . . . an essential perspective in the creation of a nation."[15] The French nationalist Maurice Barrès used to say that the fatherland is an ancient cemetery, owned by all.[16] What Barrès implies is that the nation is based on ancient history, which according to him is inscribed on graves, and not on the present-day popular will. Some nations depict a "golden age" in their history books, while others emphasize historical continuity, historical states, and historical events. Historical myths, according to Boyd Shafer, are "not true but real,"[17] and are a constitutive element of any nationalism. Thus, Kemal Atatürk's Turkish brand of nationalism "adopted" the Hittites and Arab history "Arabized" the history of old Mesopotamia and made an Arab hero out of the Muslim-Kurdish Salah al-Din (1137/8–1193), while the French made a nationalist hero out of Jeanne d'Arc (1412–1431) even though there was no French nation in her time. In a similar fashion, Kurdish nationalists used to portray Salah al-Din as an early Kurdish national leader, although he fought the Crusaders as a Muslim, not as a Kurd. They no longer do, since they now realize that he secured nothing for the Kurds. In a similar fashion the PKK (Kurdistan Workers' Party) also "nationalized" the tribal revolts against the Ottomans. As Michael Eppel aptly observes in the next chapter, the Kurdish national discourse borrowed from real and imagined events in the history of Kurdistan.

At its peak, nationalism was closely associated with national language. "One language, one nation, one state" was a widely held nationalist creed. The German nationalist Johann Gottfried von Herder identified every people's right to national autonomy or independence on the basis of his philological research about "folk languages."[18] Italian Giuseppe Mazzini demanded that the political boundaries in his new Europe be established according to linguistic boundaries. Like almost any other nationalist, he was inconsistent when it suited him, as when he demanded that the German-speaking South Tirol be part of Italy because "the landscape there speaks Italian." Modern social scientists like Benedict Anderson and Ernst Gellner have also stressed the role of language in the growth of nationalism. Anderson spoke about the role of "print language" in unifying dialects and creating national languages (e.g., High German or the King's English), while Gellner emphasized the role of literary language in a statewide school system to convey the idea of "homeland."[19] There is no doubt that national customs and culture are also inextricably connected to language.

In the Kurdish case, language has certainly played a major role in attempts to foster nationalism. As early as 1920 Bedir Khan, the secretary of the Committee for the Independence of Kurdistan and a former member of the Ottoman parliament, said, "We have nothing in common with the Turks. . . . The Turks speak a language composed of Chagatay, Arab and Persian while the Kurds speak their own language with its origins from Pahlavi."[20] According to Amir Hassanpour, "nationalists in Kurdistan as elsewhere in the world envision their people as a linguistically, culturally, ideologically and politically united entity. This nationalism emphasizes language as a major indicator of Kurdishness."[21]

In his chapter in this volume, Nader Entessar also stresses linguistic nationhood when he claims that the differences between the Kurdish dialects (Sorani, Gurani, and Kermanshani in Iran, for instance) should not be overstated. David Romano remarks that the young Kurdish generation in Iraqi Kurdistan no longer speaks any Arabic.[22]

These examples clearly illustrate not only how a language contributes to nationalism, but also how nationalism creates, strengthens, or purifies a national language, as has also been the case in post-1789 France, in Greece after 1820, and in present-day Wales and Scotland.

Michael Eppel observes elsewhere in this volume that Kurdish nationalism developed so late because of its "linguistic weakness"—that is, the lack of an ancient written language and the variety of dialects among the different tribes. Denise Natali mentions the lack of a "standardized" language. One should recall, however, that the French, Italian, and German linguistic maps were not much different, at least not until nineteenth-century nationalism transformed a wide variety of dialects into national languages. Sometimes political-national history upgrades a dialect, which eventually develops into an independent national language (like Flemish and Afrikaans, both of which were formerly considered Dutch dialects). This may still be the evolution in Kurdistan, should Iraqi, Syrian, Iranian, and Turkish Kurds each go their own way politically, without uniting in a pan-Kurdish state.

Even the fact that a national leader hardly speaks the national language, as was the case with PKK leader Abdullah Öcalan, whose Turkish is better than his Kurdish, is not unique. Zionist leader Theodor Herzl, the Algerian Ferhat Abbas, and Irish nationalist leaders are similar in that sense.

Religion often plays an important role in nationalism. It divided the Serbo-Croat linguistic-cultural group into Serb-Orthodox, Croat-Catholic, and Bosnian-Muslim nations. It identified the Polish and Spanish nations with Catholicism and Sinhala and Burmese nationalism with Buddhism. Iranian, Turkish, and Arab nationalisms, which vehemently oppose Kurdish nationalism, are all intrinsically linked with Islam. Kurdish identity is also Muslim, so that Islam does not differentiate the Kurds from the Turks, Persians, and Iraqi and Syrian Arabs. Sunni Islam is nevertheless part of the Kurdish national identity and contributes to their differential identity in a largely Shi'i Iran, and since 2003 also in a Shi'i-dominated Iraq. Furthermore, Sufism, too, is widespread amongst the Kurds, much more so than among the other Muslims in Iraq.

Territory, too, is a vital ingredient of any nationalism. According to Anthony Smith,

nationalism is always whatever other aims it may have about the possession and retention of a land; for it is only in and through such possession
that the practical business of nation-building can be carried on. Only in
and on a homeland, too, can ethnic members come to feel their political
fraternity and social cohesion . . . only those ethnies with homelands or
real chances of obtaining a homeland of their own, can seriously pursue
the route towards nationhood.[23]

The national identity of diasporas (Armenians, Jews) was connected
to a "homeland." The same held for divided communities (Italians and
Germans in the nineteenth century). Nationalism and geography are also
connected through a belief in "natural borders"—the Atlantic and Pacific
Oceans for the Americans, the Rhine River for the French. The same
holds for island nations like the Irish and the Japanese. The Swiss, Scottish, Lebanese-Maronite, Druze, Berber, and Tibetan identities are deeply
connected to the mountains they inhabit, and Egyptian nationalism is unthinkable without the Nile Valley. A nation is not just an imagined community, but an imagined community with an imagined homeland—often
with pronounced geographic features.

Geography and topography also play a significant role in Kurdish nationalism. The mountains of Kurdistan sheltered the Kurds and provided
a barrier between them and "others," and have thus become part of their
identity. They clearly share the memory of a "mountain pastoral nomadic
past."[24] The Kurdish nationalist İsmet Şerif Vanlı asserts that "our oppressors have described us . . . as a primitive mountain population."[25] Kurdish
nationalists will retort that they are not a primitive mountain population,
but a proud and ancient people, deeply connected to the mountains of
Kurdistan.

A nation is not based only on real or imagined "objective" components, like ethnic origin, language, religion, history, and territory. It also
needs a "subjective" dimension, with components like solidarity, consciousness, a common will, and aspirations for autonomy and statehood.
Due to this very subjectivity, a nation is a dynamic concept. A population that was not a nation in the past—like the Germans and Americans in the eighteenth century, the Palestinians in the nineteenth, and the
Kenyans in the twentieth—can very well become a nation. Renan rightly
said that "l'existence d'une nation est un plebiscite de tous les jours" (The
existence of a nation is a daily plebiscite).[26] The Kurds were not a nation
in the nineteenth century. Their identity was tribal, local, or communal-
religious until well into the twentieth century, which is why most tribal

rebellions collapsed for lack of support and unity. This does not, however, contradict the existence of a tiny elite with nationalist aspirations for autonomy, statehood, and unity. Theirs was an elite nationalism, a non-nation-based nationalism (that is, nationalism without a nation) that lacked popular support. Only mass support transforms elite nationalism into real, "nation-based nationalism," or in other words, a "nationalism with a nation."[27] For Kurds, this development occurred sometime in the second half of the twentieth century in Iraq and Turkey, and apparently also in Syria and Iran. Pan-Kurdish feelings of solidarity and anger could be observed when Iran crushed the short-lived Mahabad Republic in the mid-1940s, when Iraq waged a genocidal war with chemical weapons against the Kurds in the 1980s, or when Turkey refused to grant entry to hundreds of thousands of Kurdish refugees from Saddam Husayn's military campaigns.[28] Feelings of solidarity are like a subjective test of nationhood, which goes far beyond "objective" commonalities of religion, language, and history.

The subjective dimension of Kurdish nationalism is highly emotional and similar to nineteenth- and twentieth-century German and Eastern European nationalism ("Eastern Nationalism," according to Hans Kohn's famous dichotomy), which emphasized origin, language, culture, religion, and history. It is very different from "Western Nationalism," which is based on the state, rationalism, legality, democracy, and the concept of the social contract.[29]

Kurdish nationalism is everywhere a minority nationalism, opposing the majority nationalism of the Turks, Persians, and Arabs and aiming at survival, self-preservation, and liberation. It is also a liberation nationalism, like the minority nationalisms of the Greeks, Poles, and Irish—or the majority nationalisms of the black South Africans and Indians—in the nineteenth and twentieth centuries, and unlike the oppression nationalisms of the British and French in their former colonies, the Germans in imperial and Nazi Germany, or the Russians in the former Soviet Union.

Kurdish nationalism is a preindependence nationalism, as opposed to postindependence nationalism. The major goals of the latter are mostly the preservation of a traditional polity and historical boundaries (such as with Imperial Ethiopia until 1974), the renewal of the social and political system (the French Revolution, Kemalist Turkey, and Nationalist and Communist China), economic liberation (Latin America vis-à-vis the United States), or interethnic integration and "nation building" (postcolonial Africa). The major aim of preindependence nationalism is independence, or at least autonomy, to be achieved through a struggle for autonomy, secession, or irredenta. This fits both the ethnocultural nationalism of the Kurds and of nations like the Basques, the Québécois, and the Tibetans as well as anticolonial American and African nationalism.[30]

An interesting question that relates to the Kurdish case is the relation between modernization and nationalism. Modernization, which is defined above all by urbanization, monetization of the economy, industrialization, modern transportation, and schooling and literacy, is in general regarded as a sine qua non of modern nationalism. The weakness of Kurdish nationalism before World War II is thus comprehensibly explained by the fact that modernization was limited. But in the Kurdish case modernization could, and did, have an impact in two different directions. It brought about assimilation, as urban, modernized Kurds adapted to the dominant societies, thus strengthening a statist territorial nationalism at the expense of Kurdish ethnocultural nationalism. The role played by urban, educated Kurds in left-wing political parties in Turkey, Iran, Iraq, and Syria is a case in point. At the same time, however, modernization had the exact opposite effect as it inculcated young people with a growing Kurdish nationalism. Already in the late nineteenth century, urban Kurds had established Kurdish schools and associations in the Ottoman Empire; they published Kurdish newspapers and became imbued with European ethnocultural-national ideas. The vast majority of the Kurds nevertheless remained illiterate, rural, tribal, and parochial, while a small, protonational or quasi-national elite grew in the cities. The elite's contact with the governments and with the West profoundly affected nationalism. It is no coincidence that the PKK in Turkey was founded by urban students, and not by traditional leaders. The urban Kurdish bourgeoisie, intelligentsia, and working class were the recruiting grounds for the Kurdish nationalist parties, like the KDP in Iraq, the PKK in Turkey, the KDPI in Iran, and the KDPS in Syria. Hechter, Kuyucu, and Sacks report that even in the European diaspora the PKK succeeded in gaining considerable support.[31]

The dual impact of modernization is well known.[32] Because of modernization some Irish became British, while others became anti-British Irish nationalists. Many enlightened Jews became Germans, French, or Hungarians, while others became Zionists. Similar divisions could be observed among Scottish people, French Canadians, and Czechs in Austria-Hungary.

Why does modernization not necessarily lead to integrative assimilation into territorial-statist nationhood? And why do Istanbul, Damascus, Baghdad, or Tehran not necessarily function as melting pots? These are questions that need exploring. In the city there is intensive competition for the "products" of modernity—money, business, workplaces, schools, and consumer items. In an ethnically pluralistic city, competition for these products easily assumes a dimension of ethnocommunal rivalry, enhancing nationalism on all sides. Another explanation for why modernization exacerbates ethnic tensions is the differential character of modernization: Some regions and populations modernize more quickly than others, and "modernization gaps" between different groups make for growing discontent. For decades, all the Kurdish areas in Turkey, Iran, Iraq, and Syria were more backward, undeveloped, and illiterate than those of other population groups, clearly fueling Kurdish nationalism. Even a gradual closing of the gap, which occurred in the 1990s in Iraqi Kurdistan and in the Syrian al-Jazeera region, has not fundamentally changed the situation. In this case we may see how subjective feelings of neglect and discrimination are transformed into objective competition for the goods of modernity. Modernization also leads to increased social mobility and to the migration of Kurds to non-Kurdish urban centers. Situations like these usually lead to rising conflicts, because there is no friction without contact, and in premodern situations of separation and distance there was no contact.

African examples show that modernization brings together local and tribal groups that share a linguistic-cultural affinity. In this process of deparochialization, large ethnocultural groups or aggregates are created. They are more likely to engage the dominant national group and to aspire to autonomy and independence.[33] The Kurds have indeed been divided and fragmented by locality, region, tribe, and religious community, but modernization has aggregated them, if not into one pan-Kurdish nation, then at least as Turkish, Iraqi, Syrian, or Iranian Kurds.

Another product of modernity is the creation of ethnic institutional structures—cultural associations, Kurdish political parties, armed militias, and, since the early 1990s, a parliament and regional government—which intensify the shift toward nationalism. Institutional segregation increases the visibility and salience of the ethnonation, and modern organizational interests become more and more involved in the national struggle. Iraqi Kurdistan is again the most notable example of this trend, but any future autonomy of the Kurds in the other three countries may still trigger similar processes.

Elections are another feature of modernity that tends to strengthen ethnocultural nationalist mobilization in a multiethnic society by appealing to nationalist feelings. The rise of Québécois parties in Canada, Basque parties in Spain, or Arab parties in Israel illustrate how modern elections may fuel ethnonationalism. Similar processes took place in Kurdistan when ethnocultural parties were allowed. In 1970, for example, the Baʿth Party in Iraq legalized the KDP after signing the March agreement on autonomy. In the wake of the foundation of the KRG in 2003, Kurdish political parties became legal again. In some states, mass support galvanized the nationalist guerrilla movement, such as the PKK in Turkey in the 1990s. There is no doubt that mass support will eventually be transferred into support for a party, should the PKK be legalized. We have seen a similar development with the Irish IRA and its political party, Sinn Féin.

In the context of modernization, the role of the traditional tribe in Kurdish nationalism is of the utmost importance. The Kurdish tribes, like the Arab, Berber, Pashtun, or Yoruba tribes, are relatively homogeneous subethnic units that are part of a larger ethnocultural group. They usually have a shared myth of common origin, a strong common identity, and political, social, cultural, and sometimes quasi-military structures and organizations.

Tribalism has both strengthened and weakened Kurdish nationalism. Fragmentation and rivalry often led to intense infighting and even to collaboration with a hated enemy—the Iraqi, Iranian, Turkish, and Syrian governments. But the overall picture is still more complex. Modern nationalists and traditional tribes also cooperated in Kurdish uprisings—in the Kurdish revolts in Turkey in the 1920s, in Iran in the 1940s, and in the rebellions in Iraq throughout the second half of the twentieth century. In Iraq, tribal leaders like Mulla Mustafa Barzani even led the nationalist revolts, which was definitely not the case in Iran and Turkey, where the leadership of the nationalist movements—the KDPI and the PKK—was not tribal, but urban. The intriguing connection between tribalism and nationalism demonstrates once more that the linkage between modernity and nationalism is complex and does not allow for an easy formulation. The same was true with regard to African anticolonial nationalism in Kenya, Nigeria, Angola, and even South Africa. Modernization can lead to both assimilation and nationalism, and tribalism can strengthen or weaken nationalism.

Conflict is endemic in the growth of nations. It transforms a population with common, "objective" characteristics like religion, language, and culture into an ethnocultural group with a distinctive identity, shared feelings, and common aspirations. The polarization of these so-called subjective commonalities, the determination to maintain or revive a state or to found a new one, are the hallmarks of nationalism. According to Charles Tilly, conflicts create nations and nations also create conflicts.[34] And indeed, the Poles became a nation through their wars against the Russians, Prussians, and Austrians, and the Croats through their conflicts with the Serbs. Greeks became conscious of being Greek because of Ottoman-Turkish repression, and Palestinian nationalism would hardly have existed without its life-and-death struggle with Zionism.

The Kurdish road to nationhood is also paved with bloody conflicts. For over a thousand years the Kurds were conquered and oppressed by Persians, Mongols, Turks, and Arabs. Since World War I they have faced hard oppression by the state nationalism of the ruling Turks, Iranians, and Arabs.

A major cause for conflict that solidifies and intensifies emerging nationhoods is the massive influx of "foreigners" into the ethnic homeland—Spaniards into Basque and Catalan territory, French *pieds noirs* from Algeria into Corsica, Chinese into Tibet and Xinjiang.[35] The Kurds also resent the penetration of Arabs, Turks, and Iranians, especially into economically vital regions like the oil-rich area of Kirkuk. If the central government actually settles "its" people (Iraqi Arabs for instance) in the Kurdish areas and expels Kurds to remote areas outside the ethnic homeland in order to bring about their integration and assimilation, a nationalist counterreaction may be expected. In the 1980s and 1990s, hundreds of thousands of Iraqi Kurds either fled to Turkey and Iran, or were expelled from their homeland to the Arab south. In Turkey, massive ethnic cleansing—through the forced evacuation of twenty-six hundred villages—took place in the 1990s. Oppression of the Kurds was indeed harsh and brutal in all countries, and there was a striking continuity between Kemalist and post-Kemalist Turkey; between Syria under the National Bloc and Syria under the Ba'th; between Reza Shah's, Mohammed Reza Shah's, and Khomeini's Iran; and between Iraq under Faysal, Qasim, and Saddam Husayn. Some weak central governments were more liberal, but, all in all, the general picture is one of oppression in all four states.

Ever since the early 1920s, there has been a regime of ethnic and cultural repression in all four countries. The Syrian Kurds were denied property rights, restricted in their mobility, and prohibited from having their own school system, while hundreds of thousands were denied citizenship. In Turkey, thousands of villages were destroyed, tens of thousands of Kurds were imprisoned, and there were mass expulsions and executions. Nor were Kurds allowed to speak Kurdish in public, to publish or import books in Kurdish, or to found Kurdish parties. Similar restrictions—with the exception of using Kurdish in public places, which was allowed—were imposed in Iran. Iranians also expropriated Kurdish lands, prohibited Kurdish dress, and forbade all schooling or communication in Kurdish.[36] In Saddam Husayn's Iraq, oppression reached barbaric, genocidal proportions. During the 1987–1988 Anfal Campaign, a war of extermination was waged against the Kurds. Thousands were executed by Iraqi death squads and became the victims of chemical warfare. All in all, the number of Kurds murdered by the Iraqi regime may have been close to three hundred thousand. In addition, four thousand villages were destroyed by the Iraqi air force.

Repression of the Poles by the Russians and Prussians, of the Italians by the Austrians, and of the Indians by the British was less continuous, systematic, and harsh than repression of the Kurds in the Kurdish regions. There can be no doubt that this history of genocide, destruction, oppression, and discrimination will have a lasting effect on Kurdish nationalism.

> Modern nationalism was born in Western Europe in the eighteenth century. It spread from there to Central and Eastern Europe, the Americas, the Middle East, Asia, and Africa by way of reaction and imitation. German nationalism rose as a reaction to the Napoleonic conquests, Arab nationalism to Western imperialism, and Indian nationalism to British colonialism. All these expressions of nationalism reflected the goals of European nationalism—namely, national self-determination, sovereignty, unity, national culture, and a return to national history. Nationalism spread through the world by imitation.[37] Nearly all peoples have at some point in time succumbed, in a domino-effect-like manner, to the temptation of nationalism.

The Kurds are no different. Wilson's Fourteen Points had a lasting effect on them, as it did on the other nations of Europe, the Middle East, Asia, and Africa. Wilson's Fourteen Points contained a clause about the need to grant an "unmolested opportunity of autonomous development" to the non-Turkish nationalities of the Ottoman Empire.[38] And, indeed, this did bring about a declaration of disengagement from British rule, a demand for independence, and the decision by the Kurdish nationalists in Iraq to hoist Kurdish flags and issue Kurdish stamps. On the basis of these Fourteen Points, the 1920 Treaty of Sèvres promised the Kurds "a scheme of local autonomy for the predominantly Kurdish areas" (Article 62) and even the possibility of independence

if within one year from the coming into force of the present Treaty, the
Kurdish peoples within the areas defined in Article 62 shall address themselves to the Council of the League of Nations in such a manner as to
show that a majority of the population of these areas desires independence from Turkey . . .[39]

The era of anticolonial nationalism intensified the Kurds' resolve to
struggle for autonomy and independence. They asked themselves why
they should not have the right to what had been granted to Arabs, Indians, and Africans. They looked at the wars of independence of the Jews,
Algerians, and Vietnamese. In this context, PKK leader Abdullah Öcalan
also mentioned the Basques and the Irish.[40]

Kurdish nationalism is certainly a reaction to the nationalism of the
Turks, Iranians, and Arabs. In the Ottoman Empire at the end of the nineteenth century, the development of an ethnonational identity among the
modern Kurdish elite may be perceived as a reaction to the change in the
Ottoman elite, which became more Turkish, ethnic, and national. In independent Iraq, Kurdish nationalism surged as a reaction to Arab Iraqi
wataniyya or pan-Arab *qawmiyya* nationalism. Similar developments could
be observed in Iran and Syria.

The Kurdish national movement in each country was also influenced
by developments in other countries. The Kurdish Mahabad Republic in
Iran boosted Kurdish national aspirations in Iraq. Kurdish rebellions
in Iraq also had a strong impact on Kurdish nationalism in Turkey. The
Kurdistan Democratic Party of Iran (KDPI) led to the foundation of similar parties in Iraq (KDP, the Kurdistan Democratic Party of Iraq), Turkey
(KDPT, the Kurdistan Democratic Party of Turkey), and Syria (KDPS,
the Kurdistan Democratic Party of Syria). The establishment of an effective Kurdish autonomy in Iraq in the 1990s fueled the Kurdish national
struggle in Turkey.

The Kurdish struggle for autonomy or independence in Turkey and
Iraq, and most recently in Syria—though less so in Iran—resembles the
internal ethnic wars of the second half of the twentieth century in Nigeria,
Sudan, Ethiopia, Angola, India, Sri Lanka, Yugoslavia, Rwanda, and Burundi. While some of these ethnic wars were about power in the state (Angola, Rwanda, Burundi), the Kurdish case resembles that of other ethnic
groups fighting for autonomy or secession (Yugoslavia, Sudan, Ethiopia).
Some of the secessionist or autonomist struggles were violent (Nigeria/
Biafra; Sudan/South Sudan; India/Nagaland), while others were not (Slovakia, Slovenia, the Baltic states). The Kurdish struggle is a mixed one.

In certain countries and periods it has been extremely violent, in other times and places more political. At times harsh repression, as in Iran since the early 1990s, makes it difficult to differentiate between the two. Some secessionist struggles are building on existing formal autonomies or federal units (the Baltic states, Croatia, Biafra); others, like the Darfuris in Sudan, Tamils in Sri Lanka, and Oromo in Ethiopia until the early 1990s, have to struggle to establish an autonomous entity. The Kurds belong to the latter group.

There is a consensus among scholars who deal with autonomist and secessionist struggles that although the causes for conflict are mainly internal, the chances of success or failure (especially for secession) rest largely on external forces. The Kurdish case fits this rule perfectly.

The internal causes for the Kurdish national struggles are varied. In all cases the Kurds were perceived to be under foreign or internal-colonial rule, governments were either dictatorial (or, in the Turkish case, dictatorial mainly in the Kurdish areas), and the state's elite circles were closed to Kurds who identified as Kurds—just as it was closed to the Irish in Great Britain, and to the South Sudanese Africans in Arab Sudan. Assimilated or at least partly assimilated Kurds could hold senior positions, but only as Iranians, Turks, Iraqis, or Syrians, not as Kurds (post-2003 Iraq excepted). In general, harsh oppression by foreigners is a blueprint for secession. The examples of many successful secessions (South Sudan, Eritrea, Bangladesh) and unsuccessful ones (Biafra, Darfur, Tibet) come to mind. The brutal oppression of the Kurds throughout the twentieth century has most certainly fueled Kurdish nationalism.

Secession is most likely when two or more large ethnocultural groups inhabit different regions, making for ethnoregional polarization. We have seen similar situations in Nigeria (the Christian Ibo in the southeast against the Muslim Hausa/Fulani in the north), Sudan (the Arab north versus the African south), and Pakistan (West Pakistan versus Bengali East Pakistan). In Turkey, the Kurdish east faces the Turkish west; in Iraq, the Kurdish area in the north faces the Arab center and south; and in Iran and Syria, too, the Kurds have their own ethnic homelands, geographically separated from the rest of the country. If the different ethnocultural regions also reveal significant modernization gaps—as in the Kurdish case—then polarization becomes even more pronounced.

Autonomist or secessionist nationalism is also very likely if the ethnocultural group fears the colonization of its homeland by foreigners—Han Chinese in Tibet, Russians in the Baltics, Arabs in Syrian and Iraqi Kurdistan (in the Kirkuk region), and Turks in the Turkish Kurdish area. If colonization is organized by the central government, the wish to disengage from the state is a quite natural response.

In his book *Ethnic Groups in Conflict*, Donald Horowitz has analyzed secession by looking at the development and wealth of the secessionist regions and the modernization of the seceding ethnic groups.[41] His analysis resulted in four groupings: first, developed regions with modernized ethnic groups (Catalans, Sikhs, Ibos); second, developed and rich regions with nonmodernized ethnic groups (Lunda in Katanga/Congo); third, undeveloped and poor regions with modernized ethnic groups (Berbers in Kabylia/Algeria, Baluba in Kasai/Congo); and, finally, undeveloped and poor regions with nonmodernized ethnic groups (Southern Sudanese, Darfuris, East Bengalis, Moro in the Philippines, Naga in India, Toubous in Chad). Horowitz found that the latter group was by far the largest. The Kurds clearly fit in with this group. Reports about Turkey, Iran, Iraq, and Syria nearly always emphasize the backwardness, poverty, and marginality of the Kurdish areas throughout most of the twentieth century.[42] In such cases, nationalists deem their homeland and people as being dominated, exploited, and discriminated against, and see in liberation through autonomy or secession the way to development, modernity, and equality.

Broken promises of liberalization, democracy, human rights, and national autonomy frequently intensify national struggles, leading to rebellion and warfare. The same is true with regard to written agreements and oral understandings that are not honored. We have seen much of this in South Sudan, Darfur, Biafra, Eritrea, and Tibet. In Iraq, agreements on Kurdish autonomy were broken repeatedly—almost continuously since the 1920s—by the central governments. Recurrent promises of autonomy were also given in Iran, though they were never honored. In Turkey promises were held out in 1922, and broken in 1923, of an "autonomous administration for the Kurdish nation in harmony with their national customs."[43] This nearly routine web of deception and of gaps between words and deeds creates inbuilt suspicion toward any government and a wish to go it alone should the opportunity arise, as it did in Iran in 1946 and Iraq in 2003.

The prospect of success for separatist nationalists is a function of both internal and external factors. The major internal factors concern the relative military strength of the central government and of separatist forces. A strong rebel army (sometimes partly based on desertions from the regular army, as in South Sudan, Bangladesh, and Biafra) will increase the probability, though not the certainty, of success. At times, rebels can mobilize a strong army of their own, without marked defections, as they did in Eritrea. In the Kurdish case, a strong guerrilla army (the Peshmerga), not based on deserters from the army, was established in Iraq.

Another crucial variable is the strength of the central army. The power of the Turkish, Syrian, and Iranian armies prevented any meaningful Kurdish gains in those countries. The recent, quite modest, cultural rights granted to the Kurds in Turkey by the AKP government resulted from PKK activities, but may nevertheless also be attributed to the European Union's pressure on Turkey to democratize. In Iraq, a strong army usually blocked meaningful concessions to the Kurds. Only when the army was relatively weak, as in 1970, did the government grant autonomy to the Kurds, albeit for just a short period of time. The weakening of the army after the first Gulf War in 1991 and its collapse in the second war in 2003 changed the military equation in favor of the autonomists and secessionists. The Kurdistan Regional Government in Iraqi Kurdistan is a visible consequence of the changed military reality.

Another important internal variable concerns the homogeneity of the relevant region. Ethnocultural homogeneity made it relatively easy for Slovenia and Bangladesh to secede. Ethnocultural pluralism and ethnic rivalry in the seceding region were major stumbling blocks for the secessions of Katanga from the Congo and Biafra from Nigeria. Interethnic and intraregional fighting also put major obstacles in the way of nationalists in Croatia, Bosnia, Kosovo, Southern Sudan, and Eritrea, all of which nevertheless achieved independence. In the past, tribal pluralism in Kurdistan has foiled a more cohesive Kurdish nationalist struggle. The weakening of tribalism in present-day Iraq and Turkey has made the Kurdish national struggle more cohesive and effective.

In nearly all cases, external involvement is part of secessionism. In the Eritrean war of secession, the rebels received outside support in the form of weapons, bases, training, and finance—from radical states like the USSR, Cuba, China, Syria, Libya, and South Yemen until 1974, and from conservative states like Saudi Arabia and Kuwait in the years 1974–1991. The central government received strong support from the United States until 1974, the USSR after 1974, and from Israel throughout that period. In the Biafran war, military supplies from Great Britain and the Soviet Union and the involvement of the Egyptian air force proved decisive. Token support for Biafra from China, France, Israel, Portugal, and South Africa could not match the strong involvement of the Soviets, British, and Egyptians. The Bengali war for independence from Pakistan was decided by the Indian invasion of East Bengal (today's Bangladesh).

The Kurdish struggle in Iraq in the 1960s and early 1970s would have been unthinkable without financial, logistical, and military support by Iran, the United States, and Israel. In the 1990s, and even more so after 2003, American support was crucial in solidifying Kurdish autonomy or quasi-independence.

The reasons for external support may include ethnic affinity (Indian involvement in Bangladesh, Ugandan support for South Sudan), irredentist-separatist "retaliation" (Iranian support for the Iraqi Kurds as retaliation for Iraqi support of the Arabs in Iranian Khuzestan), or more often real-politik. Thus all four states of Greater Kurdistan supported Kurdish guerrillas in the neighboring states, although only occasionally and up to only a certain point, in order to weaken their regional rivals. The United States and the Soviet Union supported the movements that fought against their geostrategic Cold War rivals such as pro-Western Turkey or pro-Soviet Iraq.

Only rarely will an external power go to war to assist secessionists in another country—India in Bangladesh and Somalia in Ethiopia are notable exceptions. Foreign powers often "betray" the secessionists when their own interests change. The most famous case is the sudden withdrawal of Iranian support for the Iraqi Kurds, after Iran signed the 1975 Algiers Accord with Iraq. The accord brought about the cessation of Iranian (and covert American and Israeli) support of the Iraqi Kurds, in exchange for Iraqi concessions in the disputed waterways of the Shatt al ʿArab. During the Cold War, the Americans and the Soviets supported or opposed the Kurds according to the "coloration" of the governments' pro-Western or pro-Soviet sympathies. The United States betrayed the Kurds in 1991 when they called on all Iraqis, including the Kurds, to rise against Saddam Husayn during the first Gulf War, and then abandoned them for a pragmatic political reason—the wish to contain Iran by "balancing" its power. Later on, the United States was to "compensate" the Kurds by establishing a no-fly zone after the war, which made the creation of the KRG possible. When Henry Kissinger was asked about the morality of the 1975 American betrayal of the Kurds, he cynically replied that "covert action should not be confused with missionary work."[44] The Soviets, too, time and again betrayed the Kurds. They supported the Kurdish Mahabad Republic in post–World War II, but withdrew their support in exchange for lucrative oil concessions. They indirectly supported the Kurds in Iraq in the 1950s by granting Mulla Mustafa Barzani shelter in the Soviet Union,[45] but later on gave their support to Saddam Husayn, whose regime was marked by oppression and massacres.

The opportunity structure of nationalist-secessionist or autonomist movements depends on a few key variables: on the one hand its unity, the quality of its leadership, the extent to which it enjoys the support of the people, and its international legitimacy; on the other hand the stability of the political regime, its cohesiveness, and the strength of its military machine.

According to these variables, today the opportunity structure of the Iranian Kurds looks quite bleak. They are institutionally weak, lack strong leadership, have a weak military, and lack international legitimacy and support. The situation of the Kurds in Turkey is different because of Turkey's European connections. The Kurds in Turkey succeeded in bringing the Kurdish question to the forefront of Turkish politics. Nevertheless, in both Iran and Turkey the governments that oppose the Kurds are strong militarily and determined not to make any meaningful concessions. Furthermore, society in Iran, and certainly in Turkey, is not closed to assimilating Kurds, which prevents all modernizing Kurds from uniting in national autonomist or secessionist movements.

The Iraqi situation is completely different, at least since the early 1990s. The opportunity structure has become more favorable to the Kurds than ever before. They are relatively united, have a recognized leadership, possess a formidable military force, and receive strong foreign support. The Iraqi government is weak and fragmented, and the Kurds have succeeded in establishing a strong foothold in it. The Iraqi military, which has Kurdish Trojan horses in its ranks, is too weak to reconquer Iraqi Kurdistan. In order not to antagonize Turkey and Iran, the Kurds have to tread carefully by abstaining from a declaration of formal independence too early or at the wrong moment. The turmoil in Syria in 2011–2012 shows that the opportunity structure may change there, too. During the internal war in Syria, which started in February 2011, the Kurdish Democratic Union Party, which is close to the Turkish PKK, has gained de facto control of the Kurdish areas bordering on Iraq and Turkey. While in Iraq the recapturing of the KRG area by the Iraqi army is highly unlikely, this will not necessarily be the situation in a post-Assad Syria.[46] In all likelihood, the disintegration of the Islamic regime in Iran would also be a precursor to profound changes. The most difficult case still seems to be Turkey, although even there the Kurds have recently achieved some cultural rights that they had not enjoyed for nearly a century.

A close look at other areas in the world shows that there is no determinism in nationalist struggles. National movements are often brutally crushed, as happened in Biafra and Tibet, but in a different political and international constellation, they may rise again and even achieve historical breakthroughs, as happened in the former Soviet Union and Yugoslavia, South Sudan, and Eritrea. The circumstances are quite different in each of the countries we have discussed, so that the solution to the Kurdish national question may also vary from country to country. Nevertheless, the winds of change *are* blowing in the Middle East, and one should not take lightly the determination of the Kurds to seize the opportunity to achieve meaningful autonomy or independence.

Historical Setting: The Roots of Modern Kurdish Nationalism

MICHAEL EPPEL

Kurdish nationalism as a political ideology and national movement is a modern phenomenon. However, the development of collective identities, signifiers, cultural traditions, and self-awareness in the premodern era constitutes a wellspring for the construction of a modern nationalist discourse and modern "imagined communities." Understanding the growth of national movements and the sources used to construct a national narrative demands a close examination of historical, social, political, cultural, and linguistic developments.

The first expressions of modern Kurdish nationalism appeared in the late nineteenth and early twentieth centuries. Shaykh ʿUbaydullah, who rebelled against the Ottoman Empire in 1878 and two years later invaded the Urmiya region in Iran, spoke about Kurdish independence. His attitude toward the Ottoman Empire was ambiguous, and his motivations and conduct were traditional, tribal, and feudal. Still, on some occasions ʿUbaydullah used the term "Kurdish nation"—"taife Kurdiye"—and expressed his wish to unify the Kurds and create a Kurdish state under his rule.[1] For his part, the poet Haji Qadir Koyi (1817–1897) contributed to the growth of a Kurdish nationalist consciousness by editing and organizing the republication of the epos *Mem u Zin* by Ahmad-i Khani, which was first published in 1695. *Mem u Zin* contained expressions of an independent Kurdish identity and hopes for a Kurdish ruler.[2] It was adopted by nationalists as a saga representing Kurdish nationalism. Another step toward Kurdish self-awareness was the publication in Cairo of the first newspaper in the Kurdish language, *Kurdistan*, in 1898. Kurdish nationalism was shaped by the process of modernization and the region's encounter with the West during the Ottoman and Iranian rule of Kurdistan. The growth of Kurdish nationalism and national discourse were nevertheless related to both a historical and a mythological Kurdish identity and to its development and role throughout pre-Islamic and Islamic history.

The purpose of this chapter is to present the historical developments and the sociopolitical structures in Kurdistan, and to point out the emergence of the Kurds, of the signifiers *kurd* and *akrad* and of Kurdish identity, Kurdish tribes, and Kurdish emirates throughout Islamic history.[3] It may be viewed as the history of Kurdistan and of the historical developments that have led to the emergence of modern Kurdish nationalism, just as the Gauls, Franks, and Merovingians are perceived as part of the history of France, Prince Mieszko and the House of Piast of Polish history, Richard the Lion-Hearted of English history, and the principalities of Kiev and Moscow as signaling the beginning of Russian history. True, the concept "national" cannot be applied here since the concept of modern nationalism developed only in modern capitalist society. However, premodern events—real or invented—as well as personalities, legends, and popular myths enabled modern national movements to construct a modern national discourse. The growth of a Kurdish national identity was based on a major development in Kurdistan that had been identified as Kurdish: Kurdish tribes, emirates, poetry, and oral traditions. Kurdish ethnic identity and the seeds of Kurdish statehood—in the form of autonomous emirates that prevailed since the beginnings of Islam until the nineteenth century—created conditions for the growth of a modern national movement. But the demise of the Kurdish emirates in the first half of the nineteenth century; the slow process of modernization and limited growth of modern social classes, and their inclination toward integration or even assimilation with the developing Turkish, Arab, and Iranian identities; and the lack of a written Kurdish tradition and standardized high Kurdish language were the main reasons for the weakness and the late development of the Kurdish national movement. Kurdish nation building and the creation of a national narrative by the modern Kurdish national movement require a closer examination of Kurdish identity, of the collective memory and historical developments that affected the development of the Kurdish language, and of the sociopolitical conditions that preceded and distinguished the dawn of modern nationalism. The international arena and the redesigning of the map of the Middle East after World War I, which left the Kurds without a state, as well as the prevailing social characteristics and processes in Kurdish society created the conditions in which a Kurdish national movement could develop. Nonetheless, understanding the origins of the movement requires an in-depth study of the history of Kurdistan and the Kurds, and of their protonational characteristics, i.e., their characteristics prior to the growth of the modern national movement.[4]

The Kurds and Kurdistan and the Growth of the Islam

The medieval Muslim chronicles and history books, as well as modern studies dedicated to the rise of Islam and its conquests in the seventh century, have primarily addressed the confrontation between the Muslims and their powerful adversaries in the Sassanid Persian and Byzantine empires, which possessed centralized government, military power, their own religions, and a written culture. However, in addition to their struggles against well-organized states and cohesive cultures, the Muslims conquered the mountainous areas north and northeast of the Tigris and Euphrates plains and the highlands of Iran, encountering *al-akrad*, nonliterate pastoral and agricultural tribal populations lacking central authority and speaking a variety of Kurdish dialects related to Persian. It was a meeting between an expansionist migratory wave of Arabic-speaking, pastoral tribes from the Arabian and Syrian deserts that were unified by a mobilizing, supratribal, Islamic ideology and pastoral mountain-dwelling tribes that spoke Kurdish dialects and lacked a dominant supratribal political authority and organized religious ideology.

Islam, which spread among the oasis-dwellers and the pastoral nomadic tribes of the Arabian Peninsula during the seventh century, already constituted a source of authority and legitimacy for the supratribal leadership and provided ideological motivation for expansion beyond the tribes' traditional areas of seasonal migration. The Kurdish tribes, on the other hand, had not developed or adopted a unifying faith and lacked any kind of unified leadership or message. Whereas there was a growing linguistic cohesion in the Arabian Peninsula even before the appearance of Islam— further accelerated by the spread of Islam and Islamic culture through the medium of Arabic—no such parallel linguistic development took place among the Kurdish tribes, and none of the Kurdish dialects gained prominence. In other words, the unifying linguistic basis was nonexistent.

The term "Kurds" (*akrad*) as a signifier of collective Kurdish identity did not constitute a basis for a stable supratribal or supralocal organization aspiring to achieve sovereignty or deepen the solidarity between the various Kurdish tribes. The Arab tribes, while admittedly preserving their identities, benefited from a considerable advantage over tribes they encountered during their expansion raids: the fact that they had a faith, an organizing principle, and a supratribal leadership with religious legitimacy. The development of a Muslim "imagined community" gave the Muslims power over population groups in which no similar process had taken place. Whereas Islam fostered the initial stages of Arab state development (at least until the end of the Umayyad Caliphate), no such development occurred among the Kurdish tribes.

The collective signifiers *kurd*, *akrad*, and *ma'qal al-akrad* (the fortress of the Kurds) appear in al-Baladhuri's (d. 892) book *Futuh al-Buldan* [The conquests of the countries], the earliest book to discuss the traditions of Islamic conquests. According to al-Baladhuri, the Muslims fought the Kurds throughout the conquests of Persia and the areas of Mosul and Azerbaijan. The Kurdish tribes apparently fought on the side of the Sassanid Persian army. After their conversion to Islam and the establishment of the Islamic state, the Kurds continued to rebel and launch attacks against travelers and merchants wherever the central government declined in strength or was weakened by rebellions and domestic struggles.[5]

Al-Tabari (838–932), the greatest of all early Muslim historians, refers to the Kurds in seventeen of the thirty-nine volumes of his book, *Ta'rikh al-rusul wal-muluk* [The history of prophets and kings], commonly known as the "History of Tabari." The reference is obviously to a mostly nomadic, pastoral tribal population, which was difficult to control and showed a strong tendency toward disobedience to the central government. Al-Tabari first mentions the Kurds as having rebelled in the third year of the reign of Caliph 'Uthman in the area of southern Loristan, near the Qarun River.[6] Like al-Baladhuri, al-Tabari points out that at the time of the Muslim conquest of Iran, the Kurds fought alongside the Persians against the Muslim advance in the areas of Fars and Ahwaz.[7] Like its predecessors, the Byzantine state and Safavid Persia, the Muslim state had difficulty imposing an effective rule upon the rebellious Kurdish tribes, due to their belligerency and geopolitical location between the Muslim and the Byzantine states.

To date, no historical sources have been found that address the issue of religion among the Kurds prior to the rise of Islam. It is quite possible that the majority of the population in Kurdistan was Zoroastrian and Manichaean, with some Christian presence. Proof of Zoroastrianism among the Kurds can be found in an anonymous poem, apparently dating from the seventh or eighth century and written in a Kurdish dialect in Aramaic script, which bemoans the destruction of the Zoroastrian temples by the Arabs in Shahrizur in southern Kurdistan.[8]

Most Kurds converted to Islam during the Umayyad and Abbasid periods. Nevertheless, the physical isolation in mountainous Kurdistan and the loose government of the Muslim state facilitated the preservation of pre-Islamic traditions and beliefs and enabled the development of heterodox sects, such as Ahl al-Haqq or the Yezidis, and the establishment of Sufism as a common religious and social component of Kurdish society.

Admittedly, the Kurdish tribes entered an Islamic religious and cultural world that was to a large extent based on the Arabic and Persian languages. The hegemony of Arabic as the language of Islamic religion, law, and culture and the dominance of Persian and Turkish in the Muslim states and in the areas of cultural and literary creativity throughout the Muslim world relegated the Kurdish dialects to a colloquial status. The hegemony of the Arabic script and the absence of a unique Kurdish alphabet promoted the dominance of the former. The lack of a written Kurdish language placed the local Kurdish dialects in a position of inferiority by comparison to the Persian language, a well-formulated language with a rich written tradition that had adopted the Arabic alphabet and had managed to adapt, survive, and develop within Islam.

Kurdish poetry, mainly in the Gurani dialect, flourished intermittently until the eighteenth century. However, in the absence of social and political forces with an interest in fostering the Kurdish language, it did not become a basis for the evolution of a literary standardized Kurdish language. This linguistic weakness also impeded the development of a modern Kurdish national movement and a unified national consciousness in the twentieth century.[9]

The Tribal-Feudal Kurdish Dynasties and the Waves of Turkish Conquest

Between the seventh and sixteenth centuries, Kurdistan was conquered several times by waves of tribal migrations and conquests—Arab, Turkish, Khwarizm, Mongol, and, later on, again Turkmen—which destroyed its social structures.

The Muslim conquest, the Seljuk Turkish takeover, the Mongol conquests, and the takeover by Turkoman clans—the Qaraqoyunlu (the Black Sheep) and the Aqqoyunlu (the White Sheep) in the fifteenth century—were carried out by great migratory waves of nomadic tribes that were organizationally and politically superior to the Kurds. The Kurdish population was not motivated by expansionism on a broad scale; there was no mass movement by tribes toward new, distant living areas beyond the mountains of Kurdistan, nor did the tribes develop strong, organized political structures motivated by a religious ideology. Kurdish tribes were actively involved in the domestic struggles of Seljuk rulers, and when the central Seljuk rule was weakened by ongoing crises, they swept down from the mountains and mountain fortresses to launch raids on settlements and highways.

Between the rise of Islam in the seventh century and the conquest and division of Kurdistan by the Ottoman Empire and the Safavid Empire in the sixteenth century, the Kurds played a role in Islamic history. They did so both as feudal-tribal dynasties involved in the power struggles of the ruling Islamic states, the centers of which were outside Kurdistan, and as members of mountain-dwelling tribes or mountainous tribal emirates that sought to extricate themselves from the yoke of a central government. As in the early Muslim period, the Kurds remained internally divided, and no Kurdish emirate or dynasty was able to dominate or unify significant parts of Kurdistan. The Kurdish tribes lacked an organized religion, a standardized written language, and a political supratribal authority. Though none of the Kurdish emirates and dynasties aroused Kurdish solidarity, they were nevertheless perceived as Kurdish, and helped preserve Kurdish signifiers and Kurdish identity.

The weakening of the Abbasid Empire from the mid-ninth century onward and its inability to impose an effective rule created the conditions for the strengthening of Kurdish feudal-tribal dynasties. The struggles within the Buwayhid dynasty, the Persian dynasty that became a major force in Baghdad and in the Abbasid Empire, and the beginning of its infiltration by Turkish tribes constituted the backdrop for the rise of the Kurdish Hasanwahid (*hasanwiya* in Arabic) dynasty (959–1095), which centered on the Barzikani tribe.[10] The areas under its control extended from southeast Azerbaijan to the Shahrizur area in the Zagros Mountains, east of Shatt al-ʿArab. This dynasty was vanquished by another Kurdish dynasty, the Annazid or Banu Annaz (990–1116), which was located in the Kermanshah and Shahrizur areas, but extended as far as Mandali, in the mountains east of the Lower Tigris and on the border between modern-day Iraq and Iran.[11]

The mid-tenth century saw the rise of the Shaddadid (Shadyanid) dynasty (951–1075), whose control extended from the Arax and Kura Rivers in the southeastern and central Caucasus to Hakkari and to areas now included in northern Iraq and on the border between modern-day Turkey and Iran.[12] Its main cites were Ganja and Dvin.

In Western Kurdistan, the end of the tenth century marked the ascent of the Marwanid (Banu Marwan) Kurdish dynasty (984–1083). It was centered in Mayyafariqin and Diyarbakır (Amed in Kurdish) and also took control of Nasibin and Jazirat bin ʿUmar.[13] The most important period was the rule of the Marwanid ruler Nasir al-Dawla Ahmad Abu Nasir bin Marwan (1011–1061) in Diyarbakır, under the formal sovereignty of the Abbasid Caliph and de facto directly subordinate to the strongman of the caliphate, Sultan al-Dawla the Buwayhid (1012–1021).[14] The long years of Nasir al-Dawla's reign were characterized by economic and cultural growth. Mosques, hospitals, and bridges were built with his support, and *ʿulamaʾ* and poets were active in his court, which was visited by envoys from Fatimid Egypt and from the Byzantine emperor.

The fall of the Kurdish dynasties resulted from the growing migration of Turkish tribes to the Abbasid Empire and the transformation of the Turkish Seljuk dynasty into a predominant force in Baghdad and throughout the empire. Between 1020 and 1041, Turkish tribes invaded areas with a Kurdish population in Azerbaijan, in the Hakkari area, and in the cities of Mayyafariqin, Hamdhan, and Diyarbakır.[15] In 1054–1055, the Marwanid ruler Nasir al-Dawla bin Marwan accepted the sovereignty of the Seljuk ruler Tughril Beg. A year later, the ruler of the Shaddadid dynasty in Ganja, in the southern Caucasus, also swore allegiance to the Seljuk ruler.[16]

The turning point in the takeover of the Abbasid Empire and areas of Kurdistan by the Turks was the Battle of Malazgird (Malazkird) in 1071, when the Seljuks vanquished the Byzantine army and proved that they were the major Muslim power.[17]

In 1075, the Seljuks, led by Sultan Alp Arsalan, vanquished the Shaddadid dynasty (another branch of that dynasty, in Ani in the Western Caucasus on the Armenian border, prevailed until 1195). The Marwanid dynasty also collapsed and fell to the Seljuks. In 1083, the last cities and fortresses controlled by that dynasty in the area of Jazirat bin ʿUmar were conquered.[18] Until the end of the twelfth century, members of the Marwanid dynasty were appointed as governors of cities or provinces; they did not, however, serve as autonomous rulers, but were subject to Seljuk sovereignty. To quench the Kurds' ongoing rebelliousness, the Seljuk rulers had to retake the Kurdish fortresses time and again, forcing the Kurds back into remote mountain areas in order to secure the main highways. In his early twelfth-century chronicles, the historian Ibn al-Athir, who was loyal to the Zangi dynasty of Turkmen rulers, described the successes of Atabeg ʿImad al-Din Zangi in the conquest of numerous Kurdish fortresses in the areas of al-Jazira, Mosul, and Hakkari (Hakariya) in 1122–1123 and 1142–1143, and in the Tikrit area in 1133–1134.[19]

Although the Kurdish dynasties collapsed with the rise of the Seljuk Turks in the eleventh and twelfth centuries, Kurdish families, especially those who found positions in the military forces led by the Turkish dynasties, achieved power under the Seljuk rulers. These were the circumstances that marked the rise of the family of Salah al-Din al-Ayyubi, from the city of Dvin in the southern Caucasus, where they had apparently served the Shaddadids. After the fall of the Shaddadid dynasty, the Ayyubis emigrated from Dvin and served the Seljuks. Salah al-Din's grandfather was appointed governor of the city of Tikrit on behalf of the Zangi ruler.[20]

In the Muslim world, Salah al-Din is perceived as the Muslim ruler who repelled the Frankish Crusader invasion. Salah al-Din became an admired historic figure among Sunni Muslims. He became an Arab national hero in the twentieth century—specifically, the national hero of Syrian Arab, Iraqi Arab, and Egyptian Arab nationalism—and was admired by Arab nationalist leaders Jamal ʿAbd al-Nasir and Hafiz al-Asad, and was a model for Saddam Husayn. Although the twentieth-century Kurdish national movement promoted the myth of Salah al-Din as the Kurdish national hero who saved Islam from the Crusaders, some Kurdish nationalists despised him for not using his strong position to advance the Kurdish cause and a Kurdish state.

The Ayyubids were the first Kurdish dynasty in Islamic history to gain real power. Their power base, however, was in Egypt, far from Kurdistan and other Kurdish-populated areas. The collective identity of the Kurds who served as soldiers and officers in the army of Salah al-Din was not "national" in the sense of modern nationalism, which aspires to statehood on the basis of a national identity and a modern national "imagined community"; rather, it was Islamic, and the Kurds' loyalty was to Islam, to their tribes, and to Salah al-Din. However, the distinction between the Kurds and the Turks, and in some cases even the Kurdish solidarity demonstrated toward the Turks in the Zangi and Ayyubi army, played a role in the struggles between its various commanders. Because of it, Salah al-Din inherited the command of the Zangi army in Egypt after the death of its commander Shirkua, thanks to the solidarity among the Kurdish commanders against the Turks.[21]

The portrayal of the Kurds in the great chronicles of Ibn al-Athir (*Al-kamil fi al-ta'rikh*) and of Ibn Khaldun (*Ta'rikh al-ʿalamat*), who drew his information from al-Athir, presents a lively picture of a pastoral, tribal society and tribal-feudal dynasties, of mountain fortresses and small, scattered cities. The Kurds are mostly mentioned in the context of "Arabs and Kurds"—not in a modern national-ethnic sense, but rather in a sociological sense—as quarrelsome, rebellious pastoral-nomadic tribesmen and feudal dynasties that ruled cities like Dvin, Ganja, Hakkari, and Diyarbakır.[22]

The Division of Kurdistan between the Ottomans and the Safavids in the Sixteenth Century

A profound change took place in the history of Kurdistan in the sixteenth century, when the area was conquered and divided by two strong rival forces: the Sunni Ottoman Empire and Iran under the Shiʿi Safavids. At the time, the Shiʿi Iranian state, which had coalesced in 1501 under Shah Ismail, put an end to the Turkmen's Aqqoyunlu dynasty, which had controlled most of Kurdistan since its victory over the Qaraqoyunlu and its Kurdish allies in 1476.[23] The coalescence of the Shiʿi Iranian state and its affinity with the Kizilbashis, a Sufi stream closely related to Shiʿi Islam and enjoying considerable influence among Turkmen tribes in Anatolia, posed a challenge to the Ottoman Empire. In view of the Shiʿi Iranian and Kizilbashi threat, Sultan Selim I opened a new front in the east, in addition to the ongoing wars in Europe against the Christian states, primarily the Habsburgs. The Ottoman-Iranian struggle, which was to go on for more than three hundred years, from 1514 to the Treaty of Erzurum in 1823, would be fought on the soil of Kurdistan. In view of the Ottoman-Kurdish hostility toward the Shiʿi Safavids and their allies, the Turkmen Kizilbashis, conditions arose for cooperation between the Kurdish emirs and tribes and the Ottoman Empire.

Cooperation between the Kurds and the Ottomans was cemented by the Kurdish statesman, cleric, and courtier Mevlana Idris Bidlisi (Bitlisi) who was the secretary of the last Aqqoyunlu ruler before that dynasty was wiped out by the Safavids, after which he went on to serve in the court of Sultan Selim I.[24] Under the command of the sultan, Bidlisi attempted to convince the Kurdish emirs to support the Ottomans. The majority of Kurdish emirs and tribes preferred the Ottomans because they were powerful, and because there was a commonality of interests against the Kizilbashis. Other contributing factors may have been the Sunni and decentralized nature of the Ottoman rule and the hope that the Kurds would be able to establish autonomy under that rule. As they saw it, the Ottoman policy of encouraging cooperation with the existing emirs and strongmen in Kurdistan was preferable to the Safavid policy, which sought to remove the strong Kurdish emirs and ruling clans, and promote members of marginal families that would be dependent on the Safavid rulers.

Following the Ottoman victory over the Safavids in the Battle of Chaldiran in August 1514, the Ottomans took control of most of Kurdistan. When the Ottoman Army encountered difficulties several months later—following the reorganization of the Kizilbashis, who had laid siege to Diyarbakır with the help of the Safavids—Kurdish tribal forces organized by Bidlisi helped the Ottomans defeat their rivals.

In the sixteenth century, a number of emirates controlled by older dynasties, namely Bidlis, Baban, Mukri, and Shahrizur, attempted to maneuver between the two ruling forces, the Ottomans and the Safavids, and switched their loyalty from one side to the other according to which side might favor the preservation of their autonomous status.[25] In the seventeenth and eighteenth centuries, most of the Kurdish emirates were under Ottoman domination, save Erdelan, which was under the domination of Iran.

In 1639, a border agreement—the Zohab (Qasr-a Shirin) Agreement—was signed between the Ottoman Empire and Safavid Iran, determining the division of Kurdistan between the two empires. Notwithstanding the agreement, the wars between Ottomans and Persians continued until the signing of the Treaty of Erzurum in 1823.

The Kurdish Emirates under Ottoman Rule in the Seventeenth and Eighteenth Centuries, and the Literary Expressions of Protonationalism among the Kurds

Under Ottoman rule, the Kurdish emirates enjoyed different and varying degrees of autonomy. Some emirates, although under the authority of the Ottoman sovereign, and loyal to it, enjoyed considerable autonomy. Others were submitted to an effective Ottoman rule that was able to limit their autonomy. The degree of autonomy depended on the power of the emir and his ability to maneuver vis-à-vis the Ottoman authorities in Baghdad, Basra, and Mosul, as well as on his connections in Istanbul.

The Ottoman Empire needed the strength of the Kurds against Iran under the Safavid and Qajar dynasties. Their location on the front line between the Sunni Ottoman Empire and its rival, the Shi'i Iranian state, emphasized the importance of the Kurdish emirates and tribes. Periods of loose Ottoman rule gave the Kurdish emirates room to maneuver and to exert their influence on the balance of power between the various local forces and the Ottoman valis (i.e., Ottoman governors of a region) in Baghdad and Mosul. Although the Kurdish emirates were under the rule of the Ottoman sultan, the Iranian shah and the Iranian governors of Kermanshah and Tabriz occasionally supported them in their struggles against the Ottoman governors.

In contrast to the relatively broad areas controlled by the Kurdish emirates in the noncentralist Ottoman Empire, there was only one significant Kurdish emirate, Erdelan, which preserved some degree of autonomy in Iran under the Safavids, as members of its ruling clan held high positions in the court of the shah. The Safavids, while availing themselves of Kurdish assistance against the Ottoman Empire, at the same time undermined the autonomy of the Kurdish forces. The Safavid shah, Abbas, sought to obtain the support of the Kurds as a fighting force against the Uzbeks to the north and the Ottomans to the west. Concurrently with this attempt at dialogue, however, the shah forcibly suppressed all autonomous Kurdish forces and all forms of uncooperative behavior among the Kurds. As part of military moves intended to impose Iranian sovereignty on the Kurds in Iran, the Iranians besieged the fortress of Dimdim near the Lake Urmiya region in 1608; they succeeded in conquering it only by killing all its Kurdish defenders.[26] One of the popular Kurdish myths adopted by the Kurdish national movement in the twentieth century was that of the heroic defense of Dimdim.

The Kurdish tribes and emirates were caught up in internal struggles and in a complex relationship with the Ottoman state. The degree of autonomy they enjoyed depended on the strength of the central government and the Ottoman valis. The strengthening and weakening of the emirates depended upon the ability of the Ottoman Empire to impose an effective centralist rule or the ability of the Ottoman valis to maneuver between the various local forces. But the struggles and rivalries between the emirates and tribes, the absence of a national consciousness, and the acceptance of an Islamic Ottoman discourse by the *Mirs* (emirs) and the tribal leadership prevented any significant Kurdish unification against the central government. None of the Kurdish emirates developed into a power strong enough to impose continued sovereignty over other emirates and tribes, nor did any of them become a focus for the growth of a central political force in Kurdistan. An additional contributing factor to this was the Ottoman policy, which aimed to prevent such a development by manipulating and exploiting the struggle within the families that controlled the emirates and the rivalries between the Kurdish tribes.

The most important sources of information on the situation in Kurdistan at the time are the writings of the Ottoman traveler Evliya Chelebi (1611–1685), who repeatedly toured Kurdistan between 1640 and 1656. On his third voyage, in 1655–1656, Chelebi spent a relatively long period in Diyarbakır and Bidlis. He also visited twelve other Kurdish emirates.[27]

Chelebi provided geographical descriptions of Kurdistan, pointing out the strategic importance of the Kurdish emirates from the standpoint of the Ottoman Empire as a barrier to Iran. His descriptions revealed a picture of economic and cultural prosperity, urban development, and the military (albeit somewhat limited) might of the Kurdish emirs. The cities of Diyarbakır and Bidlis (Bitlis) were described as cultural centers of excellence, with highly educated *ulama*', merchants, and craftsmen. Religious and intellectual activities took place in the mosques and the *madrasas*, and influential Sufi orders, the *Naqshbandiyya* and *Baktashiyya*, were also involved in these activities.

Chelebi described 'Abd al-Khan, the ruler of Bidlis, as someone with a broad education about a wide range of subjects including architecture, poetry, medicine, and painting; a scholar of several languages; and a patron of the arts and sciences.[28] His library contained thousands of books, including a collection of European literature.[29] According to Chelebi, he could call up seventy thousand fighters (a figure that appears to be somewhat inflated). Chelebi also noted that Kurdish *ulama*' in al-Khan's court wrote poetry in several Kurdish dialects.

One of the highest points of religious, literary, and intellectual activity was the poem *Mem u Zin*, which was written in the Kurmanji dialect by the poet and cleric Ahmad-i Khani and published in 1695.[30] The basic narrative on which the poem is built is a love story, which previously appeared in various versions throughout the Arabic- and Persian-speaking Muslim world; this work nonetheless may be considered to include distinct expressions of Kurdish protonational identity. Its introduction includes a description of the Kurds' tragic geopolitical situation vis-à-vis the Persians, Arabs, Turks, and Georgians.

> Look, from the Arabs to the Georgians
> The Kurds have become like towers.
> The Turks and Persians are surrounded by them.
> The Kurds are on all four corners.
> Both sides have made the Kurdish people
> Targets for arrows of fate.

They are said to be keys to the borders,
Each clan forming a formidable bulwark.
Whenever the Ottoman Sea [the Ottomans] and the Tajik Sea
    [the Persians]
Flow out and agitate,
The Kurds get soaked in blood
Separating them like an isthmus.[31]

The explicit mention of Kurdish political dreams and of the Kurds as a collective entity constitutes a distinct expression of the concept of Kurdish protonationalist uniqueness. The poem includes expressions of personal Kurdish identity, put in the mouths of popular figures:

I am a peddler, not of noble origins
Self-grown, not educated.
I am a Kurd, from the mountains and distant lands.
These are a few stories from the *Kurdawari* [i.e., Kurdish way
    of life] . . .[32]

Another passage reflects the longing for a Kurdish king—that is, for Kurdish diplomatic and military power. This may have been a response to the elimination of the Bidlis Emirate by the Ottomans.

If the Kurds had a king . . .
These Rumis [Ottomans/Turks] would not defeat us,
We would not become ruins in the hands of owls;
We would not become doomed, homeless,
Defeated by the Turks and Tajiks and subjugated by them.[33]
If we had a king
and God befitted him a crown,
And a throne had been appointed for him,
a fortune would appear for us;
certainly also we would have marketability.[34]

Ahmad-i Khani was certainly not a Kurdish nationalist in the modern sense. He may, however, be regarded as a harbinger of Kurdish self-awareness, and as a precursor of the nationalist concept that developed in the nineteenth and twentieth centuries.[35]

Kurdish poetry in the Gurani dialect flourished from the fifteenth to the eighteenth centuries, mainly in Sina (Sanandaj), the capital of the Emirate of Erdelan in Iran, and in other places in southern and eastern Kurdistan.

Another very important expression of Kurdish ethnic identity was the chronicle *Sharafname History of the Kurdish States and Emirates*, which was first published in Persian in 1595 by Sharaf Khan al-Bidlisi. It traced the history of the Kurds through the prism of the dynasties of the Kurdish emirs and rulers in southern and eastern Kurdistan. The book is an extremely important source of information on twelfth-through-sixteenth-century Kurdish history.[36]

These protonationalist intellectual trends, however, did not continue. A change in discourse was needed for the continuous development and dissemination of incipient Kurdish nationalism, and for its growth as an important factor in political and social reality. None of the emirates was capable of accumulating enough power to impose its sovereignty, to promote a collective identity and common interests, or to create state-building dynamics. In Kurdistan, conditions did not arise for the development of an urban bourgeoisie or an aristocracy as a social class with supra-tribal, supralocal, or supraemirate discourses and interests.

Some of the emirates lost their autonomous status as early as the sixteenth and seventeenth centuries, becoming Ottoman administrative districts (*sanjaks*) headed by governors appointed by the central government in Istanbul. At times, these governors were members of the emirs' families; at others, they were total strangers. At the same time, emirates maintained varying degrees of autonomy, depending on the strength of the emir and his ability to maneuver among the Ottoman authorities in Baghdad, Basra, and Mosul, as well as his connections in Istanbul.

The strength of the Ottoman state, the tenuous and decentralized nature of its rule in Kurdistan notwithstanding, exceeded the ability of the separate Kurdish emirates to withstand it. The first developments of a literary Kurdish language and culture and a Kurdish administration failed, and the Kurdish dialects reverted to a demotic style.

The Elimination of the Kurdish Emirates: Causes and Implications

The administrative, political, and socioeconomic transformations in the Ottoman Empire and the changes in the international regional relations from the early nineteenth century onward had far-reaching implications for the political situation in Kurdistan and for a regional system dominated by the Ottoman Empire and Iran ever since the sixteenth century. The centralization of administration was an essential part of the reforms in the Ottoman Empire under Sultan Mahmud II (1808–1839) and throughout the Tanzimat period (1839–1876), but it aggravated the conflict between the Ottoman state and the Kurdish emirates, which sought to preserve their autonomy. The growing British and Russian interests and influence in both the Ottoman Empire and Iran—along with the end of a century of warfare between Iran and the Ottomans, brought to a close by the First Erzurum Treaty of 1823 and the Second Erzurum Treaty of 1847—changed the regional and international arena, to the detriment of the autonomous Kurdish emirates.[37] The end of the Ottoman-Iranian war deprived the Kurdish emirates of their prominence as an Ottoman border force and reduced their capacity for maneuvering between the Ottoman and Iranian governments and other local forces.

At the end of the reign of Tsarina Catherine the Great (ruled 1762–1796) and during the reign of her successor, Tsar Paul I (ruled 1796–1801), Russia took over most of the Caucasus. The proximity of Russia to Iran following the takeover of the Caucasus and the increased Russian activity in Iran gave rise to British concerns and affected British relations with Iran and the Ottoman Empire. At the same time, the strengthening of the East India Company's economic interests in the Persian Gulf impelled Britain to increase its efforts and its activities in Mesopotamia and Kurdistan, with a view to halting Russian infiltration. The strategy adopted by Britain was intended to preserve the existence, unity, and status of the Ottoman Empire as a barrier to Russian expansion toward India. The regional international system with regard to Kurdistan changed from a bipolar Ottoman-Iranian system to a quadrilateral one, in which Russia and Britain also played roles.

Conflicts developed between tribal Kurds and sedentary Assyrian peasants as tensions mounted between Muslims and Christians due to the reforms in the Ottoman Empire, a closer encounter with the West, and a tightening of the relations between local Christian communities and the Western powers. In the second half of the nineteenth century, mainly after the 1877–1878 Russian-Ottoman war, conflicts arose between Kurds and Armenians as well.

The Weakening of the Baban and Hakkari
Emirates in the Early Nineteenth Century

Upon the conclusion of the Ottoman-Persian wars with the Treaty of Erzurum in 1823, the Kurdish emirates of Baban and Hakkari lost their importance, and their ability to maneuver vis-à-vis the Ottoman Empire was reduced. Both the Baban Emirate, which was centered in Sulaymaniyya and was relatively influential in Baghdad, and the Hakkari Emirate to the west of Lake Urmiya on the border with Iran lost their status. They were weakened by internal struggles and international events, and were finally eliminated in the 1830s. Much of the information on the political situation of the House of Baban and the relations among the various local forces in Basra, Baghdad, and southern Kurdistan in the first two decades of the nineteenth century can be found in the writings of Claudius Rich, an agent of the East India Company in Basra and Baghdad.[38]

The emirs of the House of Baban, who had been centered in Sulaymaniyya since 1787, exercised considerable influence on the political developments in Baghdad for some three decades. The House of Baban played an important role in a complex and dynamic system of forces, which included the local Mamluk rulers, the valis appointed by the government in Istanbul (with the aim of reinforcing the central government's control of the vilayets of Iraq), and the strong Bedouin tribal federations. The closeness of the Babans to Baghdad and the crucial military role they played in restraining Iranian influence gave them an edge in the political struggles in Baghdad.[39] The Babans began to lose power and political leverage as a result of protracted struggles within the family, which were fostered and exploited by the Ottoman valis and the Iranian governors of the Erdelan region. Thus by the early 1820s the Ottomans had managed to significantly reduce the emirate's autonomy.

The end of the Ottoman-Iranian wars were a debilitating factor as well, depriving the House of Baban of its importance as a border force for the Ottoman Empire and detracting from its ability to manipulate and exploit the Ottoman-Iranian rivalry. The elimination of the Mamluks in Baghdad in 1831 by the forces of Sultan Mahmud II, as part of his efforts to wipe out the autonomous forces throughout the empire and establish a centralized administration, further undermined the House of Baban's position. Admittedly, the Babans continued to head the emirate until the 1850s, but their appointment was issued by the Ottoman authorities, and the extent of their autonomy was gradually reduced until it was ultimately totally eliminated.

The Rise and Fall of the Soran Emirate

With the weakening of the Emirate of Baban, the two remaining prominent emirates were Soran and Botan. The first (today in the Kurdish Region in northern Iraq, near the cities Erbil-Hewler and Rawanduz) was
headed by the powerful emir Muhammad Kor ("the Blind," as he was
called because he was blind in the left eye); the second was centered in al-
Jazira and headed by Emir Bedir Khan. The other emirates, Hakkari and
Bahdinan, were embroiled in internal struggles within the ruling clans.
In addition, there was also a mosaic of smaller, less significant tribes and
local khans.

The rise of Muhammad Kor was set against the Ottoman weakness
following the war with Russia in 1828–1829 and the conquest of Syria
by the Egyptian ruler Muhammad ʿAli in 1831. Muhammad Kor, who inherited the rule of the Emirate of Soran in 1814, developed and fortified
its capital, the city of Rawanduz, where he established a *diwan*, or advi-
sory council. Known for his religious fervor, he obtained the support of
the local ʿulamaʾ. Muhammad Kor established an army that included cavalry, infantry, and even some artillery. Most of the military force relied on
the tribes, but it also included a regular army unit.[40] At the same time,
he developed workshops for the manufacture of swords, rifles, and even
cannons. Other expressions of his self-centered ambitions included the
minting of coins bearing his name and the mention of his name in Friday
sermons in the mosques of the emirate.[41]

Admittedly, his status and achievements were far below those of Muhammad ʿAli, or even those of ʿAli Bey, the Mamluk ruler of Egypt in the second
half of the eighteenth century. Nonetheless, Muhammad Kor reflected the
trends that had been developing among the autonomous rulers throughout the Ottoman Empire since the mid-eighteenth century, to which the
empire responded in the nineteenth century with reforms, especially the
modernization and centralization of its government and administration.

In the 1820s and early 1830s, the Emirate of Soran under Muhammad
Kor became the principal force in southern and central Kurdistan. During this period he enforced his sovereignty over the Hakkari Emirate and
the Baradost, Surchi, and Mamash tribes, taking over Rawanduz, Zakho,
Dohuk, and Amadiya, the capital of the Bahdinan Emirate.[42] Only the
Emirate of Botan remained free of his dominance. In 1833, following his
oppression of the Yezidis and the conquest of Bahdinan, Muhammad Kor
cast his eye on Botan and easily conquered its capital, Jazirat bin ʿUmar.
Bedir Khan's forces, however, found shelter in a series of fortresses, which

Muhammad Kor attempted to take. The resistance by Bedir Khan and his supporters, along with the revolts that broke out in Amadiya and other places, forced Muhammad Kor to break off his offensive.[43]

In the summer of 1834, the Ottomans launched an offensive against Muhammad Kor; his success in repelling it boosted his confidence.[44] It may well be that this was the mainstay of his activities among the Kurdish tribes in Iran, as well as his attempts to maneuver between Iran and the Ottoman Empire. In practice, this move gave rise to Iranian suspicions, to fears among the Russian residents in Teheran and Tabriz that Iran's power could be waning and that this could be exploited by Britain, and to British fears that Russia might exploit Ottoman weakness. Notwithstanding the discrepancies between the policies of the two European powers, these policies may be seen as exhibiting a diplomatic pattern that would recur throughout the nineteenth, twentieth, and into the twenty-first century. Generally speaking—and especially when crucial decisions were to be made—the European powers preferred to safeguard their own interests and secure the existence of Iran and the Ottoman Empire (and, after World War I, of Turkey) rather than support the Kurds, the nineteenth-century emirates, and the Kurdish national movement in the twentieth and early twenty-first centuries.

Fearing the cooperation between the forces of Muhammad Kor and Muhammad ʿAli in Syria, and in accordance with his own policy of putting an end to semi-independent forces, Sultan Mahmud II ordered the governors of Mosul and Baghdad to help the commander of the forces in southern Anatolia to crush Muhammad Kor. The Ottoman offensive in the summer of 1836 forced Muhammad Kor to retreat and entrench himself in Rawanduz. The loyalty of the Kurdish tribes depended on his ability to intimidate them. When it became apparent that the Ottomans were prevailing, the tribes opted for their own interests and refrained from helping him any further. In Soran itself, a dispute with the *ulama* broke out over the mention of his name in the Friday sermons, instead of the name of the Ottoman sultan.

In light of his increasing isolation, Muhammad Kor entered into negotiations with the Ottomans. The British also played a role in these negotiations. A British diplomat, Richard Wood, came to Rawanduz in an attempt to convince Muhammad Kor to surrender to the Ottomans in return for their agreement to let him remain as governor of the Emirate of Soran.[45] It is quite possible, however, that Wood attributed too much importance to his own role in convincing Muhammad Kor to surrender to the Ottomans.

Muhammad Kor's position was also weakened by the tenuous nature of his tribal alliances, as each tribe ultimately favored its own interests. Faced by the strength of the Ottoman Empire, his tribal allies preferred to lay down their arms. He was dealt an additional blow by the *'ulama'* in Rawanduz, who (possibly under Ottoman influence) proclaimed they were against a conflict with the sultan; the city mufti went so far as to issue a *fatwa* prohibiting war against the sultan.[46]

In light of the Iranian unwillingness to assist him or to give him shelter, and in view of his isolation and helplessness against Ottoman power and its British backing, Muhammad Kor agreed to surrender and go to Istanbul, apparently on the basis of a promise by the Ottoman commander Rashid Pasha that if he surrendered and accepted Ottoman sovereignty, he would be allowed to continue to govern in Soran.[47]

Muhammad Kor set out for Istanbul, hoping to meet with the sultan. During the six months that he spent in Istanbul, he was given Ottoman promises that he would continue to control the emirate, although his autonomy would be limited and he would have to accept Ottoman sovereignty. On his way back to Soran via the Black Sea, he disappeared; it is safe to assume that he was murdered by the Ottomans.

The Emirate of Soran and its ambitious ruler had fallen victim to the changes in the international arena. The growing involvement of Britain and Russia, the cessation of belligerence between Iran and the Ottoman Empire, and the accelerated reforms and trends toward centralization in the Ottoman Empire had led to its downfall.

The Emirate of Botan: Caught in the Tangled Web of Muslim-Christian Relations

After the fall of Soran, Botan remained as the last significant Kurdish emirate and the strongest local force in Kurdistan. Its ruler, Muhammad Bedir Khan, supported the Ottomans in the Ottoman-Egyptian war and even held an Ottoman military rank. He sought to exploit his standing and his connections with the Ottomans to fortify his autonomous position within the Ottoman Empire. As the strongest local figure in Kurdistan, Bedir Khan began to expand his areas of influence. In light of the de facto dissolution of the Hakkari Emirate, Bedir Khan extended his protection over that area as well.

In the 1830s, American and British Protestant missionaries who sought to convert Christian Nestorians to Protestantism began their activity in the Hakkari area. The splits and struggles in the Assyrian Church, one of the oldest Christian churches, attracted various Western Christian denominations. The increased missionary activity echoed the growing involvement and interests of the West in the Ottoman Empire, and the intense competition among the missionaries increased the internal rivalries among the Assyrians.

The American missionaries exploited concessions to build churches that had been granted them as part of the Tanzimat reforms. This aroused the suspicion of the Kurdish Muslim population in Hakkari, which feared Christian infiltration and the strengthening of the local Christian population.[48] Mir (Emir) Nurullah Beg, the ruler of Hakkari (southeast of Van Lake), was officially the suzerain of the Nestorians. The relations between Nurullah Beg and the Nestorians deteriorated in the 1830s. Ottoman officials, annoyed by Western activities in the area, encouraged Nurullah Beg to impose his authority over the Nestorians. In the face of Hakkari's weakness, he approached Bedir Khan in 1839 and asked for his help. Bedir Khan used this opportunity to strengthen his patronage over the weak Emirate of Hakkari.[49]

The influence of the 'alim (religious scholar) Shaykh Taha of Nehri also appears to have affected Bedir Khan's conduct. The American missionaries and British travelers who reported on these events emphasized the Islamic religious fanaticism that characterized both Emir Bedir Khan and Shaykh Taha.

According to British travelers and American missionaries, Bedir Khan's forces massacred seven thousand to ten thousand Assyrian Christians in 1843.[50] The Muslim-Christian tensions and clashes in Kurdistan took the form of Kurdish-Assyrian struggles. The traditional struggles and tensions between Kurdish Muslims and Assyrian and Armenian Christians at times reflected the socioeconomic rifts between the Kurdish and Turkmen pastoral, tribal population and the sedentary Christians, who were peasants as well as merchants and craftsmen. There were also tensions and power struggles between the tribal Kurds and the nontribal Kurdish-speaking peasants, who were often not even seen as Kurds.

With the exception of missionary activities, which directly contributed to the disturbance of the local equilibrium, Western influence in Kurdistan was indirect, stemming principally from the general developments in the Ottoman Empire and the impression that, compared to Britain and Russia, the empire was weak. British travelers who visited Kurdistan in the 1830s and 1840s heard from their Kurdish interlocutors that they had high hopes the increased strength of Britain and Russia would release them from Ottoman rule.[51] Admittedly, the Kurds' resentment and suspicion of the Ottoman authorities increased in light of the empire's efforts to impose a centralistic administration and reforms that were perceived as threats to Kurdish tribal autonomy. At the same time, however, the Kurds feared that the European powers would give the local Christians—whose self-confidence was strengthened as a result of the activities of Western missionaries and who were perceived as natural allies of the Christian powers—their backing.

It is quite plausible that Bedir Khan was manipulated by the Ottoman authorities, who sought to call a halt to Western Christian activity.[52] The slaughter of Christians, reported by Western missionaries and travelers in Kurdistan, gave rise to strong British protests and pressure to overthrow Bedir Khan.[53] From the Ottomans' double perspective, they apparently used him to weaken Western Christian activity while at the same time seeking to block him from becoming too strong a local force.

Bedir Khan's coalition with Emir Nurullah Beg of Hakkari and Khan Muhammad of Mush could not withstand the might of the Ottoman army, which had been modernized and trained by Prussian officers. Moreover, Yezdansher Khan, a relative of Bedir Khan and one of the most prominent commanders of his army, had switched to the Ottoman side. In light of the Ottoman strength, Bedir Khan surrendered in 1847 and was exiled from Kurdistan. He was later pardoned, awarded the title of pasha, and served the Ottoman state for several decades. Two hundred members of the Bedir Khan family underwent the process of Ottomanization, like many other members of the Kurdish tribal feudal elite that immigrated or were exiled to Istanbul and integrated with the Ottoman establishment.[54] His grandchildren Sureyya (1883–1938), Celadet (1893–1951), and Kamuran (1893–1978), however, became the most important speakers for Kurdish nationalism in the first half of the twentieth century.

The conflict between the Emirate of Botan under Bedir Khan and the empire was an expression of the Kurdish opposition to Ottoman trends toward centralization and reform. The elimination of the emirate stemmed from the Ottoman effort to impose a centralized authority over the peripheral semi-independent forces and to strengthen Ottoman rule in eastern Anatolia and Kurdistan. The chain of events that led to the elimination of Bedir Khan's rule included the deterioration of Muslim-Christian relations and their connection to Britain's influence during the Ottoman reforms.

In the mid-nineteenth century, the Ottoman Empire was admittedly weakened as the strength of the Western powers increased. Nonetheless, the relative strength and capabilities of the modernized and reformed Ottoman state, government, and army increased by comparison to the Kurdish emirates, which were unable to unify around a Kurdish identity or to define a common interest.

The Revolt of Yezdansher (Izz al-Din Shir) at the Margins of the Crimean War, and the Kurdish-Russian Connection

Russian ambitions in the Balkans and in the Black Sea basin, and the attempt by the Ottoman Empire to withstand pressures exerted by Russia, led to the outbreak of the Crimean War in 1853. The Ottoman Empire received military aid from both Britain and France, both of which sought to forestall the empire's collapse and to prevent Russia from becoming the dominant force in Istanbul. The war, which had turned into an armed conflict between European powers, primarily took place in the Balkans and the Crimean Peninsula on the Black Sea. A secondary front covered areas within and to the south of the Caucasus, some of which were populated by Kurds. The weakness of the Ottoman army and its defeat by Russia on the Caucasian front, primarily in the Kars area, served as the background for a massive yet brief Kurdish revolt in the autumn and winter of 1854–1855.[55]

Among the participants in the battles in the Kars area in December 1853 was an irregular force of approximately fifteen thousand Kurdish cavalry. Both the Russians and the Ottomans mobilized Kurdish tribes to fight on their side. Following the defeat of the Ottoman forces in December 1853, fourteen Kurdish notables approached the Russians with a view to reaching an agreement. Some of the Kurdish forces that had been recruited by the Ottomans changed sides and went over to fight for Russia. A Russian colonel, Loris Melikov, was put in charge of relations with the Kurdish tribes. An additional defeat suffered in 1854 by the Ottoman army at the hands of the Russians severely detracted from the Kurds' willingness to continue assisting the Ottomans.[56]

The most prominent Kurdish personage the Ottomans sought to recruit was Yezdansher, who was given a senior Ottoman military rank as a reward for his betrayal of Emir Bedir Khan in 1847. Yezdansher was disappointed, however, by the Ottomans' refusal to give him sovereignty over the lands of the Botan Emirate and other areas of Kurdistan. Left with no alternative but to continue serving the empire, his personal disappointment nonetheless constituted an important motive for his attempted revolt.

In light of their losses at the Russian front and the Kurds' declining willingness to help them, the Ottomans assigned to Yezdansher the task of recruiting Kurds from the al-Jazira (Cizre) and Mosul areas as irregular units of the Ottoman army. Following their victories in the summer of 1854, the Russians sent a message to Yezdansher, asking him not to assist the Ottomans. In the autumn of the same year, relations between Yezdansher and the empire began to decline.

Although the relations between Yezdansher and the Ottomans undoubtedly constituted the main reason for the Kurdish revolt, the revolt also resulted from both the economic distress of the Kurdish population during the war and the weakened Ottoman image following repeated defeats of the empire by Russia, which was perceived as a rising force. Between December 1854 and February 1855, Yezdansher conquered the cities of Bidlis and Midyat. Seemingly, the scope of the revolt was broad, arousing the fears of Ottomans and British alike. Its location, to the south of the Ottoman forces that were holding back the Russian army in the north, created a strategic threat, especially since his forces were joined by Arabs from the Mardin area. According to a book by L. I. Averyanov, a Russian intelligence officer who reviewed Russian-Kurdish relations at the end of the nineteenth century, Yezdansher commanded from sixty thousand to one hundred thousand soldiers. This figure appears to be quite exaggerated, however. His tribal forces were not a regular army and were motivated mainly by a desire for booty; their loyalty was primarily tribal. It further appears that his hold on the cities he conquered was tenuous and brief.

Yezdansher attempted to coordinate his military activities with the Russians and to obtain their support, but without success. At the same time, he corresponded with Kurdish notables and influential leaders in the Van, Bidlis, and Mush areas. As the Ottomans saw it, the revolt of the rearguard in their front against the Russians constituted a serious threat. In January 1855, the British general William Fenwick Williams, who commanded the Ottoman forces and the British officers in the Kars area, conveyed a warning to Yezdansher that any conflict with the Ottomans would be viewed as a conflict with Britain. Given the absence of any hope of Russian cooperation and in view of the combined pressure exerted by the Ottoman army in Kurdistan and of the British threat, Yezdansher surrendered without having entered into direct combat with a much superior Ottoman army. The exact circumstances of his surrender are not clear.[57]

His forces, which seem to have been tribal and poorly organized, apparently crumbled entirely. It is also possible that Yezdansher's shifting alliances, as expressed in his betrayal of Emir Bedir Khan during the latter's revolt against the Ottomans in 1847, contributed to the decline of his own rebellion, even before any real clash with the Ottoman forces could take place.[58]

The revolt apparently inspired hopes for one of the most important harbingers of a modern Kurdish national movement, the poet Haji Qadir Koyi, who mentioned Yezdansher, the leader of the revolt, throughout his works.[59] On the whole, the revolt is mentioned only rarely by the advocates of Kurdish nationalism. It should be remembered that Yezdansher contributed to the defeat of the Kurds by switching to the Ottoman side after betraying Emir Bedir Khan, whose descendants had helped shape a Kurdish historical narrative in the first half of the twentieth century. The descendants of Bedir Khan hence saw him as a traitor and opportunist. Nonetheless, the subsequent nature of the relations between the Ottomans and Yezdansher, like those that prevailed between Bedir Khan and the empire after Khan's surrender, hints at the tribal-feudal characteristics of the leaders of both revolts, as well as at the prevailing political reality. After brief periods of exile, both were appointed to senior positions in the Ottoman administration, in provinces at a great distance from Kurdistan. Both ended their lives as Ottoman governors, far from Kurdistan and any modern Kurdish national commitment.

The rebellions of the Kurdish emirs and magnates in the nineteenth century were not motivated by Kurdish solidarity or Kurdish nationalism. However, they helped raise a consciousness of Kurdishness and of Kurdish identity.

The Beginnings of the Kurdish National Movement

In the late nineteenth and early twentieth centuries, when national movements began to develop in the Middle East and after the reshaping of the regional map following World War I, the situation of the Kurds was much worse than that of the Arabs, the Turks, or the Persians. The seeds of Kurdish statehood, i.e., the autonomous Kurdish emirates, had been wiped out in the first half of the nineteenth century as a result of Ottoman reforms and changes in the international arena. During the last decades of the Ottoman Empire, the tribal, feudal Kurdish elite—especially those who had been exiled or had immigrated to Istanbul and Izmir and integrated into the Ottoman state—became Ottomanized, and therefore were unprepared to exert itself and regain its leadership status in Kurdistan.[60] During the years from 1914 to 1924, as the political map of a post-Ottoman Middle East was drawn, the Kurds lacked leaders capable of filling a role parallel to that played by the Hashemite emirs in the emerging Arab national movement.

While the Ottoman state was strong enough to eliminate the Kurdish emirates, it failed to impose an effective rule in their stead. This resulted in a general sense of insecurity: rapidly deteriorating public order, outbreaks of violence, robberies, and incursions by tribal, often pastoral, populations against sedentary peasants. The vacuum resulting from the elimination of the emirates created conditions for a strengthening of tribal and clannish solidarities and for raising the status of Sufi shaykhs. Many of the leaders of the twentieth-century Kurdish national movement came from the clans and tribes of Barzani, Barzinji, Talabani, and Zibari, which emerged with the elimination of the Kurdish emirates.

Kurdistan, with its complex geographical conditions and its lack of any natural resources before the petroleum era that could have aroused Western economic interests, was exposed to the global capitalist market economy to a limited extent only. In other regions, integration into the global economy had disastrous consequences, but economic exposure to the West also created conditions for social change and for the growth of nationalism and national movements. The development of urban centers, an urban society, and modernized social strata was limited in Kurdistan and in this respect lagged behind the Levant, Anatolia, Egypt, and the Tigris and Euphrates plains. Kurdistan was geopolitically peripheral and lacked an outlet to the sea; its contacts with the West were tenuous and indirect, and its society remained basically tribal. The lack of a standardized written Kurdish language, the plodding pace of modernization, and the slow development of a modern Kurdish bourgeoisie and middle class to challenge the strength of tribal social patterns delayed the development of a Kurdish national movement and national consciousness.

To some degree, Kurdish identity pertained to a tribal, partially pastoral population and to the last remnants of a clannish-tribal aristocracy. The small, modern Kurdish middle class was concentrated in Istanbul and Izmir, had absorbed Turkish and Arab culture, and had integrated into the Ottoman establishment. In their eyes, Kurdish identity was synonymous with backwardness, conservatism, and poverty. It would best be eliminated by integration into the Ottoman (later Turkish) and Iranian states and by the adoption of a Turkish, Iranian, or Arab identity. This orientation was encouraged by the states that had split up Kurdistan: the Ottoman Empire and Iran until World War I, and afterward Turkey, Iran, Iraq, and Syria. They had dominated Kurdistan for centuries and had a vested interest in either wiping out all traces of a Kurdish identity (as in Turkey and, in a different way, Iran) or leaving the Kurds as a discriminated minority (as in Iraq). At any rate, the prevailing interests dictated the suppression of a Kurdish national movement, so that achieving autonomy, not to mention a state of their own, was no longer an option.

Although modern Kurdish nationalism developed in the context of modernization, the encounter with the West and the domination of the Turkish, Iranian, and Iraqi states after World War I played an important role in the emergence of a Kurdish national discourse and Kurdish national consciousness. The development of modern Kurdish nationalism accelerated after the end of the World War I with the demise of the Ottoman Empire and the ascendancy of Turkish nationalism and Atatürk's ideology. But tribal, clannish, and local solidarities nevertheless remained dominant in Kurdish society. Only with the foundation of the Kurdish Democratic Party in 1946 (later renamed Kurdistan Democratic Party, or KDP) did the modern national movement become a central force. Kurdish identity, tribal-feudal sociopolitical structures, oral traditions, and the pre-Islamic signifiers *kurd* and *akrad* had persisted throughout the history of Islam. Altogether, the Kurdish national discourse borrowed from real and imagined events in the history of Kurdistan, resting on the historical and social signifiers of a premodern Kurdish identity. Hence, a thorough examination of the historical and sociopolitical developments in Kurdistan, the expressions of Kurdish identity since the beginnings of Islam, and the development of the Kurdish language is essential for a better understanding of the modern Kurdish nation.

The Dual Relationship between Kurdish Tribalism and Nationalism

ELI AMARILYO

This chapter considers the relationship between Kurdish tribalism and nationalism from the emergence of Kurdish nationalism at the end of the nineteenth century to the creation in 1946 of the first Kurdish national political entity, the Republic of Mahabad, which marked an important phase in the Kurdish national movement. It implies that the relationship between Kurdish tribalism and nationalism is a dual one. On the one hand, as a military system, tribalism has served as a backbone for Kurdish national revolts, constituting the primary framework by which the Kurds conducted their national revolts. On the other hand, tribalism as a cultural system, with its tendencies toward divisiveness and rivalry, retribution, and short-lived alliances, has created an ongoing obstacle to Kurdish national unity. The situation was easily exploited by central governments to split Kurdish society, crush most Kurdish revolts, and undermine the national Kurdish movement. This chapter refers to tribalism as a multifaceted phenomenon, with some characteristics that serve as a basis for the development of national movements and other traits that constitute barriers to national unity.

Kurdish Tribalism and Nationalism

There are two opposite approaches to the relationship between Kurdish tribalism and nationalism. The first approach, advocated by Martin van Bruinessen, argues that Kurdish tribalism is the backbone of Kurdish nationalism. The ultimate evidence for this argument is the fact that all prominent national Kurdish leaders hailed from a tribal society and used their tribal prestige and allegiances to promote the Kurdish national cause. Van Bruinessen adds that at least until the 1920s, popular support for the Kurdish national movement was motivated by loyalty toward the tribal leaders rather than by national sentiment. He stresses that tribalism remained the prominent force in the Kurdish national movement even after the 1920s, when nationalism became a significant motivating force within Kurdish society.[1] According to the second approach, which is advocated by Kendal Nezan and Hussein Tahiri, tribalism is the main barrier to Kurdish nationalism. Nezan stresses that a tribal political culture of switching allegiances and maintaining divisions constitutes the main reason for the failure of nearly all Kurdish revolts aimed at setting up an independent Kurdish state. According to Nezan, the fact that the tribes are under the leadership of chiefs divided by quarrels over political and economic supremacy, vendettas, and the tendency to form short-lived political alliances impedes the development of long-term Kurdish unity. For his part, Tahiri stresses that the tribal culture prevents the Kurds from uniting and establishing a nation-state, while enabling central governments to exploit tribal rivalries and crush any revolt by inciting one tribe against another. Tahiri concludes that as long as tribal culture dominates Kurdish society, the Kurds will not be able to form a Kurdish state of their own.[2]

The question of whether both approaches could be right should probably be answered in the positive. Tribalism is a complex and multifaceted phenomenon. As a military and political system, it may serve as leverage for nationalism, so that tribes can organize as a powerful military force (though usually in loose coalitions) and revolt under the banner of nationalism. At the same time, tribalism as a cultural system is rarely conducive to cohesiveness and may have an adverse effect on nationalism that could even result in the disintegration of a nation. In this chapter, I suggest that both perspectives are right with regard to the present discussion. My approach combines the two and focuses on the dual relationship between tribalism and nationalism. I suggest that tribalism contains some elements that promote national movements and some that impede national cohesiveness and the ability to form a stable nation-state.

Before we move forward, a more thorough discussion of tribalism is required. As the terms "tribe" and "tribalism" may convey different meanings,[3] I would like to clarify that I refer to a tribe as a political, military, social, and cultural organization whose members share a common identity and demonstrate mutual solidarity, and to tribalism as a political, military, social, and cultural system and a framework of identity and solidarity that exists even in so-called "modern societies." The tribe can define itself by genealogy, territory, or both. Kinship is usually the backbone of tribal society, but frequently nontribal people join the tribe to enjoy its protection in exchange for subordination to the tribal leaders.[4] Tribalism encompasses a cultural set of values and codes that include retaliation, an inclination to divisiveness, and a tendency to create short-lived political alliances and preserve some autonomy from the state, as well as moral codes and customary laws.[5]

Frequently, tribes in the Middle East are affiliated with a specific ethnic group (i.e., a group of people sharing common cultural myths and memories rather than kinship), so that tribalism and ethnicity are interrelated. Bassam Tibi refers to tribes as subethnic units. Tribes in the Middle East, Tibi suggests, are subdivisions of ethnic groups, like the Kurds, Alawites, Druze, Berbers, Yezidis, Assyrians, and Pashtuns.[6] As tribalism and ethnicity are interrelated, one cannot deal with tribalism without taking into account ethnic affiliations. Nationalism and ethnicity are also interrelated. Nationalism may rest on ethnic identity. As Anthony Smith suggests, nationalism is a modern ideological movement based on ethnic solidarity that developed at the end of the eighteenth century.[7] Smith's theory is particularly relevant to the Kurdish national movement, which is based on ethnic identity and is frequently referred to as an ethnonational movement. Kurdish nationalism seems to have developed out of cultural consciousness (based on a common history, language origin, and territory). A Kurdish cultural consciousness developed at the end of the nineteenth century as a result of the growth of Armenian, Turkish, and Iranian nationalism in the region. As the Kurds could not engage with any of those national movements, they developed a Kurdish national movement by politicizing their own ethnic identity. With no substantial Kurdish middle class or intellectual elite that could lead a Kurdish national struggle, the only individuals who could mobilize the Kurds, raise the flag of Kurdish nationalism, and fight for Kurdish national independence were the tribal chiefs.[8]

However, tribal leaders rarely lead national movements. Therefore, we can consider the Kurdish national movement as quite unique. Traditionally, tribal leaders, especially those on the periphery, tend to follow the logic of tribal politics, i.e., protecting the tribe's interests by securing extensive autonomy from the state and getting as many services and political posts from the state as they wish. When negotiations with central governments fail, they often revolt under the banner of tribalism, rarely under that of nationalism. Kurdish tribal leaders, however, revolted under the banner of nationalism. We can assume that the reason for this was their understanding that nationalism had become the most effective political agenda for creating a new political entity capable of protecting their tribal interests.[9]

It is noteworthy that the modernization processes of the twentieth century eroded tribal identities, leaving much room for the development of a Kurdish national identity based on the ethnic Kurdish identity. However, tribalism continued to play an important role in the social and political life of the Kurds. In these circumstances, the middle class had no choice but to cooperate with the Kurdish tribal leaders, who possessed the military and financial resources to rebel against the central governments. Yet the national discourse offered the tribes a political language that could give a broader meaning to their revolts. Eventually, cooperation between tribal leaders and the middle class led to the development of the Kurdish national movement.[10]

Tribalism is deeply rooted in Kurdish society. With the emergence of Islam in the seventh century, the term "Kurd" became indicative of nomad tribes only.[11] Since then, as the Kurdish population increased and settled, the term came to refer mainly to rural society, rather than to pastoral nomads.[12] For several hundred years, at least until the tenth century, "Kurd" referred only to tribesmen organized in large confederations, but the Kurdish tribal organization underwent deep changes over time. In the sixteenth and seventeenth centuries new tribal Kurdish confederations (usually called emirates) were established in Kurdistan under Ottoman supervision. The emirates, which functioned as quasi-states, included both tribesmen and nontribesmen.[13] By the middle of the nineteenth century, the Ottoman Empire had demolished the Kurdish emirates, and the tribal organizations in Kurdistan had disintegrated into smaller units. A few failed rebellions were staged by family members of the emirs aiming to restore power. Under these circumstances, a number of mystic (Sufi) leaders became very influential among the tribes, to some extent filling the void created by the collapse of the emirates. These shaykhs became the new leaders of the Kurdish tribes, working side by side with the *aghawat* (the Kurdish tribal leaders).[14] The prominent Sufi families that emerged throughout the nineteenth century in Kurdistan included the Barzinjis, who were named after the village of Barzinja near Sulaymaniyya and controlled all the Kurdish tribes in the region of Sulaymaniyya (with the exception of the Jaf). The Sadate Nehri, who had settled in the village of Nehri near Hakkari, became Naqshbandis (they had previously been Qadiris) at the beginning of the nineteenth century and headed the tribes in the area between Hakkari and Baradost. In the region of Kirkuk the prominent family was Talabani, a Qadiri family.[15] Another leading Sufi family was Barzani, a Naqshbandi family. Its leader, Shaykh ʿAbd al-Rahim, originally from Sulaymaniyya, relocated in the village of Barzan at the beginning of the nineteenth century to make it the center of his activities. The family, which took its name after the village of Barzan, became very influential in the area. ʿAbd al-Rahim's son, ʿAbd al-Salam, succeeded his father and also became a powerful figure.[16] The shaykhs of Barzan and of Nehri joined forces and helped the Naqshbandis spread throughout Kurdistan.[17]

The First Stages of Kurdish Nationalism

Kurdish nationalism never dissociated from the Kurdish tribal milieu. A Kurdish national school of thought evolved at the end of the nineteenth century, promoted mainly by tribal leaders' sons exiled in Istanbul, where Turkish nationalism was developing at the time. Those national activists/intellectuals included Emir Ali Bedir Khan Bey, General Sharif Pasha, and Shaykh Abdul Qadir (the son of ʿUbaydullah of Nehri). By the beginning of World War I those activists/intellectuals had founded a number of national organizations, albeit not very influential ones, primarily because they operated far away from the territory of Kurdistan.[18]

In the eyes of many Kurds, however, Shaykh ʿUbaydullah of Nehri was still the first Kurdish national leader. ʿUbaydullah's national agenda was vague, but his decision to lead an uprising under the banner of Kurdish nationalism was quite remarkable. Historically, there are grounds to consider his revolt against Ottoman rule as the first Kurdish uprising held under the banner of Kurdish national independence. ʿUbaydullah came from an important dynasty of high religious status. His father, Shaykh Taha, was an outstanding spiritual Sufi leader. When Taha died, ʿUbaydullah inherited his estate as well as his religious influence. In those circumstances, he could recruit the tribesmen in his sphere of influence, i.e., the territory of Hakkari-Baradost in southern Kurdistan (the areas bordering on Turkey, Iraq, and Iran), whenever he wanted.[19] ʿUbaydullah was a traditional leader. According to the American missionary traveler Joseph Plumb Cochran, who had met with him, Shaykh ʿUbaydullah was both a religious man of great prestige and a "civil monarch" who served as supreme judge, settling his people's disputes. According to Cochran, the shaykh, who wished to strengthen his local autonomy, regarded the Turks and Persians as deceptive and expressed his reluctance to pay tribute to the Ottoman administrators. He was interested in the world's situation and very much aware of the worldwide nationalist tide.[20]

In October 1880, 'Ubaydullah invaded Persia to show his discontent with the Ottoman and Persian local authorities for their harsh treatment of the tribes in his sphere of influence, and to fight back rival tribes, most notably the Herki and Shikak. When the Kurdish tribes of Mamash, Mangur, Zaraza, Gowrik, and a few others joined him, each for local and tribal reasons of their own, the shaykh's troops, which included about eighty thousand fighters, captured the Persian town of Sauj Bulaq (Mahabad). They then proceeded toward Miandoab, occupied it, and were eventually joined by other tribes (sections of the Herki and Begzadeh tribes in Mergever and in Somay Baradost). They then besieged Urmiya but found it impossible to proceed to Tabriz. Eventually, the Ottomans and the Persians crushed the revolt in October 1882, using rival Kurdish tribes to this end. The Ottomans arrested the shaykh and exiled him to Istanbul, from where he escaped to Hijaz, where he died in 1883.[21]

Even though he was a religious-tribal leader, 'Ubaydullah used a national terminology that worried both the Ottomans and the Persians. He called for the establishment of a Kurdish state and argued that the Kurds were a nation like any other and therefore entitled to a state of their own. In his correspondence with foreigners, the shaykh spoke of the Kurds as a distinct people. He also complained about widespread corruption in the Persian and Ottoman administration.[22] He was definitely not the first Kurd to call for a Kurdish state—the Kurdish poet Ahmad Khani had made a similar appeal as early as the late seventeenth century—but he was almost certainly the first Kurd to lead a revolt under that flag. It seems that the shaykh used nationalist vocabulary or slogans in response to the Armenian struggle for an independent state, fearing appeals to Armenian nationalism would limit his geographical area of influence, as many Armenians were living in Kurdistan. Well aware that the Russians were supporting the Armenians, he sent emissaries to the Russian consuls in Erzurum and Van to check the czarist government's approach to the Kurdish issue. At the same time he looked for support from the British, all the while leaving the door open for negotiations with the Ottomans on local autonomy under their rule.[23]

It seems that although 'Ubaydullah's call for Kurdish independence aimed to extend his influence among the Kurds outside his territory (in the Hakkari-Baradost area), in reality he was leading a local rather than a national revolt, and tribes outside his sphere of influence ignored him in most cases.[24] Furthermore, 'Ubaydullah's national lexicon was rich in terms expressing loyalty to the Ottoman sultan and conveying a desire to secure local and tribal interests. All this seems to indicate that his national ideas were not yet sufficiently crystallized. In 1880 the shaykh sent a message to William Abbott, the British consul-general in Tabriz, explaining that the Kurds were a distinct nation and wanted to run their own lives. At the same time, eager to protect local tribal interests, he also expressed his loyalty to the Ottoman sultan. Henry Trotter, consul-general at Erzurum, wrote during the revolt: "I believe the Shaykh to be more or less personally loyal to the Sultan; and he would be ready to submit to his authority and pay him tribute as long as he could get rid of the Ottoman officials, and be looked *de lege* as well as *de facto* the ruling chief of Kurdistan."[25] This was consistent with what Trotter himself had been told by his vice-consul in Van a year earlier, namely that the shaykh was quite willing to show allegiance to the sultan. Shaykh 'Ubaydullah confirmed this when he met Abbott in Tabriz. When Abbott asked him about his ambitions, the shaykh replied that nobody could ever doubt his loyalty to the sultan, adding, however, that he had a very poor opinion of the pashas (i.e., the provincial administration). Therefore, it seems that the shaykh was indeed more eager to achieve autonomy under the sultan than national independence.[26]

A closer look at the initial stages of Kurdish nationalism may lead to the conclusion that tribalism does not necessarily contradict nationalism. Shaykh 'Ubaydullah's revolt shows that tribal leaders may raise the flag of nationalism in order to recruit their tribesmen to the national cause. It seems that, as a military system, tribalism provided leverage to promote a Kurdish national struggle, even though its national agenda was weak, while tribal culture, which was manifested in tribal rivalries and divisions, served as a barrier that prevented its further expansion. In those circumstances, the Ottoman and Persian governments easily exploited tribal rivalries, inciting the tribes against one another and thus crushing the revolt. The ambivalence of the shaykh's political agenda was evident, not least because of the prevalent tribal political culture: While the shaykh called for Kurdish independence, he also at the same time showed his readiness to compromise on Kurdish autonomy under the Ottoman sultan, in a way similar to that of tribes negotiating with central governments to defend their local interests. Furthermore, as a man commanding religious prestige, it was probably not easy for the shaykh to turn his back on the sultan (who was regarded as caliph, or leader of the Muslim community).

Development of Kurdish Nationalism
and the Role of Tribalism, 1914–1924

The collapse of the Ottoman Empire during World War I created a new situation in Kurdistan. The establishment of new states and the creation of new borders in the 1920s left Kurdistan divided between Turkey, Iraq, Iran, Syria, and the Soviet Union. Each of these states attempted to integrate the Kurdish population into their territories and crush the Kurdish national movement. Nevertheless, the Kurdish national movement continued to develop, and tribal chiefs led revolts against the central governments, often under the banner of Kurdish nationalism.

One of the prominent leaders of these revolts was the Qadiri shaykh of Sulaymaniyya, Mahmud Barzinji. The shaykh, who was a descendant of a revered Qadiri shaykh, became the most powerful man in Sulaymaniyya during World War I. His activities, however, were inconsistent: On the one hand, he acted as a local tribal chief striving to preserve his autonomy under the aegis of the central government, and on the other hand, when his tribal ambitions were thwarted, he used nationalist slogans and fought for the establishment of an independent Kurdish state. On the eve of World War I, Shaykh Mahmud established his first contacts with the British, expressing his willingness to cooperate with them and build an autonomous rule in the area under British protection.[27] At the end of 1918, he turned again to the British to gain their support and establish a Kurdish government in Kurdistan under British supervision. The shaykh handed the British a document signed by nearly forty chiefs, asking for British protection.[28] Acting on their behalf, the British appointed Barzinji as governor (*hukmdar*) of the Sulaymaniyya division. However, Barzinji, aspiring to greater autonomy, did not cooperate with them and operated as an independent ruler. In response, the British cut his salary, increasing the shaykh's hostility toward them.[29] On May 23, 1919, Barzinji organized a force of three hundred men from Persian Kurdistan to rebel against the British and arrested a number of British officials in Sulaymaniyya. The revolt spread and Barzinji consolidated his authority, but by mid-June the British, assisted by his sworn tribal rivals (mostly the tribal leaders of Jaf and Pizhdar), had sent troops against him and defeated his forces. The shaykh was arrested and exiled from Sulaymaniyya.[30]

Even though the revolt was tribal and local, Barzinji used national slogans throughout: he called for the liberation of Kurdistan from British rule, introduced himself as a Kurdish national leader, and declared himself chief ruler of all Kurdistan. He used national symbols of sovereignty, such as a Kurdish national flag (a red crescent on a green background) and his own postage stamps, as well as Kurdish administrative posts and organized military force. During the revolt, he also called for jihad, apparently because he wanted to gain the support of Kurds who were not attracted to the national cause but were motivated by religion.[31]

Barzinji's revolt reflected, more than anything else, a local and tribal struggle for local autonomy, thus exploiting the vacuum created by the Ottoman withdrawal during the war. Like many other tribal leaders who looked for protection by a major power, Barzinji too sought British support, only to rebel when Britain tried to undermine his local autonomy. The shaykh's power was local. He enjoyed the support of the Kurds in the area of Sulaymaniyya only, while Kurdish tribes outside the area were either indifferent to his struggle or supported British attempts to crush it. During the rebellion, however, national aspirations blended with religious ones, and tribal interests emerged. It seems that the shaykh took Kurdish nationalism a step forward: not only did he call for the liberation of Kurdistan and declare himself a chief ruler of all Kurdistan, but he also used symbols of national sovereignty. Although the tribesmen seemed to be motivated more by tribal and religious concerns than by national interests, the idea of Kurdish nationalism seems to have become widespread in Kurdistan after the revolt, especially in the Sulaymaniyya area.[32]

Barzinji resumed his activities upon his return to Sulaymaniyya in September 1922. He consolidated his position as an autonomous ruler in the region, formed a government one month later, issued postage stamps, and published a formal newspaper. In November 1922, after persuading tribal leaders in Sulaymaniyya and its vicinity to recognize him as the head of an independent Kurdistan, he crowned himself King of Kurdistan. In the hinterlands of Sulaymaniyya, sections of Jaf in Halabja, and the Pizhdar of Qala Diza, his former antagonists now seemed willing to join him. On March 3, 1923, the British launched air attacks on Barzinji's forces, which fled. As a result, the situation improved for the British, who took control of the areas where the shaykh was in command, i.e., Koya, Rawanduz, and Sulaymaniyya. He continued to engage in guerrilla activities, but in December 1923, after advance warning, the British bombed the shaykh's headquarters in Sulaymaniyya, including his home in May 1924. Iraqi forces entered Sulaymaniyya in 1924. Barzinji fled to the mountains in 1927, where he continued to be a thorn in the side of the British. He persisted with the guerrilla warfare against the British until he was captured in May 1930. The British offered him a salary and moved him to the town of Hilla in southern Iraq, far away from Sulaymaniyya.[33]

It is obvious that national elements became much more evident in the activity of Barzinji during the revolt of 1922. The Treaty of Sèvres, which was approved in August 1920 and provided for an autonomous Kurdish state in eastern Anatolia, apparently increased the shaykh's ambitions to achieve an independent state under his rule, at the very time when the threat posed by the Arab administration in southern Kurdistan under the Iraqi state became more serious. As a result, Barzinji managed to gain enough power to continue his fight for the Kurdish national cause. But tribal rivalries undermined his power so that he found it difficult to sway tribes outside the area of Sulaymaniyya and create a broad, sustainable national alliance under his rule.

The revolt of Isma'il Agha of Shikak, who managed to establish his authority in the north of Iranian Kurdistan during the years from 1919 to 1922, provides another example of the continued Kurdish struggle for independence. Isma'il Agha, known as Simko, was the chieftain of the Shikak tribal confederacy, the second-largest Kurdish tribal confederacy in Iran (smaller only than Kalhur). The Shikak tribe inhabited the areas of Somay and Baradost, the area west of Salmas, and Urmiya (the borderland between Iran, Iraq, and Turkey) and numbered about two thousand households (nontribal subjects not included) in 1920. During World War I, the Shikak territory was occupied in succession by the Turks (January 1915), the Russians (1916–1917), and, once again, the Turks (1918). The 1918 armistice marked the end of the Turkish presence in those areas, while the Iranian government tried to impose its power by appointing governors there. The only effective authority with a strong power base in the territory of the Shikak, however, was Simko, who was reputed to be a daring warrior and bold raider, having repeatedly looted the towns of the area and plundered their main economic resources. He was in regular contact with Shaykh Taha of Shamdinan, the grandson of Shaykh 'Ubaydullah of Nehri. Together with Shaykh Taha, Simko created (for tribal reasons) a formidable cross-border Iraq-Turkey bloc after 1918.[34]

In 1919, Simko started showing an interest in Kurdish independence. He expressed his aspirations in a letter addressed to the civil commissioner of Iraq in February 1919, demanding an independent Kurdish state. Shortly afterward, probably after he understood that his aspirations would not materialize without a struggle, he started a rebellion in the Shikak territory, taking control of the town of Dilman and ransacking Khoy. In the autumn of the same year, Simko's forces came under attack from Iranian forces and suffered heavy losses. In 1920 he regained control of the plains of Urmiya, Salmas, and the southern part of Khoy. A growing number of tribes, including the Herki, Mamash, Mangur, Piran, Zaraza, and Pizhdar, recognized his authority because of his repeated victories over Iranian troops. By the middle of 1921 the area under Simko's control covered all of the Iranian territory west of Lake Urmiya and to the south as far as Baneh and Sardasht, as well as the northwestern district of Iraq. In October 1921, his troops occupied the town of Saujbulakh (Mahabad). By July 1922, Simko's territory had extended as far east and south as Sain Qaleh and Saqqez, and Kurdish tribal leaders from Iraq and Turkey had established friendly relations with him. In 1922, however, the Iranian government launched a massive attack against him and managed to suppress his revolt. As his power declined, Simko fled to Iraq. In 1930 he was finally killed by Iranian forces in Iranian Kurdistan.[35]

A close analysis of the revolt leads to the conclusion that it was too untimely to be called national in the fullest sense. Although there was a call for Kurdish independence, no national program seemed to have been in place and no formal national foundations were established. As a military system, tribalism played an important role in forging a nucleus of local power leading the revolt. Tribal alliances were established, but they were short-lived: tribal chiefs joined Simko when his rebellion seemed successful and abandoned him when it weakened. The reason for this was the lack of a common denominator among the tribes. While tribalism played an important role as a military system (at least until the Iranian military intervened) and partly as a political system (of short-lived alliances), the tribal culture of divisiveness and rivalry remained a main obstacle to Kurdish unity. National feelings in Kurdistan were still too weak, and tribal divisions prevailed.[36]

Cooperation between Nontribal National Activists and Tribal Chieftains, 1925–1946

During the period between 1925 and 1946 an important development in the Kurdish national movement took place, starting in 1925 with the revolt of Shaykh Saʿid of Piran in Turkey, which is considered the first instance of strong cooperation between a tribal chief and Kurdish nontribal middle-class national activists. It ended with the formation in 1946 of the Republic of Mahabad, in which tribal chiefs cooperated with modern Kurdish national activists to establish a Kurdish nation-state for the first time. This contributed significantly to the spread of national thought among the Kurds, while tribalism, too, continued to be dominant in this movement.

The revolt of Shaykh Saʿid swept over a large area of Turkish Kurdistan. Saʿid, a charismatic and powerful Naqshbandi shaykh who controlled the western area around Lake Van, used his religious prestige and financial resources to establish a Kurdish state. His revolt was initiated and prepared by a modern national political organization that exploited the shaykh's charisma to mobilize the mass following that it lacked. The tribesmen themselves were probably more motivated by their loyalty to the shaykh than by true national sentiments.[37]

Preparations for the revolt were completed in 1924, the same year the Turkish government abolished the caliphate. This aroused a deep sense of unease among the Kurds, who were generally committed to Islam. But a greater reason for discomfort among the Kurds was the series of steps taken by the Turkish government against the Kurdish national movement, which included forbidding the use of the Kurdish language in the public sphere, opposing any kind of Kurdish tribal autonomy to create a more centralized administration, and arresting Kurdish national activists and intellectuals. The measures reinforced Kurdish national sentiment. Azadî (freedom), a national Kurdish organization founded in 1923, used Kurdish grievances against the Turkish government to propagate its ideological message. The organization, whose members were mainly Kurdish officers in the Turkish army, called for Kurdish independence. They contacted Kurdish tribal leaders, first and foremost Shaykh Saʿid, and proposed that, for security reasons, they become the overt leaders of the revolt. Shaykh Saʿid coordinated the planning of the revolt and called on the tribes to join it in the name of jihad against the Turkish secular government. The revolt broke out in March 1925 and spread rapidly. Though the rebels advanced toward a number of key towns such as Kharput, they failed to occupy important centers like Diyarbakır and Malatya. The tribes engaged in the struggle expelled the Turkish officials from their areas of dominance. A month later, however, the revolt was suppressed by the Turkish army. Shaykh Saʿid was caught and hanged on September 4, 1925. Even so, the revolt continued, with the shaykh's followers organizing as guerrilla forces against the Turkish government. In 1928 the Turkish government proclaimed an amnesty, and most of the fighters surrendered their arms, though guerrilla attacks continued in the region until the end of the decade. While many tribes remained aloof during the revolt, some tribal leaders turned against Shaykh Saʿid and assisted the Turkish government in crushing the revolt.[38]

We can conclude that even though an unprecedented level of cooperation emerged between modern nontribal national activists and tribal chiefs under the national flag, tribalism remained the dominant force. It provided the military and material basis for the national struggle, while the tribal culture of divisiveness constituted a barrier that prevented the expansion of rebellion. The revolt seemed neither purely religious nor purely national, but a mixture of both, as manifested by the shaykh's call for both jihad and national independence. Nationalism in itself did not seem to be a sufficient motive for joining the revolt. This was clearly brought to the fore during the revolt in a manifesto that asserted Shaykh Saʿid's aspirations to create a Kurdish government while at the same time calling for the restoration of the caliphate.[39]

Another prominent leader who contributed significantly to the cooperation between tribal chiefs and the modern middle class, which culminated in the establishment of a Kurdish republic in the Iranian town of Mahabad on January 22, 1946, was Mulla Mustafa Barzani. At the time, the tribal leaders continued to be the most influential leaders in Kurdistan, while the middle class expanded.[40] This situation promoted a closer cooperation between tribal chiefs and the middle class, thus preserving the special status of the former.

Cooperation between Barzani and the middle class was preceded by a large-scale revolt against the Iraqi government, waged under the Mulla's leadership between 1943 and 1945. The revolt, which was generally viewed as a tribal and local struggle, paved Barzani's way to the leadership of the national Kurdish movement. Unlike his brother Ahmad, Mulla Mustafa was not a religious leader, but he nevertheless gained prestige from the family's religious status. He was a warrior and charismatic tribal leader who had developed his national agenda step by step. He joined his brother's local revolts against the Iraqi government in the 1930s, and by the 1940s had become experienced enough to lead a revolt.[41]

In September 1943, Barzani and his followers in the village of Barzan (in Iraqi Kurdistan, very close to the Iranian border) attacked an Iraqi police post in the area and started a revolt that lasted about two years, during which Barzani's followers ambushed Iraqi troops and attacked Iraqi police positions. During the revolt, Barzani demonstrated remarkable political capabilities, forcing his sworn enemy, Mahmud Agha of the Zibari tribe, to cooperate with him for a common goal, that is, to break away from an Arab Iraqi administration imposed upon them. Barzani was also joined by Agha Mahmud Khalifa, head of a section of the Baradost tribe, by the tribal leaders of the Duski, and by several other tribal chiefs. Others, however, such as Shaykh Rashid Lolan and Gharib Agha from Surchi, chose to support the Iraqi government in its struggle against Barzani because of tribal rivalries.[42]

Since the revolt was tribal and local, Barzani was ready to compromise with the Iraqi government on Kurdish autonomy within the Iraqi state. In October 1943 the Iraqi prime minister Nuri al-Saʿid expressed his willingness to reach a compromise with Barzani. He appointed Majid Mustafa, a Kurd from Sulaymaniyya, as minister without portfolio and dispatched him to conduct negotiations with Barzani. As a result of his meeting with Majid Mustafa in January 1944, Barzani visited Baghdad to meet with senior Iraqi government officials. Nuri al-Saʿid was prepared to accept Barzani's demands, which included the establishment of a new Kurdish province in the Dohuk area in Iraq, the appointment of a Kurdish representative in the Iraqi educational system to preserve Kurdish cultural identity, and the investment of additional resources to improve the agrarian and social situation in the Kurdish areas. Following the refusal of Regent ʿAbd al-Ilah and the majority of Iraqi ministers to accept his position, Nuri al-Saʿid submitted his resignation in June 1944.[43] Since his demands were not met, Barzani continued to rebel and was joined by additional Kurdish tribal leaders.[44] In September 1945 the Iraqi army launched a large-scale attack against Barzani and his supporters, using his tribal rivals to crush the revolt. Barzani crossed the border into Iran with about forty-five hundred of his men and settled in the village of Mahabad, from which he launched attacks against the Kurdish tribal leaders who were operating against him. He called these opponents "the traitors of the Kurdish issue."[45]

In Mahabad, Barzani joined the national Kurdish activists who had occupied the area under the aegis of the Soviet Union, which had penetrated into the area during World War II with a view to strengthening its power in the region. The Republic of Mahabad, established on January 22, 1946, was the first national entity created by the Kurds. Barzani cooperated, for the first time, with middle-class Kurdish national activists. The partnership apparently influenced his political thinking, which became more nationalistic.[46] The newly established republic boasted national institutions and a national agenda. On January 22, 1946, a Kurdish parliament was elected with 134 representatives, including many tribal leaders. They established a Kurdish administration and began collecting taxes. Many Kurds across Kurdistan supported the republic. The establishment of the Republic of Mahabad contributed to the perception that an independent Kurdish state in Kurdistan was not beyond the realm of possibility.[47] The Kurdish language and culture flourished: textbooks and newspapers were published in Kurdish (at a time when the central governments of Iraq, Turkey, and Iran harshly restricted Kurdish publications), and the primary language of study in the schools was Kurdish, which led to a growing national awareness. The cooperation between the tribal chiefs and an educated middle class was exceptional. While Barzani and his followers were in charge of the military force, the middle class contributed to the spread of Kurdish national culture. Still, tribal rivalries did not disappear, so that the fact that Barzani controlled the military became a source of concern for rival tribal chiefs. The common denominator of Kurdishness nonetheless seemed to prevail.[48]

In February 1946, Barzani, joined by a Kurdish nationalist lawyer, Hamza ʿAbdullah, and tribal leaders, established the Kurdistan Democratic Party (KDP) of Iraq, creating an alliance between tribal forces and modern middle-class national activists. The KDP became the most influential party in Kurdistan in the following years and contributed to the spread of Kurdish national thought. The party was founded when Mulla Mustafa Barzani, together with Hamza ʿAbdullah, approached the son of Shaykh Mahmud Barzinji, Shaykh Baba ʿAli, asking him to participate in the creation of a Kurdish party that would amalgamate all the Kurdish national organizations in Iraq under one umbrella. This resulted in the establishment of the KDP.[49] Barzani was elected as its president. Two Kurdish tribal leaders, Shaykh Latif, the son of Shaykh Mahmud Barzinji, and Ziyad Muhammad Agha, head of the Kakai tribe in the Sulaymaniyya area, were chosen as Barzani's deputies. Hamza ʿAbdullah was appointed the party's secretary general. The party adopted an agenda that ostensibly set two contradictory goals: "Absolute independence for Kurdistan" and a "struggle for the establishment of a federal state in Iraq which would be the democratic federal state of Kurdistan," implying either that the party wanted to leave open the option of negotiations with the Iraqi government on autonomy within the state of Iraq (thus reflecting traditional tribal politics), or that the national movement in Iraq was still too immature to define its final goals.[50]

The Republic of Mahabad collapsed in December 1946, after the Soviets had left the region (under U.S. and British pressure) and enabled the Iranian army to deploy in the area. Barzani and his forty-five hundred followers escaped to Iraqi Kurdistan on April 17–18, 1947, but some of them were captured by the Iraqi government and executed. Barzani himself refused to surrender and fled through Iraq, Turkey, and Iran before reaching the Soviet Union, together with about eight hundred followers. He remained in the Soviet Union until the collapse of the Iraqi monarchy in 1958.[51]

The case of the Republic of Mahabad and the establishment of the KDP show that tribalism as a military and political system may contribute significantly to a national cause. While the tribal culture of divisiveness hinders the development of national unity, it also tends to erode as national awareness develops. Tribal identity is not necessarily contradictory to national identity, and national awareness may develop among tribesmen over time, especially when cooperation with a modern middle class is encouraged.

Conclusions

This chapter considers tribalism as a multifaceted phenomenon with an equivocal impact on nationalism, both constructive and destructive. Duality is therefore the term best used to describe the relationship between tribalism and nationalism in the Kurdish national movement. On the one hand, tribalism gave leverage to the Kurdish national struggle, as the tribes were the only military and economic entities within Kurdish society that could engage in any kind of struggle against the central governments in Kurdistan. Political tribal alliances enabled the Kurds to stage rebellions over quite large areas. On the other hand, the tribal culture of divisiveness and rivalry led to short-lived alliances and impeded the creation of national unity, which could have led to a much larger national struggle.

Unlike what Kendal and Tahiri imply, it seems that tribalism was not the only obstacle to Kurdish nationalism; it may not even have been the main obstacle, and indeed there were other substantial barriers such as military inferiority and lack of international support. Turkey, Iran, and Iraq had such strong armies that they could have suppressed any revolt, even if the Kurdish people had been more unified. It seems that without international support and a strong army to protect their independence, the unification of the Kurds would have been insufficient. As far as van Bruinessen is concerned, the negative effect of tribalism on nationalism cannot be underestimated, as tribalism is in many ways responsible for the weak national cohesiveness among the Kurds.

It is quite clear that tribalism does not necessarily contradict nationalism. The Kurdish tribal chiefs, who were deeply involved in the Kurdish national movement, apparently did not find an inherent contradiction between tribalism and nationalism, and used nationalism as an overall political framework with which to protect their tribal interests. Tribes therefore can engage in a national movement and lead it. There is no clear-cut dichotomy between Kurdish nationalism and tribalism, as many Kurdish intellectuals and activists came from a tribal milieu, especially from leading tribal families. In the modern era of multiple identities, a person may identify both as a tribesman and a nationalist. This applies to Kurdish society, too. It seems that only close cooperation between the educated middle class (which has grown over time) and tribal leaders has enabled continuous development and crystallization of the Kurdish national movement. Thus, tribal divisiveness has eroded while nationalism has increased in popularity.

During the period under discussion, the Kurdish national movement still seemed to be weak, which is why tribal, religious, and national interests blended together and no cohesive political agenda had emerged. Nevertheless, this movement had gone a long way since its beginnings, a fact that should not be underestimated, as nationalism had evolved from being a slogan used by tribal chiefs to a more crystallized agenda. Though the creation of strong national consciousness takes time, tribal solidarities, which may impede this process, will not necessarily prevent it. The erosion of tribal loyalties and organizations in modern times often paves the way for stronger national solidarity, even though tribal rivalries have not vanished.

PART II

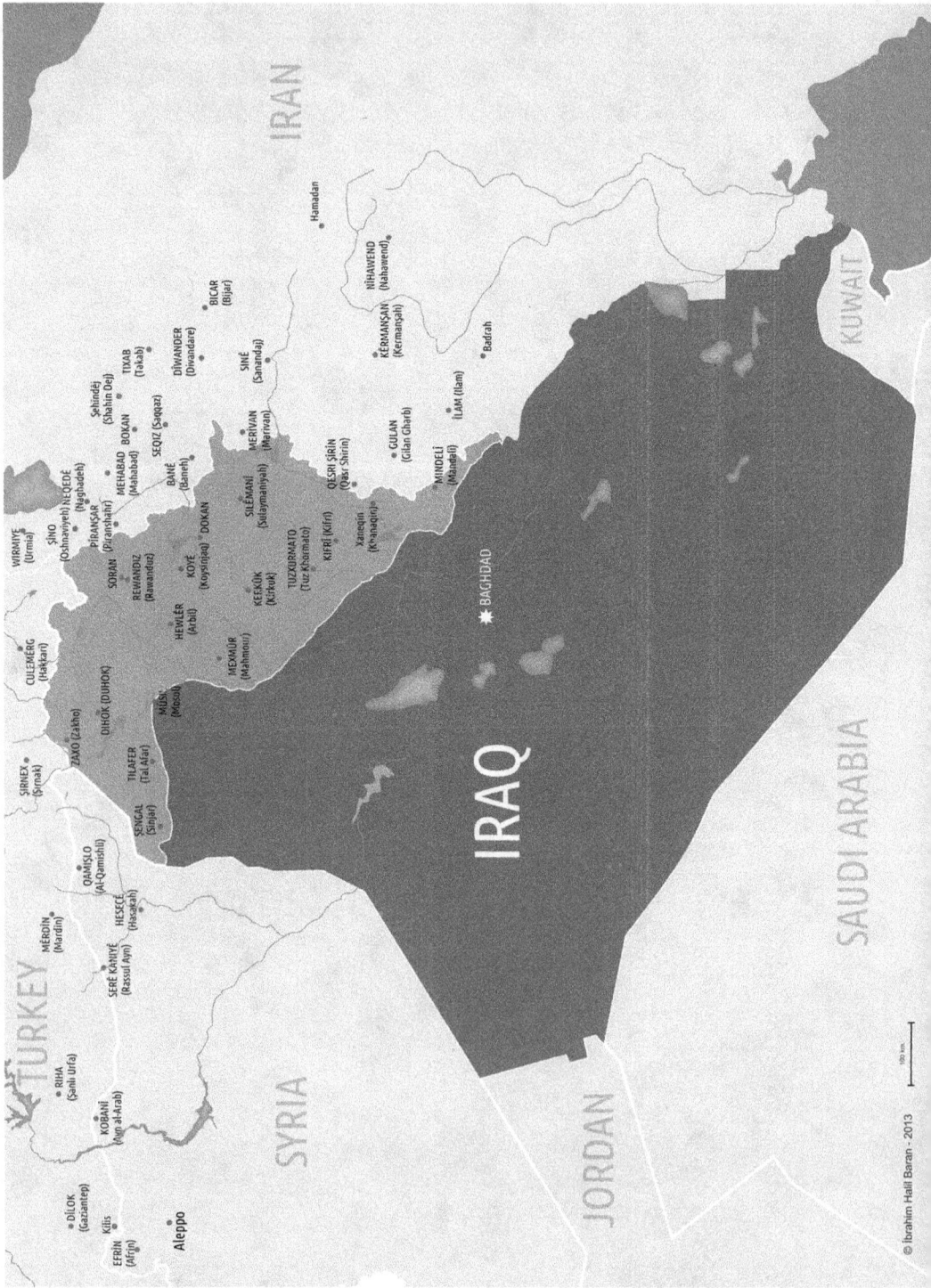

TURKEY

DÎLOK
(Gaziantep)

Kilis

EFRÎN
(Afrin)

Aleppo

RIHA
(Şanlı Urfa)

KOBANÊ
(Ayn al-Arab)

MÊRDÎN
(Mardin)

SERÊ KANIYÊ
(Rasül Ayn)

QAMIŞLO
(Al-Qamishli)

HESEKÊ
(Hasakah)

ŞIRNEX
(Şırnak)

ZAXO (Zakho)

DIHOK (DIHOK)

ŞINO
(Oshnaviyeh)

NEQEDÊ
(Naghadeh)

WIRMIYÊ
(Urmia)

CULEMÊRG
(Hakkari)

SÊNÊ
(Sanandaj)

SILO
(Sine)

MÛSIL
(Mosul)

TILAFER
(Tal Afar)

ŞENGAL
(Sinjar)

SYRIA

JORDAN

SAUDI ARABIA

IRAQ

BAGHDAD

HEWLÊR
(Arbil)

MEXMÛR
(Makhmour)

REWANDIZ
(Rawanduz)

SORAN
(Diyana)

PÎRANŞAR
(Piranshahr)

MEHABAD
(Mahabad)

BANÊ
(Baneh)

SEQIZ (Saqqez)

Şehîndej
(Shahin Dej)

BOKAN

TIXAB
(Takab)

BÎCAR
(Bijar)

DIWANDER
(Diwandare)

MERIVAN
(Marivan)

KOYÊ
(Koysinjaq)

DOKAN

SILÊMANÎ
(Sulaymaniyah)

KEFKOK
(Kirkuk)

TUZXURMATO
(Tuz Khurmato)

KIFRÎ (Kifri)

Xaneqîn
(Khanaqin)

QESRî ŞÎRîN
(Qas Shirin)

GILAN
(Gilan Gharb)

MINDELÎ
(Mandali)

ÎLAM (Ilam)

KÊRMANŞAN
(Kermanşah)

NIHAWEND
(Nahawend)

Hamadan

Badrah

IRAN

KUWAIT

100 km

© Ibrahim Halil Baran - 2013

Kurdish Integration in Iraq: The Paradoxes of Nation Formation and Nation Building

SHERKO KIRMANJ

The Question of National Identity

Scholars investigating the meaning of identity and nation formation have sought to explain these concepts from primordialist, ethnosymbolic, or modernist (instrumentalist and constructivist) points of view. For primordialists, identity is an objective entity with inherent features such as race, territory, language, and kinship. In this view, all people are born into an ethnic/national context that has a profound effect on every aspect of their lives.[1] In contrast, the modernist theoretical approach is based on the notion of "rational choice." Modernists suggest that identities are not given; rather, they are artifacts constructed under particular circumstances and discarded, adjusted, or traded for others under different conditions.[2] Furthermore, modernists argue, a nation is the product of modern conditions, in particular early industrialism, that go hand in hand with social mobility and a need for mass literacy and public education.[3] A third perspective is what Anthony D. Smith calls the ethnosymbolic approach, in which it is argued that while a nation may seem modern, it has retained its premodern ethnic roots.[4] In other words, the nation carries most of the elements of an ethnic group, such as shared ancestry, symbols and myths, shared historical memories, and a collective cultural identity.[5]

The methodology used here to examine the integration of Kurds in Iraq inclines toward the ethnosymbolic approach. The reason for this is that ethnosymbolism emphasizes the importance of memories, values, myths, and symbols, including flags, anthems, frontiers, services for fallen heroes, shrines and museums, history textbooks, even flower and animal totems, all of which are at the heart of the Iraqi case.[6] For example, the clashes among the Kurdish, Iraqi, and pan-Arab nationalisms very often involve the pursuit of territorial rights, symbolic goals, the language of teaching in the educational system, the preservation of ancient or religious sacred sites, and the right to worship according to one's own traditions. These goals have often led to protest and bloodshed. Yet, modernist theories tend to marginalize these issues, especially the critical component of common memories, shared ancestry, and attachment to a historic homeland. The other argument in support of the ethnosymbolic approach is that Iraq's ethnic groups often view their identities in primordial or essentialist terms, at least at this stage of Iraq's history. In view of all of the above, the idea that collective identity is situational, negotiated, or culturally constructed does not contribute adequately to the creation of a model that would help us understand the flaws facing a unified national Iraqi identity.

At this stage, defining "nation" will be helpful in examining the paradoxes and obstacles confronting nation formation in Iraq. This chapter draws heavily on the definitions of nation put forward by Montserrat Guibernau and Smith.[7] The concept of nation refers to a social group conscious of its shared community, common memory, culture and ancestry, and sense of solidarity; that is strongly attached to a clearly demarcated territory and a common project for the future; and that claims the right to self-rule.

In the light of the above definition, theoretical perspectives, and a review of modern Iraqi history, two sets of problems appear to be at the forefront of nation formation in Iraq. The first is systemic, having to do with the paradoxical makeup of Iraqi society itself: it is related to questions of common memory, ancestry and history, shared culture and language, and attachment to a historic homeland. The second is intermittent, related to successive Iraqi regimes' policies of discrimination and exclusion, and to the monopoly of power by a specific ethnic or sectarian group—Sunni Arabs from 1921 until 2003, Shi'i Arabs since 2003. The latter has been studied and documented quite extensively.[8] While this study examines both sets of difficulties, its emphasis is on the first set.

Postwar Violence: Questions at the Roots of the Conflict

In comparison with the early years of the U.S. occupation (2003–2007), Iraq has recently seen slight improvement in the security situation and a relatively decline in violence. In fact, by mid-2007, fatalities resulting from ethnic and sectarian violence had declined by nearly 90 percent according to the U.S. Department of Defense.[9] Statistics compiled by Iraq Body Count 2011 indicate that the number of civilian deaths further decreased from an average of 2,300 per month in 2006 to 322 per month in August 2011. After two rounds of elections to the Iraqi National Assembly in 2005, Iraq also staged three successful elections in 2009 and 2010: provincial elections in January 2009, elections to the Kurdistan Regional Government in July 2009, and elections to the Iraqi parliament in March 2010. In contrast to the 2005 elections, when Sunnis boycotted the process, later rounds enjoyed a high participation rate across all ethnic and sectarian groups.[10]

Despite the promising picture of progress and some security gains until 2011, the situation in Iraq remains unstable, primarily because the underlying sources of its instability have yet to be resolved. The Iraqi problem cannot be understood without close scrutiny of the structure of Iraqi society, in particular the question of identity. That is why Iraq's current political predicament, especially the ethnonational and sectarian conflict, should not be attributed exclusively to insurgency and terrorism. Indeed, conflict and disputes among Iraq's ethnonational and sectarian groups are the crux of the dilemma that has torn Iraq apart since its establishment by Great Britain in 1920.[11]

Scholars have reached different conclusions as to the roots of the current predicament facing Iraq regarding nation building, national reconciliation, and security. Some blame the U.S. administration for making a series of blunders that resulted in what they describe as a fiasco. According to this view, a lack of knowledge about Iraqi society and politics, the deployment of insufficient military forces, the dismantling of Iraq's armed forces, and the process of de-Ba'thification are just a few factors that have contributed to the current Iraqi problems.[12] Others go further and blame the Americans for fostering ethnic loyalty.[13] In this chapter, however, it will be argued that the core issues are in fact national identity and the lack of ingredients vital to forming a unified nation—in other words, nation formation.

The Paradoxes of Common Memory and Shared Ancestry

Most theoretical approaches, in particular ethnosymbolism, see common memory as an essential ingredient in forming a nation. Historical sources and related common memory written from the Iraqi Arab (Sunni and Shi'i) or Kurdish perspectives reveal the contradictory and/or paradoxical nature of these two communities, which supposedly constitute one Iraqi nation with a shared memory.[14]

Uniform mass education, which was introduced in Iraq in the 1920s and 1930s, was used to "build" a nation. As part of a uniform educational strategy, textbooks (history textbooks in particular) were used to present so-called facts that would contribute to an apparent sense of unity. Iraqi textbooks are hence worth examining. Meanwhile, after the formation of the Kurdistan quasi state in 1991, the textbooks produced by the Kurdistan Regional Government (KRG) were modified, if not reconstructed, to reflect the Kurds' vision of nation building. They, too, will be examined. The aim of this chapter is to identify the paradoxical nature of the common memory and ancestry of the Iraqi and the Kurdish communities in Iraq.

The paradox is clearly evident in the way Kurdish and Iraqi authorities highlight the 1948, 1952, and 1956 uprisings and the 1958 revolution. The textbooks published by the Iraqi government or the KRG underscore the importance of these events as part of a common memory and representation of Iraq's history.[15] Ironically, after more than four decades (1968–2003) of pan-Arab projects, albeit failed ones, and eight years (2003–2011) from the collapse of the Iraqi Ba'th regime, no history school textbooks were dedicated to Iraqi history. During their six-year high school education, Iraqi students studied *History of Old Civilizations*, *Arab-Islamic History*, *Modern and Contemporary History of the Arab Homeland*, *History of Arab-Islamic Civilization*, *the European Modern and Contemporary History*, and *The Modern and Contemporary History of the Arab Homeland*. While the Iraqi textbooks in the pre- and post-Ba'th era presented Iraqi events as part of an overall Arab history beyond Iraqi borders, the KRG textbooks described Iraqi Kurdish history as part of an overall Kurdistan history beyond Iraqi-Kurdistan borders. This reflects the paradoxical nature of the self-image of the two major Iraqi communities, the Kurds and the Iraqi Arabs. It is part of another identity crisis, namely that of Arab and Kurdish national borders beyond Iraqi state borders. Reflecting a pan-Arab vision, Iraqi textbooks paid, and still pay, particular attention to the April 1941 coup led by Arab nationalist officers. In fact, they depicted the last Ba'thi coup, the July Revolution of 1968, as "the legitimate heir" of the April 1941 revolution.[16] The KRG textbooks emphasize other events, such as the Black September of 1930, when the Kurds protested against the British-Iraqi Treaty that ignored Kurdish rights.[17] Both the April 1941 coup and Black September were significant events in contemporary Iraqi history. The total disregard of the April revolution in the KRG textbooks and of Black September in Iraqi textbooks can only be understood in the light of the different views Kurds and Arabs hold of Iraqi history.

Several important events are etched in the recent memory of the Iraqi Kurds, such as the collapse of the 1974–1975 Kurdish revolt, the 1988 genocidal *Anfal* operations and the chemical attacks on the city of Halabja, and the 1991 uprising and the subsequent Kurdish mass exodus.[18] None of these occupies a significant space in the memories of Iraqi Arabs or in Iraqi textbooks, apart from the 1991 uprising, in which Shiʻi Arabs also participated. However, as the Shiʻis generally designate their dates according to the Islamic Hijri calendar, their commemoration date does not coincide with that of the Kurds, who use the Gregorian calendar. To be more specific, while the Kurds commemorated the 1991 uprising in 2011 between March 5 and 21, the Shiʻis marked it in August of that same year. Contrary to the positive image that the Shiʻis and the Kurds have of the 1991 uprising, excluding its suppression and the subsequent repercussions this had, the Sunnis generally view the uprising as one of the darkest episodes of Iraqi history. Official Iraqi (until 2003) and Sunni-inclined sources still call those days *safhat al-ghadr wal-khiyana* (the chapter of treachery and treason) and the participants—heroes to both the Kurds and the Shiʻis—are labeled *al-ghawghaʼiyyun* (demagogic mobs).[19]

The myth of a real, or imagined, shared ancestry, like that of common memory, provides a psychological focus on the unity of a nation. Generally speaking, both the Iraqi Sunnis and the Shiʻis trace their ancestry to Semitic Arabs who migrated from the Arabian Peninsula to Iraq. The Kurds, however, claim that they do not come from the same stock. This has created another paradox for nation formation in Iraq. The Kurds believe, whether accurately or not, that they are the descendants of the Medes, and thus are of Aryan ancestry.[20] Indeed, the pre-Islamic Median Empire (612–549 BC) shapes the first formative memories of Kurdish nationalism, as echoed in the Kurdish national anthem:

We [Kurds] are the children of Medes and Kai Khosrow [Cyaxares],[21]
Both our faith and religion are our homeland.[22]

By the same token, 612 BC, the year the Medians defeated the Assyrian Empire and established the Median Empire, is now marked as the start of the Kurdish calendar.[23] The textbooks published by the KRG devoted separate chapters to the Kurdistani and the Mesopotamian civilizations in order to give the Kurds distinct historical roots; the purpose was to portray the Mitani and Medes civilizations as Kurdistani and the Sumerian, Assyrian, and Babylonian civilizations as Iraqi.[24] Paradoxically, during the Saddam era the Iraqi textbooks portrayed the Median people as "foreigners" and "destroyers" of Mesopotamian civilization.[25] Although the current Iraqi textbooks no longer contain these negative terms, they are still written from a pan-Arab and pan-Islamic perspective. Not only are the Kurds not mentioned in the current textbooks, but the term "Iraq" itself is only mentioned as part of the Arab world and national history. This is evident in the titles of high school textbooks, such as the two titles dedicated to Arab world history (year three intermediate and year six preparatory), the two titles covering *Arab Islamic History and Civilization* (year two intermediate and year four general); one title of *Old Civilizations* (year one intermediate); and one title about *European History*. The history of Iraq, Iraqis, Kurds, and Kurdistan is almost entirely absent from Iraqi textbooks.

The semi-independent Kurdish principalities between the sixteenth and the mid-nineteenth centuries provided another formative memory for the Kurds as their self-rule set up a precedent the Kurds admire today. In the twentieth century this was reflected in the historical narrative of the Kurds in general and of Kurdish nationalists in particular.[26] The latter period witnessed the Shaykh Mahmud revolts of 1919, 1922, and 1926 as well as the first and second Barzan revolts of 1931–1932 and 1943–1945. Evidence of these can be found in the current textbooks studied in the KRG-controlled region schools.[27]

Labeling the Medians "invaders" and "destroyers" of Mesopotamian civilization in Iraqi textbooks (until the collapse of the Saddam Husayn regime) and ignoring Kurdish history and Kurdistani civilization in current Iraqi textbooks—the exact opposite of the Kurdish portrayal of the Medians as their forefathers, as reflected in KRG textbooks—shows the inherent difference between the Arab-Iraqi nationalist and Kurdish nationalist visions. It also demonstrates the difficulties facing people residing on Iraqi territory, be they Arab or Kurdish, in building a unified nation.

The Extension of Ethnonational and Sectarian Borders beyond the Nation-State

One of the systemic obstacles to the formation of the Iraqi nation is that major Iraqi ethnonational and religious communities have links beyond the designated territorial borders of the state. Arabs (Sunnis and Shi'is)

live in four countries (Syria, Jordan, Saudi Arabia, and Kuwait) border-
ing Iraq, and they share more culturally, linguistically, and politically with
each other than they do with their supposed "co-nationals," the Kurds.
This is particularly true of the Sunnis. Similarly, Iraqi Kurds have ethnic-
based co-nationals in three neighboring countries: Iran, Turkey, and
Syria. As for the Shiʻis, although they share a common ethnicity with the
Sunnis, they are of the same religious denomination as Iranians or as other
Shiʻi Arabs residing in the neighboring Gulf States. All these ties lead to
a disjuncture between loyalty to the state, Iraq, on the one hand, and to
co-national/religious groups across the Iraqi border on the other. The sub-
sequent existence of at least two current nationalisms, pan-Arab and pan-
Kurdish, is a reflection of this reality. Both nationalisms call for Arab or
Kurdish unification, as an irredentist or unificationist movement.[28]

The early Kurdish national movements in the late nineteenth and early
twentieth centuries called for an independent, united Kurdistan, akin
to Arab national movements. But the situation was complicated by the
clash of these two strands of nationalism, in particular when Iraq became an independent state. Nevertheless, after World War II the Kurds
usually adapted to the situation, aspiring to less ambitious goals such as
autonomy or federalism. Likewise, pan-Arabism, which was the major
political current to engulf the Arab world after World War I, lost its allure
in the late 1960s.

In this context, another obstacle that further complicated Kurdish integration into Iraq was the fact that in bi- or multiethnonational states,
the state was generally identified with one ethnonational group. In the
context of Iraq, the state was perceived as an Arab state. This notion was
enshrined in successive Iraqi constitutions until 2004, when for the first
time Iraq was not identified as part of an Arab nation. Nonetheless, all
three recent Iraqi prime ministers, Iyad ʻAllawi, Ibrahim al-Jaʻfari, and
Nuri al-Maliki, stressed an uncompromising vision of the Arab identity
of Iraq.[29]

In the absence of harmony between the Iraqi ethnonational groups
and belief in a common destiny uniting all Iraqis, it is natural for the Iraqi
communities to incline toward their co-national or religious groups outside Iraqi borders. This is particularly evident with Iraqi diaspora groups
such as the Iraqi Kurds, who form ongoing associations with the Kurds
from Iran or Turkey, and the Iraqi Shiʻis, who identify with Saudi Arabian, Kuwaiti, and Bahraini Shiʻis rather than with their "co-citizens"
from Ramadi and Mosul. One of the reasons for this is their strong sectarian and ethnonational affiliation, as well as the weakness of Iraqi patri-

otism compared to Arab and Kurdish nationalism. The explanation for this lies in another paradox facing nation formation in Iraq, namely the paradox of imagined communities.

The Paradox of the Imagined Community

The term "imagined community" was coined by Benedict Anderson in 1991.[30] Anderson asserted that in the mind of each member of a community lives the image of that community. The significance of imagination is that "nations are built in the imagination before they are built on the ground."[31] When Iraq became a state, it already comprised two ethno-nationalisms, each of which had its own "imagined community." In this context, it is worth looking at the emergence of Arab and Kurdish ethno-nationalism and their imagined communities to understand the weakness of Iraqi state nationalism (or patriotism).

The idea of the "nation" was adopted by educated Arabs and Kurds prior to the complete disintegration of the Ottoman Empire in 1918. Several reasons were behind the strengthening of Arab and Kurdish nationalism. Among them was the introduction of a series of reforms, known as *Tanzimat*, by the Ottomans in 1864.[32] The reforms were aimed at reorganizing the relations between the center and the peripheries, whereby the ethnic-based principalities lost their autonomy. As part of the reforms, many Ottoman officers were sent to Europe for training and Europeans were asked to train the Ottoman army. Upon their return, officers from diverse ethnic groups established the Young Ottoman Movement in 1865, hoping to reinvigorate the Ottoman Empire, often labeled "the Sick Man of Europe." In 1880 the Young Turks ethnified the Ottoman Empire. When the Young Turks assumed and consolidated their power in 1909, however, they revealed a nationalist ideology of their own—namely, Turanism or Turkism.[33] This move further strengthened non-Turkish (Arab, Kurdish, and Armenian) nationalist sentiments,[34] and separate associations, clubs, and leagues were established within these communities. They published books and newspapers, thereby improving communication among the intelligentsia of the Arab and the Kurdish communities. They also took drastic measures against many of the recently established non-Turkish associations, with the result that clubs and societies that had previously operated freely turned clandestine.

Within the Arab community, the most active of these associations were

Jamʿiyyat al-Arabiyya al-Fatat (the Young Arab Society), founded in Paris in 1911, and Jamʿiyyat al-ʿAhd (the Society of the Covenant), founded in Istanbul in 1913.[35] These organizations demanded autonomy or independence from the Ottomans. Their demands culminated in the 1916 Arab Revolt during World War I. By the end of the war, all Arab lands had been liberated from Ottoman rule. As a result, the Arab nationalists believed that they were on the verge of realizing their dream of a national state.[36] However, these hopes soon evaporated as colonial powers divided the Arab lands among themselves.

After World War I, a more sophisticated current of Arab nationalism, identified with Satiʿ al-Husri and Michel Aflaq, emerged. Both prewar and postwar models of Arab nationalism made a common language and history the primary basis of nation formation and nation building.[37] However, the distinguishing characteristics of both models were their imagined homelands. While the homeland of prewar Arab nationalism was the Arab part of Asia (the Arabian Peninsula, Greater Syria, and Arab Iraq), that of postwar Arab nationalism included all of what is now known as the Arab world, from the Persian Gulf to the Atlantic Ocean.

Parallel to Arab nationalism, Kurdish nationalism took shape before the creation of Iraq. It also emphasized territorial and linguistic unity. It emerged first in the realms of language and literature in the sixteenth century, when Kurdish poets broke the monopoly of Arabic and Persian in literary production. The most important literary manifestation of political awareness was Ahmad Khani's popular epic *Mem u Zin*, which he composed in 1694. In the epic, Khani was explicitly modern in his conceptualization of the Kurds as a nation, since he referred to Kurds, Arabs, Persians, and Turks not in the then prevailing sense of a "religious community," but rather in an ethnonational sense.[38] He laid the foundations of Kurdish nationalism and urged Kurds to liberate Kurdistan and establish a state of their own. In 1596, long before Khani, Sharaf Khan al-Bitlisi had defined the ethnographic boundaries of a Kurdish "imagined community" and of the Kurdish homeland.[39] Remarkably, both al-Bitlisi and Khani lived before the rise of modern nationalism, and their idea of a state based on ethnic or national groups predated the French Revolution of 1789, which is often thought to be the true beginning of the nation-state concept. Another godfather of Kurdish nationalism, Haji Qadiri Koyi (1817–1897), a poet, urged the Kurds to unite and form an independent state. Both Khani and Koyi emphasized the importance of using language, literature, and newspapers for mass communication.[40] *Kurdi-*

stan, the first Kurdish newspaper, was published in 1898, one year after Koyi's death. The name shows the significance of what Kurds perceived as their homeland.[41]

Like Sharif Hussein of Mecca, who used practical means to achieve statehood, Kurdish religious and nationalist leaders led a string of revolts from 1880 to 1925.[42] In addition, several Kurdish organizations were established by Kurdish urban intellectuals and officers residing in Istanbul in a way very similar to the founding of Arab organizations. The first, *Komeley Taraqi u Ta'ali Kurdistan* (Society for the Rise and Progress of Kurdistan), was established in 1908. A second organization, *Komeley Hevi Kurd* (Kurdish Hope Society), whose members came from all over Kurdistan, was founded in 1912. The aims of these organizations ranged from autonomy to full independence.[43] At the end of World War I, the idea of forming separate Arab and Kurdish states occupied the minds of a sizable proportion of Arab and Kurdish intellectuals. The Kurdish and Arab "imagined communities" are demonstrated on the front covers of Iraqi and Kurdistani textbooks: the former display the map of the Arab world, and the latter a map of Greater Kurdistan.[44] The current Iraqi textbooks do not display the Arab world map, but the title and the content of the books remain nearly intact.[45]

The major impact of these two evolving nationalisms, namely the weakening of Iraqi patriotism and the identification of Kurds and Arabs with Iraq, resulted from the fact that their "imagined communities" did not coincide with the actual communities in which they were living. On the one hand, the Arab and Kurdish hoped-for communities overlapped, and on the other hand they cut across Iraq's territory and the imagined community created after the formation of Iraq. The other problem associated with this is that both the Kurdish and the Arab nationalisms aimed at assimilating Iraq, partially or fully, into the Arab nation in the case of Arab nationalism, and into a Greater Kurdistan or Iraqi Kurdistan in the case of the Kurds.

Historically, two other external factors strengthened the ethnonational-based aspirations of the Kurds and the Arabs. The first was Woodrow Wilson's famous Fourteen Points put forward in 1918, and the second was a promise of statehood held out by the French and British colonial powers to several ethnonational groups in the Ottoman Empire during World War I. Undeniably, Wilson's Fourteen Points and the Allied promises envisaged ethnic and linguistic-based states. Indeed, point twelve of Wilson's declaration was particularly tempting as it emphasized that non-Turkish nationalities within the Ottoman Empire "should be assured

The Arab imagined community on the front cover of an Iraqi textbook.

The Kurdish imagined community on the front cover of a KRG textbook.

. . . [of] an absolutely unmolested opportunity of autonomous development."[46] This point was understood by the Arab and Kurdish elites to mean that every ethnonational group (e.g., Kurds and Arabs) within the Ottoman Empire should enjoy the right to establish its own state. This was clearly indicated by the way Shaykh Mahmud, the leader of the Kurdish revolts of 1919–1930, confronted the British authorities during his trial in 1919 by presenting Wilson's Fourteen Points and the French and British declaration of 1918, both of which recognized the right of people to self-determination.[47] His main argument was that he had full rights to fight for the freedom of his people on the basis of these points and of British promises of independence.[48] Indeed, Shaykh Mahmud had the text of Woodrow Wilson's twelfth point and the Anglo-French declaration of November 7, 1918, strapped to his arm like a talisman when he was fighting the British forces in 1919.[49] Likewise, Iraqi Arab intellectuals, among them Sa'd Salih and Muhammad Rida al-Shabibi, who later played a critical role in Iraqi politics, debated among themselves whether Wilson's Fourteen Points should provide the basis for their demand for Iraqi independence.[50]

The British promises to the Arabs were documented in July 1915 in a letter from Henry McMahon, a British official, to the Sharif of Mecca. McMahon promised to free the Arabs from the Turkish yoke and assist them in establishing their own state.[51] In a memorandum submitted to the Conference of Allied Powers at the House of Commons, Prince Faysal, who would later become the king of Iraq, reminded them of the promises they had made to his father. Faysal argued that his father "considered that in view of the pledges given to him, the essential unity and independence of the Arab-speaking provinces of the Turkish Empire were secure in the event of the success of the Allies."[52]

The British had also made several promises to the Kurds. They recognized the Kurds as a distinct ethnonational group and separated them from the Arabs both ethnically and territorially.[53] Indeed, soon after their occupation of Iraq, the British published a newspaper in Kurdish, *Tega-yishtini Rasti* (Understanding the Truth). This was part of a strategy to win Kurdish hearts and minds and to encourage the Kurds to rebel against the Ottomans. The logo of the newspaper stated that its aim was "to serve the Kurdish unity and freedom."[54] Later these promises were inscribed in the Treaty of Sèvres (1920), which recommended the establishment of a Kurdish independent state but was superseded by the Treaty of Lausanne (1923), which made no mention of Kurdish statehood.

These provisions and promises had a significant impact on the mind-sets of Arabs and Kurds and served to strengthen both ethnonationalisms. However, after its formation, Iraq became identified as Arab as a result of which Iraqi Arabs were more willing to accept the newly created state. Moreover, by the time the Kurdish-populated areas were annexed to Iraq in 1926, the idea of an Arab state had already taken root. This created the next generations' position on Iraq as part of the Arab world and as an Arab rather than a binational state. In opposition to this approach, the Kurds have challenged the Arab identity of Iraq ever since, firstly because they are convinced that every nation has its own genius and ought hence to have its own state. Secondly, the Kurds see statehood as a prerequisite for maintaining their political and territorial identity. Thirdly, as states are generally identified with one national group, for the Kurds to accept Iraqiness would mean to subsume themselves into a larger national group, namely the Arabs.

The emergence of Arab and Kurdish nationalisms before the establishment of Iraq, as well as the mind-sets of the two population groups arising from the promises made by the colonial powers and Wilson's Fourteen Points, meant that the balance turned in their favor vis-à-vis Iraqi state patriotism. This was true both before and after Iraq became an independent state.

The Paradox of Attachment to a Historic Homeland

Not only is Iraq's history perceived in contradictory ways, but its name and its territory are also not agreed upon by the different Iraqi ethnonational groups. Iraq as a state is modern; however, many Iraqi Arabs, and some scholars, trace the name "Iraq" to the Sumerian city Uruk. For example, al-Istrabadi argues that "when medieval Islamic geographers referred to 'Iraq,' they meant roughly the same place we mean now."[55] This contradicts historical facts because the current territory of Iraq was referred to in history by three distinctive terms with separate territories. The first, al-'Iraq al-'Arabi (a Persian term), referred to what is now a southeastern Shi'i-populated area of Iraq. The second is al-Jazira, which covered much of the current Sunni-inhabited provinces of Anbar and Ninawa (and beyond into Syria). The third, Kurdistan, is used to describe the areas north of al-'Iraq al-'Arabi and east of al-Jazira (the northeastern parts of the current Iraq).[56] Although the term 'Iraq al-'Ajam was also used to describe the areas located to the north of al-'Iraq al-'Arabi, the borders of 'Iraq al-'Ajam were nevertheless never identified, as opposed to those of al-'Iraq al-'Arabi. Furthermore, in 1925 a committee of experts on the Mosul problem presented a report to the League of Nations indicating that, historically, Iraq's territory extended as far north as the Hamrin Mountains, the natural borders of Kurdistan.[57]

Although Iraq's current borders owe much to the British, Iraqi Arabs largely stress its historical roots.[58] Many Muslim historians and geographers used the term "Kurdistan" between the ninth and the fourteenth centuries, despite the fact that Kurdistan was not an administrative political entity until the eleventh century. In 1150, the Seljuk sultan Sanjar granted the Kurds autonomy over some Kurdish-inhabited areas and used the name "Kurd Ustani."[59] Gradually, Kurd Ustani turned into Kurdistan.[60] While arguing for their own and Kurdistan's deep-rootedness, the Kurdish nationalists stress the "manufactured nature" of the Iraqi state. In fact, its creation is seen by the Kurdish nationalists as a "grave mistake."[61]

More importantly, there is evidence that Arabs lack an emotional attachment to the Kurdish-populated areas of Iraq. During this author's visits in 2005 and 2011 to several Arabized villages in the district of Dibs, in Kirkuk Province—several years after most of the Arab settlers had left the area—he found that although the villages had been occupied by Arab settlers between 1975 and 2003 (that is, for twenty-eight years), none of them buried their family members in the local cemeteries or anywhere else in the area. Instead, they always had their dead taken back to their places of origin in the southern and central parts of Iraq.[62] When asked about this, they replied that "the land belongs to its people."[63] While this example might seem anecdotal, it nevertheless signifies the importance of people's attachment to their homeland. It demonstrates that the Arab settlers did not regard the Kurdish areas as their homeland; rather, they considered their ancestral territory as their only motherland. This also shows that the current territory of Iraq consists of two homelands—Kurdistan and Iraq.

The Paradox of Shared Symbols

The Kurds and the Iraqi Arabs do not share the same national symbols and values. This is significant because the social bonds between members of any nation can be formed by producing and using a repertoire of shared values, symbols, and traditions. Flags, anthems, costumes, monuments, and ceremonies can remind people of their shared heritage and cultural values and reinforce a sense of common identity.[64] Even after living in the same country for more than ninety years, one can hardly, if at all, find a single Kurdish household that raises the Iraqi flag. In a survey conducted in May 2008 by the Kurdistan Institute for Political Issues (KIPI), only 9.07 percent of the people surveyed in the Kurdistan region considered the current Iraqi flag as theirs;[65] meanwhile, 84.13 percent regarded the Kurdistani flag as their national flag.[66] Indeed, until the removal of the Baʿth symbols (the three stars) from the Iraqi flag, it was banned even from state institutions in Kurdistan—with overwhelming public support.[67] Despite this modal change, the Iraqi flag is still not an all-encompassing symbol for Iraqis. Many former and pro-Baʿthist organizations and Sunni groups still use the old version of the Iraqi flag.[68]

Last but not least, while Iraqis generally regard the palm tree, falcon, and sword as their national symbols, the Kurds consider the oak, partridge, and dagger as theirs. In addition, the Kurds have used *Ey Raqib* (hey enemy) as their national anthem since 1946. The Iraqis, on the other hand, have had several national anthems, including the current *Mawtini* (my homeland) and *Ard al-Furatayn* (the land of two rivers) (1979–2003). The Iraqi national anthems emphasize Arab and Islamic glory, while the Kurdish anthem is a departure from religion. It is well possible that the only national anthem in the Islamic world to state overtly that "our faith and religion are our homeland" is the Kurdish one.

Some modernists believe that states are largely responsible for the invention of public ceremonies and the production of public monuments.[69] However, states cannot create national symbols and ceremonies out of nothing. The Iraqi state was neither able to impose July 17 (the day the Ba'thists assumed power in 1968) as Iraq's national day, nor to abolish 'Ashura (the commemoration of the killing of Imam Husayn by the Shi'is) or Newroz (the Kurdish national day). Every invention has to be based on a myth or an event involving a national or religious group, and related to a common memory or shared ancestry. The difficulty in establishing an all-Iraqi national day is an indication of the Iraqi identity crisis, a crisis that stems from not only the failure of successive Iraqi governments' efforts of nation building but also the absence of essential ingredients for nation formation.

Conclusion

The facts and myths discussed in this chapter testify to the competing and contradictory visions of history held by Iraqi ethnonational groups, especially the Iraqi Arabs and the Kurds.

In the context of nation building, nationalists often glorify history, endowing their nation with deep historical roots. However, in the case of Iraq, such glorification creates more problems than opportunities for nation formation. As discussed, the "invention" of a Mesopotamian-inspired tradition and identity excludes the Kurds, for they trace their ancestry to the Medes. In the case of Iraq, interpretation of past memory and ancestry is likely to stimulate as much tension as harmony. Generally speaking, Iraqis neither share a unifying common memory, ancestry, or culture, nor are they united by symbolic values, all of which contain critical ingredients for nation formation and nation building.

In short, one of the major obstacles facing nation formation in Iraq is related to the manifold identities that not only compete with one another but are often contradictory. The people living in Iraq have neither a deep, historic common memory and ancestry, nor a collective destiny. Most scholars and political analysts do not pay enough attention to these complex issues;[70] rather, they limit the Iraqi problem to the absence of democracy and to the discriminatory policies that Iraqis have experienced in the last forty years of Ba'thi rule. While it is true that a lack of democratic values has complicated Iraq's quest for nation building, this cannot explain the failure completely. Abstract concepts of democracy and democratization are not sufficient in themselves to address the question of Iraqi nation building.

The Evolution of National Identity and the Constitution-Drafting Process in the Kurdistan-Iraq Region

RACHEL KANTZ FEDER

The study of constitution making in Middle Eastern contexts has been treated with a hefty dose of cynicism. Political scientists and historians have relegated it to the margins of legal history, owing to the perception that such studies would be futile because of the authoritarianism of Middle Eastern regimes. Nonetheless, even drafting histories of authoritarian regimes—and certainly that of the Kurdistan-Iraq Region—can provide valuable insights into questions of national identity and social and political dynamics.[1] The literature on the Kurdistan Regional Government's constitutions and the 2005 Iraqi constitution consists mostly of journalistic accounts. The academic contributions have been written mainly by former advisers to parties involved in the negotiations, or by the negotiators. Such valuable firsthand accounts provide a more nuanced understanding of constitutions than does a mere reading of constitutional documents. Barring some exceptions, the academic discourse can be characterized as a struggle between legal advisers to frame the narrative of constitution making and to assert their version of how the final constitutional product was conceived and how it should be understood.[2]

The only scholarly work written on the 2009 Kurdistan Regional Government (KRG) draft constitution was authored by Michael J. Kelly, a legal consultant to the Kurdistan Parliament.[3] Kelly's most valuable contribution lies in his intimate knowledge of how the KRG draft constitution was designed to coexist with the Iraqi constitution and exploit its loopholes, particularly those concerning oil and gas contracts. While Kelly does provide important insights, the scholarly analysis of constitution making in Kurdistan-Iraq could benefit from a more disengaged vantage point and from new questions of a different nature.

From a sociological perspective, constitution making is best under-stood as a "deliberate attempt at institution-building at the fundamental level of laying down the normative and legal foundations of the political order. Framing a constitution always purports to be an act of foundation; an act intended to break with the past, and with the existing cultural and institutional traditions . . ."[4] Following Iraq's 2005 provincial elections, the Kurds of Iraq were operating from a position of strength, and their political leadership appeared poised to commit itself to a new political order and a break with the turbulent Kurdish past. However, it seems that due to a confluence of political and economic considerations, Kurd-ish politicians are content with a de facto state, preferring tranquil rela-tions with Baghdad and Washington. They shelved the ratification of the 2009 draft constitution and their historical quest for independence lest the monumental gains achieved after 2003 be jeopardized.

This chapter will survey the various official and nonofficial KRG draft constitutions in an attempt to explore issues of national identity in Kurdistan-Iraq since 1991, the year of the Kurdish uprising against Sad-dam Husayn and of the enforcement of a no-fly zone by the international community. It investigates and contextualizes elements of change in the draft constitutions and strives to ascertain what the latter reveal about national identity, politics, and society at the official, institutional level. It should be made clear that most conclusions and findings relate to how the political elite—not the general populace—regards the issues discussed in this study. What do the drafts disclose about the internal social and politi-cal dynamics in Kurdistan-Iraq and their impact on the ruling elite's rep-resentation of national identity and related core issues, such as commu-nal membership, ideological orientation, and self-determination? What is the relationship between a localized Kurdish and a pan-Kurdayeti identity throughout the drafts? Is the relationship stable, or does it fluctuate?

If competition to define the collective identity of a society and estab-lish a legitimate order of meanings typifies the transformation of a politi-cal system, the drafts' preambles are of the utmost importance, as they are the arenas in which social organizations and political parties compete to construct a national identity.[5] Based on a comparative analysis and con-textualization of the preambles and articles, this chapter contends that the 2009 draft reflects the Kurdish political elite's recognition of the need for compromise on central components of Kurdish politics, society, and national identity so as to accommodate a number of internal and exter-nal actors. The 2009 draft constitution demonstrates a redefinition of the political elite's national objectives. It expresses their stated commitment to democracy and to inclusivity in their definition of national community and identity in Kurdistan-Iraq. Furthermore, within the context of the Kurds' political and economic exigencies, the draft conveys a distinct preference for and promotion of a localized Kurdish national identity at the expense of pan-Kurdish belonging. Yet this is not to imply that the political leaders have intensified their pursuit of local nationalist aspirations. On the contrary, they have deemphasized their historically recognized right to self-determination, even at the perilous risk of distancing themselves from their constituents.

Kurdish constitution making is an incomplete and discontinuous process that began in earnest in 1992 and produced several drafts, none of which have been ratified. In 2003 a committee was formed and charged with adapting the KRG's 1992 draft constitution to the new realities created by the U.S.-led invasion of Iraq. The 1992 draft was the result of the KRG's first attempt at constitution making since the 1991 Kurdish uprising against Saddam Husayn. It came on the heels of the Iraqi government's total collapse of authority in northern Iraq and the 1992 elections for the Kurdistan National Assembly. The Committee for Revising the Draft Constitution of the Kurdistan-Iraq Region was headed by Firsat Ahmed, then secretary of the Kurdistan National Assembly,[6] and law professor Nouri Talabani, who was one of the chief architects of the original 1992 draft. Its mission was completed in June 2006, after three years of upheaval, violent turmoil, and newly forged reconciliation and power-sharing agreements between the two major Kurdish political factions, the Kurdistan Democratic Party (KDP), led by KRG president Mas'ud Barzani, and the Patriotic Union of Kurdistan (PUK), led by the Iraqi president Jalal Talabani.[7] During these three years, Iraq's Constitutional Committee of the National Assembly also drafted Iraq's federal constitution, which was adopted by referendum.

In August of 2006 the Kurdistan National Assembly approved the draft, with modifications, yet it was not until June 2009 that it was released to the public. In this intervening period, political newcomers mounted a challenge to the traditionally uncontested dominance of the KDP and the PUK. On June 26, 2009, the Kurdistan Parliament (previously referred to as the Kurdistan National Assembly) approved the revised draft, which was slated for a referendum to take place that July. The draft, which was authored in Arabic and translated into Kurdish, has not been ratified. Although the official explanation for the postponement was "technical reasons," it is likely that pressures from Baghdad, Washington, and neighboring capitals were at play. Kurdish lawmakers have periodically raised the issue and requested a date be set for the referendum, but to no avail.

Omissions and Additions: Pan-Kurdayeti Identity versus a Localized Kurdish Identity

In tandem with trends in the literature on nationalism and national identity formation, various approaches have been applied to the Kurdish case: the primordialist approach, which views Kurds as an ancient nation yearning for the establishment of a nation-state; the modernist approach, which regards Kurdish nationalism as an inherently modern phenomenon and political construct aimed at legitimizing aspirations to popular sovereignty; and the ethnicist or ethnonational approach, which treats Kurdish ethnicity as the primary basis for political claims and identity formation.[8] A growing critical mass of scholarship has upheld the centrality of Kurdish ethnonationalism in the study of Kurdish nationalism and identity, but more recently some scholars have adopted an alternative approach. They regard the diversity of the Kurds' "other" as the driving factor in Kurdish national identity, particularly as the explanation for its fragmentation and transnational character.[9]

Abbas Vali argues that the major contours of national identity construction within the community are unstable and consequently "subject to the mutation in the balance of forces in the community, a mutation which underpins the changing relationship between the self and the other and defines the essentially unstable character of national identity."[10] In her book *The Kurds and the State: Evolving National Identity in Iraq, Turkey, and Iran*, Denise Natali employs the notion of political space to explain the "uneven and changing nature" of Kurdish nationalism and identity formation.[11] By focusing on the nation-building strategies of host states, opportunity structures, and particularist Kurdish experiences, she paints a complex picture of the evolution of Kurdish national identities.

These approaches, taken into consideration alongside the dynamic political conditions and contexts since 1992, are useful in determining and analyzing the relationship between a localized Kurdish identity in Kurdistan-Iraq and pan-Kurdish national identity in the draft constitutions. Comparative analysis of the available drafts from 1992 to 2009 provides a glimpse into the fluctuations in this relationship and highlights how it has evolved in conjunction with the Kurds' experience with autonomy, state building, and the upheavals in Iraq.

How does the KRG refer to the constituents for whom the draft constitution ostensibly speaks? What type of social unit do the citizens of Kurdistan-Iraq constitute according to the drafts? Are they a nation, a people, or both? To answer this line of inquiry, judicious attention to the exact terms employed in the original Arabic text is imperative. The authors of the various unofficial and semiofficial English-language drafts have provided an inaccurate translation, misusing politically loaded terms such as homeland, nation, and people—all of which are of critical importance in the draft constitution's description of the polity, the Kurdish population it represents, and Kurdish political ambitions.

The 2009 draft opens with "we the people of Kurdistan-Iraq" (*nahnu sha'b Kurdistan–al-'Iraq*) and goes on to describe the "oppression, persecution, tyranny and campaigns of genocide" inflicted upon them by the Iraqi state.[12] Some writers have translated *Kurdistan–al-'Iraq* as Iraqi Kurdistan or the Iraqi Kurdistan Region and have failed to take note of the new phrasing the KRG officially uses to define its polity.[13] Here, *al-'Iraq* is not an adjective that describes Kurdistan; nor should it be translated as "Kurdistan of Iraq." Previously, when Kurds residing in Iraq sought to refer to themselves, not to Kurds outside Iraq, they would either use the more provocative term *Kurdistan al-Janubiyya* (Southern Kurdistan), which demonstrates commitment to a Greater Kurdistan, or *Kurdistan al-'Iraq* (Kurdistan of Iraq).[14] Kurdish nationalists striving to stress territorial and national affinity with Kurds residing in countries neighboring Iraq use the term "South(ern) Kurdistan," (*Kurdistan al-Janubiyya*), which accentuates Kurdish identity and was contemptible in the eyes of the Ba'th regime.[15] Hyphenation in compound words demonstrates that the two elements have a combined meaning. Therefore, the inclusion of hyphenation between the terms *Kurdistan* and *Iraq* renders the two parts a compound word, negating the grammatical possibility that *Kurdistan* should be modified by *al-'Iraq*. Hence, in order to avoid a terminology that would too rigorously or erroneously define the relationship between Kurdistan and Iraq, the authors preferred to add hyphenation. The last thing the KRG would want is to call its polity *Kurdistan al-'Iraqiyya*, or Iraqi Kurdistan, which is how the Ba'th regime referred to it.

The usage of the term *sha'b* is nondescript, and the word is commonly used in other Middle Eastern constitutions. In modern political parlance it is typically the equivalent of *people*, as in the Preamble to the U.S. Constitution, "We the people." It connotes a social unit of organization associated with the masses or the governed.[16] Its place in the text of the preamble to the Kurdish draft constitution, coupled with the term *Kurdi-*

stan–al-ʿIraq, strongly suggests that it is not meant to denote an ancient nation called *Kurdistan–al-ʿIraq*, but rather refers to the residents of Kurdistan-Iraq.

The preamble to the draft contains the word *watan* (homeland),[17] or derivations thereof, three times. It first appears in a sentence that conveys admiration for the Kurdish Liberation Movement, its Peshmerga fighters, and their "defense of our homeland" (*himayat watanina*). Authors of English-language texts have generously translated *watan* as "nation," although its meaning is clearly homeland, the object of local patriotism. The second time it appears is in the preamble's depiction of the Kurds' aspiration "to establish a civilized Kurdish society . . . and unleash the energy of its sons to build Kurdistan as a united homeland for all . . ." Again, the texts incorrectly render the derivation of *watan* as nation. Its final occurrence is in a sentence portraying the convergence between the Iraqi Kurds' "choices [that] have become unified" and the will of "the people of Iraq and its national forces (*shaʿb al-ʿIraq wa qiwahu al-wataniyya*)."[18] In this case, *al-wataniyya* is an adjective that describes Iraq's primary political actors. Thus, while the former two derivations point to local Kurdish patriotism, none are indicative of a Kurdish nation or nationalism.

A derivation of the term *qawmiyya* (nationalism) appears twice in the preamble.[19] In contrast to *wataniyya*, the affinity to one's homeland, *qawmiyya* has been used to describe wider pan-national movements and ideologies, such as pan-Arab nationalism or pan-Kurdish nationalism.[20] The first time it appears is in a sentence that depicts the Kurdish suffering caused by the Iraqi state's policies "forcing them to change their nationality" (*ajbaruhum ʿala taghyir qawmiyyatihim*). The second time is in the same sentence: ". . . striving to establish a developed and civilized Kurdish society comprised of its ethnic and religious groups . . ." (*wa liʾiqamat mujtamaʿ Kurdistani mutamaddin yazhu bimukwwanatihi al-qawmiyya wa al-diniyya*). Here, the English-language translations have rendered *bimukwwanatihi al-qawmiyya wa al-diniyya* as "ethnic and religious groups." This use of *al-qawmiyya* seems to mirror a much earlier usage of *qawm*. It denotes a form of social organization that is rooted in a claim to collective ancestry. Thus, in using the adjective *al-qawmiyya*, the authors likely intended to refer to heterodox communities that populate Kurdistan-Iraq, such as the Kakais, the Ahl-e Haqq, the Yezidis, or the Shabak, not to nationalist groups with political claims to statehood. In the two instances where the Arabic text contains any derivation of *qawm*, it is used to depict an act that was forced on the Kurdish population or, as an adjective, to convey tolerance toward Kurdistan-Iraq's minority populations. In neither case does it declare affinity with Kurds residing in other countries. In other words, these uses do not underscore the existence of a broader, pan-Kurdish nationalism.

What is excluded from the text of the 2009 draft, and what is the significance of such omissions? One of the most notable omissions concerns Kurdish nationhood. In an edited collection published in 2006, Michael Gunter asserted that the preamble of the 1992 draft constitution attempts to justify what the Kurds seek to accomplish:

> The Kurds are an ancient people who have lived in their homeland of Kurdistan for thousands of years, a nation with all the attributes that entitle it to practice the right of self-determination similar to other nations and peoples of the world.[21]

In the 2009 draft, as well as in the previous draft translated by the U.S. government in October 2008, the preambles reflect a glaring change: the (primordialist) definition of the Kurds as an ancient people dwelling in their homeland for thousands of years was omitted. The omission followed the publication of the paper in which Gunter made his assessment, casting doubts on what was commonly perceived as the aims the Kurds sought to accomplish. It diluted the political elites' self-definition of the Kurds as an ancient people and nation, leaving ample room for conjecture concerning how their self-definition and political aims were to materialize.

Moreover, in preambles of early drafts, emphasis was placed on pivotal historic junctures such as President Woodrow Wilson's 1918 declaration of the Fourteen Points and the 1920 Treaty of Sèvres — two defining events that have been invoked as unequivocal pronouncements of international recognition of the Kurdish right to independence and statehood. In Wilson's Fourteen Points, the political principle of self-determination was promoted as an essential term for world peace and an objective for the post–World War I order. Although Wilson did not specify how self-determination was to be implemented, his declaration aimed to legitimize the creation of new states, in particular the Kurds' claim to independence. Similarly, the Treaty of Sèvres, signed by the defeated Ottoman Empire and by delegates of the Allies, acknowledged the Kurds' aspirations to independence and detailed provisions for statehood.[22] In a striking departure from earlier drafts, the 2008 and 2009 drafts omitted any reference to these critical events, which bear symbolic significance in bolstering Kurdish political claims and found expression in draft constitutions as late as 2006.

What explains this seemingly self-defeating omission? Perhaps, in the context of the Kurds' extraordinary gains in the Iraqi political arena, Kurdish leaders' self-confidence was at a peak and they no longer saw the need to justify their claims, at least not in their constitution. Another, more plausible explanation is that they were concerned about strong opposition from neighboring countries should Kurdish statehood be included in the claims. Not only statehood but also the issue of nationhood was problematic. During the negotiations for the drafting of Iraq's new constitution, when the issue of Iraq's affinity with the greater Arab nation arose, Kurdish negotiators did not raise a reciprocal request, although, according to Hussein Tahiri, Kurdish negotiators had gone to Baghdad with the intention of demanding recognition that the Kurds are one nation.[23] 'Adnan Mufti, the president of the Kurdistan Regional Parliament, recounted that Sunni Arab negotiators actually suggested to their Kurdish counterparts that they request a parallel statement that the Iraqi Kurds are part of the Kurdish nation. However, they refrained from doing so, lest they invite trouble from Iraq's neighbors, who were keen to thwart any developments that might stir up their own restive Kurdish populations.[24] The need to express a broader Kurdayeti identity did not seriously arise in the constitution drafting process, nor has it appeared in recent draft constitutions for Kurdistan-Iraq.

Similarly, the preambles of later drafts do not offer a geographical description of what constitutes the entity represented in the draft constitution. Article 2 of the 2009 Draft Constitution of the Kurdistan-Iraq Region stipulates that the "political borders of the Region of Kurdistan-Iraq shall be determined through the implementation of Article 140 of the Federal Constitution," which mandates a process for normalization in the mixed Arab-Kurdish city of Kirkuk and calls for a referendum to determine the status of disputed territories. The geographical description of Kurdistan-Iraq is not included, since there has not been any resolution with the Iraqi government to dispel regional opposition from Iran, Turkey, or Syria over the disputed territories. Article 2 does, however, describe Kurdistan-Iraq as a "geographical and historical entity."[25] This wording differs from the 2008 draft constitution, which defines the region as a "geographical, historical, and political entity."[26] By way of further comparison, in a 1992 draft provided by Nouri Talabani, Article 2 not only describes Kurdistan-Iraq as a geographical, historical, and *politi-*

cal entity but also declares explicitly that Iraqi Kurdistan is part of Kurdistan.[27] Whatever their exact reasoning may have been, these omissions—that is, of the definition of the Kurds as an ancient people that had lived in their homeland for thousands of years, of any reference to the Fourteen Points and the Treaty of Sèvres, and of a description of the nature of the Kurdish entity—serve to weaken any semblance of a pan-Kurdish identity and quest for statehood as it appears in the text.

In addition to the political pressures that partially explain these omissions, another explanation touches upon the core of the identity-formation process. Abbas Vali posits that "Kurdish nationalism is the politics of the affirmation of Kurdish national identity," and that resistance to the denial of Kurdish identity is a fundamental motivation of the Kurdish opposition.[28] Many scholars concur with Vali's view on the emergence of a more stringent local Kurdish identity after 1991. Ofra Bengio observed that "during the exceptional decade of the 1990s, the most important achievement has been the forging of a stronger Kurdish identity . . . made possible through a combination of Kurdish maturity, born of bitter experience; vital support from the outside world; and the complete disappearance of the Iraqi central government from Kurdistan." She found that self-identity manifested itself in real and symbolic forms, such as the development and usage of the Kurdish language in the public sphere and the broad employment of national symbols such as flags, hymns, and statues.[29] Owing to the Kurds' newfound political space, it seems that a more cohesive local Kurdish identity in Iraq is in the ascendancy—one that is increasingly exclusive of the greater pan-Kurdish community. This trend is reflected in the 2009 draft constitution: since the powerful symbols of pan-Kurdish nationalism are omitted, the ambiguity with which it defines the political and social unit of organization of Kurdistan-Iraq and the additions to the draft suggest a more local Kurdish association. This is not to say that the identity of the Kurds of Kurdistan-Iraq is an exclusively localized identity; clearly, multiple identities fluctuate according to political, economic, and social circumstances. Rather, at the official, institutional level, the various drafts underscore a surge in localized Kurdish identity and a decline in expressions of pan-Kurdish identity.

Furthermore, the 2009 draft constitution reveals salient compromises on a plethora of identity-related issues and indicates the political elite's steadfast commitment to the democratic experiment. The draft bears a more nuanced understanding of and increased dedication to the cultivation of a democratic government and society than did earlier drafts. Whereas the term "democratic" appears only once in the 2002 draft, it appears many times in later versions.[30] Significantly, the 2009 draft includes a repugnancy clause meant to defend the principles of democracy that was entirely absent from earlier drafts.[31] Moreover, later drafts delineate a sharper separation of powers in government and enumerate new rights and freedoms—from rights regarding freedom of movement,[32] expression, assembly, and communication, to rights relating to academic freedom and the practice of sports.[33]

The depiction of Kurdish society and government as democratic correlates to what has been identified as a historical shift in the nationalist project in Kurdistan-Iraq. Denise Natali, a scholar and experienced international humanitarian aid worker, observes that since 1991, the nationalist project has undergone a significant transformation whereby nationalism in Kurdistan-Iraq has disassociated itself from leftist revolutionary ideology and asserted its Western democratic character. She argues that the nationalist project in Kurdistan-Iraq has been redefined as an experiment in democracy, replete with all of the trappings of a liberal democratic society, its ideology, institutions, and norms. According to her, the political elites have regarded their commitment to democracy as a source of legitimization for their cause on the international level. Natali contends that the protracted international aid that has served as the exclusive lifeline to Kurdistan-Iraq at least until 2003 has been contingent upon the KRG's affirmation and demonstrable adherence to democratic norms and practices.[34]

On the one hand, her inference that the KRG's shift to democracy is somewhat instrumental is seemingly vindicated once the authoritarian nature of politics and governance in Kurdistan-Iraq is taken into consideration. The gulf between the political leadership's commitment to democracy and political realities suggests that profound democratic political and social change has not been implemented. Some even argue that authoritarian Baʿthist patterns have been replicated in Kurdistan-Iraq.[35] On the other hand, this view dismisses Kurdish parties' historical affinity with democracy. The Kurdistan Democratic Party of Iraq (KDP), founded in August 1946, has supported the establishment of a democratic republic in Iraq since 1954.[36] Its official party line has always promoted democracy, since its leadership has traditionally viewed democratic systems as the most conducive to their demands for autonomy and to their cohabitation with Arab Iraqis in the Iraqi state. As early as 1992, KRG president Masʿud Barzani and other politicians proclaimed Kurdistan as a model of democracy for the Middle East.[37]

At times, Kurdish leaders have invoked their democratic merits to gain political and economic capital. In 2008, President Barzani restated the KRG's dedication "to a federal, democratic Iraq" and conveyed his pride that Kurdistan-Iraq "is both a model and gateway for the rest of Iraq" as well as "a thriving civil society in the heart of the Middle East."[38] Kurdish politicians have marketed their democracy as the United States' natural ally and an attractive venue for global economic investment. Given the significance of the democratic model to the Kurdish political elite and the involvement of international legal consultants in the process of constitution making, it is not surprising that the 2009 draft highlights an enhanced dedication to democracy, even if reality may be at odds with self-definition as stated in the draft constitution.

The 2009 draft constitution also reveals the leadership's pragmatic response to new internal political and social dynamics. For example, the 1992 and 2002 drafts do not contain any mention of Islam. It was not until the 2006 draft that "Islamic identity" was recognized as that of "the majority of the people (*sha'b*) of Kurdistan" and "one of the main sources of legislation."[39] In the 2009 draft, the invocation *bismillah al-rahman al-rahim* (in the name of God, the most compassionate, the most merciful) was affixed to the first page of the preamble, imbuing the document with a religious hue. However, the 2009 draft also downgrades Islam from "one of the main sources of legislation" to "one of the sources of legislation" and coupled the article with a repugnancy clause, which invalidates any law that is contrary to principles of democracy.[40] Still, the recognition of Islam as a component of Kurdish identity and a source of legislation speaks to Kurdish Islamist ascendance and a general challenge to the KDP and PUK's monopoly on power. This concession runs counter to the previously avowed secularism of Kurdistan-Iraq and represents a political compromise.

Additional concessions were made to ethnic and religious minorities on the issues of official language and the notion of communal membership. The 1992 and 2002 drafts assigned Kurdish as the official language,[41] but Article 14 of the 2008 and 2009 drafts designate both Kurdish and Arabic, while guaranteeing "the right of the citizens of the Kurdistan Region to educate their children in their mother tongue, including Turkmen, Assyrian, and Armenian, in the government's educational institutions and in accordance with pedagogical guidelines." The article also allows for Turkmen and Syriac to serve as official languages in "administrative districts that are densely populated by speakers of Turkmen and Syriac."[42]

A similar progression toward inclusivity regarding the question of who constitutes the people of Kurdistan-Iraq is discernible throughout the drafts. The 2002 draft states that "the people (*shaʿb*) of the Kurdistan Region consist of the Kurds and the national minorities of Turkmen, Assyrians, Chaldeans, and Arabs."[43] In the 2009 draft, minority status is deemphasized and Kurdish ethnicity is no longer the primary marker of the concept of citizenship.[44] This change, together with the concessions on national language and Islamic identity, betrays a trend toward a less ethnic-based definition and presentation of national identity in Kurdistan-Iraq.

Finally, an unmistakable hallmark of national identity pervades the draft constitutions: the collective memory of persecution perpetrated by the Iraqi state. As exemplified by various drafts and other official and nonofficial self-narratives of Kurdish society, national identity is conditioned by and expressed through a discourse of victimization and trauma. Although the 1991 Kurdish uprising against Saddam Husayn and the experience with autonomy and self-governance represent an important threshold in forging identity and collective self-confidence, the suffering inflicted upon the Kurds, particularly in the 1980s, remains a cornerstone of national identity. Shafiq Qazzaz, the KRG minister of humanitarian assistance and cooperation, observed that "the Kurds see their present identity mostly in terms of what has happened in the last two or three decades. They therefore see Kurdish identity through persecution and suffering: Arabization, Halabja, and Anfal operations."[45] Indeed, the opening sentence of the 2009 draft's preamble reinforces Qazzaz's sentiment. It details Iraqi governments' oppression and injustice and outlines "crimes against humanity," "mass genocide and ethnic cleansing," and the altering of "the demography of large parts of Kurdistan-Iraq." It also depicts the "use of chemical weapons . . . against civilians in martyred Halabja, Ballisan, Garmiyan, Bahdinan, and other large areas," and recounts that "thousands of Fayli Kurdish youth were led to their death into chemical experimentation fields and mass graves . . . [T]heir remaining families were displaced outside Iraq and stripped of their Iraqi citizenship, which was followed by mass genocide campaigns . . . called the Anfal . . ."[46] The 2009 draft even contains an article that obliges the government to prevent forced expulsions, hardly a mainstay of typical constitutions.[47] Thus, in addition to the draft's omissions and additions that convey a preference for localized Kurdish identity versus a broader pan-Kurdish identity, the 2009 draft also promotes the idea of a thoroughly democratic government and society in Kurdistan-Iraq; it demonstrates the leaders' attentiveness to internal dynamics that impelled compromise and inclusivity, and sets forth a notion of communal membership deeply affected by experiences of victimhood and trauma.

Leaving the Door Ajar: The Question of Self-Determination

The crucial issue of self-determination continues to persist as a divisive and elusive topic in Kurdistan-Iraq. Since the 1918 declaration of Woodrow Wilson's Fourteen Points and the establishment of the state of Iraq, the quest for Kurdish self-determination has been characterized by an ebb and flow stimulated and recontextualized by political developments in Iraq and by relations between Baghdad and Kurds. How has self-determination been interpreted by the political elite since 1991? Does self-determination imply autonomy or an independent state, and how do the various drafts treat this thorny issue?

The Arabic phrases for self-determination or the right of self-determination as employed in international law—*taqrir al-masir* or *haqq taqrir al-masir*—do not appear in the 2009 draft constitution. The draft certainly discusses the right of self-determination, albeit without invoking the aforementioned key phrases. The preamble comes closest to doing so in its last paragraph; in expressing the reasons for cherishing and appreciating the Peshmerga fighters, it describes the fighters' protection of the homeland and of "the recognition of our right in determining our fate" (*wa al-iqrar bi haqqina fi taqrir masirina*). Article 7 of the same draft also outlines the idea of self-determination, without actually using the loaded term, when it declares "the people of Kurdistan-Iraq have the right to determine their fate by themselves" (*lisha'b Kurdistan-al-'Iraq al-haqq fi taqrir masirihi binafsihi*). This article also declares that they "have chosen, out of their own free will, to be a federal region within Iraq, as long as Iraq abides by the federal, democratic, parliamentary and pluralistic system, and remain committed to the human rights of individuals and groups, as stipulated in the federal constitution."[48] While Article 7 conveys the same fact—namely that the KRG has actively and freely elected to maintain Iraq's territorial integrity by defining itself as a federal region (contingent upon Iraq's adherence to its constitutional obligations)—it does so without explicitly invoking the phrase "self-determination." The upshot of this exclusion, which brings to mind the notion of a historic and internationally recognized right of self-determination afforded to nations and to be acted upon, should not be underestimated.

Although initially this may seem to be merely a matter of semantics, the lack of the exact terminology constitutes a discrepancy compared to the 1992 and 2002 drafts. The latter state in the first sentence of the preamble that "The Kurds are an ancient people . . . a nation with all the attributes that entitle it to practice the right of self-determination similar to other nations and people of the world," and were first recognized by Woodrow Wilson and later on entrenched in international law.[49] After stating their historical experience with self-determination, the preambles of both drafts stress the KRG's voluntary commitment to federalism as the most viable and peaceful solution to a Kurdish-Arab cohabitation in Iraq. In a 1992 draft provided by Nouri Talabani, the preamble also clarifies that

> the recognition of the right of the people of Iraqi Kurdistan to self-determination does not necessarily mean its inevitable separation from Iraq, but living with the Arab people of Iraq in a voluntary federation, in a democratic system that recognizes the right of the Kurdish people to self-determination, that guarantees basic human rights and freedom of expression, and a multiplicity of political parties and organizations that will ensure the existence of such a federation and its survival.[50]

In fact, all drafts from 1992 until 2009—whether they explicitly or implicitly mention self-determination—emphasize that despite the Kurds' right to self-determination, they have of their own volition opted for autonomy or a de facto state, not a de jure polity. In remarks delivered at a conference at Princeton in 1994, Nouri Talabani explained this voluntary commitment to federalism, arguing that the Kurds were in fact *exercising* their right to self-determination:

> The Kurdish parliament adopted the principle of federalism for two reasons: first, to safeguard the Kurdish people in Iraq from further atrocity, as the federal system contains provisions available in neither decentralized nor autonomous systems, and second to emphasize the desire of the Kurdish people in Iraq to maintain the integrity of Iraq, alongside the Iraqi Arabs, *while exercising their right to self-determination*. For this reason, the parliament has demanded neither independence nor confederation [italics added].[51]

However, there seems to be an internal contradiction between Talabani's assertion that voluntary commitment to federalism is an act of *im-*

plementing self-determination and early drafts of the constitution. Article 75 of the 2002 draft stipulates that "the structure of the entity and the political system of the Federal Republic of Iraq cannot be changed without the consent of the Kurdistan Regional Assembly. Action contrary to this shall afford the people of the Kurdistan Region the right of self-determination."[52] This article implies that, though the constituents' right of self-determination has been recognized, it has not been *implemented*. And it conditions the execution of self-determination on any modification of the structure of the Federal Republic of Iraq, which takes place without the approbation of the Kurdistan Regional Assembly. In other words, the draft states both that by opting for voluntary federalism Kurds are in fact exercising their self-determination, and that changes to the structure of the entity and the political system of Iraq will result in granting self-determination to the people of the Kurdistan Region.

Article 75 may be construed as a mechanism that legitimizes or at least allows room for a future push toward an independent state.[53] Notably, its content is altogether absent from the 2006 draft, and from all subsequent drafts. The changes in the documents' approach to self-determination cannot be understood as an innocuous oversight. Rather, the changes are part and parcel of the evolving political context in post-Saddam Iraq and of the geopolitical dimensions involving major political forces, as well as foreign actors such as the United States, the international community, and Iraq's anxious neighbors, which are home to restive Kurdish populations.

The deemphasis on self-determination in the 2009 draft constitution, too, represents a sharp dissonance between public discourse on the right of self-determination and the political elite's interpretations of the principle. Whereas some politicians have tried to disseminate the notion that Kurds in Iraq are in fact exercising their right to self-determination by choosing to remain a federal region, the Kurdish Referendum Movement, which emerged shortly after the 2003 invasion, suggested that the populace view the matter differently. The Kurdish Referendum Movement (KRM), initiated and led by independent local Kurdish intellectuals and diaspora activists, agitated for a referendum on the future of "South Kurdistan" (the Kurdistan-Iraq Region) as early as December 2004. In the memorandum that the KRM submitted to the United Nations, they claimed that the "People of South Kurdistan do have the inalienable right to self-determination and we are strongly demanding the UN to enable us exercise this right" [*sic*].[54] Thus, according to the movement's leadership, voluntarily remaining a federal region of Iraq is not an act of self-determination; only a referendum and application of its results would sufficiently fulfill this right. In response to demonstrations staged by the KRM, the Iraqi Interim Government president, Ghazi al-Yawar, chided the demonstrators and ratcheted up the rhetoric, stating, "What we do not accept is the issue of secession because it is an act of treachery and we will fight it drastically. We will fight those who stand up for separation."[55] Following this caustic remark, many Kurds came to believe that not only Iraqi Arab leaders but also Iraqis at large oppose Kurdish self-determination, a realization that has contributed to an increasing nationalist sentiment and will for independence.[56]

The contentious referendum was conducted concurrently with the Iraqi parliamentary elections on January 20, 2005. Around 98 percent of participants urged their leaders to push for an independent state, not autonomy; and Kurdish politicians fared well in the Iraqi elections, receiving 27 percent of the vote and seventy-five seats in Parliament.[57] On election day, Kurdistan-Iraq regional president Masʿud Barzani declared that "an independent Kurdish state is indeed going to be established, but I do not know when," and that in the meantime, a democratic and federal system "is the best solution for Iraq." When the results of the referendum were announced a few days later and showed overwhelming support for an independent state, President Barzani insisted, "When the right time comes, it will become a reality. Self-determination is the national right of our people."[58] On February 14, 2005, around ten thousand activists marched for independence in Sulaymaniyya, but the political elite disregarded the popular demand. Instead, Kurdish leaders opted to consolidate their gains and harness their newfound influence in Baghdad, lest they invite intrusive opposition from Turkey, Iran, Syria, and/or the U.S. administration that would jeopardize their achievements. Thus the political leadership postponed self-determination—as defined by Barzani, not by Nouri Talabani—and the early draft constitutions in favor of a more conducive geopolitical climate. Despite the populace's aspirations, the political elite focused its efforts on translating their gains into a Kurdish-friendly Iraqi constitution, an objective that would reignite the issue of self-determination in Kurdistan-Iraq's public discourse.

During the negotiations for the Iraqi federal constitution, Kurdish negotiators pushed for a clause similar to that of Article 75, one that would enshrine the Kurdish right to self-determination, leaving the door ajar for an independent Kurdish state should Iraq violate its constitutional obligations toward Kurdistan-Iraq. Jalal al-Din Saghir, a cleric who is believed to be close to Grand Ayatollah Sistani, closed ranks with Sunni negotiators in a public effort to torpedo the Kurdish bloc's demand for an article reminiscent of Article 75. PUK leader and Iraqi president Jalal Talabani tried to allay the fears of the major Iraqi political forces as well as Iraq's neighbors, who were intently observing the negotiations. He defended the self-determination option in the constitution as a measure to protect the Kurds against potential Arab violence, while insisting that there were not any plans for a Kurdish secession. On August 15, 2005, thousands of Kurds took to the streets again to demand the inclusion of such an article, but Kurdish politicians capitulated to American pressure so that its inclusion was no longer a precondition for negotiations.[59] Given the political elite's acquiescence to external pressures and their subsequent decision to abandon the popular thrust for self-determination (in the sense of statehood), it is not surprising that the 2006–2009 draft constitutions omit the loaded terms *taqrir al-masir* and *haqq taqrir al-masir*, thus effectively divorcing the notion of self-determination from the idea of an independent state in the draft. This omission is a function of the geopolitical constraint and the conflict with Baghdad (and Washington) caused by the question of self-determination.

Likewise, whereas the 2002 draft constitution designated the city of Kirkuk, located in the strategic oil-rich governorate of Kirkuk, as the state's capital, drafts from 2006 through 2009 have chosen Erbil as the capital, while retaining the option to select another city at a later time. The hotly contested fate of the ownership of Kirkuk has become a nearly intractable problem given its strategic and economic importance, the perception that it will stimulate Kurdish independence, and the ethnicization of the conflict between Kurds and Arabs.[60] Thus the decision to name Erbil the capital also should be seen as an important concession, an attempt to placate Baghdad and, by extension, Washington. These discrepancies, which center on core issues of national identity in landlocked Kurdistan-Iraq, are reflections of the political elite's calculations made in light of profound considerations of political and economic expediency.

Conclusion

The Kurdish experience with autonomy since the imposition of a no-fly zone and safe haven in 1991 has been an unequivocally important factor in forging Kurdish national identity in the political and cultural sphere. Despite the Kurds' heavy reliance on the international community, their experience of autonomy has bolstered Kurdish self-confidence and demonstrated that they are able to conduct their own affairs as long as they maintain the peace and contain the KDP-PUK enmity. In the post-Saddam era, new institutional arrangements with Baghdad have shifted much of the previous dependency on the international community to a new type of financial dependence on the Iraqi state and private international investment. Thus, as Denise Natali claims, the Kurdish national agenda now must coexist with Kurdistan-Iraq's development and stability. Crudely put, "Kurds must choose between electricity and independence, international legitimacy and pan-Kurdish nationalism, and external patronage and extended territorial claims."[61] The 2009 draft constitution demonstrates that for the Kurdish political elite, the opening of political space and the sharp decline in the negation of Kurdish identity in post-Saddam Iraq has mitigated their nationalist aspirations. While the populace has chosen self-determination in the form of an independent state, the leadership has chosen political and economic expediency. This does not prevent Kurdish leaders from brandishing the self-determination card before their detractors in Baghdad at pivotal moments. As recently as December 11, 2010, at a time when Kurdish political support was critical to then Iraqi prime minister-designate Nuri al-Maliki, President Barzani boldly called for self-determination at the opening session of the KDP Congress in the presence of al-Maliki, Speaker of Parliament Usama al-Nujayfi, and Iranian and Turkish representatives—only to emphasize his desire to remain part of a federal Iraq a few days later.[62]

While the issue of self-determination hangs in the balance—both in reality and in the 2009 draft constitution—other aspects of national identity in the draft constitution are more clear-cut. As a result of the experience with issues of autonomy, with the political contexts in post-Saddam Husayn Iraq, and the evolving internal dynamics in Kurdistan-Iraq, the ruling political elite has declared its ambition to cultivate a society that is more democratic, inclusive, and cohesive. The 2009 draft constitution demonstrates that whether due to the ascendance of new political forces or to genuine pretensions to democracy, the political leadership has made significant concessions to minority and pressure groups. Comparative analysis of the drafts also indicates a distinct decline in expressions of pan-Kurdish identity and a preference for localized Kurdish identity. In the 2009 draft constitution, it is the Fayli Kurds and the victims of the Anfal and Halabja campaigns that constitute the subjects and beneficiaries of the document, with virtually no mention of the Kurds dispersed throughout Syria, Iran, and Turkey.

At present, the 2009 draft constitution remains a document with an indefinite status and future, which perhaps aptly represents the fragility of the nationalist project and of national identity in Kurdistan-Iraq. The quest for national identity is in flux and subject to numerous external factors. Apparently, as of this writing, the political leadership is not ready for the profound foundational act of constitution making. For now, the benefits of political stalemate are too high for the leadership to gamble away, although the future trajectory of Baghdad-Erbil relations could change this equation. In Shafiq Qazzaz's view, one thing remains certain: "This dichotomy of autonomy versus independence will no doubt continue to loom large in current and future political thinking . . . [And] this dichotomy will make the search for a Kurdish identity somewhat less conclusive."[63]

Forging Iraqi-Kurdish Identity: A Case Study of Kurdish Novelists Writing in Arabic

RONEN ZEIDEL

Kurdish nationalism and Kurdish identity in Iraq have reached a dramatic stage. Over the last two decades, significant progress has been made in homogenizing the various groups that live in this part of Kurdistan and the region has achieved de facto autonomy, placing it on the verge of independence. In Iraq, the mainstay of that process was to assert Kurdish identity, e.g., through the use of the Kurdish language, as opposed to Arabic. Similar processes are taking place in other countries with Kurdish populations, such as Iran and Turkey. Literature, as Benedict Anderson has shown, plays an important role in the process, giving expression and shape to national aspirations.[1]

Among the few outstanding scholarly works on the relations between Kurdish literature, particularly the novel, and nationalism is Hashim Ahmadzade's *Nation and Novel: A Study of Kurdish and Persian Narrative Discourse*.[2] Though focusing on Kurdish literature in Iran, the author writes about the dissimilarity between the state-based and state-oriented novel—the Persian novel in his study—and the stateless and nation-oriented Kurdish novel. This definition is applicable to the situation in Iraq, in particular with regard to the little-studied literature in Kurdish, which enjoyed a renaissance with the appearance of new publishing houses in Erbil and Sulaymaniyya. Fitting Kurdish literature in Iraq into that model becomes more complicated and nuanced when one adds novels written by Kurdish writers in Arabic. These novels will be the topic of this chapter as I will try to explain how writing in Arabic, a loaded issue for the Kurds, affects the content of a novel and is, in turn, affected by the personality of the writer.

According to Ahmadzade, the Kurdish novel in the Kurdish language is a recent phenomenon, dating back only from the last decades of the twentieth century. Right from the beginning, the novel in Kurdish has been confronted with scores of problems. The most serious problems, however, have been the prohibition and strict limitations on the public use of the language in Turkey, Iran, Syria, and, to a lesser extent, in Iraq; the lack of standardization of the Kurdish dialects; the lack of publishing houses; and a limited reading public. For a long time, writing in Kurdish was a liability for Kurdish writers eager to assimilate into the intellectual circles of their countries or to become known throughout the Arab world. Historically, Kurds wrote in Persian, Turkish, or Arabic. Authors began writing in Kurdish only in the sixteenth century, and even so only to a limited extent.[3] In fact, writing in Arabic seems to have been the norm.

One of the major Kurdish writers in Iraq was ʿAbd al-Majid Lutfi (1906–1992). Lutfi, who lived all his life in Iraq, is considered one of the pioneers of Iraqi prose and a close associate of famous Arab writers and poets, with whom he established the Association of Iraqi Writers in 1959. In the late 1920s he moved to Baghdad, where he lived until the end of his life. Like many other Iraqi writers, including those to be discussed in this chapter, he was a member of the Iraqi Communist Party (ICP) and a frequent contributor to its organs. While Lutfi was known mainly for his short stories, his most important work, *ʿUruq al-Ballut* [The veins of the oak], is an epic novel on the struggle of the Kurdish people. He died in Baghdad, but had asked to be buried in his hometown, Khanaqin.[4] In 2009 the Kurdish authorities organized an event in Khanaqin, commemorating Lutfi, praising him both as an Iraqi and as a Kurdish writer.[5]

The writer and playwright Muhyi al-Din Zangane (1940–2010) also moved to Baghdad, where he studied Arabic at the university in the late 1950s. After graduation, he worked for some years as a teacher of Arabic in the Arab south of Iraq. He was a prominent playwright and received several awards from the Baʿth regime: he won the award for the best Iraqi writer in 1970 and the best playwright in 1976 and 1989. After the fall of Saddam Husayn in 2003, he moved to Sulaymaniyya. Despite the fact that he had cooperated to some extent with the Baʿth regime, the Kurdish content of his work was highlighted after his death by Kurdish intellectuals, who added, somewhat apologetically, that his work was Kurdish "even if written in Arabic."[6]

For Kurdish writers, the decision to write in a language as politically and nationally loaded as Arabic was not just a question of commercial success or failure. From the outset, granting an official status to the Kurdish language in Kurdistan and Iraq was one of the main demands of the Kurdish national movement.[7] The language was given official status in Iraqi Kurdistan in 1970, and despite the severe limitations under the Baʿth regime, particularly with regard to freedom of expression, the subsequent years constituted quite a long time span for the creation of a reading public in Kurdish. For Kurdish writers, writing in Arabic also signified targeting an Arab public and conducting a dialogue. Since the number of Kurds who could read Arabic was quite limited, they may even have forsaken the Kurdish public for the Arab one.[8]

Writing in Arabic, the hegemonic language, was the Kurdish writer's way of assimilating. Most of the writers I will discuss moved from their hometowns to Baghdad when they were quite young. Lutfi, Zangane, Burhan Shawi, and others were at home in Iraqi Arab literary and political circles. Therefore, the decision to write in Arabic also involved personal and even political considerations. By targeting the Arab public, they mitigated their Kurdish nationalism, making it "softer" than the version propagated by the Kurdish parties.

This chapter is based on the reading of four novels by four Kurds who wrote in Arabic. Together with Lutfi and Zangane, they form a sample of six writers who write in Arabic. First, I will discuss their lives, underlining certain aspects that link them more intimately to Iraqi nationalism and life in Iraq, and then I will explore how their views are expressed in every one of the novels. I will explain how each novelist came to write about the Kurds, since this point is significant in the construction of their particular version of a hybrid (Kurdish and Iraqi) national identity.

The reviewed novels are *Efin . . . wa Intizar al-Fajr* [Evin . . . and the waiting for dawn] by Azad al-Ayyubi, published in 2004;[9] *Tahawwulat* [Transformations] by Zuhdi al-Dahoodi, published in 2007;[10] *al-Bum wal-Miqass* [The owl and the scissors] by Haval Amin, published in 2008;[11] and *al-Jahim al-Muqaddas* [The holy hell] by Burhan Shawi, published in 2008.[12]

As we shall see, Azad al-Ayyubi is unlike any of the other authors. Holding a Ph.D. in English literature, he left Iraq in the 1990s, traveling first to Europe and then to Libya, where he worked as a university lecturer. He wrote mainly in English and Kurdish, and *Efin . . . wa Intizar al-Fajr* was to be his first book in Arabic. Though some of the other writers have a relatively long bibliography in Arabic, they never published a book in Kurdish. Al-Ayyubi's book includes a critique of Arab governments, which he accuses of being unable to achieve Arab unity. Despite the fact that his book is in Arabic, al-Ayyubi criticizes the Arabs, Arab culture, and Arabism. Clearly, his choice of Arabic in *Efin . . . wa Intizar al-Fajr* stems from the need to say something to the Arabs about their own culture, as well as about Kurdish culture. The Kurdish landscape is an integral part of his personality, whereas the Libyan desert is not. In a long passage, his grandfather, who was a landowner in Kurdistan, tells his version of Kurdish history, which starts with the words "when God created a valiant people thousands of years ago and called them Gurd [thus in the original], meaning courageous."[13] As a member of the al-Ayyubi family, Azad al-Ayyubi describes himself as a descendant of Salah al-Din al-Ayyubi, a personality who connects between the Kurds and the Arabs. No other Kurdish writer personifies the desire to fuse the two cultures as he does.

Unlike al-Ayyubi, Zuhdi al-Dahoodi started his literary career in Baghdad in 1962 and continued his work throughout his German exile. He wrote several novels, all of them in Arabic and German. Born in a village near Kirkuk, he joined the ICP in his youth and was arrested several times. His bitter experience led to his decision to leave Iraq, a country he referred to as his "homeland," in the 1960s.[14] Haval Amin started his literary career in Holland. His writing echoes life in exile, with the need for roots and for belonging, as well as the social and cultural confusion of the exile, especially for one who is both an Iraqi and a Kurd.[15]

Burhan Shawi was born in Kut, in the Arab Shi'i province Wasit, in 1955. Following his brother, he joined the ICP and became a student activist. He moved to Baghdad to pursue his studies. At the same time, he started publishing in the Iraqi Communist press. He was a friend of eminent Iraqi poets, such as Sa'di Yusuf. In 1975 he was enlisted in the army and sent to serve in Kurdistan. Despite his Kurdish origins, this was his first encounter with Kurdistan and with Kurdish reality, an experience that was to mark his literary work. It was during this time that he learned about the crimes committed by the Iraqi regime against his fellow Kurds in Kurdistan. In 1978 he was arrested by the Ba'th and tortured. After his release he fled Iraq, first to Moscow, where he studied cinema, and then to Berlin. He returned to Iraq in 2005 and has been the director of the Iraqi Forum of Communication and Information (*Hay'at al-Ittisalat wal-I'lam al-'Iraqiyya*) in the Ministry of Culture since 2009.[16] In 2012 he returned to Germany, following allegations of involvement in a major corruption case in his department.

Some common features stand out in these brief biographies. Nearly all the writers for whom we have detailed personal histories (Zangane, Lutfi, Dahoodi, Shawi) moved to Baghdad as youngsters to pursue their studies in high school and at university. Due to a lack of appropriate institutions of higher learning in Kurdistan, moving to Baghdad was almost an imperative for a Kurdish youngster intent on continuing his education. Baghdad accepted them with open arms, and soon after moving there they became active in literary or political circles, often in both. While most of these writers never returned to Kurdistan, Zangane did go back, but only after the fall of Saddam Husayn. Interestingly, four out of the six did not hail from the three Kurdish provinces of Iraq, but came from either the Kurdish periphery (Kirkuk, Khanaqin) or the Kurdish communities in Arab Iraq (Kut). This fact could be of some significance since those writers were surrounded by speakers of Arabic, so that their Kurdish was very often limited to domestic usage and thus not fit for literary writing. Khanaqin, the hometown of Lutfi and a mixed town in Baghdad's orbit of influence, saw many of its people migrate to the capital.[17] Kut, Shawi's birthplace, was a hotbed of Communist activity.

Consciously trying to break the primordial ties in the Iraqi population, the ICP accepted many Kurds into its ranks, some of whom even reached leading positions in the party. In 1963, for example, Kurds constituted 23.1 percent of the Central Committee of the ICP, much higher than their percentage in the total population at the time.[18] Though its ideology was antinationalist, the Communist Party always tried to be in contact with the Kurdish movements and considered the Kurdish struggle to be part of a joint struggle against the regime.[19] When other parts of Iraq became too dangerous, Communists found refuge in the relative safety of the Kurdish mountains, where they were under the protection of the two Kurdish political parties that had armed militias. Although many Arab activists of the ICP only came to know Kurdistan and the Kurds in the 1970s and 1980s, Communists had become active in Kurdistan much earlier. In his novel *Mudun Fadila* [Utopias], the Iraqi Arab Shi'i writer Zuhayr al-Jaza'iri describes life in those camps in Kurdistan. Though most of his characters are Arab Communists, he also shows the impact of their presence on local Kurds, especially the younger generation, who joined the Communist Party in defiance of traditional Kurdish society and its representatives in the villages. It is quite possible that al-Jaza'iri has unintentionally described the political upbringing of the writer Zuhdi al-Dahoodi, who grew up in one such village.[20] However, these rare periods of solidarity between the Kurds and the Communist Party were brief and frequently ended in clashes between the parties, as the Communists were no longer an asset to the Kurds.

As we learn from al-Jaza'iri's novel, the encounter between Kurds and Arabs within the framework of the Communist Party was complicated. For the Arabs it was the first encounter with the unfamiliar environment of Kurdistan and what they perceived as a hostile topography and an often-treacherous population that was still living in "primitive" conditions. For al-Jaza'iri, who as a child had never been fond of excursions, the experience was a revelation. It helped the Arab activists of the Communist Party visualize their homeland as something much larger geographically and more complex than they had imagined, with people who were suffering greatly and needed their help. Arabs like al-Jaza'iri had mixed feelings toward the Kurds: they identified with them as an oppressed minority and pitied them for their marginality and "primitiveness," yet disliked their nationalism. For Kurds like al-Dahoodi, membership in the Communist Party was a tool for modernizing and transforming Kurdish society. For others, like Shawi and Lutfi, as will be elaborated later, it was a way to bridge the multiple facets of their hybrid identity. All of them, Arabs and Kurds, needed a national alternative to the Kurdish and Arab nationalist trends, but the ICP supplied them with a rather vague Iraqi nationalism at best. Yet as members of a national minority, the Kurdish writers sometimes found themselves uneasily compromising their Kurdishness in favor of Iraqi nationalism. Thus, when a conflict broke out between the Kurdistan Democratic Party (KDP) and the ICP, Lutfi, a member of the ICP, published an article in *al-Ta'akhi*, KDP's organ in Arabic, calling on the leader of his party, ʿAziz Muhammad (a Kurd himself), to resolve the conflict.[21] The Communist Party presented the most serious political platform for Arab-Kurdish partnership in Iraq. At times, the camaraderie of those years even survived exile and the political transformations of the ICP and the people involved.[22]

Remarkably, two of the six writers (Lutfi and Shawi) are Fayli Kurds. The Faylis are a small Shiʿi minority among the Kurds. Most of them do not live in the Kurdish areas of the north; their largest community is in Baghdad. The Faylis suffered abuse from both the Kurds and the Arabs. Arab regimes repressed them as Kurds and Shiʿis. Unlike other Iraqi communities, the Faylis were not given Iraqi nationality, a circumstance that was exploited to expel large numbers of them to Iran in the 1970s and 1980s. With the exception of ethnic Persians, no other Iraqi community was as deeply affected by the expulsions. Hundreds of thousands of Fayli Kurds were taken from their homes to the Iranian borders and left there. More than thirty years later, most are still unable to retrieve their Iraqi citizenship and possessions.[23] Many Fayli Kurds strongly reject the term "Arabized Kurds," used by scholars to refer to the Faylis. In November 2007 I met Saʿd Eskander, the director of the Iraqi national archive and a Fayli Kurd; he strongly criticized a Western scholar for using that term, arguing that it diminished Faylis' Kurdishness. "I am 100 percent Kurd and an Iraqi," he said.

Faylis are also deeply connected to their Shi'i sectarian identity, and some of them have benefited from it as it helped them get jobs in post-Saddam Husayn Iraq. Lutfi, a Communist and author of a book about 'Ali bin Abi Talib, founder of the Shi'a and the Fourth Caliph, was deeply influenced by Shi'i religious ceremonies that he attended in his childhood—as was Burhan Shawi, another Communist.[24] Theirs is a hybrid identity: they are Shi'i, Kurdish, and Iraqi at the same time. As Shi'is, they are a minority among the Kurds and a majority among the Arabs. Shi'i identity is rich in content and produces emotional identification that is reinforced in a Shi'i environment. As Kurds, they are a minority among the Arabs. An Iraqi identity could be a way out of their predicament, but not having Iraqi citizenship interferes with their attachment to Iraq. This situation has encouraged many Faylis to join the ICP and fight discrimination. It could be argued that by doing so they are playing down an Arab ingredient in their overall identity: indeed, most of them use Arabic for working and writing, grew up in Arab areas, and never found a place in the national Kurdish struggle. Past personalities, like 'Aziz al-Hajj, a prominent breakaway member of the ICP,[25] and later on Eskander and Shawi show that Faylis are much better suited to life in Arab Iraq than are other Kurds. Their personal history as Faylis and the misfortune of their community is what made Lutfi and Shawi such ardent Iraqi patriots. The personal histories of all these Fayli writers, with special emphasis on their past and current jobs in the Iraqi administration—Shawi, for instance, is a senior employee of the Ministry of Information and Eskander a director of the Iraqi National Archive—prove their commitment to a united Iraq, as do their descriptions of Iraq in their novels, in which Arabs and Kurds fight an evil regime. This is their version of Iraqi patriotism, which is as strong as their Kurdish identity.

Four out of the six writers experienced exile in Europe. For any writer, exile in the West is a perplexing experience, but for Kurdish writers from Iraq it was even worse. Aside from differences of mentality, economic problems, or the threat of persecution by the Iraqi secret services, they also faced other concerns. Should they join the circle of Iraqi intellectuals abroad or the circle of Kurdish intellectuals from all over Kurdistan? Did they have a homeland? Where was that homeland? Was it in Iraq? In the Kurdish provinces in Iraq? In the whole of Kurdistan? Faced with a disparate environment, they asked themselves to what extent they felt Kurdish. The reality of life in exile included choosing Arabic as the language of writing (Amin and al-Ayyubi published their first novels in Arabic in exile). The rationale behind this decision was not only the lack of Kurdish-language publishers and readers but also the wish to communicate with other Iraqi exiles, and thus to show that they were all part of the same discourse.

Of all the novels reviewed in this article, Haval Amin's *al-Bum wal-Miqass* bears the strongest imprint of exile. It is an autobiographical novel, located in Erbil and Holland, but its central motif is the extent to which life in Holland and his spiritual quest for meaning led to a fuller appreciation of the art of storytelling, personified by his Kurdish grandmother, who hailed from Erbil and died there: in other words, it is an appreciation of his cultural roots. However, Amin's hero writes poems in Arabic, goes on a spiritual trip to Damascus, and, finally, is sought by the Iraqi exiles in Holland to be their leader; he thinks they are not so different from the current Arab leaders, however. Most importantly, his frame of reference throughout the book is mainly Iraq, not Kurdistan, and in exile he meets Iraqi, not Kurdish, intellectuals. Nevertheless, the novel is a constant attempt to achieve a clear manifestation of Kurdishness, and as such is the most Kurdish of all the novels presented here. This emerges most clearly at the end of the novel in the form of a girl singing a Kurdish folk song, "The Grain of Sand," and playing the Kurdish flute. The song was actually performed by the Kurdish singer Zayrab, who used to travel between Iraq and Iran. In the symbolic final scene, which takes place near his grandmother's tomb in Erbil, the hero and the girl walk toward each other to the tune of Zayrab's song. A symbolic fusion between the two is implied.[26] What emerges is a very confused portrayal of a person torn between his homeland and Western exile, both of which shape his identity while pulling him in opposite directions.

Before examining each novel, we must take a closer look at what motivated each author to write his novel. By looking at the formative experiences behind each book, we may better understand the authors' personal positions on the Kurdish question. In this part I will only discuss four writers. Al-Ayyubi was involved in the Kurdish struggle until his arrest after the great setback in the rebellion of 1975. For some reason, he left Iraq only in the early 1990s and settled in Libya. This is a rare case of an Iraqi Kurd finding refuge (and a job) in an Arab country. Clearly, his alienation from Arab (mostly Bedouin) Libya with its arid landscape and social conservatism as well as his impossible love affair with one of his students prompted him to write his novel. Al-Ayyubi seems to be saying that the Arabs, hardened by bigotry, cannot accept people who, while wholly immersed in Arab culture, are descendants of Salah al-Din—and this simply because they are Kurds, and not of Arab stock. He wanted to be accepted by the Arabs. Before going to Libya, he lived in Europe, where he had relations with many women, but like Haval Amin he was searching for something more spiritual that could only be found in the Orient—*evin*, the Kurdish term for sublime, platonic, spiritual love. He willingly goes to Libya, with its particularly strong Arab identity, where he ultimately finds the spirituality he was searching for. In this novel one can see the strong wish to be accepted by the Arabs as equal, and the bitter disillusionment that comes with rejection leads to a tragic end.

In Amin's novel, the difficulties of assimilating in Holland are the motivating force behind the author's quest. He is not exactly down and out: he works, has a Dutch girlfriend, studies at the university, and is even active in Dutch literary circles. Although he criticizes Iraqi exiles in the Netherlands for not assimilating, his Dutch exile sharpens his identity as an immigrant. Taking a Sufi point of view, he is introspective and in constant search of spiritual mentors. These are varied, starting with a Syrian friend in Damascus, who helps him understand the medieval Sufi scholar and philosopher Ibn al-ʿArabi and his universalist spiritualism; then there is a Dutch poet, who encourages him to publish a poem in Arabic; a university lecturer; a Hungarian immigrant, who teaches him to appreciate the significance and art of storytelling, as did his grandmother in Erbil. His search leads him in narrowing circles, from the universal to the Kurdish, and finally to his cultural roots.

In al-Dahoodi's novel the motives are more mundane. His autobiographical novel revolves around his membership and activities in the ICP between 1958 and the mid-1960s. During these problematic years, al-Dahoodi left his mother and brothers in their village to become one of the activists in Kirkuk. He lived through the Baʿthi repression of February 1963 and got caught up in the growing armed conflict between the ICP, the government, and the KDP. As a member of the ICP, he criticized the incompetence of its leadership during these troubled times, stating that it bore responsibility for the ensuing calamity. As a Kurd active in Kurdish areas, he also criticized the KDP for conducting a very problematic relationship with the ICP after 1963. At the same time, he writes about his absolute loyalty to the party: he went to prison for his loyalty and, after his release, refused to sign a letter denouncing his membership in the party, even though he was not allowed to work as a teacher due to his ICP ties. Unable to find a job, he started thinking about leaving the country. Feeling that he was paying a heavy price when he had to leave his homeland, he likened it to his own funeral—not knowing, however, whether the coffin contained his body or his soul.[27] Al-Dahoodi was mainly motivated by the need to describe what made him emigrate and to name the people responsible for what befell the ICP.

Shawi was exposed to the Kurdish problem when he served in the army near Sulaymaniyya. Although he was a Kurd himself, nothing in his former life had prepared him for the experience of military service. He saw atrocities, executions, and operations against Kurdish villages in which innocent civilians were targeted. He also felt that neither he nor the Iraqi army actually belonged there: it was not the environment he knew, and the Iraqi army, with its Arab soldiers, was also misplaced. But he was in an ambiguous situation since he was not only an Iraqi soldier in Kurdistan, but also an Iraqi Kurd. Therefore, in *al-Jahim al-Muqaddas*, he splits up his own persona: on the one hand, the main character, ʿAbdullah, is an Arab soldier serving in Kurdistan; on the other hand, ʿAli al-Fayli is a Communist Kurd in Baghdad.[28] The symbolism of this split stands out as it is the only example in which a Kurdish writer exposes his Arab side. Unlike the other writers, Shawi discovered the Kurdish problem when he was already nearly totally assimilated into Arab Iraq. In my personal correspondence with the author, he drew a dividing line between Kurdish writers in Arabic such as himself and nationalist Kurdish writers.

An Analysis of the Narratives

Sherko, a veteran of the Kurdish struggle and the hero of al-Ayyubi's novel *Efin . . . wa Intizar al-Fajr*, leaves Iraq in the 1990s and, after traveling in Europe, settles in Libya in search of *evin*—that is, the type of relationship he could not maintain with a Western woman. He finds this kind of love with Zaynab, his student and a local Arab woman of tribal origins. Their love cannot transcend local mores and prohibitions, and Zaynab is eventually admitted to a mental hospital. Later he discovers that her family had convinced her that he was killed in Kurdistan, and married her off to a cousin, by whom she had a son, Sherko. Unable to bear her fate, she kills herself. As in Haval Amin's novel *al-Bum wal-Miqass*, the spiritual love is related to Kurdish nationalism: Sherko perceives *evin* as compensation for the tragedy of the Kurdish people. Zaynab's suicide therefore shatters him, and not only on a personal level as her lover. Events are shown in a series of flashbacks, when the hero is in his hotel room, anticipating dawn and his own suicide. It ends on a mystical note: Sherko and Zaynab's graves are haunted as people swear they see the lovers together, "for every fire turns into ashes, but the fire of love . . . the fire of *evin*."[29] This is not a personal narrative in any sense, but one in which the national and even the metanational (Kurdish and Arab) transcend individual lives to reach a symbolic union. It is quite evident that the author found inspiration in the Kurdish national epos *Mem u Zin*. However, in the sixteenth-century epos the love story, which also ends tragically, is between two Kurdish lovers torn apart by borders, whereas in this novel the lovers are torn apart by ethnicity.[30]

Similarly, in Amin's autobiographical novel, the hero is looking for a spirituality that he cannot find in Western exile. We do not know much about his life in Iraqi Kurdistan, before he left for Holland, but his quest for spirituality in Holland leads him to literary circles, to university studies in journalism, and even to the tomb of the Sufi philosopher Ibn al-ʿArabi in Damascus. Finally, he finds the essence of spirituality in his late grandmother's stories, which were an essential part of his childhood in Erbil, and he reinterprets her *al-Bum* (owl) stories as the struggle between the weak and witty and the powerful—no doubt an allegory of the Kurdish disposition. In the end, he returns to Erbil and, in an act of bonding with his grandmother, falls asleep on her grave. Then, when he wakes up, he hears a well-known Kurdish melody, "A Grain of Sand," by the Kurdish singer Hasan Zirak, who used to move back and forth between Iran and Iraq, depending on the political situation. The tune is played on a Kurdish flute by a young girl. She reminds him of his Dutch girlfriend, who waded into the sea playing the flute and drowned. He and the girl, who is still playing the song, move toward each other.[31] Amin's is probably the most national of the four novels: his spiritual search is introspective, leading him to Kurdistan and ending in a scene that binds him to his ancestors, his culture, and the future, personified by the girl. The function of the other characters in the novel is either to show him the way, or to show him what he should not be, i.e., like the Iraqi exiles he meets.

The other two novels are political and lack any spiritual dimension. Dahoodi's autobiographical novel reads mostly like a documentary and is of very little literary value. Most of it takes place in a rural Kurdish environment. The hero, Zorab, grew up in a small Kurdish town and moved to Kirkuk, where he graduated from the local teachers' seminary. He joined the ICP and witnessed the onslaught against the party in 1959 and 1963, as well as in subsequent assaults. He eventually was forced to leave Iraq. Looking more deeply at the simplistic narrative, one sees interplay between the Kurdish environment and the overall framework of a patriotic (*watani*) Iraq. On the one hand, Zorab praises the simple life in the Kurdish village where he grew up, and on the other he criticizes the

KDP, the political personification of Kurdish nationalism. He describes a multiethnic reality, in which members of different groups cooperate and are influenced by developments in Baghdad, but on his one brief visit to Baghdad, as a prisoner on his way to yet another prison, he is upset by people's indifference to the fate of others. What makes him eventually leave the country is a feeling that Iraq has betrayed him. Somehow, the last two novels, which are political and less nationalist and Iraq-oriented, are more pessimistic.

Shawi's short novel is a comprehensive attempt to discuss the Kurdish problem. Set in Kurdistan and Baghdad, the main story is about ʿAbdullah, an Arab soldier with a Communist background, who does a stint in the army in the Kurdish countryside in the late 1970s. He witnesses atrocities and expresses his support for the Kurdish struggle. After a cruel attack on the nearby Kurdish village, he is ordered to accompany a frightened Kurdish-speaking woman, Shirin, to the military corps headquarters. ʿAbdullah helplessly witnesses the ordeal of the young woman, as she is repeatedly raped by Arab officers and sergeants. Arab soldiers did indeed use rape as a weapon against the Kurds. A museum in Sulaymaniyya even addresses these atrocities. In this scene, Shawi was influenced by an important and exceptional Iraqi novel from the 1970s, *Shaqqa fi Shariʿ Abi Nuwwas* [A flat in Abu Nuwwas Street], written by the Arab novelist Burhan al-Khatib, in which a Kurdish woman is raped by one of the roommates while another watches helplessly.[32] Parallel to that story, the novel follows the travel to Baghdad of an elderly Kurdish mother searching for her imprisoned son, Hayman, and a nephew, ʿAli al-Fayli, a Communist activist who has been arrested for alleged complicity in a "conspiracy." Fayli lives in an apartment building run by the hospitable Umm Tariq and symbolizing Iraq under the Baʿth. Two other tenants are a Daʿwa activist and a nonpolitical artist. They are all arrested by a fourth tenant, a Tikriti informer of the Mukhabarat. ʿAli and the Daʿwa member are killed in jail. So is the son of the elderly Kurdish woman. On the way, the truck that takes ʿAbdullah and Shirin to Mosul is hit by a Kurdish Peshmerga militiaman fighting the government. (The name "Peshmerga" literally means "those who face death.") Shirin is saved and protects ʿAbdullah from certain death. At that point he pleads with his Kurdish captors—one of whom is an Arab from the south (a Shiʿi)—to accept him into their ranks. But he is shot in the back by the Arab truck driver, who calls him a traitor, and dies.

A novel is not a political agenda. One should not expect to find a "solution" in its pages. There are few allusions as to how the author envisions the problem: Kurdistan is portrayed as a separate area, in which Arabs, especially Arab soldiers, do not belong; the Kurdish guerrillas are not "saboteurs," but rather "oppressed [people] asking for their rights," and the Iraqi army is sent to Kurdistan to turn it into a hell.[33] But such allusions are few and far between. However, 'Abdullah's death does call for symbolic interpretation: first, he gives his gun to Shirin and together they pull the trigger. Then she takes his gun and joins the Peshmerga.[34] Possibly, it was not the author himself who sacrificed the Arab soldier in that final act, but Shawi's own helplessness. By giving the gun to a woman, the epitome of weakness and the real victim in this novel, he empowers her and adds a moral dimension to the Kurdish struggle. Nonetheless, Shawi wrote an Iraqi novel, in which Baghdad and Kurdistan are intertwined.

Finally, a short comparison with a novel written in Kurdish (and translated into French) will show the hybrid nature of the novels in Arabic. Ibrahim Ahmad's *Jan-i Gal* [The agony of people], originally published in the 1960s, tells the story of Jwamer from Sulaymaniyya, who is imprisoned for ten years for his Kurdish patriotism. Meanwhile, his wife dies in childbirth, having given birth to a baby who dies as well. Upon his release, Jwamer becomes aware of the terrible conditions in which his people live and joins the liberation movement to continue their struggle. The author, who was a leading political figure in Kurdish politics at the time (and not a prolific novelist), emphasizes the notion that throughout history the Kurds were under the domination of other ethnic groups and calls on them to break out of this vicious circle. The novels discussed here have a different drift, which is less nationalist. None of the heroes of these novels joins a Kurdish movement, and in al-Ayyubi's novel one of them, an exhausted veteran of the struggle, refuses to return to Kurdistan in the 1990s. Another character, in al-Dahoodi's novel, suffers from the struggle between the ICP, of which he is a member, and other Kurdish movements. More often than not, the search for identity is not expressed solely in the political arena, as seems to be the case in Ahmad's novel, but is transferred to the personal and cultural sphere, and is hence more thorough.

Conclusions

No matter the differences between them, all the novels discussed in this chapter share a strong yearning to belong to something broader than the Kurdish people. This explains the loaded choice of Arabic as a writing tool, since the wider framework could be Iraq or the Arab world. It is quite possible that this is not the case with literature written in Kurdish. Arabic is thus not only a language in these novels, but also a political signifier. By contrast, after long years of ignoring the Kurds, the Iraqi novel has recently started fitting them into the Iraqi national fabric. Iraqi writers, however, generally downplay Kurdish separatist feelings, quite unlike the writers discussed above.[35]

All of this puts the Kurdish writers in Arabic in a category apart: they do not conform to the norms of writers in Kurdish, nor do they write like their Arab Iraqi counterparts. Significantly, despite the large number of Kurds who collaborated with various Iraqi regimes, these writers were not collaborators.[36] They were also unique in some other respects: as members of the ICP, as exiles, and, in the case of Lutfi and Shawi, as Fayli Kurds. Writers of a minority group who write in the language of the majority often find themselves set apart. This is the case of Israeli Arab writers writing in Hebrew. Whether or not they compromise the contents of their novels as a result of the choice of language, the dialogue they conduct across ethnic lines is open to various interpretations and to debate. The fact that writers like Lutfi and Zangane were warmly accepted into the pantheon of Kurdish literature (Zangane even moved to Kurdistan after April 2003) is a sign of moderation and forgiveness in contemporary Kurdish nationalism.

Unlike Arab writers who write in Hebrew, especially Sayyid Qashuʿa and Ayman Siqsaq, the Kurdish writers discussed here hardly ever use Arabic as a cover to criticize Kurdish politics and society. In such a situation, the writer chooses a foreign language because he can be certain that his books will hardly be read by people of his ethnic group. This allows him to be more daring in his criticism of his own society. Torn between an Arab reading public, their own Kurdish identity, and the urge to represent the Kurdish cause within an Iraqi discourse, Kurdish authors were not in the position to take an introspective look at the wrongs of Kurdish society.

To what extent can they be viewed as Arab writers? Some, like Shawi, are more so than others, and probably more so than they themselves would admit. All of them have faced accusations of not being Kurdish enough, to which they retorted by mentioning similar allegations by Arab writers who accused them of being "Kurdish nationalists." The term "Arabized Kurds" is not appropriate in their case. It is appropriate for people of Kurdish ancestry who have lived for generations as Arabs and adopted the Arab language, customs, and political thinking. Taha Yasin Ramadan, Saddam Husayn's deputy, was an "Arabized Kurd." Yet when personalities like Saʿd Eskander were labeled as such, they were justly irritated. It is more appropriate to refer to these writers as Iraqi Kurds. In the final account, Arabic for these writers is a cultural means of expression and a linkage to other groups in Iraq; it is not an identity. Their identity is Kurdish and their Iraq is not only, nor even predominantly, Arab.

To what extent can they be considered Iraqi writers? This is another sensitive question, which some of them would probably seek to evade. The answer is to be found in the novels and in the overall approach of the novelists. None of the novels are located solely in Kurdistan. The narratives take place in Kurdistan and Baghdad (Shawi), Kurdistan and the diaspora (al-Ayyubi, Haval Amin), or in a mixed area (al-Dahoodi). Shawi, whose writings are more ideological than the others, chooses an Arab as his main character and bases that character largely on himself. The end of Shawi's novel is a call for Arab-Kurdish solidarity in the framework of a unified Iraq. Al-Dahoodi grieves bitterly for having to leave his homeland Iraq, and blames the Arabs and Kurds who forced him to do so. Even the more nationalist al-Ayyubi and Amin, who do not mention other, non-Kurdish parts of Iraq, conduct a dialogue with Arabs in Arabic. They do not easily fit into the narrow and parochial constraints of an exclusively ethnic Kurdish nationalism.

This identity, the Kurdish-Iraqi one, was once a real option. As political developments separate the Kurds from the Arabs, Kurdish nationalism rises, and the number of Arabic readers in Kurdistan declines, the Kurdish-Iraqi option is rapidly disappearing from the scene. How rare the phenomenon is can be glanced from the following anecdote: in February 2011 an American student of mine, who speaks fluent Arabic, visited Iraqi Kurdistan. I asked her to buy me any book in Arabic she could find, especially novels. Having browsed the bookstores (and sidewalks) of Erbil, Sulaymaniyya, and Dohuk, she returned with only one book. There was no other book in Arabic in Iraqi Kurdistan.[37]

PART III

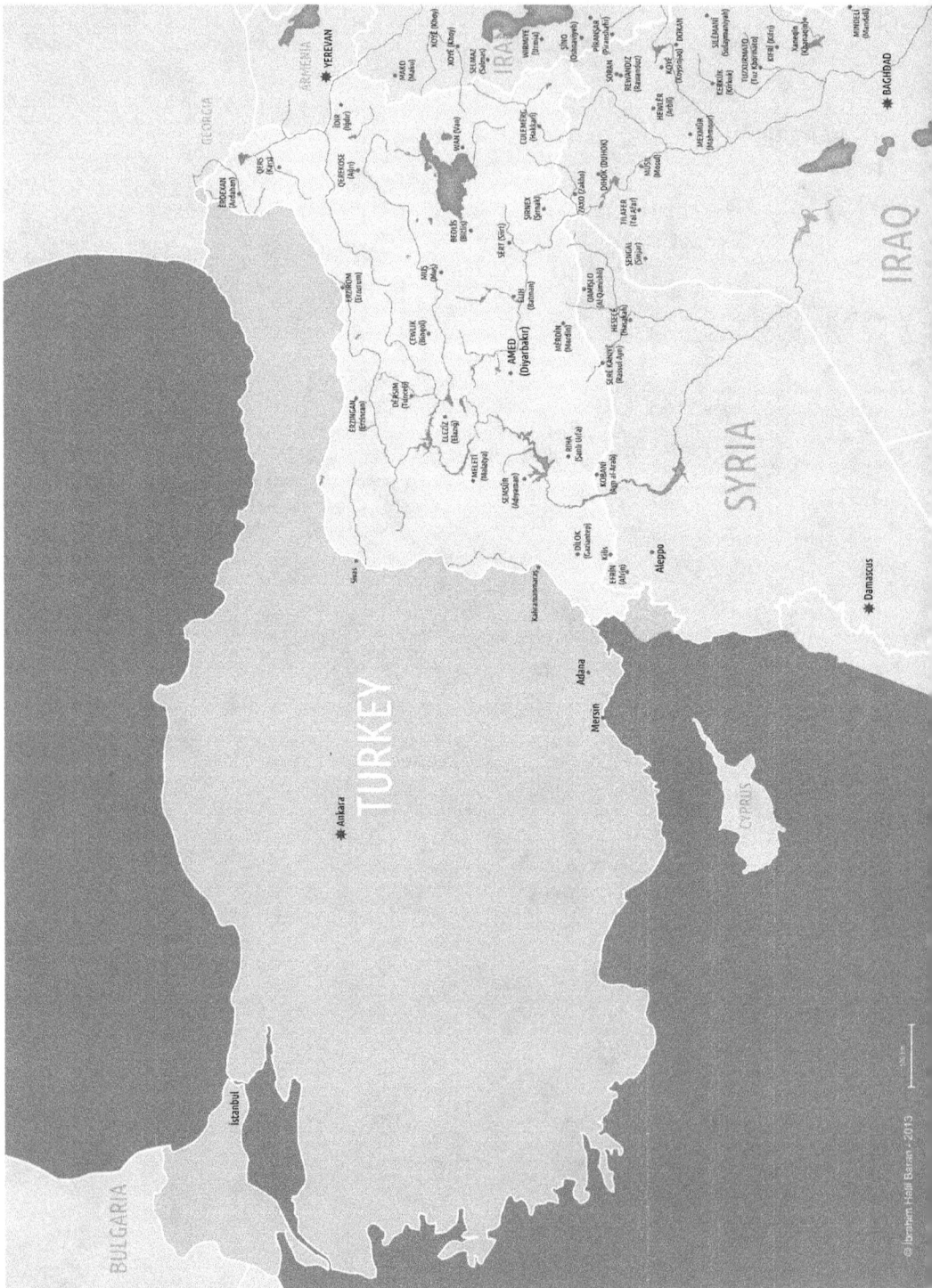

A Tale of Political Consciousness: The Rise of a Nonviolent Kurdish Political Movement in Turkey

HAY EYTAN COHEN YANAROCAK

We are not the enemy of the Turks; we support the ideals of brotherhood;
we want justice and freedom. Today, Tunisia, Egypt, and Libya are crying
out for their freedom; believe me, our cry will be much greater than theirs.[1]
AHMET TÜRK, KURDISH POLITICAL LEADER

This chapter focuses on the evolution of the nonviolent Kurdish political movement in Turkey and its symbiotic relations with its violent counterpart. The struggle for Kurdish political and civil rights in Turkey began with the enactment of the Treaty of Sèvres on August 10, 1920. The treaty, reluctantly signed by the last Ottoman government of Sultan Vahdettin with the Allies at the end of World War I—among them the United Kingdom, France, and Italy—led to the dissolution of the Ottoman Empire. Articles 62, 63, and 64 of the treaty paved the way for considerable local Kurdish autonomy, potentially leading to full independence.[2] The treaty envisaged a future Turkish state that would include only Istanbul and central and northern Anatolia, with access to very few resources and practically no freedom of action in the economic sphere.[3]

The enactment of the Treaty of Lausanne in July 1923, following the Turkish War of Independence from 1919 to 1923 and the establishment of the Turkish Republic in October 1923, defeated the goal of Kurdish independence. The treaty between the Turkish Grand National Assembly (Türkiye Büyük Millet Meclisi, TBMM) representatives and the Allies was signed on July 24, 1923. Articles 37–42 define the minorities, as well as their rights and obligations. In point of fact, only non-Muslim Turkish citizens were identified as "minorities."[4] In the Turkish political discourse, the Kurds were seen as first-class citizens who should not seek minority rights.

The Kemalist revolution created a monist type of nationalism that ignored ethnic and cultural differences.[5] After the Turkish Republic was formally declared, the caliphate—separated from the sultanate since November 1922—was abolished on March 3, 1924, and the last caliph, Abdülmecit (Abd ul-Majid), sent into exile. These changes were embodied in a new constitution, enacted on April 20, 1924. In 1926 Turkey abandoned the old, Islamic civil and penal codes in favor of secular codes based on those of Switzerland and Italy. The compulsory change from Arabic letters to Latin script and the revocation of Islam as the religion of the state upended the relationship between the Turks and the Kurds.[6] Turks and Kurds were bound together by Islam.[7] Since Islam was virtually excluded from the political sphere, the Kurds of Turkey began to see themselves as a different ethnic political entity. However, the Turkish state's nationalist discourse, which was based on Ziya Gökalp's definition of nation, rejected their claim.

Ziya Gökalp, a Kurd who greatly influenced Mustafa Kemal Atatürk, is widely regarded as the architect of the core theories of Turkish nationalism. Gökalp defines "nation" as follows: "[a] nation is not a group of people who came from the same racial roots, geography, or political view, but a group of people who share the same language and religion—in short, people who have received a similar education."[8]

To form a monist society, Turkey adopted denial of Kurdish identity as state policy. The Kurds were never acknowledged by successive Turkish administrations—as either a different ethnic group or a minority. In May 1932, the Kurds of Turkey were classified as "Mountain Turks" for the first time.[9] The term referred to a group of people who had forgotten their own Turkish identity and roots.

The Kurds reacted to the Kemalist revolution with a series of rebellions, such as the Koçgiri (1920), Sheikh Said (1925), Ağrı/Ararat (1927), and Dersim (1937) rebellions. These upheavals had an ethnonational and Islamic character that threatened the new Kemalist regime. As a result, the Kurds suffered increasing oppression so that Kurdish national consciousness became less visible, at least until the 1960s.

The nonviolent Kurdish political movement came into being in the 1960s with more active involvement in left-wing political parties. However, the establishment of nonviolent student unions strengthened Kurdish consciousness and paved the way for a violent Kurdish political movement.

Beginning in 1990, a rising Kurdish consciousness found its political expression in Kurdish political parties. Naturally, a symbiotic relationship emerged between the nonviolent movement and its violent counterpart, so that the policies of all Kurdish political parties were inevitably affected by the violence.

This chapter will address the following questions: What kind of relationship developed between the nonviolent and the violent Kurdish movements? What were the achievements of the nonviolent Kurdish movement for Kurdish society? What role did the Kurdish nonviolent movement play in the Turkish polity as a whole?

First Steps of the Nonviolent Kurdish Political Movement

In the 1960s the seeds of the Kurdish political movement began to germinate within the Kurdish intellectual awakening, which was manifested in the Kurdish radio broadcasts that were first transmitted from Cairo and Yerevan. The Kurdish intellectual Musa Anter launched a daily newspaper, *İleri Yurt* (i.e., homeland forward), in 1959, the first Kurdish publication since the Dersim rebellion. The Dersim rebellion was the fourth serious Kurdish uprising against Kemalist Turkey; it resulted in 7,954 deaths between April and December 1938. Its leader, Seyit Rıza, was captured and hanged.[10] The repercussions of the Dersim oppression were felt by the Kurds as late as the 1960s. The Menderes government eventually banned *İleri Yurt* and imprisoned fifty Kurdish intellectuals in 1959. They were accused of being communists. As one of the intellectuals was killed in custody, the case became known as the "49ers." All forty-nine prisoners were set free during the military coup d'état in 1960.[11] The 49ers case and the banning of *İleri Yurt* marked a milestone for Turkey's Kurds, who began to emphasize their ethnic origin and their objection to Turkey's assimilation policies.

The 1961 constitution made the establishment of a socialist party possible. The Turkish Labor Party (Türkiye İşçi Partisi, TİP) was founded in 1961 and became a legal political home for many Kurds.[12] Many Kurds became very active in the labor party, which claimed that Kurdish people in eastern Turkey confronted policies of assimilation, suppression, and violence in their daily lives.[13] The party's statement with regard to the Kurdish situation provoked an earthquake in the Turkish political arena. The 1961 constitution and the establishment of the TİP did not put an end to Kurdish alienation from Kemalist Turkey, however. On the contrary,

Kurdish alienation was exacerbated by a provocative article that appeared in the Turkish magazine *Ötüken*, the journal of the rightist Nationalist Movement Party (Milliyetçi Hareket Partisi, MHP), in April 1967.[14]

The anonymous writer claimed that the Kurds were a backward people without historical roots and, even worse, accused them of wanting to bring about the disintegration of Turkey. Moreover, the author suggested that Kurds be expelled because Turkey was for the Turks only. President Cevdet Sunay went even further when he declared that "those who are not Turks may go away from Turkey."[15] The *Ötüken* article and Sunay's comments sparked the first important Kurdish demonstrations, also known as Doğu Mitingleri (Rallies of the East) and supported by TİP, in Silvan and Diyarbakır in August 1967.[16] The government accused the organizers of treachery. The meetings aroused Kurdish consciousness, leading to the establishment of numerous Kurdish organizations in the region.[17]

A new era began in 1969 with the foundation of the Devrimci Doğu Kültür Ocakları (Eastern Revolutionary Cultural Hearths). Urban Kurds organized the DDKO in response to provocative anti-Kurdish articles that inflamed Kurdish public opinion.[18] The word "East" (Doğu) in DDKO, which symbolized Kurdistan, is noteworthy.[19] In the 1960s the new concept of "Doğuculuk" (Eastism) emerged. It can be understood as a campaign that called for the development of Turkey's badly neglected eastern provinces. Doğuculuk served as an intellectual basis for the birth of the Kurdistan Workers' Party (Partiya Karkerên Kurdistan, PKK).[20]

The main concerns addressed in the DDKO monthly bulletins were the economic problems of eastern Turkey, the oppression of the Kurdish villagers by (Kurdish) landlords and tribal leaders, and the brutal and violent behavior of the Turkish army units in Kurdish villages.[21] In 1970, Abdullah Öcalan, the founder of the PKK, took part in DDKO activities in Istanbul. The DDKO were later destroyed and all their leaders were arrested during the 1971 military coup.

The Rise of the PKK and Kurdish Representation in Turkish Politics

The DDKO paved the way for an ideological Kurdish political movement. Its banning persuaded some of the members to form a new organization, which would differ from the DDKO. In 1973, Abdullah Öcalan and a group of supporters decided to form the PKK in Çubuk, a town in the province of Ankara. The organization's main ideology was Marxist-

Leninist and its goal was to achieve the independence of the Kurdish people.[22]

The 1980 coup d'état put an end to the TİP, which provided a political platform for the Kurdish political movement. Toward the end of the 1980s the Social Democratic Populist Party (Sosyal Demokrat Halkçı Parti, SHP), which had taken the place of the TİP, adopted a critical stance on Turkey's Kurdish policy. In 1986 the SHP prepared what it called a "South East Report," since the use of the word "Kurdish" constituted a legal risk. According to the report, "eastern Turkey had become a sort of concentration camp where every citizen was treated as a suspect and where oppression, torture and insult by the military were the norm."[23] Due to SHP's new Kurdish policy, many Kurds became active members of the party.

Mehmet Ali Eren, SHP member of Parliament, made a landmark speech demanding that TBMM "overcome the taboo" against using, or even discussing, the term "Kurdish question." Eren stated that the taboo of modern Turkey is "the Kurdish problem." He went on to say that "the Kurdish problem should be dealt with in all its facets, realistic solutions should be proposed and a detailed debate is necessary."[24] In April 1988, Mehmet Ali Eren proposed an amendment to outlaw the ban on the Kurdish language.[25]

In September 1989, former president Turgut Özal hinted at a change in his Kurdish policy. In a meeting with the Turkish Industrialists' and Businessmen's Association (Türk Sanayicileri ve İşadamları Derneği, TÜSİAD), he stated that "the government engaged in a quest for a serious model for solving the Kurdish problem in a manner that goes beyond police measures."[26] The following year, signaling a serious change in policy, Özal annulled the ban on the use of the Kurdish language, which had been implemented in October 1983 under Law 2932.[27]

Even after the ban was lifted, the use of the Kurdish language still remained limited. Its use in official agencies, publishing, or teaching was still considered a crime. The following year, Özal made a revolutionary move and suggested sixty- or ninety-minute programs in the Kurdish language in the Southeastern Anatolia Project TV Network (Güneydoğu Anadolu Projesi, GAP).[28]

Despite Özal's Kurdish policy-opening initiative in the fall of 1989, Kurdish members of the SHP were expelled from the party because of their attendance at the Paris Kurdish Conference, which was perceived as a pro-PKK gathering, opposed to Turkish national interests. This event created a split in the SHP; the more left-oriented members of Turkish origin and eleven SHP members of Kurdish origin formed the People's Labor Party (Halkın Emek Partisi, HEP) in the spring of 1990. From the start, HEP members were fully aware of the limits of freedom of speech in Parliament and hence avoided red-flag words such as "Kurdistan." HEP stated its goals as "solving the Kurdish problem through peaceful and democratic methods in line with Universal Declaration of Human Rights, the European Convention on Human Rights and the statutes of Helsinki Final Document."[29]

In 1990, HEP activities were formally initiated. The party openly called on the Özal government not to intervene in the Gulf War in order to protect pan-Kurdish interests. Its most vital show of force came at the 1991 Istanbul Newroz gathering, as the Turkish flags were removed from the congressional center. Pressure against the HEP reached a peak when the party organized its first official congress. In the final document of the congress, government policies toward the Kurds and the region were harshly criticized. Due to the party's increasing influence in Turkish politics, the spate of attacks on Kurdish party members in 1990–1991 triggered violent clashes between the police and civilians in southeast Turkey.[30]

Vedat Aydın, the HEP chairman in Diyarbakır, was taken from his home by a group of people disguised as policemen;[31] a few days later, his body was found in the city of Elazığ. Aydın's funeral took place amidst violent clashes between the protestors and the police, resulting in fourteen civilian casualties.[32]

In a spate of mysterious killings, a total of 1,310 Kurds were assassinated between 1993 and 1997.[33] To this day, many Kurds believe that the killings were carried out by a group associated with the Islamic Turkish Hizbullah (Party of God)[34] and the Gendarmerie Intelligence and Fight against Terrorism (Jandarma İstihbarat ve Terörle Mücadele, JİTEM), a covert Turkish state-sponsored antiterror squad.[35]

In November 1991 a respected Turkish journalist, İsmet İmset, interviewed the PKK leader Öcalan at his headquarters in Lebanon. For the first time the PKK leader emphasized that, like the Kurdish political party HEP, the PKK was no longer interested in creating an independent Kurdistan, but rather in Kurdish political and human rights inside Turkey.[36] In that same year, Kurdish deputies who were younger, more radical, and less experienced began entering the political arena. New HEP members formed informal contacts with PKK. PKK flags, banners, symbols, and pictures of Öcalan began to appear at HEP meetings and demonstrations. As a party policy, HEP refused to condemn PKK actions against the state.[37] It is quite clear that with the "Lebanon Declaration" of Öcalan to İsmet İmset, a symbiotic relation was formed between the violent Kurdish movement, the PKK, and the nonviolent political Kurdish movement, the HEP. In a sense, one can argue that the HEP and its successors began to act as the unofficial political wing of the PKK.

1991 was a crucial year for HEP. The then Turkish prime minister Turgut Özal's ascendance to the presidency paved the way for an early election in Turkey. According to the election law of 1991, only parties that fulfilled the organizational requirements as expressed in the law (i.e., that had representative offices in at least half the Turkish cities and managed to organize a formal congress six months prior to the election) were eligible to participate in the elections. HEP could have organized itself six months before the ballot, but it could not meet the criterion of organizing its first congress in time. When the party found itself one week late, HEP requested that the elections be postponed by seven days, but its demand was rejected by the ruling Motherland Party (Anavatan Partisi, ANAP). HEP members decided to form an election alliance with the SHP. HEP-listed members managed to secure twenty-two parliamentary seats. On December 6, 1991, the swearing-in ceremony took place in the TBMM, the National Assembly. The SHP-listed Kurdish HEP members of Parliament were sworn in. Members of Parliament of Kurdish origin emphasized that they were taking the oath solely because it was a constitutional obligation and not because they believed in it. Moreover, at the end of the oath they added the following sentence in Kurdish: "I read the oath for the brotherhood of the Turks and the Kurds."[38] The event caused an earthquake in Turkish politics since this was the first time that the Kurdish language was used in Parliament and the first time the Kurdish question was mentioned openly in the TBMM.

In the summer of 1991, public prosecutor Nusret Demiral launched an investigation against HEP. Finally, on July 14, 1993, the Constitutional Court of Turkey dismantled the party. The party's closure derived from articles 78, 80, 81, and 82 of the Turkish Political Parties Law (No. 2820), which prohibited any party activity that would lead to territorial separation, the creation of minorities, the abolishment of the unitary state principle, and regionalism. Articles 98 and 101 granted the Constitutional Court the jurisdictional power to determine the destiny of political parties.[39] It should be noted that the law was not designed to ban individual party members from politics, but only the party as an institution. Consequently, former party members were still allowed to establish a new political party under a new name. The HEP deputies therefore managed to keep their parliamentary seats, namely by forming the Demokrasi Partisi (Democracy Party, DEP) prior to HEP's breakup.

In February 1994 the PKK bombed Istanbul's Tuzla train station, targeting military cadets. In an interview for Turkish television, DEP chairman Hatip Dicle argued that "during wartime, soldiers in uniform are targets."[40] He emphasized the PKK's role in a potential peace process, while another DEP member, Mahmut Kılınç, stated that the PKK was a political party.

Turkey's general chief of staff Doğan Güreş suggested that instead of casting about for the bandits in the Bekaa Valley of Lebanon, they should look for them in Parliament.[41] In March 1994 the TBMM repealed the parliamentary immunity of six DEP members of Parliament, who were accused of being in a direct relationship with the PKK. Dicle's and Kılınç's statements were sufficient for the Constitutional Court to ban the newly founded DEP. The oath ceremony or, as they were popularly named, the "DEP trials" were concluded in December 1994. Orhan Doğan, Selim Sadak, Hatip Dicle, and Leyla Zana were sentenced to fifteen years of imprisonment.[42]

In July 1994 the People's Democracy Party (Halkın Demokrasi Partisi, HADEP) was established by a lawyer, Murat Bozlak. The HADEP ran in the national elections in 1995 and received 4.2 percent of the votes.[43] It is noteworthy that the HADEP won landslide victories of 65 percent in Diyarbakır and Van, where the Kurdish population is dense.[44] Like its predecessor, the HADEP congress of June 1996 proved the existence of a symbiotic relationship between the PKK and the nonviolent HADEP. On that occasion, a masked man lowered the Turkish flag, threw it on the floor, and raised the PKK banner in its place. A few HADEP members and some party leaders were arrested. After pro-PKK magazines were discovered in the offices of HADEP members, the public prosecutor argued that HADEP was an extension of the PKK.[45]

The capture of PKK leader Abdullah Öcalan by the Turkish National Intelligence Organization (Milli İstihbarat Teşkilatı, MİT) in Nairobi, Kenya, in the spring of 1999; his sentencing to death by the State Security Courts, which was later amended by Parliament to life imprisonment;[46] the arrests of thousands of pro-Kurdish activists; and a nationwide bombing campaign by militant Kurdish groups placed an additional strain on the HADEP.[47]

After Öcalan's capture, MİT released a report that accused HADEP of supporting the PKK. HADEP became more critical of the Turkish state:

it demanded the abolition of the 10 percent voting threshold, constitutional reforms, the abolishment of the death penalty, decentralization, and reforms in the field of education, including the use of the Kurdish language. And finally, it accused Turkey of adopting assimilation policies against its Kurdish citizens.[48]

The 10 percent Turkish elections threshold was, and still is, a significant challenge for the Kurdish parties. Viewing it as a deliberate obstacle to Kurdish representation in Parliament, Ahmet Türk, a former DEP member—and later the head of the Democratic Society Party (Demokratik Toplum Partisi, DTP)—demanded that the 10 percent threshold be decreased to 3 percent. However, the European Court of Justice's decision states that the existence of a 10 percent threshold does not constitute an obstacle to the right of free election.[49] In the 1999 national elections, the votes for the HADEP increased from 4.2 to 4.7 percent, but the party could not get a seat in the TBMM because of the 10 percent threshold.

In 2002, in the context of Turkey's accession to the European Union, a reform package was passed in the TBMM that abolished the death penalty and granted limited cultural rights such as broadcasting and private education in the Kurdish language to Turkey's Kurds. In March 2003 the Constitutional Court accused the HADEP of aiding the PKK; consequently, the party was abolished.[50] In other words, Turkish policy is a classic example of the carrot-and-stick approach. On the one hand, by approving the reforms, Turkey improved the Kurds' civil status in the country. On the other hand, by closing down their political party, Turkey showed that it would not be that tolerant with the Kurds.

HADEP was replaced by DEHAP, the Democratic People's Party (Demokratik Halk Partisi). In the November 2002 elections, the DEHAP won 6.2 percent of the national vote.[51] It was one of the shortest-lived political parties in Turkey: it dissolved in 2004 and joined the Democratic Society Movement (Demokratik Toplum Hareketi, DTH), which was established by former DEP members, to form a new political party, the Democratic Society Party or DTP.

On October 22, 2004, former DEP members Leyla Zana, Orhan Doğan, Hatip Dicle, and Selim Sadak founded the DTH, which can be described as a political decision-making movement that aimed to unify all Kurdish political groups outside Parliament. It should be noted that the DTH was not a political party, so that the Constitutional Court could not use articles 78, 80, 81, and 82 of the Turkish Political Parties Law to close it. In order to form a political party, DTH members held a meeting in Ankara, where they established the DTP. Aysel Tuğluk and Ahmet Türk were elected as chairmen of the new party. On November 9, 2005, the DTP became legally registered.[52]

The party's program could be differentiated easily from that of other Turkish parties. Its main goal was to force the state to accept a "Kurdish political identity." Ultimately, it strove to define "Turkishness" as an overarching identity, as opposed to being the sole identity by law and constitution.[53]

On November 9, 2007, the DTP published its Political Stance Document. In it, the party accused the Republic of Turkey of assimilating the different ethnic groups by blending everyone under one Turkish identity. The DTP emphasized that the ethnic Turkish national concept was unacceptable. Instead of the term "Turkish people," the DTP suggested the "people of Turkey" (Türkiyeli). This term would refer to territory instead of ethnicity. The DTP stated in its Public Stance Document that it supported not secession policies, but rather greater democratization policies that might lead to regionalism and allow for the use of regional symbols and regional languages.[54]

In 2006 the DTP came up with a new strategy. Confirming the continuous, symbiotic relationship between the PKK and nonviolent Kurdish political parties, PKK leader Abdullah Öcalan decided (via his lawyers) that the DTP would run in the national elections as "independent" candidates in order to overcome the 10 percent threshold.[55] Once candidates were declared independent, they were immune from the national threshold. The DTP participated in the general elections with this new election strategy. Twenty members of the DTP entered TBMM as independents, reuniting later under the umbrella of the DTP. The party's conspicuous policy on the Kurdish question, its pro-PKK slogans during political meetings, public demonstrations, and statements by DTP members resulted in a campaign of political lynching against it. Devlet Bahçeli and his MHP accused the DTP of being an extension of the PKK.[56]

Public Prosecutor Abdurrahman Yalçınkaya first appealed to the courts on November 16, 2007, demanding the closure of the DTP. He argued that the party had become a "center of activities aimed at damaging the independence of the state and the indivisible integrity of its territory and nation."[57] The indictment called for 221 members of the DTP, including eight sitting members of the Turkish Parliament, to be banned for five years from membership in a political party.[58]

Following demands by the Constitutional Court that the DTP be dismantled for a series of violations of Turkish law, the party held a public meeting on November 25, 2007. At the meeting, Selahattin Demirtaş, a member of the DTP, emphasized that a "lynch campaign" was being mounted against the party.[59]

On October 5, 2008, following a PKK raid against the Aktütün gendarmerie station that resulted in fifteen casualties, the Turkish General Staff requested that the Turkish government expand the general staff's jurisdiction over counterterrorism issues and take the necessary steps against the "political party, local administrations, labor unions, foundations and clubs, which are affiliated with the PKK."[60] Following a request by the Turkish Armed Forces (Türk Silahlı Kuvvetleri, TSK) to discuss the new policy against the PKK and the Justice and Development Party (Adalet ve Kalkınma Partisi, AKP), the government convened the "Struggle against Terrorism Summit" and decided to form a civil committee under the auspices of the Ministry of Defense, in which TSK members, too, could be represented.[61]

Besides its violent activities, the PKK was also involved in Turkish political life. In his April 19, 2009, statement, PKK's de facto leader Murat Karayılan emphasized his party's relations with the DTP and called upon the Kurdish citizens of Turkey to support the party. Karayılan defined the DTP as the only legitimate democratic platform for raising the voice of Kurdish politics in Turkey.[62] At the same time, DTP members showed their solidarity with the PKK, with Kamuran Yüksek, the vice-chairman of the DTP, stating, "They ask us to condemn the PKK, but we won't do it; and we are ready to pay the price. If they close our party, the Kurds will desert their struggle on legal grounds, and will choose the other option."[63]

Similarly, in an interview with CNN Türk televison's Cüneyt Özdemir, DTP cochairman and Member of Parliament Aysel Tuğluk was asked whether the DTP was getting its orders from the PKK. Tuğluk's response proved the link between the PKK and the DTP: "It should be clear that our main supporters also support the PKK. Of course these people can influence our policies. You should not see the PKK as composed of 5,000–7,000 fighters but rather as a political entity in Turkey."[64]

In May 2008 the European Parliament adopted the report it had released on Turkey. Since the PKK was perceived as a terrorist organization, the European Parliament demanded that the DTP detach itself from the PKK. Moreover, it also insisted on the disarmament of the PKK.[65] The PKK's de facto leader in the Qandil Mountains, Murat Karayılan, accepted the European Parliament's position in an interview dated September 2010, restating that if local autonomy were to be granted to the Kurds, the PKK would concede its weapons to the United Nations.[66]

During its 2007 Congress, the PKK also formed the Union of Communities in Kurdistan (Koma Civakên Kurdistan, KCK).[67] The KCK was created as a clandestine nonviolent organization and functioned as an extension of the PKK in the cities. Its most important venture was to take on state responsibilities, including establishing courts, schools, and the means to administer punishments. In other words, since the PKK did not operate in the cities, the KCK in effect brought the PKK "down from the mountains" into the cities.[68] After April 2009, according to Article 314 of the Turkish Penal Code, most of the eighteen hundred people affiliated with Kurdish political parties—the DTP and later on the BDP (the Peace and Democracy Party or Barış ve Demokrasi Partisi)—were arrested on the allegation of being members of an illegal organization.[69]

Prime Minister Recep Tayyip Erdoğan's ruling AKP wanted to marginalize the DTP by removing its raison d'être in Turkish politics. By introducing much-needed reforms for the good of the citizens of Kurdish origin, the AKP gained widespread support among the Kurds. Another landmark in the government's handling of Turkey's Kurdish question was the "Kurdish opening" policy, which allowed for the launching of a new twenty-four-hour Kurdish-language television station. TRT 6 began its broadcasts on January 1, 2009, introduced by preliminary messages from Turkey's president, Abdullah Gül, and Erdoğan.

On February 24, 2009, DTP chairman Ahmet Türk stated that "the prime minister is speaking Kurdish in TRT 6's opening ceremony. In fact all people should speak freely in their native language. Speaking Kurdish in parliament should not pose any problems. I will therefore speak Kurdish in today's party session in parliament."[70] Since Türk spoke in Kurdish, the state-owned TRT 3 TV channel, which broadcast parliamentary sessions live, stopped broadcasting and issued the following statement: "The Turkish constitution and the Law on Political Parties only allow speaking Turkish in the political party meetings. Speaking any other language is not permitted. Here we have to stop broadcasting."[71]

Like the other Kurdish parties before it, the DTP was perceived as a threat to the Turkish unitary state. The legal bases of the accusation were Article 68 of the Turkish constitution and Articles 101 and 103 of the Political Parties Law (No. 2820), which were legislated to oppose any act contradicting the inseparability of the homeland. Consequently, on December 11, 2009, the DTP was banned by the Turkish Constitutional Court, and DTP leaders Ahmet Türk and Aysel Tuğluk were banned from politics for five years.[72]

However, before the banning of the DTP, forty-two Kurdish politicians with links to the DTP formally applied (on May 9, 2008) to the Turkish Ministry of the Interior to found the Peace and Democracy Party (BDP). The party succeeded the DTP and became the new watchdog of Kurdish consciousness.[73] On December 23, 2009, former DTP members, including mayors affiliated with the party, joined the BDP. In 2010 the BDP had twenty seats in Parliament and ninety-eight municipalities throughout Turkey.

Like the DTP, its predecessor, the BDP advocated constitutional amendments that would emphasize a variety of identities. The BDP advised that the decentralized 1921 constitution, which remained in force until 1924 and described Turkish citizens as "the people of Turkey," be adopted again. Moreover, the BDP called for the right to education in the mother tongue (Kurdish would be studied officially in the schools), for the reduction of the 10 percent election threshold, and for optional rather than compulsory religious instruction in the schools in order to preserve the rights of Turkey's minorities, such as Alevis, Christians, Yezidis, and Jews.[74]

In December 2010, BDP members gathered in what they called the Democratic Society Congress (Demokratik Toplum Kongresi, DTK), which combined all pro-Kurdish, nongovernmental organizations under one roof. Hence the congress published a final document—called "Turkey's democratization process, and a solution with regard to the Kurdish Question Stance Document"—in which the BDP advocated following the French example, i.e., the removal of the term "unitary state" from the French constitution and the granting of further liberties to the minorities. It called for the introduction of a regional flag, an official language, and even a regional government that would be accountable for security, foreign relations, and finance. Finally, the BDP underlined the importance of freedom of expression and of finding a long-term solution to the ongoing conflict.[75]

On March 23, 2011, BDP chairman Selahattin Demirtaş declared that his party had submitted its four conditions to the AKP government so that a consensus on the Kurdish question could finally be reached. The conditions were securing the right to education in the mother tongue, setting political prisoners free, ending military operations, and abolishing the 10 percent election threshold. Demirtaş stressed that unless they received a concrete answer from the government, the BDP would begin a "civil disobedience" campaign.[76] Indeed, it seemed that the BDP had adopted Gandhi's civil disobedience doctrine. This meant that the party would encourage its supporters to carry out protests all over Turkey without clashing with the security forces. In other words, BDP supporters would not express their protests by violent means.[77]

The earthquake in Turkish politics with regard to the BDP occurred on April 18, 2011, when the Turkish High Election Authority (Yüksek Seçim Kurulu, YSK) prohibited twelve independent candidates from standing for election. Eminent party leaders, such as Leyla Zana, Hatip Dicle, Gültan Kışanak, and Sabahat Tuncel, were banned from running for election because of their criminal records.[78] BDP leader Demirtaş accused the election authority of creating a chaotic situation.[79] The party supporters' civil disobedience strategy did not last long. BDP supporters in the eastern provinces of Turkey began to protest the decision. The dominant picture to emerge from the protests was one of Molotov cocktails and police intervention.[80] On April 21, 2011, the YSK revoked a ban that it had itself imposed on BDP candidates, and the crisis was finally resolved.[81]

Considering the state of the Kurdish political parties in the June 12, 2011, elections, the BDP achieved quite astounding election results. As in the previous elections, the BDP candidates ran as independent candidates to overcome the threshold obstacle. By the end of the elections, the BDP had gained 36 seats in a 550-seat TBMM. The BDP received 2,826,031 votes in Turkey, or 6.58 percent of the total.[82]

Although the election authority had authorized the candidacy of imprisoned candidates from the BDP, the Republican People's Party (Cumhuriyet Halk Partisi, CHP), and the MHP before the elections, the election authority retroactively disqualified BDP's Hatip Dicle and several other elected opposition party candidates. To justify its ruling, the election authority referred to Article 76 of the Turkish constitution.[83] According to this article, individuals who have been sentenced to a prison term of one year or more, or were involved in acts of terrorism or incitement and encouragement of such activities, cannot be elected as deputies, even if they have been pardoned.[84]

As a result, the BDP openly declared on June 23, 2011, that as long as Hatip Dicle remained barred from attending parliamentary sessions, the party would boycott the TBMM.[85] Due to the election authority's decision, the candidate who achieved the largest number of votes after Dicle, in this case AKP's Oya Eronat, was appointed as the Diyarbakır deputy.[86] The BDP's parliamentary seats were hence reduced to thirty-five.

Those BDP members who were not sworn in did not rest, however. On July 14, 2011, the DTK unilaterally proclaimed "democratic autonomy" in Diyarbakır. Aysel Tuğluk, BDP member of TBMM, read the declaration of autonomy. The DTK openly called for a change in the 1982 constitution by referring to the 1921 constitution as the most democratic constitution ever established in Turkey. The declaration emphasized that the Treaty of Lausanne and the 1924 constitution had worsened the Kurdish political situation in Turkey by ignoring Kurdish identity. However, Tuğluk also pointed out that "democratic autonomy" should not be understood as separatism; on the contrary, it encouraged local people's involvement in politics. And lastly, once again certifying the symbiotic relationship between the PKK and BDP, the declaration called for a less harsh treatment of the "Kurdish people's leader and architect of the idea of democratic autonomy, Abdullah Öcalan."[87] Prime Minister Erdoğan reacted very harshly to this unilateral declaration, stating that Turkey would never accept the regional administration's autonomy.[88]

On July 30, 2011, an event crucial to domestic Kurdish politics took place. Kurdish politician and author Kemal Burkay, who also represented nonviolent Kurdish resistance, returned to Turkey from Sweden after thirty-one years of exile. Upon Burkay's arrival, BDP's Demirtaş commented that Burkay should not undermine his people's struggle.[89] In an interview with CNN Türk, Burkay rejected all BDP claims that he had become a tool in the hands of the AKP government for fragmenting the Kurdish electorate and weakening the BDP. Burkay emphasized that, unlike the PKK, he supported nonviolent methods to achieve a federation rather than the autonomy for which the BDP was striving.[90]

Although the BDP did not attend the official TBMM opening ceremony because of Dicle's imprisonment, on October 1, 2011, the party participated in a second oath ceremony in order to prevent Erdoğan and Burkay from having the last word on the Kurdish question. As for the Kurdish parties, from HEP to BDP, there were no prominent changes in the party manifestos. Traditionally, the policies of the Kurdish parties were in correlation with those of the PKK. Consequently, the vast majority of the Turkish public regarded the BDP and previous pro-Kurdish parties as a nonviolent branch of the PKK. This perception derived from the BDP's refusal to label the PKK as a terrorist organization, to keep its distance from the PKK, to view talks with Abdullah Öcalan or Karayılan as the means to end the conflict, and, lastly, to take political decisions in accordance with the PKK position, like in the 2010 referendum that was boycotted by the Kurds.[91] Murat Aksoy, columnist of the daily *Yeni Şafak*, saw the relationship between Abdullah Öcalan, the PKK, and the BDP as a patriarchal hierarchal triangle that forced the BDP to follow in the path of its predecessors and obey Öcalan and the PKK. Aksoy argued that the capture of Öcalan gave him immunity from Kurdish political criticism.

Hence, despite his imprisonment, Öcalan was a crucial actor in the Kurdish political movement. Consequently, the BDP and its predecessors were
unable to formulate their own policies, but instead followed policies imposed by Öcalan or by PKK headquarters in the Qandil Mountains. The
parliamentary boycott initiated by the BDP to protest the closure of the
DTP was canceled, as stipulated by Öcalan. This event was regarded as
evidence of Öcalan's political influence in the party. The non-Kurdish political players were also aware of the status quo.[92] In March 2011, Erdoğan hence openly accused the BDP of being an extension and mouthpiece
of the PKK.[93]

Conclusion

The Kurdish political movement made significant progress, establishing
political legitimacy and achieving considerable political gains. With the
enactment of the Lausanne Treaty the Kurds had lost their right to exist as
a distinct people, but the 49ers, TİP, and DDKO paved the way for a more
developed sense of Kurdish identity. Turkey's policy of denial of Kurdish
identity provoked an even stronger Kurdish response.

With the emergence of the TİP, Kurds became involved in Turkish politics. The establishment of the PKK on a Marxist basis, its rejection of the
feudal *agha* system of Kurdish tribalism, and the involvement of Kurdish
women in the struggle contributed much, both politically and socioeco-
nomically, to Kurdish society. In addition, one could also argue that the
PKK's violent activities shaped Turkish politics, making the political arena
more flexible so that hitherto untouched taboos could be broken. While
the PKK put the Kurdish question at the top of Turkey's critical issues,
the Kurdish political movement continued to work toward its political
goals, such as removing the ban on speaking Kurdish; gaining acceptance
of the existence of a Kurdish people, with explicit reference to the issue as
the "Kurdish question" instead of the "Southeast problem"; and obtaining licenses for an official Kurdish broadcasting TV channel, private radio
stations, Kurdish institutes, and so forth. Naturally, while Turkey became
more democratic, the Kurdish parties' demands grew. Speaking Kurdish
was banned in October 1983, but twenty-eight years later BDP members
unilaterally declared democratic autonomy, demanding education in the
mother tongue and even the redefinition of Turkishness.

Non-Kurdish actors in Turkish politics were also deeply influenced,
both by the armed groups and by the political Kurdish movement. The

landmark speech of Turkish prime minister Recep Tayyip Erdoğan on August 15, 2005, was revolutionary. Erdoğan stated: "There are ethnic elements. There are Kurds, Lazs, Circassians, Georgians, Albanians, Turks. All of them are 'subidentities.' We also have a more prominent identity, which is being citizens of Turkey."[94]

Therefore, while Erdoğan again included all citizens in Turkey as a state, he allowed the ethnically non-Turkish citizens to identify themselves as they wished. With Erdoğan's speech, the huge gap between Turkey's former policies of denial toward non-Turks and the current policy of recognizing different "subidentities" became evident. However, the opposition parties, the CHP and MHP, did not share the same viewpoint and criticized Erdoğan very harshly.[95]

Between 2005 and 2011, the CHP, too, could not resist the winds of change, and thus adopted a new policy with regard to the Kurdish question. CHP head Kemal Kılıçdaroğlu made an unexpected move when he organized a political rally in the city of Diyarbakır, with its higly concentrated Kurdish population. During the meeting he called for the establishment of committees to investigate mysterious killings and for reduction of the 10 percent election threshold;[96] more importantly, Kılıçdaroğlu emphasized that there would be no secession if local autonomy administrations were established.[97]

However, the winds of change did not affect MHP's Devlet Bahçeli as they did the CHP. In the speech he gave during his visit to Diyarbakır, Bahçeli emphasized that the seeds of the Kurdish problem derived from socioeconomic problems and criticized Kurds who demanded the right of education in the mother tongue, querying, "When the right of education in the mother tongue is recognized, will you be sated?"[98] In other words, he questions whether using Kurdish will resolve the severe economic problems they endure.

The parties' policies on the Kurdish question were also reflected in the June 2011 election polls. According to the Konda public opinion research company, in June 2011, 43.9 percent of the Kurds voted for BDP while 38.9 percent voted for AKP and 8.6 percent for CHP. It is obvious that Bahçeli's MHP was wiped off the map. The same research shows a drastic increase in pro-BDP votes in highly Kurdish-populated southeast Turkey. In the 2007 local administration elections, the BDP received 29.7 percent of the votes, while it achieved 34.4 percent in the 2011 elections.[99] Despite the AKP and CHP Kurdish opening policies, BDP scored a major success in the elections, which proved that further reforms would not affect the BDP's raison d'être in Turkish politics. One should not forget that the drastic change in Turkey's policy on Kurdish rights was a direct consequence of the Kurdish reawakening that dates back to 1959. It should also be noted that this reawakening process involved both violent and nonviolent Kurdish political actors. In other words, their synthesis was the determining factor that led to a détente of Turkish policies on the Kurdish question. Nevertheless, the impact of the nonviolent Kurdish political movement should not be underrated. Compared to the 1960s, the present-day improvements in Kurdish civil rights and the rise in Kurdish consciousness are quite remarkable.

The Role of Language in the Evolution of Kurdish National Identity in Turkey

DUYGU ATLAS

Language, which is the essence of our human condition, sets us apart from other living creatures. It is not only a crucial medium of communication, but also the most notable and prominent marker of both individual identity and community membership. People develop a strong bond with their mother tongue as a means of expressing their culture, tradition, and identity. Therefore, the rise of nation-states and concurrent projects for establishing unitary national identities in what had once been multiethnic societies have affected many languages by reducing them to minority status. As strong symbols of ethnic identity, languages of minorities became the most obvious targets of nation-states. In the case of Turkey, the creation of a Turkish national identity came at the expense of its various ethnic groups and their languages, as speaking Turkish was seen as the defining characteristic of Turkish citizenship.

Since the dynamics that define the relationship between the secular-civilian and military establishments are shifting, Turkey has started to re-conceptualize its relations with its minorities. The question of civil liberties and minority rights has moved to the forefront more forcefully than ever. The Alevis are seeking official recognition and state support for their faith; the Circassian and Laz minorities are demanding language rights. In a landmark event, religious services were permitted for one day at the Armenian Church of the Holy Cross in the city of Van in September 2010, and sporadic discussions still continue regarding the reopening of the Theological School of Heybeliada, the main Greek Orthodox seminary in Turkey. A recent decision also made it possible for minority assets that were confiscated by the state to be returned to their owners. But the problem Turkey seems to be grappling with the most is its Kurdish minority's demands for recognition of Kurdish ethnic identity and cultural rights. These demands are viewed with great suspicion within Turkey and are deemed divisive and threatening to the cohesiveness of the Turkish state and society. The reason for this lies in the saliency of the Kurds' strong ethnic consciousness, which resisted all efforts of assimilation. That the Kurds inhabited the same territories for centuries and were hence not migrants relocated to a new land, and that they had a loosely based relationship with the Ottoman political structure, were among the factors that bolstered their strong sense of ethnic identity and helped them maintain their traditional social structures and language.[1] Furthermore, armed conflict led to the relegation of the Kurdish question to a terrorist problem, on the one hand hampering the ability of Turkish governments to navigate through such a multilayered issue while on the other hand adding to the frustrations of a Kurdish population already disgruntled by state policies.

Today, Kurds of all ranks and political leanings unite in their demand for a broadening of Kurdish cultural rights, most particularly the freedom of education in their mother tongue. Since the 1960s, when the Kurdish political movement in Turkey became a force in its own right, the Kurdish language has played an increasingly important role in Kurdish politics. It was not only central to the Kurdish demand for recognition of their collective identity, but also served as a point of reference by which Kurds have come to measure their own worth in relation to the Turkish state. In this regard, the denigration and suppression of the Kurdish language by the state contributed to Kurdish identity formation, strictly centered on ethnicity. As an ethnic marker that bore the brunt of draconian state policies after the establishment of the Turkish Republic, the Kurdish language unmistakably emerged as an effective political tool in the hands of the Kurdish political movement. It became a rallying point around which the Kurdish masses mobilized, regardless of whether or not they were part of the Kurdish political movement represented by the Peace and Democracy Party (Barış ve Demokrasi Partisi, BDP). The pressure generated by mass protests and campaigns for language rights has forced the Turkish state to reconsider its past approaches and to produce satisfactory policies, suited to the realities of Turkey's multicultural character and need for greater democracy.

This chapter is an attempt to map out the development of the Kurdish political identity, with heavy emphasis on the Kurdish language. In order to achieve this objective, the relationship between language and nationalism will be analyzed first, followed by a look at the changing state policies with regard to the Kurdish language, from the early Republican period to the 2009 "democratic opening" initiative ("Milli Birlik ve Kardeşlik Projesi," also known as "Demokratik Açılım" and "Kürt Açılımı") of the ruling Justice and Development Party (Adalet ve Kalkınma Partisi, AKP). The period following the initiative was marked by significant growth of Kurdish political activity, in which the calls for language rights became ubiquitous and were extended to every possible official and societal domain on a hitherto unprecedented scale. Lastly, the obstacles to imparting Kurdish language rights at a political and societal level will be examined.

Language and Nationalism

Language has always been a significant element in the construction of groups and in the way individuals define themselves and others. Throughout history, the expansion of major civilizations has been accompanied by the spread of their language. Alexander the Great's Hellenization project brought about the diffusion of the Greek language. The use of Latin increased greatly throughout the Roman Empire, and Arabic became a prominent language with the appearance of Islam. As Fernand de Varennes demonstrates, however, most ethnically diverse empires and civilizations of the past did not impose their language on the territories they had subdued.[2] The level of correlation between the dominant civilizations and their lingua franca took a new turn in the nineteenth century with the rise of a Western European concept of nationalist ideologies and the subsequent emergence of nation-states in all parts of the world. Local languages that had been left intact until that time came under attack by the centralizing tendencies of the nation-state. More than any other cultural symbol, language has provided nation-states with a strong proof of commonness among the people the state claims to represent, thus endowing them with a much-sought-after basis for legitimacy.

The firm correlation between language and nationalism is often traced back to the influential eighteenth-century German philosopher Johann Gottfried von Herder (1744–1803). In Herder's ideological construct, the German language became the defining characteristic of the German ethnocultural nation and attested to its historical continuity. Stressing the ethnic aspect of nationalism and putting language at the core of his ideology, Herder argued that no true and successful nation could be created unless it was constructed on the basis of a mother tongue. Thus, Herder equated nations with language groups. In the same line of thought, another German idealist, Johann Gottlieb Fichte (1762–1814), believed that only the Germans possessed an original language—not a derived one such as French or English—and therefore a true culture that crowned the Germans as the only people capable of bringing "the great historical movements to fruition."[3] It was Herder's and Fichte's strong emphasis on language as the main criterion of nationhood that eventually paved the way for the hegemonic equation of language and nation.

In contrast, the approach to language of modern theories on nationalism can be described as both accommodating and dismissive. One of the most potent critics of nationalism, Elie Kedourie, takes a skeptical approach to language as a relevant criterion for drawing a political conclusion such as determining what is a nation. Kedourie, who regards nationalism as a misguided invention based on a distortion of Immanuel Kant's notion of autonomy, discards cultural particularities on the grounds that they do not constitute a sufficient reason for the foundation of a state. "The world is diverse, much too diverse, for the classifications of nationalist anthropology," he says. "Races, languages, religions, political traditions and loyalties are so inextricably intermixed that there can be no clear convincing reason why people who speak the same language, but whose history and circumstances otherwise widely diverge, should form one state, or why people who speak two different languages and whom circumstances have thrown together should not form one state."[4] Contrary to Kedourie's views, in Ernest Gellner's theory of nationalism, cultural classifications are of great importance. Unlike in agrarian societies, where the social structure and roles of individuals were clearly circumscribed, in modern society culture fills the void left behind by the disappearance of old social structures and becomes the new bond among people, providing them with a sense of belonging and solidarity. Gellner uses the terms "culture" and "language" almost interchangeably in the context of modern, industrialized societies.[5] In his theory, one's linguistic identity becomes one's national identity and language becomes the criterion for nationhood.[6] He asserts that "in stable, self-contained communities culture is often quite invisible, but when mobility and context-free communication come to be of the essence of social life, the culture in which one has been taught to communicate becomes the core of one's identity."[7] Language therefore contributes to the growth of nationalist movements. Benedict Anderson also places great emphasis on the role of language. According to him, the advent of print capitalism and the subsequent dissemination of vernacular languages have led to the emergence of people's awareness of their membership in specific groups. Thus, print languages "laid the bases for national consciousness" by enabling people to be unified along imaginary links.[8]

In the post–Cold War period, the issues of ethnicity and human rights moved to the forefront of the international agenda, largely due to the ethnic atrocities in the Balkans. To prevent similar disasters in the future, international bodies prioritized minority rights, thus putting nation-states under unprecedented scrutiny in their treatment of minorities. The ensuing process of "transnationalization of human rights"[9] has thus encouraged recognition of the needs of minorities. Scholars have long deliberated on solutions to conflicts and tensions arising in multilingual societies. One solution proposed by Stephen May is to support minority language rights. May argues that "changing the language preferences of the state and civil society, or at least broadening them, would better reflect the cultural and linguistic demographics of most of today's multinational and multilingual states." According to May, such a step can better ensure the survival of a language and lead to an improvement in its speakers' socioeconomic conditions.[10] Taking this viewpoint a step further, Tove Skutnabb-Kangas merges language rights with human rights and argues that Linguistic Human Rights (LHR) can be adopted against a wide range of problems inflicted on minorities, from "linguistic genocide" (linguicide) to "forced assimilation."[11]

Language Policies of the Turkish Republic and Their Effect on Kurdish National Identity

Since the foundation of the Turkish Republic in 1923, the state language policies have revolved around two interconnected projects. The first was to establish Turkish as the only official language of the new republic and to incorporate it into the overall project of nation building. The second project focused on what Geoffrey Haig has termed the "invisibilisation" of all languages other than Turkish as part of language planning in Turkey.[12] The state policies on non-Turkish languages, especially Kurdish, were aimed consistently at eradicating signs of otherness in an attempt to further consolidate the homogeneity of the emerging nation.

There was, however, a more accommodating approach to the Kurds in the pre-republican period. The best example, often cited by Kurds in Turkey today as a proof of earlier Turkish acceptance of Kurdish autonomy, was the 1921 constitution (Teşkilat-ı Esasiye Kanunu), which portrayed

Kurds as "an ethnic group with the right to self-rule."[13] The difficult war-time conditions of the pre-republican period forced the future founders of the republic to adopt a policy of recognition toward this large Muslim minority and to abstain from alienating it. In fact, the Kurds were the only minority that was willing to fight alongside the Turks and build a joint future, while the other, non-Turkish Muslim subjects (the Arabs and Albanians) seceded from the Ottoman Empire and what eventually became Republican Turkey. This accommodating perception, however, underwent a major change after the signing of the Lausanne Treaty and the subsequent establishment of the Turkish Republic in 1923. The Lausanne Treaty (July 24, 1923) included, inter alia, provisions for the protection of minorities (Articles 38–44). As to the use of language, Article 39 stipulated that "no restrictions shall be imposed on the free use by any Turkish national of any language in private intercourse, in commerce, religion, in the press, or in publications of any kind or at public meetings." Furthermore, Article 40 allowed minority groups to "establish, manage and control at their own expense, any charitable, religious and social institutions, any schools and other establishments for instruction and education, with the right to use their own language."[14] However, the composition of the Lausanne Treaty eventually resulted in the exclusion of the largest minority in the country, the Kurds, as it recognized only non-Muslim groups as minorities and made it impossible for Kurds to use their language without restrictions. In contrast, the constitution of 1924 recognized the existence of ethnic and religious groups other than Muslim Turks, but it did not allow for the institutionalization of their cultural rights within this legal system. As Mesut Yeğen argues, "in 1924, the Republic recognized the presence of the Kurds, but not as peoples whose collective cultural rights could be recognized."[15] The 1924 constitution's declaration of Turkish as the official language as well as the exclusive language of education meant that Kurds could not have an educational system in their mother tongue.

In addition to the early policies of "invisibilisation," the central place of the Turkish language in forming a Turkish national identity was further consolidated by the introduction of the Sun-Language Theory (Güneş Dil Teorisi) an extension of the Turkish History Thesis (Türk Tarih Tezi).[16] The Sun-Language Theory traced the origin of all languages to a primal Central Asian language and argued that only Turkish spoken in Asia Minor was a "continuation of this original form of Turkish."[17] The glorification of the Turks' pre-Islamic past both in historical and linguistic theory not only helped solidify the unitary characteristic of the nation but also promoted a Western-style secular identity, which Turkey strove to emulate. Ilker Aytürk argues that "both theses put the ancient Turks on the highest pedestal possible, extolled their contribution to civilization and reminded the western nations that they had to acknowledge the Turks as a part of their family, as a nation which contributed most generously to their civilization."[18] The language revolution, however, in its strongly national character, "disregarded all particularities that were seen as dangerous for the healthy formation of a new Turkish nation."[19]

The theories, aimed at solidifying the basis of Turkish national identity, were supplemented by additional steps such as the enactment of the Settlement Law of 1934. The law divided Turkey into three groups on the basis of language and ethnicity: "localities to be reserved for the habitation in compact form of persons possessing Turkish culture; regions to which populations of non-Turkish culture for assimilation into Turkish language and culture were to be moved; regions to be completely evacuated."[20] The law was designed to accelerate the assimilation process of non-Turkish groups into a homogeneous society in the making, through the evacuation of some areas and the relocation of the Kurdish population in mainly Turkish-speaking areas.[21] According to the plan, a population of five hundred thousand Turkish-speaking people was to be settled in Kurdish-inhabited areas to dilute the Kurdish population east of the Euphrates.[22] Although the plan was not carried out in its entirety, it is characteristic of the policies of the 1930s, in which the "physical assimilation" of Kurdish ethnic markers was under way.[23]

After the suppression of the last of the Kurdish uprisings, the Kurdish question almost seemed to have reached a state of inertia. It was not until the 1960s that the Kurds finally found a relatively democratic platform for political expression. Ironically, the 1960 military coup and its upshot, the 1961 constitution, ushered in a period of political awakening in which the emerging leftist organizations, modeled after the youth movements in the world, became an important venue for Kurdish political participation. The Turkish Labor Party, which was founded in 1961 and whose Marxist message of equality resonated with the Kurds, quickly became their first address. The party's inaction on the Kurdish issue, however, soon led the Kurds to form their own parties and organizations. The first was the Kurdistan Democratic Party in Turkey (Türkiye Kürdistan Demokrat Partisi, TKDP), founded in 1965. Inspired by the example of the Kurdish uprising in Iraq led by Mustafa Barzani, the TKDP's aim was to gain "autonomy or even independence."[24] The place of Kurdish cultural rights in party discourse was made evident by the letter Mustafa Remzi Bucak (cousin of Faik Bucak, the party's leader, who was assassinated in 1966) wrote in 1963 to the then prime minister, İsmet İnönü. Nesrin Uçarlar explains that in this letter "Bucak made a comparison between the rights of the Turkish-speaking community in Cyprus and the Kurds in Turkey, and proposed a federative administration for the Kurdish region in which education would be in Kurdish."[25] It was, however, the formation of the Eastern Revolutionary Cultural Hearths (Devrimci Doğu Kültür Ocakları, DDKO) in 1969 that marked a new phase in the Kurdish nationalist movement. Mass demonstrations held in the late 1960s in Kurdish-inhabited areas were indicative of the growing frustration and disaffection of the Kurdish population, as the relative liberalism of the period was not reflected in the field of Kurdish civil liberties. Among other measures, the military regime initiated a campaign to replace non-Turkish place-names.[26] Following the 1971 coup d'état, giving Kurdish names to children was also prohibited by Birth Registry Law 1587, enacted in 1972.[27] Amir Hassanpour illustrates the effect of these policies on the Kurdish-speaking population by documenting the steady increase in the number of people declaring Kurdish as their second language, which could be interpreted as the "success of Turkification" policies.[28]

The formation of a Kurdish identity along ethnic lines was further accelerated by the 1980 military coup and the uncompromising policies of the military junta that ascended to power. The reason given for the military takeover was to "strengthen the state and to restructure Turkish politics" in the face of ongoing violence, which, it deemed, resulted from excessive liberties granted by the 1961 constitution.[29] Yet another goal was to curb a growing Kurdish nationalism, the first of two "divisive and destructive forces" threatening the stability of the Turkish state, the other being the threat of Islamism.[30] Oppressive measures such as banning the Kurdish language were to eliminate this perceived threat. In particular, Law 2932, Publications and Broadcasts in Languages other than Turkish (Türkçe'den Başka Dillerde Yapılacak Yayın Hakkında Kanun), was aimed precisely at the Kurdish language. This 1983 law prohibited "the declaration, circulation and publication of ideas in a language which is not the first official language of a State recognized by Turkey."[31] The law unintentionally accelerated the standardization of Kurdish, based on its Kurmanji dialect, by the Kurdish diaspora in Europe in an effort to counter the attempts to downgrade its status.[32] In the aftermath of the 1980 coup, as part of state measures, Kurdish children were placed in the compulsory schooling system to ensure their assimilation.[33] In an effort to underscore "the extent of its power over its citizens," the Turkish state undertook yet another wave of renaming Kurdish villages.[34] The state of emergency proclaimed in Turkey's southeastern provinces in 1987 and the Anti-Terrorism Law actually made it impossible to speak of Kurdish cultural rights. These measures only reinforced the Kurdish language as a rallying point around which the Kurdish nationalist movement grew and the Kurdish identity was further consolidated. For Kurds, grievances no longer emanated from the strains of economic underdevelopment, but from the state's constant suppression of their ethnic identity—especially language. Apart from honing the Kurdish sense of identity, the draconian policies of the junta regime of the 1980s increased the appeal of the PKK in the eyes of the Kurdish population.[35]

In the 1990s, restrictions on the use of Kurdish were eased somewhat during Turgut Özal's term as prime minister. He rescinded Law 2932 and legalized the use of Kurdish in the private sphere in 1991, although it remained banned in education. He advocated the free use of the mother tongue in the public sphere without violating the principle of one official language.[36] Özal's attempt to accommodate the cultural differences within Turkey was an early sign of recognition that a solution to the Kurdish problem should not be sought through military action, but by granting cultural rights to the Kurdish minority. However, as Hassanpour points out, Özal's policy did not "indicate a change in the ideology and politics of the Turkish state."[37] Therefore, when Leyla Zana, then the elected representative from Diyarbakır, took her inaugural oath of loyalty in parliament in Kurdish, the reaction was fierce. Zana was arrested for her attempts to demonstrate the existence and relevance of the Kurdish language in an official context. She was sentenced to fifteen years in prison and released in 2004 after ten years' imprisonment. In a similar event, a widely celebrated singer of Kurdish origin, Ahmet Kaya, was forced into exile when he generated fury at an awards ceremony by stating that he intended to produce music and music videos in Kurdish. He was sentenced to prison in absentia and died in exile in Paris in 2000.

Turkey's European Union accession bid marked a turning point in its democratization process and, inextricably, its Kurdish question. Turkey was declared a candidate for EU membership by the Helsinki European Council of 1999, and formal accession negotiation talks began five years later.[38] Turkey's efforts to meet the Copenhagen criteria led to some general, yet limited, improvements in its human rights record. The Copenhagen criteria are a key set of rules that define a country's eligibility to become a member of the European Union. They require that the candidate country have "stable institutions that guarantee democracy, the rule of law, human rights and respect for and protection of minorities; a functioning market economy"; and "the ability to assume the obligations of membership, in particular adherence to the objectives of political, economic and monetary union."[39]

In the field of language rights, amendments were made to Articles 26 and 28 of the constitution to allow local language courses and to prepare the groundwork for broadcasting in local languages.[40] Following the EU-prodded reforms, the expectations for greater cultural freedom and protection of rights grew among the Kurds. The frustration over the slow pace of reforms was translated into campaigns, at the core of which lay demands for language rights. These campaigns were reminiscent of earlier, smaller-scale protests, such as those staged in 2001–2002 by Kurdish university students demanding education in the Kurdish language under the banner "I want to be taught in my mother tongue."[41] These actions were precursors of a more systematic strategy to be adopted by the Kurdish political movement as well as the Kurdish masses in the years ahead. The strategy was to permeate rapidly through the eastern provinces after the "democratic opening" initiative period and attested to the fact that the government had to put more effort into accommodating cultural rights, the call for which only seemed to have gained strength.

The AKP's Democratic Opening Initiative and the Kurdish Language

The "democratic opening" initiative of the ruling AKP, launched in mid-2009, marked a turning point in the government's approach to the Kurdish question. First labeled the "Kurdish opening" and then the National Unity and Brotherhood Project to cushion the growing criticism directed against it, the AKP's initiative sought a solution to the Kurdish problem by attempting to advance the democratization process. As laid out in the official brochure about the initiative, democratization was considered the key to solving Turkey's festering problems that interfered with the country's upward momentum. The party saw economic development and success in both internal and external politics as inseparable from the development of democracy at home. Therefore, the initiative was designed to target all issues inhibiting Turkey's progress at all levels—social, economic, and global. The party asserted that the Kurdish problem was only one such issue, along with other minority-related grievances and economic problems requiring a solution.[42]

Despite the lack of substantial achievements to date and unabated criticism and speculation, the initiative was nevertheless a watershed in the wider historical context of Turkey's Kurdish question. First, it heralded a period in which a Turkish government made an attempt to make amends for having ignored the country's multiethnic character. This marked a clear shift from denying Kurdish existence and seeking to assimilate it to recognizing the Kurdish reality and Turkey's multicultural makeup. The AKP contended that they set out to eradicate inequalities based on cultural and ethnic differences by fostering individual rights and freedoms.[43] In turn, AKP's novel approach initiated a lively debate at all levels of society regarding Turkey's democratic deficit on issues such as multiculturalism and democratization, thus breaking the taboo about discussing the Kurdish question. In this process a highly nationalist discourse, which occasionally translated into physical confrontation, was heard. At the same time, there were positive, accepting voices that regarded the initiative as a helpful tool for unearthing Turkey's fault lines and sensitivities, and that eventually could be used to the advantage of a democratic Turkish society.

On a policy level, the AKP government started off by introducing initiatives regarding the use of the Kurdish language. As a first step, a state-run TV channel, TRT 6, which broadcasts entirely in Kurdish, was launched on January 1, 2009, with a message in Kurdish by Prime Minister Recep Tayyip Erdoğan, which read "TRT şeş bi xer be" (may TRT 6 be prosperous). Erdoğan stated that the new channel would "further solidify the unity and fraternity of the people" and "strengthen [Turkish] democracy."[44] The TV initiative was followed by an announcement from the Turkish Board of Higher Education (Yükseköğretim Kurulu, YÖK) that courses in the Kurdish language and on Kurdish culture would be allowed at universities.[45] In October 2009 the Living Languages Institute (Yaşayan Diller Enstitüsü) for the study of regional minority languages, including Kurdish, was established at Mardin Artuklu University for postgraduate students. The disappointment over the naming of the institute, in particular the avoidance of the word "Kurdish," was mitigated when YÖK gave its approval in March 2011 for the opening of an undergraduate Kurdish Language and Culture Department at the same university.[46] In the 2011–2012 academic year the department admitted its first twenty-one undergraduate students.[47] Other regulations, introduced within the framework of the "democratic opening" initiative and through an appeal to the Ministry of Interior, included the reintroduction of original Kurdish place-names and permission to give Kurdish names to children.[48] In

March 2010 the Parliamentary Constitutional Commission also accepted an amendment allowing for political propaganda in languages other than Turkish during election campaigns.[49]

Despite these policy revisions, which led to the increasing use of Kurdish, the focal point of the initiative remained the right to be educated in the mother tongue, Kurdish. The AKP's stance on the issue did not change, however. Although it was laid out in the initiative's official brochure that the party did recognize Turkey's cultural differences and considered "cultural activities including broadcasting in languages other than Turkish not to be harmful but a means to strengthen and consolidate [our] country's unity and integrity," it did not intend to regulate the use of different languages spoken in Turkey as languages of education.[50] Meanwhile, the government has been willing to move forward with private Kurdish courses and Kurdish-language institutions, but it does not support Kurdish as a mother tongue and considers it innately contradictory to the principle of "one nation, one state, one language." However, the Turkish government's solution of the Kurdish problem on the basis of individual rights is juxtaposed and countered by the Kurdish political movement's insistence on collective rights, such as the official use of Kurdish in education and public services. According to the BDP's vision of democratic autonomy, as outlined in its 2011 elections manifesto, "Turkey will be separated into 15–20 autonomous regional governments," in which "regions will use other second and third languages according to their specific needs," that is, besides the official Turkish language.[51]

The incongruity between Kurdish demands and what the AKP was willing to provide soon turned the issue of language into a central tenet of Kurdish protests, around which the Kurdish political movements and masses mobilized. Conditions were ripe for a political outburst when the AKP's "democratic opening" initiative fell through the cracks. The entrance through the Habur gate on the Iraqi border of thirty-four PKK militants in guerrilla attire on October 22, 2009, and the jubilant welcome they received from ecstatic Kurdish crowds signaled the beginning of a downward spiral in the opening process.[52] In the eyes of those who had single-heartedly opposed the initiative since its launch, this incident served as a reaffirmation of fears that the government was trying to appease the PKK. Although the government hoped to put an end to the conflict by dissolving the PKK, it did not take into consideration the force of Kurdish nationalism among the Kurdish masses. The Habur incident not only exacerbated Turkish nationalist fears, but also turned the supporters of the "democratic initiative" against it by its very negative impact.

The deterioration continued with the closure of the Kurdish Democratic Society Party (Demokratik Toplum Partisi, DTP) in December 2009 and the roundup of its representatives that same month, and with a crackdown against the Kurdish Communities Union (Koma Civakên Kurdistan, KCK), the urban wing of the PKK. The banning of the DTP, which increased Kurdish suspicion toward the initiative, followed the killing of seven Turkish soldiers in a PKK ambush on December 7, 2009, in the Reşadiye district of Tokat. The killing of four police officers in the Dörtyol district of Hatay and the subsequent attack by Turkish nationalists on the local headquarters of the BDP only portended the growing Turkish-Kurdish rift. The initiative unintentionally aggravated Kurdish feelings of being ostracized, as well as feelings of distrust on the Turkish side.

Kurdish disgruntlement with the turn the initiative had taken found its immediate expression in acts of civil disobedience starting on March 24, 2011. Within the framework of these acts, which began with a sit-in by a crowd of twenty thousand in the eastern city of Batman, demands for Kurdish language rights became more systematic and planned. To increase the visibility of the language, the use of Kurdish was extended to different social domains and official contexts. Although the chairman of the DTP, Ahmet Türk, delivered his speech partly in Kurdish at his party's group meeting in Parliament in 2009 and caused Meclis TV to stop its broadcast, this did not create an uproar similar to the one in 1991 following Leyla Zana's speech. Later on, as part of a civil disobedience campaign, the BDP—together with the Democratic Society Congress (Demokratik Toplum Kongresi [DTK], a Kurdish umbrella structure for Kurdish nongovernmental organizations) and the Peace Mothers Group—set up the Democratic Solution and Peace Tents in many cities around Turkey. Calling for a peaceful solution to the Kurdish question, they became a platform for voicing Kurdish demands. Among the four main demands, presented by the BDP co-chair Selahattin Demirtaş, was the lifting of all restrictions on the use of Kurdish, both in the public and private spheres, in education, and alongside "the release of political prisoners, an end to military and political operations [against Kurds] and the elimination of the 10 percent [election] threshold."[53] The BDP deputy and independent representative from Diyarbakır, Emine Ayna, emphasized the language rights dimension of the tent sit-ins, saying that "without the right to pursue an education in their language, people are culturally held in a state of arrested development, prevented from practicing and appreciating their group identity."[54]

The call for Kurdish language rights soon spread to the religious domain, where it merged with criticism against state-run religious mosques. During the tent protests, the BDP had the call to prayer (*adhan*) recited in Kurdish for the first time in the BDP-run municipalities. Interestingly, the *adhans* are recited in Arabic in Turkey. The BDP's move therefore can be regarded as an attempt to distance themselves and the Kurdish masses from state-controlled Turkish Islam. Commenting on the event of *adhan* recitals in Kurdish, BDP Şanlıurfa provincial head Müslüm Kaplan said that "worship [will be] carried out in Kurdish. The Kurdish *adhan* started last week. In the processes to come [i.e., in the future], the *adhan* will continue to be recited in the dominant language of the community."[55] Reciting the *adhan* in Kurdish was part of a boycott staged by Kurdish worshipers against state-controlled mosques. They began conducting their prayers in protest tents instead of mosques and called for the right to hear sermons in their own language. Moreover, according to the BDP, the state was sending "political imams" to the region and using "religion as a means to fight terrorism."[56] In a similar manner, the head of Diay-Der (Din Alimleri Yardımlaşma ve Dayanışma Derneği, the association of the Kurdish clergy), Zahit Çiftkuran, also stated that the government had ignored their pleas to allow sermons in Kurdish; instead, they sent "10,000 new imams [. . .], who have no connection to this land. So it is a kind of religious assimilation."[57]

In the judicial arena, Kurdish was made part of a high-profile case against the KCK, in which 151 suspects, including twelve mayors from the BDP, were put on trial. The trial soon became widely publicized because of the defendants' demands to deliver their defense speeches in Kurdish. When one defendant attempted to do so, the presiding judge claimed that the defendant spoke in an "unknown language presumed to be Kurdish."[58] The judge's response outraged the Kurds. Consequently, the court's refusal to hear testimony in Kurdish led the defendants' lawyers to boycott the trial, so that the case ended in gridlock.[59]

On another front, many municipalities and small-scale businesses in the Kurdish-populated regions adopted multilingualism following a BDP initiative to spread and reinforce the use of Kurdish in everyday affairs. As a first step, they replaced Turkish-only signs with bilingual signs in municipal buildings and on street signs. The move followed a statement by Interior Minister Beşir Atalay claiming that the government looked favorably upon the use of original place-names.[60] Diyarbakır Municipality took the lead in applying these changes, and soon other municipalities such as Cizre, Şemdinli, and Şırnak followed suit.[61] However, lacking a consistent strategy, the Interior Ministry opened an investigation on a similar initiative by the Bismil Municipality.[62] This was reminiscent of a 2007 verdict against the multilingual municipal initiative by Diyarbakır's Sur Municipality, which was investigated by the Ministry of the Interior, resulting in the sacking of Mayor Abdullah Demirbaş.

In a similar manner, Kurdish masses also mobilized through civil initiatives and campaigns for language rights. The January 2011 "Ez zimanê xwe dixwazim" (I want my own language) signature campaign in Batman and the march organized the following month in Van are illustrative of the extent of the Kurdish population's involvement and concern.[63] Kurdish Language Celebration Day, held every May 15 since 2006 to commemorate the launching in Damascus of the Kurdish magazine *Hawar* on that same date in 1932, acts as another platform for making a stand for Kurdish language rights. On the occasion of the 2011 celebrations of Language Day, Filiz Koçali and Hamit Geylani, the BDP chairpersons at the time, declared in a joint statement that "the ban on a mother tongue is the heaviest punishment," especially for the Kurdish population.[64]

On a cultural level, the accounts of Kurdish experiences related to a denial of cultural rights, especially of education in the mother tongue, have received more attention. In his book *Bir Dil Niye Kanar* [Why does a language bleed?], published in 2010, Muhsin Kızılkaya, a prominent Kurdish writer, recounts the shock he experienced upon realizing that his language, which until he started school he had deemed as simply a means of communication, could become a source of fear for him. Kızılkaya explains that the transition to self-expression in an imposed language means stepping into a new, unfamiliar world.[65] Many recent accounts of alienation due to similar language-related early school traumas can be found in *Bildiğin Gibi Değil: 90'larda Güneydoğu'da Çocuk Olmak* [Not like what you know: being a child in the Southeast in the 1990s], which presents accounts of childhood memories of individuals who grew up in eastern Turkey in the 1990s during the most violence-ridden years of the conflict. Another example that brought the severity of the situation to public scrutiny is the 2008 documentary movie *İki Dil Bir Bavul* [Two languages, one suitcase], which follows a Turkish teacher from Denizli to his post in a remote Kurdish village and displays the difficulty of providing education in a communicational void between the teacher and his students.

Many reports shedding a new light on the situation of minority-language speakers in Turkey have been published in recent years. In seeking to create a deeper understanding of the issue by providing statistical data and encompassing information, these reports aimed to contribute to the ongoing discussion about minority rights and to transform the prevailing majority perception through grounded scholarly work. A 2010 report by Eğitim-Sen (Education and Science Works Union) entitled "Eğitimde Anadilinin Kullanımı ve Çiftdilli Eğitim: Halkın Tutum ve Görüşleri, Türkiye Taraması 2010" [Usage of Mother Tongue in Education and Bilingual Education: Society's Approach and Opinions, Scanning Turkey 2010] pointed out the flawed reasoning in Turkey regarding education in a mother tongue. The reasoning was based on the belief that allowing education in minority languages would be harmful to the official language and eventually would result in the minority languages supplanting the official one. The Eğitim-Sen report revealed an interesting picture, according to which 48 percent of the 781 participants from various ethnic and socioeconomic backgrounds expressed the view that education in one's mother tongue is a right that should be granted to all, while 27.7 percent declared that they were completely against this principle. Twenty-five percent said that the issue should not even come up for discussion. One extremely telling finding concerned the loss of a mother tongue through the generations. The report states that for children whose mother tongue is not Turkish, the percentage of communication in the mother tongue drops to a mere 27 percent, while the percentage stands at 72 percent with their parents.[66] Thus, in the absence of regulated education and state support for maintaining their language, minority-language speakers struggle to transfer their language to the next generations, resulting in the slow erosion of Turkey's cultural richness.

Another study comparing the levels of education between Kurdish- and Turkish-speaking populations shows that the number of people who have not graduated from primary school stands at an alarming 46 percent within the Kurdish-speaking population, while it drops to 9 percent among Turkish speakers.[67] According to another report on bilingualism and education in Turkey, the literacy rate in the southeastern and eastern parts of Turkey is 73.3 percent and 76.1 percent respectively—much lower than in other parts of the country.[68] Unfamiliarity with the language of education has deleterious effects on the future educational performance of the Kurdish-speaking population, which in turn deeply affects the overall quality of life. A similar study suggests that in addition to the endemic economic and security problems the region suffers, speaking a language other than the one in which education is conducted is a major contributor to feelings of estrangement from the educational system.[69] The study, entitled "Dil Yarası" (language wound), delves further into the matter and analyzes the extent of "psychological, educational, linguistic and social problems" induced by the ban on Kurdish in education.[70] In a concluding remark, the study states that this measure leads to repressive relations between students and teachers, to the students' failure to complete classes, to their dropping out of school, and to their being stigmatized for speaking Kurdish.[71] Overall, the emergence of such a body of literature, which brings the Kurdish question into focus through personal accounts and reliable data, is important in creating a broader understanding of the politicization of Kurdish identity as well as in increasing the prospects of finding mutually agreeable solutions.

Obstacles Inherent in the Turkish Perception regarding Kurdish Language Rights

There are two main, interrelated reasons why approaching the issue of Kurdish language rights solely on the basis of cultural and human rights turns out to be highly problematic for Turkey's government and society alike. First and foremost is that the idea of equal language rights is incompatible with the nature of the Turkish state, which was shaped by the secularist policies of the 1920s and is still governed with a highly authoritarian conception of secularism and of the nation-state. In the process of nation building, secularism was used to limit the role of religion to the private domain, while the modernization project set out to create an advanced and prosperous society devoid of traditional structures such as those represented by Kurdish tribal and feudal mechanisms, which were met with profound antagonism by the republican ruling elite because they were associated with the "backward, pre-modern and tribal past" of the ancien régime.[72] In addition, the traumatic dissolution of the Ottoman Empire left the following generations with a psyche tarnished by fears of division and a persistent Sèvres syndrome—the imprint of the 1920 Treaty of Sèvres, which was signed between the Allies and the Ottoman Empire at the end of World War I and foresaw a partitioning of Ottoman lands. As a result, the Turkish state largely ignored the multicultural character of Turkey and the pressing issue of cultural rights. The reaction displayed by Turkish society and its government alike to this issue reveals that, despite the recent positive steps taken on minority-related issues, Turkey's past still shapes the manner in which the country deals with its minorities. Therefore, the question of minority rights is not dealt with in terms of its relation to the principles of democracy and freedom, but instead has been taken hostage by Turkish nationalist fears, which are not limited to the Kemalist secular elite and the military, and which strike a sensitive chord on a societal level as well.

Second is the fact that cultural issues, such as language and education in the mother tongue, are overshadowed by the conflict associated with the Kurdish question, which has embroiled Turkey in a bloody dispute for almost three decades. Therefore, insufficient heed is paid to the need to divorce the cultural symbols of Kurdish identity from the political ones and to regard them as part of multiculturalism in Turkey. On the contrary, expressions of Kurdish identity often lead the majority to question the Kurdish population's loyalty to the Turkish state and, therefore, to doubt Kurds' entitlement to Turkish citizenship. The blurred line between citizenship and national identity engenders a lack of understanding that individuals may hold multiple identities and that particularist identities do not necessarily conflict with one's duties and loyalty as a citizen of a state. As such, a strict understanding of the universality of citizenship, coupled with the nationalist and secular characteristics of the Turkish Republic, overrides Turkey's multicultural texture and often becomes exclusionary in its fierce attempt to melt down differences by blocking expression of diversity and preventing its incorporation into society as a positive value.

Conclusion

Turkey's own nation-building experience is a fitting demonstration of the hermetic relationship between language and nationalism. The project of creating a unitary, monolingual state was carried out by creating an ideological basis for a Turkish nation premised on a linguistic and historical background, and by incorporating into that homogenized society the ethnic and cultural particularities that define minority groups. Throughout this process, Turkey's linguistic richness was diluted in favor of monolingualism by means of repressive state policies. As Turkey's biggest minority group, the Kurds were the hardest hit. Over the years, the armed conflict over the Kurdish question thrust aside the issue of cultural and linguistic rights, which accelerated the politicization of Kurdish identity. Against this backdrop, Kurds were mobilized more forcefully around the ethnic markers of their identity, especially their language, which was catapulted onto the highest cultural pedestal in the eyes of the Kurdish population. As the most demonstrable and observable ethnic marker, it became the most visible and obvious political tool of the Kurdish political movement. The issue of language rights, specifically the demand for education in the mother tongue, emerged as a central catalyst for mass political activism. In this respect, the BDP's actions, as well as its civil initiatives and campaigns, illustrated the solidification of Kurdish nationalism in Turkey—a slow-developing process that can be traced back to the beginning of the Kurdish political movement in the 1960s.

In terms of the state's approach to the Kurdish question, the AKP's "democratic opening" initiative marked a turning point. The 2009 initiative of the ruling AKP introduced some long-needed positive steps by opening the way to a democratic solution to the Kurdish problem and underscoring the need for democratization. Despite the relaxation of Kurdish language regulations, the government's position on allowing education in the mother tongue and the introduction of multilingualism in official domains remain a source of Kurdish criticism, thus feeding continued Kurdish protests. Moreover, the AKP's emphasis on common Islamic ties as the basis for a solution led the Kurdish political movement to reconfigure itself strictly around Kurdish ethnicity, specifically the Kurdish language. From demands for equal citizenship to demands for greater civil rights, all issues touching on the status of the Kurds in Turkey merged with the struggle for the accommodation of linguistic rights.

As tensions mounted amid renewed PKK attacks and subsequent responses by the Turkish army, the platform for dialogue that was created following the launch of the "democratic opening" initiative became largely muted, risking a further widening of the Turkish-Kurdish rift. Against this backdrop, imparting language rights to Kurdish citizens through dialogue and a mutually agreeable solution might act as a positive step not only for Turkey's overall democratization process, but also toward a long-lasting solution to the country's blood-ridden Kurdish conflict.

The Kurdish Women in Turkey: Nation Building and the Struggle for Gender Parity

HEIDI BASCH-HAROD

Since the mid-twentieth century and continuing into the twenty-first cen-tury, Arab and Iranian women of the Middle East have used the state apparatus to negotiate and gradually gain some measure of civil and po-litical rights. In fact, in the case of Iran and Egypt, this relatively rich history of political activism and pioneering for social change dates as far back as the mid-nineteenth century. Yet Kurdish women, stateless and lacking any sort of coherent political recourse until the current Kurdish nation-building project got under way in the 1980s, cannot claim the same legacy. Consequently, the majority of Kurdish women continue to endure a dual-faceted struggle against discrimination and disenfranchise-ment, both as Kurds in an ethnocentric Turkish nation and as second-class citizens simply by having been born women in their community.

As of 2009, statistics gathered in Turkey indicate that nearly 42 per-cent of all Turkish and Kurdish women older than fifteen and 47 percent of women living in rural areas (a majority of whom were Kurds) experi-enced physical or sexual violence at the hands of a husband or partner at some point in their lives.[1] The 2010 Report on the Eastern and South-eastern Anatolia Region, published by the Human Rights Association (IHD) Diyarbakır Branch, documented that 72 women were murdered in the area between March 2010 and March 2011 and that their deaths were categorized as suspicious deaths, honor killings, domestic violence, and rape; 10 of these victims were under the age of eighteen. In the same time period, 113 women committed suicide and 73 women attempted to do so. The organization also found incidences of violence against women by security forces, including harassment and rape, as well as seven cases of women who were forced into prostitution.[2] Millions of Kurdish women in Turkey continue to suffer from domestic violence, illiteracy, and political disassociation in higher percentages than their non-Kurdish Turkish counterparts.

More than 70 percent of Kurdish women have not completed primary school and less than 0.5 percent have completed a secondary education.[3] Unlike Kurdish men, who learn Turkish during their compulsory army service, Kurdish women in rural areas often do not speak Turkish, a trend that prevents them from receiving an education, pursuing employment, and accessing public services.[4]

Paradoxically, over the past three decades, especially since the 1990s, tens of thousands of Kurdish women in Turkey have played an increasingly active and essential role in the Kurdish ethnonation-building movement that is taking place in the Turkish state. Parallel to this activism is an ongoing campaign, led by Kurdish women, to promote the rights of women and to create a society that does not view half of its population as subhuman. In today's Turkey, Kurdish women are parliamentarians, political organizers, social activists, guerrilla fighters, poets, artists, and academics. While the socioeconomic, political, and structural obstacles they have faced and continue to confront are, to put it mildly, quite astounding and persistent, they continue their struggle on a hitherto unprecedented scale. This chapter seeks to reconcile the dissonance between the statistics of deprivation and disadvantage suffered by Kurdish women with the rising number of women who, by participating in and contributing to the nation-building struggle, do no less than change their destiny, rewriting their own historic legacy in the process.

Prominent Women in Kurdish History

Throughout the Middle East there have been remarkable, politically active women who overcame the barriers of traditional, conservative, and tribal societies, which are particularly limiting for women. Notably, following the end of the British Protectorate in the 1920s in Egypt and during France's process of decolonization and departure from Tunisia and Morocco in the 1950s and 1960s, women used the infrastructure of the modernizing state to secure rights and positions of power previously unattainable to them in the Middle East. The women of Iran played a significant role in the 1979 overthrow of Mohammad Reza Shah Pahlavi, although the outcome of the revolution and the subsequent establishment of the Islamic Republic of Iran was not the desired objective for the majority of women who participated in the revolt.

In the case of the Kurds, however, prior to the 1980s and the rearticulation of a Kurdish nation-building movement, only particular circumstances enabled a Kurdish woman to transcend the boundaries surrounding her gender and the societal functions delegated to women as mothers and daughters, i.e., as sources of reproduction and labor. As was customary throughout Kurdish history, women who rose to positions of power were the daughters and wives of notables, emirs, and wazirs. Toward the late nineteenth century and into the early twentieth, they were also the daughters, wives, and sisters of Kurdish intellectuals and nationalists. The current phenomenon of ordinary women rising in the ranks through political mobilization and social activism is largely unprecedented in Kurdish history.

Early evidence of these claims is found in the writings of the Turkish traveler Evliya Chelebi, who authored *Book of Travels* in the seventeenth century. According to Chelebi, in Shahrizur (in today's Iraq), customary law (*qanunname*) contained provisions allowing succession to power by daughters. He observed that it was a common enough occurrence to extrapolate that such a custom was generally accepted by the Kurds.[5] In fact, Chelebi came into direct contact with one of these Kurdish daughters, Khanzade Sultan, who, during the reign of Sultan Murad IV (1623–1640), ruled over the dual principality of Harir and Soran (east and northeast of Erbil in Iraq) and commanded twelve thousand foot soldiers and ten thousand mounted archers.[6]

Another notable example is Kara Fatima Khanum (Black Lady Fatima), a female chieftain of a Kurdish tribe from Marash (present-day Kahramanmaraş in southeastern Turkey), whose reign reportedly spanned the 1850s.[7] Acting as the leader of one of the largest tribes in Eastern Anatolia, she replaced her husband after his imprisonment and sought to win the favor of the Ottoman sultan so he would free her husband.[8] At the beginning of the Crimean War between the Ottoman Empire and the Russian Empire in 1853, Kara Fatima, chaperoned by her brother, journeyed to Constantinople with three hundred warriors on horseback to request an audience with the *padişah* to show support and offer assistance. According to a German observer, Kara Fatima, who showed up for the war wearing men's garb, had a "manly look."[9] Her activities were also documented in the *Illustrated London News* on April 22, 1854, under the headline "Lioness of Kurdistan."[10]

E. B. Soane (1881–1923), a British officer who traveled the areas of today's Iraq, Iran, and Turkey from the early 1900s through approximately 1920, provides one of the most extensive accounts of a ruling

Kurdish woman. Disguised as a Persian and claiming to be a traveling scribe and merchant, Soane came under the employment of the beloved and renowned Adela Khanum, the Kurdish wife of Uthman Paşa, the Ottoman government's appointee as governor (*qa'immaqam*) of the district of Shahrizur. In his chronicles, *To Mesopotamia and Kurdistan in Disguise*, Soane described Adela Khanum as a "woman unique in Islam, in the power she possesses, and the efficacy with which she uses the weapons in her hands."[11] Soane recounted how, during her husband's regular absences, Lady Adela gradually accumulated official power. In this capacity she built a prison, instituted a court of justice and designated herself as its president, and "so consolidated her own power that the Paşa, when he was at Halabja, spent his time smoking a water pipe, building new baths, and carrying out local improvements, while his wife ruled."[12]

According to Janet Klein, urban Kurdish women made their debut on the stage of modern Kurdish-Ottoman politics in 1913, when a Kurdish writer informed the readers of his publication *Kurdish Press* that the entire West and parts of the East were preoccupied with the "woman question."[13] In the context of rising nationalist awareness, the woman question was presented as a social issue whose solution would contribute elements of progress, modernity, and prosperity to the pursuit of Kurdish nationhood.[14] In the same year, Ulviye Mevlan, the wife of Mevlanzade Rifat, Kurdish journalist and opposition member, supervised the publication of *Women's World* (*Kadınlar Dünyası—Monde Féminin*), which touched upon the woman question and saw two hundred issues go to print.[15] The publication became a voice for all Ottoman women, regardless of religion, sect, or ethnic group, and had a reputation for being "serious."[16] When the Society for the Advancement of Kurdish Women (Kurd Kadınları Teali Cemiyeti) was founded in 1919 as a branch of the Society for the Advancement of Kurdistan (Kürdistan Teali Cemiyeti), *Women's World* printed its regulations with the aim of encouraging women to participate in the national awakening.[17] Another notable woman of the period was Emine Xanim, the Kurdish granddaughter of Mehmet Ali Paşa of Egypt, who served as the head of the Society for the Advancement of Kurdish Women. She took advice from two Swedish female friends, both well-known progressives on the topic of women's rights.[18]

Nevertheless, Klein argues that in the early twentieth century the woman question was not so much about women themselves, but instead garnered its importance from men who deemed women as useful and significant symbols for the burgeoning nationalist discourse. As a result, the woman question was intertwined with other issues, such as culture, religion, the economy, and nationalism.[19] Regardless of the sincerity of the intentions to include the woman question in the nationalist discourse, in the aftermath of World War I the political situation in which the Kurds found themselves halted further development of any distinctively Kurdish political, social, or cultural reform.

In 1920 the Treaty of Sèvres, signed between the Ottoman Empire and the Allied Powers of World War I (the British Empire, France, Italy, and Japan), stipulated that "Kurdistan" should remain under Turkish sovereignty. Six months after the treaty came into force, a commission composed of three members chosen by the British, French, and Italian governments drafted "a scheme of local autonomy." The treaty also guaranteed the possibility of establishing a Kurdish state by stipulating that the Kurds could petition the League of Nations for independent statehood within one year. In addition, Turkey committed itself to renouncing all rights and claims of ownership over that territory, should the international body find it suitable for independence.[20] However, when Mustafa Kemal Atatürk, the founder of modern Turkey, successfully led his troops to reoccupy the territory partitioned by the Allied Powers, the area designated as Kurdistan also fell under his authority. The 1923 Treaty of Lausanne, which reestablished "complete and undivided Turkish sovereignty" over nearly all the territories that comprise modern-day Turkey, in effect canceled all articles pertaining to the Kurds in the Treaty of Sèvres.[21] In response to this betrayal, as some Kurdish forces—under the impression that their demands for sovereignty would be fulfilled—helped Atatürk reclaim territory, various Kurdish tribes rose in rebellion against Atatürk's authority and the enforcement of a Turkish ethnocentric state. To counter insurgent forces, Atatürk imposed the Law for the Maintenance of Order and effectively quelled the efforts of the Kurdish nationalists and tribal leaders to achieve any measure of autonomy.[22] In the repressive atmosphere of the following decades, activities promoting Kurdish nationalism, including examination of the woman question, were suspended.

Overall, unless a Kurdish woman belonged to a prominent family endowed with private monetary wealth, property, and connections to a regional ruling power, few to no opportunities for public involvement were available to them. Possibly, an exception to the rule was Rabiʿa, a lower-class woman (notably from an urban rather than a rural setting) who became head of the bakers of Sulaymaniyya in the early 1920s. During an economic crisis, she negotiated with the municipality on a fixed price for bread, all the while maintaining "admirable discipline among her colleagues in the craft who were second only to the butchers."[23] Perhaps there were other such women, but Rabiʿa's image is not representative of the popular characterization of Kurdish women. Even in Kurdish folklore, the heroism of women is confined to defying prearranged marriages or disguising themselves as men to save their men from captivity. Once the mission is accomplished, the story usually ends with the woman succumbing to the male, either sexually or politically.[24] As in real life, in Kurdish folkloric imagination, the common Kurdish woman is ultimately hemmed in by the needs and demands of men and the constraints of traditional society.

Kurdish Women Arise

Shortly after the establishment of the Republic of Turkey in 1923, rebellions by Kurdish nationalists led to the enforcement of a canon of laws that sought to erase Kurdish history and identity. Kurdish names of cities in southeastern Turkey were given Turkish names, and the Kurdish language became practically banned from usage.[25] After Turkish forces quashed the 1937 Dersim rebellion, the years between 1938 through 1968 came to be known as the "silent decades" of the Kurdish struggle.[26] In this time span the Law of Maintenance of Order, displacement, and the resulting breakdown of Kurdish society succeeded in suppressing public expression of Kurdishness, both politically and culturally. Only in the late 1960s did the Kurds once again begin to organize against the Turkish establishment, in the spirit of worldwide sociopolitical revolutions and leftist-radical movements, and as a side effect of the domestic political climate of Turkey.

In 1966, in the Turkish capital Ankara, Kurdish youth were spurring a quiet but defiant Kurdish movement, smoking "Bitlis" cigarettes (the *Kurdish* name for the city where they were manufactured), attending mass meetings for democratic rights, and protesting oppression.[27] At this time, Abdullah Öcalan, the future founder and leader of the Kurdistan Workers' Party (Partiya Karkerên Kurdistan—PKK), the longest-standing Kurdish nationalist organization to date, was living in Ankara, where the political activities transpiring around him awakened his political consciousness. In 1978, after a decade of repeated terms of imprisonment and having joined and left various Kurdish associations, Öcalan and a small group of university dropouts, both young men and women, gathered to plan a campaign for an independent Kurdish state under the auspices of the PKK.[28] While the first PKK members took advantage of the leeway provided by the economic and political crisis wreaking havoc throughout Turkey, the

crackdown on dissident activities that followed the 1980 military coup instituted an era of repression reminiscent of the silent decades.

Following the coup, the Constitution of the Republic of Turkey was
redrafted in 1982, declaring Turkish as *the* mother tongue (as opposed to
the official language) of all Turkish citizens and ushering in an era during
which the very use of the words "Kurd" and "Kurdistan" was viewed as
treasonous.[29] In 1983 the new military leaders enacted Law No. 2932,
which banned the use of the Kurdish language in Turkey, even in private.[30] But despite these legal measures, defiance persisted, and the veil
of silence over the Kurdish question gradually lifted. When a measure of
democratic rule returned to Turkey in 1984, under Öcalan's directive the
PKK launched an armed uprising against the Turkish government and
the Turkish forces.[31] Öcalan realized, however, that to succeed he needed
the strong backing of the Kurdish people.

To shore up support for the PKK, he implemented the party's Marxist ideology on the gender question, turning to the untapped resource of
Kurdish women and enjoining them to participate as real actors in the
fight for the cause. Thus from its inception the PKK played a considerable
part in incorporating Kurdish women into the nation-building effort. Of
course, there was no way to predict the empowering effects that such integration into the movement would have on the Kurdish women who had
joined the ranks of the PKK or who were merely observing events, and
the extent to which they would become empowered.

Initially, the PKK sought to recruit women for two reasons: its Marxist ideology dictated a view of women based on the principles of gender
equality, and the party wished to overcome the social realities of severe
gender discrimination, which Öcalan viewed as one of the main obstacles
to mobilizing the Kurds. However, between 1978 and 1990, Öcalan faced
a recruitment crisis resulting from the fact that most Kurds preferred to
rely on the security provided by their tribes and families. To undermine
this, Öcalan decided that the feudal family and tribal structure had to be
dissolved. He decided that altering the role of women, who were at the
bottom of the tribal Kurdish hierarchy, was the best way to disperse tribal
loyalty, replace the tribe with the party, and substitute the party leader—
himself—for the tribal leader.[32] In fact, the tactic of inviting women to
join the PKK served as the most effective way to challenge the "religious"
and largely feudal Kurdish society.[33]

Based on its ideology, the PKK's early educational program included
bringing about a social revolution based on both men's and women's sovereignty. At one point, Öcalan, and subsequently the party, labeled the

PKK as the Movement of Women's Emancipation.[34] Consistently, and to the present day, Öcalan has called for the double liberation of Kurdish men and women, as "the rebirth of free woman will inevitably result in general emancipation, enlightenment and justice."[35] Nevertheless, early voluntary recruitment of women proved unsuccessful. To circumvent this challenge, the PKK initially recruited young women by kidnapping them.[36] According to David Romano's research, reports of PKK units kidnapping youths aged sixteen to twenty-five appeared in Turkish news sources in the late 1980s.[37] This tactic "forced families whose children were already a member of the organization to cooperate . . . creating both a myth and sensation of curiosity based on the idea that women in the organization were 'free.'"[38] However, the term "kidnapped" may have been employed and circulated by the PKK to avoid reprisals by the Turkish authorities against Kurdish communities accused of colluding with the PKK.[39] Either way, the strategy apparently worked—Kurdish women continued to voluntarily present themselves for service in the PKK.

From the beginning, the PKK allowed women to undertake nontraditional activities, such as combat and noncombatant military functions, and to serve as party journalists.[40] Nevertheless, while the PKK espoused a particular ideology of equality, gender rights, and an end to feudal tribal practices, membership in the organization did not translate into the immediate rejection of the patriarchal culture and customs such social systems foster. For example, in the early days, female militants carried out military operations together with their male counterparts until the number of sexual harassment incidents forced a separation of the units by gender.[41] Moreover, at that time women were precluded from holding top leadership positions.[42] By the mid-1980s, however, a rapidly escalating insurgency forced the PKK to put women in leadership positions; by the early 1990s female participation in the PKK had increased to such an extent that special women's units for female militants were created.[43]

In an interview conducted by journalist and filmmaker Kevin McKiernan, one female PKK member revealed that the reduced status of women in Kurdish society, where they were subject to virginity tests before marriage and honor killings on suspicion of having had premarital sex, played an important role in many women's decision to join the guerrillas.[44] In exchange for their support against the Turkish authorities, PKK women were promised equality and assured that if they fought for their freedom with their "own hands in the war, no one can take it away."[45] Nevertheless, for both Kurdish men and women there was still a gap between the rhetoric of this social revolution and sociocultural reality.

In the mid-1980s the Women's Association of Kurdistan (YJWK) came into being as a PKK affiliate. Its platform stated that all forms of violence and oppression faced by Kurdish women resulted from the Turkish occupation of Kurdistan.[46] The YJWK advocated first and foremost a free Kurdistan, only then to be succeeded by women's liberation.[47] At that point the YJWK-PKK thus prioritized national liberation over women's liberation, an agenda that was accepted and promoted by PKK women themselves. Thus at the same time that the PKK advocated equality between men and women for the purpose of recruitment, PKK women themselves pushed forward a somewhat different plan in that they chose to join the PKK to escape the constraints on their gender. They failed, however, to take the necessary steps to actualize the PKK discourse on women's emancipation that, for Öcalan, was a foundational tenet of the party's ideology. But the prioritizing of the nation's rights over women's did not last very long.

In the late 1990s, 30 percent of the PKK's seventeen thousand armed militant recruits were women, who sometimes rose to the rank of commandos. Women demanded equal participation in the party rank and file; more importantly, they succeeded in having their demands met.[48] Despite the early self-imposed limitations in the quest for equality within the PKK-created microcosm of Kurdish society, the PKK ultimately created a legitimate and socially acceptable alternative to marriage and to the traditional, subservient role apportioned to women in Kurdish society.[49] Consequently, when the PKK launched its militant, pro-Kurdish campaign and effectively politicized the peasantry in 1984, unprecedented numbers of women were included—for the first time in Kurdish history.[50] At the end of the twentieth century it became clear that the PKK had initiated the first truly mass movement in Kurdish history, as it enjoined and attracted the participation of Kurdish women from all walks of Kurdish society.

Since the mid-1980s, and largely through activism in the PKK, thousands of Kurdish women have internalized the political and social implications of their involvement. According to Metin Yüksel, the militarization and popularization of Kurdish nationalism in the 1980s and 1990s (primarily facilitated by the PKK) also led to the development of "a womanhood and/or feminist consciousness" among Kurdish women that questioned the prevalent sexism of Kurdish society and the limitations it has placed on women.[51] Furthermore, it has also given Kurdish women the tools and the confidence to ascend to positions of leadership and, gradually, to defy the status quo.

This development is clearly illustrated by the story of Kesire Yıldırım, Öcalan's former wife and a cofounder and member of the PKK. She was a member of the PKK Politburo until 1988. Although the details of the affair are still unclear, in the late 1980s Yıldırım attempted to remove her husband from his position as chairman of the Politburo and lead in his stead. Following her failed attempt, she fled with her fellow dissidents to Europe, where she tried to establish an alternative PKK politburo. Martin van Bruinessen uses this case to illustrate that, even though she failed, Yıldırım's attempt "showed that the idea of a woman becoming a political leader through her own strength has become conceivable" in Kurdish society.[52] Apparently, as Yüksel states, "the unintended consequence of Kurdish nationalism" has been the emergence of politically independent Kurdish women, a phenomenon not previously seen in Kurdish society.[53] The PKK, the first organization to include women in its national struggle, has been the singularly most influential factor in this development.

As PKK members continue their efforts to bridge the gap between the rhetoric and the reality of gender relations and equal rights in Kurdish society, ongoing attempts are made to institutionalize women's place in the nation-building struggle. For instance, in 2003 the PKK issued an edict stating, "All laws reflecting male domination should be annulled. Violence against all women, all forms of control on women's bodies and lives resulting from outdated custom and traditional habits, and bride prices should be forbidden."[54] As of 2007, the PKK's armed wing for self-defense has a 40 percent mandatory female quota for women commanders.[55] Moreover, if a woman decides to contribute to the nation-building movement via the PKK, she learns self-defense, receives an education, and learns—together with the men—about her rights as a Kurd and a woman. The PKK provides a place for Kurdish women where gender is no longer a direct or indirect obstacle to personal mobility.

In addition to the alternative lifestyle that Kurdish women have chosen merely by participating in the PKK, both women who are members and women who are not affiliated with the party vouch for the vital role the PKK has played in triggering a demand for national and gender rights. According to the testimony of Nazan Bagikhani, a female PKK member, her political involvement conferred upon her confidence and pride in her identity. It provided a context in which, she claims, a Kurdish woman could become an active agent in her own history.[56] Similarly, based upon her research in Istanbul among members of displaced Kurdish communities, particularly women, Anna Secor found that ". . . women frequently attributed their own active self-positioning as Kurds to changes in Turkish society since the early 1980s," citing one Kurdish woman who claimed that "the expression of Kurdish identity was more possible today than it was 20 years ago and . . . those who did try to explain these changes pointed toward the effects of the PKK's armed uprising."[57]

Today, the PKK continues to be the most popular and accessible way for Kurdish women in Turkey to participate in the ongoing nation-building movement, as well as in the struggle for gender rights. It continues to attract Kurdish women from all socioeconomic sectors—from rural areas, urban centers, universities, and also from the Kurdish diaspora of Europe.[58] In the past couple of years, volunteers from Iraqi Kurdistan have also joined the struggle. Kurdish women who are escaping honor killings either elect to join the PKK or are sent by their families to seek refuge by joining the party, whose operative cells are mainly in the Qandil Mountains of northern Iraq.[59] Not only are these women's lives saved, but they are also instilled with the PKK brand of feminism. Kurdish women from Syria and Iran are also joining the ranks of the PKK, in search of alternatives to the lives their communities expect them to lead, and to flee retaliation for breaching the social contract of traditional Kurdish society.[60]

While the PKK continues to carry out acts of violence against Turkish forces and civilians, the movement has diversified and has at times claimed its commitment to peaceful and democratic change. As a result, additional umbrella organizations sprang up, such as the High Commune of Women (KJB), which coordinates PKK-sponsored programs that offer coaching on the rights of women, a "practical unit" that addresses problems of inequality, and a section that oversees the female military role in the PKK.[61] The KJB and other PKK programs that educate men and women on gender rights, including the required course for PKK fighters, called "kill the man in you," continue to attract women.[62] Women such as Commander Rengin, who joined the PKK in 1990 at the age of fourteen to fight for Kurdish rights and women's rights, elected to "go to war" because "women grow up enslaved by society. The minute you are born as a girl, society inhibits you. . . . If I am a woman, I need to be known by the strength of my womanhood, to get respect. Those are my rights," she claimed.[63] Through the vehicle of the PKK, Kurdish women have become active, influential players in building the nation and, taking that role one step further, are dictating what the Kurdish nation should be for them, as women.

The Case of Leyla Zana

Parallel to the cadres of female PKK fighters, other Kurdish women, like Leyla Zana, have discovered alternative avenues to fight the dual battle for the right to express their national identity and for equal (or at least improved) rights for women. Until 1980, Leyla Zana—former political prisoner in Turkey, three-time Nobel Peace Prize nominee, controversial figure for the Turkish government, and inspiration to Kurds, especially women—described her life as a long pursuit of "Turkishness" since to be a Kurd was a disgrace.[64] As a Kurdish woman and "as a matter of destiny," she resigned herself to a fate of servitude to her male counterparts, as well as to her situation as a Kurd in Turkey.[65] Her attitude changed, however, when she started a campaign for the release of her husband, Mehdi Zana, a Kurdish nationalist who was serving a thirty-year prison sentence following his conviction for treason. The campaign included visits to her husband and other Kurdish prisoners, and demonstrations outside the prison walls where the men were serving prison sentences. On these visits she met with Kurdish men and women seeking justice and freedom for their incarcerated family members. Her interactions with fellow Kurds inspired Zana to question her own identity and what it meant to be a Kurd. Leyla Zana has since developed a career in politics, advocating Kurdish rights and, in particular, Kurdish women's rights. In the June 2011 Turkish national elections she was elected for the second time to the Turkish Parliament (this time as an independent candidate) by a majority of voters in the Diyarbakır district, and became one of eleven Kurdish female candidates to win a seat in the Turkish governing body.[66] On October 1, 2011, she was sworn in as a member of the Turkish Parliament, stating that what had once more brought her to the podium of the Turkish National Assembly was her belief in peace.[67]

Still, Leyla Zana attributes the participation of women, and indirectly her own involvement, in the Kurdish nation-building movement to the incorporation of women into the PKK and to Öcalan's ideological commitment to gender equality. In the 1980s, when she discovered that Kurdish women were carrying guns, she said, "I was moved to action. This changes everything, I told myself, a woman is also a human being."[68] In her view, the struggle for freedom—as Kurds and as women—propelled Kurdish women into a period of rapid transformation, in which the PKK was the principal outlet through which Kurdish women could dictate the terms of their own metamorphosis. Presently, however, Kurdish women's options have broadened significantly—over and beyond that of becoming militants or associates of the PKK. This development has made it possible for Kurdish women to pursue nonviolent ways to participate in the nation-building movement, as well as to enlist otherwise hesitant international supporters for their cause.

Kurdish Women's Political Activity Today

In the latter half of the 1990s, the organized political activism of Kurdish women in Turkey flourished through the publication of journals such as *Roza, Jujin, Jin u Jiyan*, and *Yaşamda Özgür Kadın* and the expansion of women's associations.[69] Moreover, female members of the Kurdish diaspora also contributed extensively to this mobilization. Roj Women's Association, for instance, a Kurdish and Turkish grassroots movement based in London, was established in 2004. Through the Internet, Rojwomen .com brings together Kurdish women in Europe as well as women in the Kurdish regions of Syria, Iran, Iraq, and Turkey. The organization has several branches, including a political section that campaigns for legal and political reforms aiming to improve the lives of Kurdish and non-Kurdish women in Turkey.[70] Kurdish Women Action against Honour Killing (KWAHK), a network of Kurdish and non-Kurdish activists, lawyers, and academic researchers, seeks to raise national and international awareness about the issue of violence against women in the Kurdish communities, particularly honor killings, both in Kurdistan and in the Diaspora.[71] Another network, the Kurdish Women's Rights Watch (KWRW), is a UK-based organization dedicated to supporting and promoting women's rights in the Kurdish community, whether in Kurdistan or in the Diaspora; it incorporates KWAHK.[72] These organizations are grassroots movements, initiated and run by a growing number of Kurdish women who are activists in their communities.

In the last decade, opportunities for mainstream, democratic political participation of Kurdish women have also increased. Within Turkey, Kurdish political factions and politicians are presently pursuing an aggressive policy of inclusion in public events and political quotas for women. For instance, until the People's Democracy Party (HADEP) was banned in 2003, its women's branch encouraged the participation of women in civil society by sponsoring local festivals and International Women's Day marches—providing housewives who were not politically active an opportunity for public political engagement.[73] Furthermore, the official party protocol of the current pro-Kurdish Peace and Democracy Party

(BDP) dictates that a woman must be one of its two chairs.[74] On September 4, 2011, Member of Parliament Gültan Kışanak was indeed elected as the female co-chair of the BDP, alongside the reelected MP Selahattin Demirtaş.[75] Out of the twenty-eight female mayors throughout Turkey, fourteen are BDP members.[76] In addition, the BDP women's quota requires that if a party mayor is male, his deputy must be female.[77] Of the twenty-eight new female parliamentary members elected in the June 2011 Turkish national elections, eleven are Kurdish.[78] Of the BDP candidates for Parliament, 30.5 percent were women.[79] Ostensibly, while the majority of Kurdish women continue to suffer under the double oppression of their Kurdishness and their status as women in Kurdish society, it appears that they will be less and less likely to suffer in silence.

Building a Legacy

While there are historical examples of Kurdish women leading armies and political delegations, or conducting negotiations over the price of food, they usually did so with the permission of men in authority or in their absence. More often than not, these women came from prominent and wealthy families connected to regional powers and leaders. In the current context of the Kurdish ethnonation-building movement, however, women from all walks of life are coming to the forefront for the first time in Kurdish history to claim their stake in their nation's sociopolitical future. Over the past thirty years, women such as Leyla Zana and Kesire Yıldırım, respectively of peasant and middle-class backgrounds, and lacking wealth, property, and the backing of influential men, have developed into powerful and influential leaders in their own right. These women and those who follow in their footsteps carry out the ongoing struggle against modern-day challenges—that is, against the "internal enemies" of tribalism, illiteracy, and limited economic and industrial growth that their female predecessors had neither the tools nor the resources to overcome.[80]

Indeed, the mid-1980s resurgence in the struggle against persistent cultural, economic, and political challenges faced by the Kurdish people of Turkey bolstered the Kurdish national struggle and, from the onset, provided Kurdish women with a prominent part. Playing the principal role in this endeavor, the PKK enabled not only Kurdish men but also Kurdish women to stand up for their sociopolitical rights. For Kurdish women, it also served as the first socially sanctioned avenue for public and political involvement. Although statistics indisputably reveal that the majority of

Kurdish women are still culturally and legally disadvantaged, these findings ignore the changes in the self-perception of women and their persistent struggle against discrimination, violence, and social ills and negate the bold steps Kurdish women have taken and continue to take. In this two-sided struggle, Kurdish women, in their roles of guerrillas, writers, poets, painters, journalists, academics, physicians, and members of Parliament, continue to defy the status quo and set impressive precedents for future generations of Kurdish women.[81]

Kurdish women are redefining the scope and scale of their participation in Kurdish society. Consequently, in addition to a national freedom struggle, they have initiated a complementary process of sociological transformation that defies the historical and traditional gender roles delegated to Kurdish women. By becoming political activists in the Kurdish nation-building movement, they are refashioning their historical legacy. Or, in the words of a Kurdish woman in Istanbul, in "that moment when one constitutes oneself as being capable of judgment about just and unjust, takes responsibility for that judgment, and associates oneself with or against others in fulfilling that responsibility," one begins to escape what used to be accepted as a Kurdish woman's preordained fate.[82]

Still, yesterday's obstacles have hardly disappeared, and Kurdish women continue to grapple with ongoing patriarchal Kurdish politics, the misogyny of Islamic groups, political repression by central governments, ongoing warfare, and a largely disintegrated economy and society.[83] Yet despite the hardships, the past thirty years have witnessed an unprecedented increase in the number of Kurdish women demanding not only participation in the political process but also the prerogative to direct that process and to define the rights they expect as Kurdish women and as citizens of Turkey. In doing so, they prove to themselves and others that Kurdish women, too, possess the power and capacity to make valuable contributions to the national struggle—thus heeding the words of Leyla Zana "to speak out, take the floor, express themselves in every way, and that no one should ever again say to us, 'Shut up, woman'!"[84]

PART IV

TURKEY

ZAXO

TILAFER
(Tal Afar)

ŞENGAL
(Sinjar)

QAMIŞLO
(Al-Qamishli)

MÊRDÎN
(Mardin)

HESECÊ
(Hasakah)

SERÊ KANIYÊ
(Rassul Ayn)

RIHA
(Şanlı Urfa)

KOBANÎ
(Ayn al-Arab)

DÎLOK
(Gaziantep)

Kilis

EFRÎN
(Afrin)

Aleppo

Adana

Mersin

SYRIA

IRAQ

Damascus

LEBANON

JORDAN

ISRAEL

© Ibrahim Halil Baran - 2013

The Kurds in Syria: Caught between the Struggle for Civil Equality and the Search for National Identity

EYAL ZISSER

The Syrian state and the Kurds have come a long way since modern Syria began to emerge in the 1920s. A large Kurdish population found itself part of the Syrian state. From the late 1940s onward, however, the Kurds were perceived—by the state and in public opinion—as a threat to the country's Arab identity. Since the spring of 2011 and the upheavals that followed, both the Kurds and the Syrian state have had to cope with a brand-new situation.

In 2011 the Kurds constituted a much more cohesive and unified ethnic group than they had in the past. Against them stood both the Syrian regime and its opponents within the country's Sunni Arab majority. All sides sought to redefine the place and status of the Kurds in Syria and to reexamine the identity and character of this ethnic group. Was it a disparate and fragmented collective, composed partly of nomadic tribes and partly of inhabitants of cities and small towns, some of which were undergoing a process of Arabization? Was it a group lacking a national consciousness, and especially leadership—a population that could not be considered a significant player in the Syrian mosaic? Or was it perhaps a national minority that deserved to be granted full rights? In any case, the questions about the relationship between the Kurds and the Syrian state remain unanswered—e.g., whether the Kurds should be treated as citizens with equal rights, or as members of a recognized ethnic minority with the right to cultural and national autonomy, or as an irredentist minority that aspired to secede from the Syrian state and join the Kurdish entity, imagined or real, that was evolving in Iraqi Kurdistan.

Meanwhile, among the Kurds themselves there is a nagging suspicion that at the end of the day, no matter what the results of the Syrian political turmoil, they will find themselves once more relegated to the sidelines and perceived by Arab public opinion and by the Syrian state institutions as a threat, or even as an enemy.

The Kurds in the Syrian Lands

The beginnings of the Syrian state can be traced back to the 1920s and 1930s, when it was promoted by the French Mandate in parts of the territory known at the time as Syria (Bilad al-Sham). As the new state's geographical borders were being defined, though as yet in crude and general outline, a large Kurdish population was included in its boundaries.

In 1945, near the end of the French presence in Syria, the number of Kurds residing in the Syrian territory was estimated at a little over 250,000, about 8.5 percent of the state's approximately 2,950,000 inhabitants. This figure did not include the Kurds living in the big cities of Syria, who had become completely or partially assimilated into the Sunni Arab population. It is estimated that by the late 1990s more than two million Kurds were living in Syria and that they constituted about 10 percent of the Syrian population and about 5 percent of the total Kurdish population throughout the Middle East.[1]

Most of the Kurdish population of Syria resides in three regions located along the northern and northeastern borders adjoining Turkey and Iraq. These areas are cut off from each other geographically, as are the Kurdish communities themselves. This circumstance has weakened the Syrian Kurdish population's ability to act as a unified and cohesive ethnic or national group and to play an active and prominent role in the political life of the country.[2]

One Kurdish area of residence is located in the northeast of the al-Jazira region, in the province of Hasaka, where the Kurds were the largest ethnic group until the 1960s. To this day, many of them maintain a tribal and nomadic or semi-nomadic way of life; the others live in the large towns of the area, Darbasiyya, 'Amuda, and Ra's al'Ayn, and in the cities, Qamishli and Hasaka. Another Kurdish area is Jarablus, the region where the Euphrates River enters Syria from Turkey, around the city of 'Ayn al-'Arab. A third area is also located along the Syrian-Turkish border north of Aleppo and extends over both sides of this divide. It is called Kurd-Dagh or Kurd Mountain (also Aleppo Mountain or Jabal Halab). The main city in this region is Efrin. As noted, to this day many Kurds continue to live in these regions in tribal settings, although increasing numbers have settled in towns and cities where Kurds constitute a majority or a sizable proportion of the population.³ Finally, significant numbers of Kurds also live in the big cities of Syria, mainly Aleppo and Damascus, but also in Hama. In these cities they tend to be concentrated in their own neighborhoods. In many cases the Kurds living in the interior of Syria underwent a process of Arabization; some of them assimilated completely into the surrounding Sunni Arab population.

It is important to note that the Kurds who lived in the Syrian state from the 1920s onward were by no means strangers to this area. For many generations they had been an integral part of the mosaic of ethnic and religious communities that characterized the area—in particular, from the time Islam and the Arabs took control of Bilad al-Sham (the Syrian lands) in the seventh century. At the same time, the areas inhabited by the Kurds and initially under the French Mandate in the Levant, but later under the rule of the Syrian state, were not perceived as an integral part of Bilad al-Sham. Rather, they were considered to be more closely connected with Iraq and the Diyarbakır region of Turkey. At most, the Kurdish areas in Syria were regarded as a kind of corridor between Bilad al-Sham and Iraq and Anatolia.

Over the years many Kurds migrated to the heart of the Syrian territory, mostly to Damascus and Aleppo, as soldiers in the armies of the Mamluk and, later, of the Ottoman rulers. In other instances, Kurds were relocated to these areas by the Ottoman authorities, who used relocation as a means of punishment. Kurds created their own neighborhoods and for the most part remained loyal to the social, tribal, and family structures that had originally linked them together. In this way they preserved their attachment to their Kurdish origins. A prominent example of such a Kurdish quarter was the Hayy al-Akrad neighborhood in Damascus, which goes back to the time of Salah al-Din's rule, and perhaps even earlier. It is still known and acknowledged in Damascus as a Kurdish place of residence. About twenty thousand Kurds, and perhaps even more, live there now. In the shadow of the cultural and political awakening of the Kurds in Syria in the 1980s, public disturbances and clashes between Kurdish youths and the Syrian security forces broke out over and over again in this neighborhood. One of the most violent confrontations took place during the Kurdish intifada of 2004.⁴

In other instances the Kurds integrated into the Sunni Arab population and in fact underwent a process of almost complete Arabization, as had members of other communities and minorities who made up the mosaic of peoples inhabiting the Syrian lands during the Mamluk and Ottoman periods. This was the story of the growth and consolidation of an elite group of notable families of Turkish and Kurdish origin in the Syrian lands in the nineteenth and twentieth centuries. They adopted and integrated into Arab culture in a process of Arabization that reached its peak at the beginning of the twentieth century, as described by Philip S. Khoury in his *Urban Notables and Arab Nationalism: The Politics of Damascus, 1860–1920*.[5] Indeed, several of Syria's twentieth-century leaders were of Kurdish origin. Ibrahim Hananu (1869–1935), hero of the struggle against the French in the early 1920s, was such a figure. Others were Husni al-Za'im (1897–1949), for a short while the military ruler of Syria in 1949, and Adib bin Hasan al-Shishakli (1909–1964), military ruler of Syria from 1951 to 1954. Even the founder and historic leader of the Syrian Communist Party (SCP), Khalid Bakdash (1912–1995), was of Kurdish origin, as were many of the other leaders of the SCP who followed in Bakdash's footsteps. Thanks to these figures, the party was nicknamed "the Kurdish party." Several of Syria's prominent religious figures also were, and still are, of Kurdish origin, like the former Grand Mufti of Syria, Shaykh Ahmad Kaftaru, and the well-known cleric Muhammad Sa'id Ramadan al-Buti, who was assassinated by terrorists in his mosque in Damascus in February 2013. They were prominent figures even though they did not belong to the hard core of the Sunni religious elite in Syria, but operated on its fringes.[6]

On the Way to the Syrian State:
The Kurds during the French Mandate Period

The establishment of a French Mandate over Syria and the delineation of its borders, which eventually became the borders of independent Syria, brought a large Kurdish population under Syrian rule. A significant part of this Kurdish population, it will be remembered, had close ties with the larger Kurdish area, which was split up between Syria, Turkey, Iraq, and Iran. Moreover, in the mid-1920s—against a background of Turkish efforts to extend the government's authority over the Kurdish regions that had recently been included in the Turkish state and to promote a process of "Turkification"—tens of thousands of Kurds migrated to the al-Jazira region, for the most part maintaining the integrity of their tribes. This migration, or flight, of the Kurdish tribes to al-Jazira led to tensions and, at times, confrontations between the newcomers and the local Arab tribes over areas of pasturage and habitation. At the same time, signs of tension between Kurds and Christians also appeared, especially when Christians of various denominations made up a large proportion of al-Jazira's population. It should be noted that many Christians also fled to Syria, mostly from Iraq, but from Turkey as well.[7]

The demographic situation in the al-Jazira region, and the fact that from the beginning its connections with the Syrian interior had been weak, aroused concern among the supporters of the Syrian national movement in Damascus over the possibility that the region might be severed from the Syrian entity, as had happened with Lebanon and the Sanjak of Alexandretta. These misgivings laid the foundations for the feelings of apprehension and mistrust that the Syrian national movement demonstrated toward the Kurdish population living in Syria, particularly in the al-Jazira region.

The French recognized the benefits they might reap from this situation by exploiting the tension between the Kurds and the Syrian national movement. They hence encouraged separatist sentiments among the Kurdish population, especially among the traditional tribal leaders. At the same time, French policy regarding the Kurds was generally marked by indecision and caution—an outcome of the possible negative ramifications that too blatant a policy might have on France's relations with Britain, which then ruled in Iraq, and on its relations with Turkey, which was also struggling with a complex Kurdish problem.

The Franco-Syrian Treaty of Independence was signed in 1936. As is widely known, it was never ratified by France. Still, it constituted an important stage on Syria's road to independence. Even though the treaty was never put into effect, it nevertheless led to the imposition of the authority of the Syrian state over Syrian territory, including Jabal al-Druze (Druze Mountain), the Alawite region, and the Kurdish-populated al-Jazira region, which had previously been subject to the state of Aleppo, albeit only in theory. One of the most significant aspects of the 1936 French move was, in effect, to put the members of the minority communities, who until that time had relied upon the patronage of the French, at the mercy of the country's Sunni Arab majority and its leadership, the National Bloc. The following years—from the integration of the al-Jazira region into a Syrian state evolving toward independence—witnessed constant tensions and incidents between the state and the Kurds. At the basis of these tensions lay the efforts of the government in Damascus to impose the authority of the Syrian state on the al-Jazira region and other Kurdish areas, with the help of the region's Arab population. There is no doubt that some of the violence that was to break out in the future was rooted in this formative period, as were the anti-Kurdish policies that were later adopted by representatives of the Syrian government as a means of retribution.[8]

The Kurds and the Independent Syrian State: On Both Sides of the Barrier

When Syria gained independence on April 17, 1946, the situation of the Kurds did not change much, because the central government of the new state was quite weak, at least in the beginning. Beyond this, however, it should be noted that the early years of Syrian independence were marked by relative tolerance toward the Kurdish minority and other religious minorities in an effort to integrate them into the Syrian state. Thus, Kurds were granted representation in the elected legislative assembly and were employed in various governmental institutions, including the army. Thus, for example, Tawfiq Nizam al-Din, an officer of Kurdish origin, held the position of chief of staff of the Syrian army in 1955. It should also be noted that the Kurds enjoyed a quite comfortable economic situation during these years, thanks to the extensive development of the agricultural sector, mainly in the al-Jazira and Aleppo regions, which had become the country's breadbasket. Another facet of the region's economic prosperity, however, was that it often led to the land being appropriated by landowners, most of whom were scions of the urban Sunni notable families.

As noted, two of Syria's military rulers in the early years after independence were of Kurdish origin, Husni al-Zaʿim and Adib bin Hasan al-Shishakli. However, these figures had no interest whatsoever in Kurdish affairs, nor did they view themselves as Kurds. They viewed as merely anecdotal the fact that they were born into families from that community. Nevertheless, Zaʿim's military coup d'état in 1949 aroused anti-Kurdish sentiments on account of his origins. The Arab press outside Syria, mainly those organs close to Zaʿim's opponents, thus described his administration as an administration of Kurds and accused him of aiming at the establishment of a Kurdish republic. Another claim against him was that his army relied on Kurds and Circassians, while members of other ethnic communities were sent to the front. Under the rule of Zaʿim and Shishakli, who succeeded him, the prevailing attitude toward the Kurds was like that toward the *shuʿubiyya* (non-Arabs).[9]

In 1957 a Kurdish political party was established in Syria for the first time. The Kurdish Democratic Party was merely a Syrian branch of the

Kurdish Democratic Party of Iraq; it was active mainly among the Kurdish population of the al-Jazira region, while in the other Kurdish areas of Syria its presence was limited or nonexistent. The party's aim was defined as strengthening and emphasizing the Kurdish presence (*al-wujud al-kurdi*) in Syria and advancing the national and cultural rights of the Kurdish people. At the same time, it accepted the principle of a Syrian state, but strove for it to become a democratic entity that would respect and preserve the rights of its minorities.[10]

The "golden age" of the Kurds in Syria, if this term can be used in connection with the early days of the country's independence, came to an end with the establishment of the United Arab Republic (UAR) in February 1958, which aimed at uniting Syria and Egypt. It goes without saying that the Kurds, like the members of other minorities in the country, had serious reservations about the new union, because they were afraid that it would dilute their proportion in the population, and consequently their power, in the Syrian state. Time proved their concern to be quite justified. With the establishment of the UAR, the Kurdish Democratic Party of Syria was disbanded and dozens, perhaps hundreds, of its activists were arrested by the local UAR security services, headed by 'Abd al-Hamid Sarraj. This step followed naturally from Jamal 'Abd al-Nasir's policy of strengthening the dedication to Arab identity in Syria so that it could become the basis of his rule there.[11]

The dissolution of the UAR in September 1961 did not change the Syrian authorities' relationship with the Kurds. Indeed, the tendency to reduce the Kurds' status in the state, signs of which had appeared even before the establishment of the UAR and which intensified during its existence, now became even more pronounced. For two years after the breakup of the UAR, until the Ba'th coup of March 1963, Syria was ruled by a government that was given the nickname "secessionist regime" (*infisali*). It relied on the notable families that had supported the National Bloc and had ruled in Syria from the time it achieved independence until the era of the UAR (1946–1958). The "secessionist" regime of 1961–1963 retained the hostile attitude toward the Kurds manifested by the UAR, an aggressive approach which may have been adopted in light of the regime's distress over Nasir's accusations that the *infisali* had stabbed Arab unity in the back. It may also have been an element of its anti-Kurdish worldview, going back to the days when notable families led the Syrian public's struggle for national independence against the French Mandate and came up against Kurdish separatism. It is also possible that the tension in Syria's relations with Iraq and Turkey throughout the 1950s increased the Syrian leaders' awareness of the need to strengthen the country's control over Syrian northern territories and ensure their connection with the Syrian state.

The Kurds as Enemies

These factors provided the background to the regime's declaration of war against the Kurdish population of Syria in 1962, especially in the al-Jazira region. The assault launched by the regime was unprecedented in both scope and outcome. The Kurds henceforth became an oppressed and persecuted minority, perceived by the ruling powers, and perhaps by the Syrian public as a whole, as an enemy.

There were two facets to the regime's assault on the Kurds in the al-Jazira region. On the one hand, the regime set out to deprive a large percentage of Kurds of their Syrian citizenship, with the aim of expelling them from the region and, if possible, inducing them to migrate back to Turkey or Iraq, from where they had come in the 1920s. On the other hand, the regime took steps to encourage large numbers of Arabs to move from the interior of Syria to the al-Jazira region in order to change the demographic balance there. Another important aim of the government's program was the establishment of an "Arab belt" (*hizam ʿarabi*)—that is, a "security" strip, inhabited by Arabs along Syria's border with Turkey and Iraq—thus placing a partition between the Kurds on the Syrian side of the border and their brethren on the other side.

On August 23, 1962, the authorities in Damascus published Decree No. 93, which called for a census of the al-Jazira region. One of its aims was to check the Kurdish population's right to Syrian citizenship. At the root of the census lay the assumption that a large percentage of the Kurds inhabiting the region, about 40 percent according to government claims at the time, had infiltrated from Turkey into Syria illegally, which was unacceptable since it threatened the Arab character of the Syrian state. On the basis of the census, Decree No. 49 was issued on November 4, 1962, denying Syrian citizenship to nearly 120,000 Kurds. It was claimed that they could not prove their connection to the region prior to the establishment of the Syrian state, since there was no record of their presence in the population registries of either the Ottoman or the French Mandate periods. Those affected numbered about 20 percent of the whole Kurdish population of Syria. The decree stipulated that they would receive the status of resident aliens (*ajanib*). It also stipulated that another 50,000 Kurds who had not participated in the census would be defined as "lacking citizenship status" (*bidun* or *maktum*) and would be removed altogether from the population registry since their citizenship status was not clear. Recently, the total number of persons in these two categories has been estimated at about 700,000.[12]

While the census was being carried out, the authorities announced a program to establish an Arab population "ring" or "belt" in certain areas, with the goal of combating the Kurdish danger and preserving the Arab character of Syria and al-Jazira. However, this project was never carried out in practice during the short-lived rule of the "secessionist" regime. Only with the establishment of the Ba'th regime or, to be more precise, only after Hafiz al-Asad's rise to power, were steps taken to realize the project.

The Ba'th and the Kurds

The relationship between the Syrian state and its Kurdish population deteriorated further following the rise to power of the Ba'th Party on March 8, 1963. It should be noted that despite the Ba'th being an Arab national movement, in the beginning it was not characterized by any declared anti-Kurdish policies. Thus, for example, Michel 'Aflaq, the founder of the Ba'th movement and architect of its ideological foundations, acknowledged that although Syria was indeed an Arab state, it could also incorporate a non-Arab population. In an article entitled "Qawmiyyatuna al-mutaharrira amama al-tafriqa al-diniyya wa al-'unsuriyya" (Our nationalist viewpoint: between religious schism and ethnic-sectarian fragmentation"), 'Aflaq wrote:

When we deal with ethnic minorities, like the Kurds, for instance . . . the question arises as to why they are afraid, or to be more precise, why some of them fear to be identified as Arabs. The answer to this is that this fear is the result of modern imperialist propaganda by the English and the French, who arrived in the Middle East fifty years ago. [This is the only possible explanation] since the Kurds have lived alongside the Arabs for hundreds of years and fought along with them to defend Arab lands . . . The ordinary Kurds want to a live a happy life just like that of the other citizens of the state, but some of their feudal leaders seem to seek some-

thing more for themselves . . . but no one suggests that the Kurds be prevented from learning their own language, on condition that they respect
the laws of the state and do not present it in a threatening way . . .[13]

However, the Ba'th regime that came to power in 1963 and the neo-Ba'th
regime that ruled Syria from 1966 to 1970 formed a series of radical governments whose policies tended toward ever-increasing extremism in regard to, and perhaps because of, the regime's opponents and enemies. The
Ba'th regime's extremism and radicalism was manifested in many areas of
Syrian life. With the Kurds it found expression in a booklet that appeared
in November 1963 and was the handiwork of Muhammad Talib Hilal,
a young second lieutenant who headed the security department (*shu'bat
al-amn al-siyasi*) in Qamishli. In this capacity he was responsible for over-
seeing the political activities of the regime's opponents in his region. The
fact that Talib was promoted and given more prestigious positions (first
as governor of Hama, and later as minister in several Syrian governments)
following the appearance of his booklet indicated, certainly in the eyes of
the Kurds, that his writings reflected the views of his colleagues in the
Ba'th Party.[14]

In a booklet entitled *Al-bahth fi al-jawanib al-qawmiyya wal-siyasiyya
wal-ijtima'iyya li-iqlim al-Jazira* [A study of the al-Jazira region from the
ethnic, social, and political aspects], Talib sought to formulate a plan of
action in the face of what he characterized as the Kurdish threat to Arab
Syria. His booklet reflected the true face of the Ba'th policies toward the
Kurds; it was certainly seen that way by the Kurds. This state of affairs
continued even after the existence of the document had become public
knowledge in 1968, and in spite of the Syrian regime's claim that it merely
represented the personal views of its author and not the position of the
Ba'th regime.[15]

The booklet contains various racist claims, the main aspect of which
is the denial of Kurdish identity. It claims, for example, that there is no
Kurdish people, since the Kurds lack a history or civilization of their own,
and since they adhere to various religious faiths and have never enjoyed an
independent status. A racist tone can also be detected in the claim that the
Kurds lived on the margins of Arab and Muslim civilization as parasites
who took advantage of the culture and achievements of their neighbors,
without contributing anything toward those achievements.

In addition to these blatantly racist accusations against the Kurds,
Talib's booklet included practical suggestions for a program of action.
The aim of his proposals was to cleanse the al-Jazira region of its Kurdish

population by expelling at least some Kurds to what Talib claimed was their place of origin in Turkey, from where, he said, they had migrated to al-Jazira.[16]

The Kurds and the Asad Dynasty

In November 1970, Hafiz al-Asad seized power in Syria. With this his long, drawn-out struggle for control within the Ba'th regime, which had started in March 1963, came to an end. Asad's rise to power turned out to be a very significant stage in the history of the Syrian state. Now, for the first time since its inception, it was to have a firm and effective central government that gave the country unprecedented stability. For the first time since gaining independence, the Syrian state had a regime that was able to implement effective domestic and foreign policies on a large number of issues. This included the Kurdish question. For the first time, a systematic and effective policy was formulated and put into practice, from a starting position in which the regime was extremely powerful. It is important that Asad cleverly integrated the Kurdish issue into his regime's regional policies and used this card, a first for any Syrian government, in his relations with Turkey and Iraq.

As a result, there were two different facets to Asad's policies toward the Kurds. On the one hand, he moderated and softened the tone of the regime's discourse and policies. There is no question that he neutralized their blatantly racist aspect. This was also the line adopted toward the other minorities, including the Jews and the members of various Christian denominations. Insofar as the Kurds were concerned, many Syrians of Kurdish origin were integrated into the Syrian regime—for example, Hikmat al-Shihabi, who served as chief of staff of the Syrian army during most of Hafiz al-Asad's reign; Mahmud al-Ayyubi, who was prime minister in the early 1970s; and clerics of Kurdish origin, such as the Grand Mufti of Syria, Shaykh Ahmad Kaftaru, and the professor of Shari'a law, Shaykh Muhammad Sa'id Ramadan al-Buti, who became prominent religious figures.[17]

At the same time, Asad's policy gave rise, if not to outright hostility to a Kurdish presence in the Syrian state, then at least to resistance against the growth, cultivation, or even expression of Kurdish cultural, ethnic, or national sentiments. The ultimate aim was clearly the Arabization of the Kurds, as the implementation of the "Arab belt" project clearly demonstrated. Beginning in the mid-1970s, and in the framework of the project, dozens of Arab villages were established in the north of the al-Jazira region, where thousands of Arab families settled while the local Kurdish population was expelled. In like manner, the Syrian regime acted firmly against any manifestation of Kurdish sentiments. Thus, for example, it forced settlements to change their Kurdish names to Arabic names, as with the attempt to change the Kurdish name of Efrin to Madinat al-Thawra. The use of Kurdish names for businesses and institutions and the registration of children with Kurdish names were proscribed. Finally, teaching or using the Kurdish language in schools was strictly prohibited, as was opening Kurdish schools. It goes without saying that the Kurds never regained Syrian citizenship, which had been taken from them in 1962, and that the prohibition on Kurdish political activity remained in force.[18]

In addition, the Asad regime established a network of relations with Kurdish forces and organizations in Iraq and Turkey. The intention was to exploit the Kurdish issue as a playing card or a means of applying pressure on the Iraqi and Turkish governments, with which the Syrian regime was in conflict. It was also a means of mitigating dissatisfaction among the Kurds in Syria. Thus, for example, the Syrian government established ties with the main Kurdish parties in Iraqi Kurdistan, namely with Mulla Mustafa Barzani's Kurdistan Democratic Party (KDP) and Jalal Talabani's Patriotic Union of Kurdistan (PUK). Indeed, the PUK was founded in 1975 at an event held in Damascus under the auspices of the Syrian regime. For many years Talabani maintained ties with the Syrian authorities and at times even found shelter and asylum in Syria. As for Mulla Mustafa Barzani and, later on, his son Mas'ud Barzani, the Syrian regime allowed them to recruit Syrian Kurds into the ranks of the Peshmerga militia. In addition, the Syrian government established ties with the Kurdistan Workers' Party (PKK), led by Abdullah Öcalan. This movement worked against the Turkish regime, which viewed the PKK as a terrorist organization. The Marxist-oriented PKK had no interest in fostering a Kurdish national identity among the Kurds in Syria. Öcalan was even credited with saying that the Kurds originated in Kurdistan and needed to return there. This approach naturally made it easier for the Syrian regime to cooperate with Öcalan and his party.[19]

Cooperation reached its peak in the 1980s and 1990s. It found expression in the steps Syria took to give shelter and training to PKK activists, at first in training camps in Lebanon, which was under Syrian tutelage at the time, and later, insofar as can be determined, in Syria itself. It seems that the Syrians even allowed the Syrian Kurds, especially those inhabiting the border areas between Syria and Turkey, to join the PKK, or at least to support the party. Also, as leader of the movement, Abdullah Öcalan enjoyed the patronage and protection of the Syrian regime, which allowed him to establish his headquarters in Damascus. During the 1990s the Turks took steps to set up projects in southeastern Anatolia, such as diverting the waters of the Euphrates River for Turkish use, to the detriment of Syria. In the wake of these initiatives and in the shadow of the improved relations between Turkey and Israel, Syria increased its cooperation with and material assistance to Öcalan and the PKK.[20]

In 1998, relations between Syria and Turkey were on the verge of confrontation on account of the PKK's intensified activities against Turkish targets. As a result, the Turks adopted a harsher tone toward Syria, with Ankara even issuing threats of war against Damascus. These threats ultimately resulted in the capitulation of Syria and its withdrawal of support to the PKK, in the expulsion of the party's activists from Syria, and, ultimately, in the expulsion of Öcalan himself from Damascus. He was captured a short time later by the Turkish security services. Following the American conquest of Iraq, signs began to appear of Turkish and Syrian cooperation, with the aim of preventing the establishment of a Kurdish state in Iraq. As Iran shared this objective, the three states joined forces, so that they ceased to use the Kurdish card against each other.

It seems that decades of oppression, culminating in Hafiz al-Asad's "iron fist in a velvet glove" policies, ultimately produced results that were the exact opposite of what Damascus was seeking. The Kurdish population of Syria, beset by years of schism and fragmentation and seemingly lacking a common denominator, gradually developed a cultural identity, a growing awareness of being an ethnic community, and nationalistic sentiments.

Manifestations of these developments included repeated clashes between Kurdish activists and the Syrian authorities. The first decade of the twenty-first century witnessed a number of demonstrations initiated and carried out by Kurdish activists in Damascus and Aleppo. It should be recalled that even earlier, during Hafiz al-Asad's rule, the Kurds were allowed to celebrate Newroz, their New Year, despite the fact that the celebrations often became a source of friction between Kurdish celebrants and the Syrian security services. Thus, for example, several Kurds were killed in clashes with the police during the 1986 Newroz festivities. The outburst of violence began in the Kurdish quarter of Damascus and spread to other regions such as Qamishli and Efrin.[21]

At the same time, the population continued to suffer because Kurdish society was fragmented. There were competing social forces, some of them traditional, and contending political parties and movements. Thus the Kurdistan Democratic Party of Syria (KDPS), which was founded in 1957, was officially disbanded during UAR rule (1958–1961). In a gradual process that reached its peak in the 1980s, the Syrian Kurds formed over twenty competing parties. They operated within three major frameworks: the Kurdish Democratic Front, the Kurdish Democratic Alliance, and the Kurdish Democratic Union. A review of all Kurdish parties reveals a complex picture, from parties accepting the Syrian state and wanting the Kurds to integrate into it, to all-Kurdish parties looking forward to a unified entity encompassing all Middle-Eastern Kurds. The Syrian regime, for its part, preferred to ignore the activities of many of these Kurdish parties, since it did not perceive them as a threat or danger to state security. This was the case mainly because many of the parties had agendas that focused almost exclusively on issues affecting the Kurds across the border, in Turkey and Iraq, while others had only cultural and social welfare agendas rather than political or national ones.[22]

The Rule of Bashar al-Asad

Hafiz al-Asad died in June 2000 and was succeeded by his son and heir, Bashar al-Asad. Bashar's rise to power aroused hopes of change, both because of the new leader's image as a man with a liberal Western worldview and the assumption that he lacked the stature and governing power of his father. Indeed, several months after Bashar came into power, the so-called Damascus Spring erupted. Calls for greater democracy and pluralism in the country's political life began to be heard all over the country, on the face of it with the backing of Bashar al-Asad himself. Debating clubs were established and held relatively free discussions, at least in comparison with the past.

The Kurdish intellectuals, whose voices stood out among those heard during the Damascus Spring, opened discussion clubs in Hasaka and Qamishli and participated in like clubs in Damascus and Aleppo.[23] However, their voices erupted and then ended just as suddenly as the Damascus Spring. The regime, afraid that it might lose control, restored its tight control over security matters. The debating clubs and discussion groups that emerged during the Damascus Spring closed down, and many of their organizers and backers were thrown into prison.

The American conquest of Iraq in the spring of 2003 and the establishment of Kurdish autonomy in northern Iraq only served to increase the tension between the Kurdish population and the Syrian regime. As is widely known, the Syrians were opposed to the American undertaking, in part because they were concerned about its negative ramifications for Syria's Kurdish citizens. At the same time, the Syrians were careful to maintain their ties with the Kurdish parties in Iraq, that is, with both the faction of Mas'ud Barzani and that of Jalal Talabani.

Meanwhile, the protest activity of the Syrian Kurds continued, even when the Damascus Spring ended. There were several reports of incidents and demonstrations by Kurdish activists, one of which related to a sit-in that had taken place on December 10, 2002, in the heart of Damascus to demand that citizenship be granted to Kurds in the al-Jazira region. Another report related to a demonstration by Kurdish children on June 25, 2003, in front of the UNICEF offices in Damascus.[24]

The Kurdish Intifada of 2004

On March 12, 2004, serious rioting broke out in the wake of a soccer game in which an Arab team from Dayr al-Zur played against a Kurdish team. During the game the Arab fans shouted slogans praising Iraqi president Saddam Husayn, to which the Kurds countered with praises not only of Jalal Talabani and Mustafa Barzani but also of U.S. president George Bush, the liberator, or perhaps conqueror, of Iraq. The clashes between the fans turned violent and spread beyond the playing field to the city of Qamishli, and from there to Kurdish towns and cities in the region and even as far as the Kurdish quarters of Damascus and Aleppo. In Hasaka, Kurdish demonstrators set fire to government and public buildings, and in Damascus they hurled rocks at the police and security personnel. Dozens of Kurds were killed in the clashes and hundreds were wounded. Although the upheaval died down after a while, its hot embers continued to smolder.[25]

The "Syrian Spring"

At the height of the winter of 2011, the so-called Arab Spring broke out, first in Tunis and Egypt, then in Libya and Yemen and even in Bahrain. It reached Syria in mid-March 2011. Initially, the demonstrations were held on Fridays. When prayers in the mosques ended, large street demonstrations were staged in towns and cities all over the country. To rally demonstrators and draw in new participants from a wide spectrum of Syrian society, the activists gave each Friday a different nickname or slogan in the hope that it would unite the anti-regime demonstrators and protestors. Thus, Friday, March 20, 2011, was called "Friday of Freedom" (*jumʿat al-huriyya*). This time, however, the demonstrators were careful to add the word *azadi* ("freedom" in Kurdish). They had two aims in doing so. One was to show that the various religious and ethnic communities making up the Syrian public agreed on the need to overthrow the regime. The other was to attract members of the Syrian Kurdish community into the ranks of the demonstrators.[26]

True, many Kurdish activists expressed support for the uprising against Bashar al-Asad's regime, but these were mostly Kurds living outside Syria. A strong Kurdish presence was also evident in worldwide demonstrations against the Syrian regime. Still, inside Syria, the Kurds remained largely onlookers. *Azadi* Friday did little to change this.

In an effort to placate the Kurds, Bashar granted them benefits that they could not even have dreamed of before the demonstrations. With the stroke of a pen, official Syrian policy toward the Kurdish population changed radically. In the al-Jazira region, more than 100,000 Kurds were granted Syrian citizenship, which significantly improved their situation. Four decades earlier, in 1962, about 120,000 Kurds had been deprived of their Syrian citizenship by an administrative act that claimed they had not been born on Syrian soil, but had migrated into the country from Turkey and Iraq. These Kurds and their descendants had been stateless ever since and thus could not enjoy the rights, social services, and other benefits granted by the Syrian state to its citizens. In April 2011, Bashar al-Asad decided to grant citizenship to a large number of Kurds to deter them from joining the protests against his regime. At the same time, he also removed many of the security restrictions that had been placed on the Kurds.

In a television interview he granted on June 21, 2011, President Asad took pains to explain his new policy regarding the Kurds:

> The first time this matter [of granting Syrian citizenship to the resident stateless Kurds] came up was in August 2002, when I visited the Hasaka region and met the local notables, including our brother Kurds. They raised this issue during my visit, and my answer was that I recognized that they had the right to hold Syrian citizenship, and, furthermore, that there was a humanitarian problem here that we must deal with. . . .

In this connection it is important for me to emphasize that the Kurd-ish brothers are part of the Syrian social fabric. Every citizen should hold citizenship that provides a basis for his existence—otherwise he will be like a migratory bird. Without one of its components, Syria cannot be a stable state like the one we know from the past. If we look at past events in our history, including our struggle against the French and other colo-nialists, we will find that the Kurds also produced revolutionaries and fighters from their ranks. This is set apart from what happened in the dis-tant past, and which is known to all of us [evidently a reference to Salah al-Din].[27]

Whether on account of the decrees issued by the Syrian government or perhaps without any direct connection to them, relative quiet con-tinued to prevail in the Kurdish areas. The head of the Kurdish Progressive Democratic Party in Syria, ʿAbd al-Hamid Darwish, explained the situa-tion in an interview he granted to *al-Sharq al-Awsat* on August 27, 2011:

Some accuse the Kurds of taking a position different from that of the other citizens of Syria, but this accusation is false. The Kurds were, and still are, the most resolute fighters for freedom and democracy in Syria simply because they have suffered more than anyone else from the heavy hand of the totalitarian government ruling Syria. They have suffered both as Syrians and as Kurds. The struggle of the Kurds is for a democratic and just solution to the Kurdish problem in Syria, and such a solution will be reached only if the Kurds and the Arabs come to an understanding. A civil war, on the other hand, is frightening and destructive. The Syrian nation is wise, and we must not go downhill this way. The Kurds are part of this nation, and they have good and strong relations with their Arab and Christian brothers in Syria. Fears of a civil war have arisen—and there were signs [that Syria was entering a civil war], among them threats made by Arab tribes in areas with Kurdish towns, where notices were published against the popular demonstrations. We have good and strong relations with the parties in Kurdistan, and especially with the Patriotic Union of Kurdistan (PUK) and its leader Jalal Talabani. But our policy derives from the actual state of affairs and the uniqueness of our situation in Syria.[28]

In other words, it turned out that the Kurds preferred to measure their steps and evaluate risks carefully, and that despite their hostility to the Syrian regime, they had decided to refrain from entering into the situation blindly, perhaps because they feared a backlash from the regime's opponents. As a matter of fact, the efforts of Kurdish activists to take part in conferences held by the Syrian opposition in Anatolia and Ankara did not turn out well, due to disputes over the question of whether the Syrian state was an Arab state or a state of all its ethnic groups and citizens. A clear example of this is the Conference for National Salvation, which activists of the Syrian opposition convened in Istanbul on July 16, 2011. Most of the political forces at work outside Syria against the Syrian regime attended this gathering. Yet, not surprisingly, the Kurdish representatives who attended the event walked out in protest because the conference had adopted a resolution whose main point was that Syria was an "Arab Muslim state." In their view, the resolution excluded the Kurds from the Syrian collective, since the Kurds constitute a separate ethnic group. A short time later, at the beginning of October 2011, all the opposition groups in Syria assembled in Istanbul and declared the establishment of a national council. Kurdish representatives were included, but of the twenty-nine council seats, only four were allotted to the Kurds.[29]

It would thus seem that the Kurds were suspicious of not only the regime in Syria but also the regime's opponents, who had their roots in the very same forces among the Sunni community, and even the Sunni elite, that had assailed the Kurds in the 1950s and 1960s. The Kurds therefore refused to become a tool in the hands of either the regime or its opponents. However, it is also possible that the Kurds were reluctant to act because they felt their community was not unified and consolidated enough to play a leading role, or even an active and prominent role, in the events unfolding in Syria.

Then on July 18, 2012, a major rebel attack in the heart of Damascus killed many in the upper echelons of Syria's security forces. This seemed to signal the imminent fall of Bashar al-Asad's regime. Sensing this, the Kurds threw off their restraints and began taking steps to gain some degree of autonomy in the areas they inhabited, which they call Western Kurdistan. At the same time, they left the door open for dialogue and even limited cooperation with both the government and the opposition.[30]

As forces of the Asad regime began to withdraw from northern parts of Syria and from al-Jazira, confrontations arose between the Kurds and some Arab tribes over control of the territory, and especially over the grain storage facilities and oil fields located there. These confrontations became sharper because of the presence of radical Islamic movements like the Al-Nusra Front (*Jabhat al-Nusra li-Ahal al-Sham*) or the "Islamic State in Iraq and al-Sham" (al-Dawla al-Islamiyya fi al-ʿIraq wal-Sham), both of which have ties to al-Qaʿida. These radicals set the tone, with the support of the local Arab tribes that are inclined to cooperate with them. Naturally, the Muslims oppose the Kurds' efforts to gain control or even some degree of autonomy in these regions.[31]

Summary

Jordi Tejel begins his book *Syria's Kurds: History, Politics, and Society* with the assertion that one cannot speak about the Syrian Kurds as a cohesive group. Rather, it is a heterogeneous group that encompasses people of different religions, identities, and languages. In his words:

> . . it became impossible to speak in terms of unique identifying charac-
> teristics of the Syrian Kurds during the first half of the twentieth century.
> For individuals and groups (e.g., clans, tribes, families), ethnic identity
> was more likely determined according to their social and political inter-
> ests and constraints and less often in terms of their linguistic and historic
> identifying traits. Up until the advent of contemporary Syria, the natural
> reference point for Kurdish groups was not found in ethnic or linguistic
> terms, but it was defined in relational terms, including geographic ori-
> gin (valley, village, quarter), family, clan, tribe, or sect (as for the Yezidis).
> In light of these factors, it is problematic to consider the Kurds as a
> "minority" in the prescriptive sense during the mandatory period.[32]

There is no doubt that the Kurds who came under the wings of the Syrian state, at first during the French Mandate and later when Syria gained its independence, constituted a quite heterogeneous group, frag-mented and separated geographically and socially, lacking all social aware-ness of a national or ethnic identity, and consequently lacking unity and consensus. They were a mixed grouping of nomadic and seminomadic tribes and residents of towns and cities, spread out over various geo-graphical areas and often lacking any connections or affinity with each other. The establishment of the Syrian state severed their ties with their fellow Kurds in Turkey, Diyarbakır, and Iraq, with which they had previ-ously had ties.

The Kurds within the boundaries of the Syrian entity were faced with an unfriendly government and, in point of fact, an unfriendly public, led by a Sunni Arab political and cultural elite that quickly came to view them as an enemy and, one might add, an easy prey because of their weakness as a group. So for eighty years the Kurds were exposed to systematic, though not necessarily unremitting, policies that backed the suppression of their cultural and ethnic identity, a widespread use of divide-and-rule policies, and ultimately steps aimed at bringing about Kurdish Arabization or, alternatively, emigration from the Syrian state.

For many years it seemed as if the policies of the successive Syrian governments had been successful in sweeping the Kurdish problem under the rug. Ultimately, however, these policies turned out to have the opposite effect of what was intended, insofar as they united the Kurds by creating a common denominator that seemed to have been lacking during the early days of the Syrian state. Kurdish cultural, ethnic, and national ideas and sentiments gradually gained a foothold. The experience of the Kurds on the Turkish and Iraqi sides of the border undoubtedly also contributed to this trend.

Indeed, as early as the 1980s, Kurdish cultural sentiments became evident, although only sporadically. As time went by, the political and socioeconomic changes taking place among the Kurds of Iraq and Turkey exerted an increasing influence on the Syrian Kurds. Following the Kurdish Intifada of 2004 and the events of the Syrian Spring of 2011, the Kurds seem to have reached a watershed. They are now a more united group, which is how they are perceived by both the Syrian regime and its opponents. Both sides now see the Kurds as a group that knows how to stand up to the state for its rights, even if they still suffer weaknesses.

The Syrian state and the Kurdish population in Syria have both come a long way since the Kurds crossed the boundaries of the Syrian entity at the beginning of the twentieth century. On the one hand, the Syrian state reversed its initial policy of tolerance and patience, which was a continuation of the policy pursued under Ottoman rule, and adopted a policy of cultural, ethnic, and national repression in which the Kurdish people were viewed as enemies of the state and the Kurdish question was treated as an issue that needed to be swept under the rug. Later on, during the reign of Hafiz al-Asad, new policies were aimed at containing the Kurdish problem and, what is more, Arabizing the Kurds. The Kurds found it difficult to defend themselves against these policies, due to their heterogeneous society and low self-awareness regarding their own identity, traits that also marked the Kurds on the Turkish and Iraqi sides of the border.

On the other hand, from the 1980s onward change became evident, mainly in the form of a growing Kurdish awakening. On the whole, it seemed as if the Kurds were no longer pursuing a separatist solution, as they may have found this option to be unrealistic.

And so after nearly eighty years of Kurdish life in Syria it became clear that all the efforts of previous and present Syrian governments—whether to suppress sentiments in favor of a Kurdish identity, or to get rid of them, or to swamp their areas of habitation with a flood of Arab migrants—had failed, and that the Kurdish problem was once again raising its head. It became clear as well that, as always, the future depended first and foremost on the Kurds themselves.

The outbreak of the 2011 Arab Spring in Syria was set against the background of weakening the Syrian state's foundations and the simultaneous emergence of a Kurdish entity in Iraq. These processes posed both an opportunity and a dilemma to the Syrian Kurds such as they had never known before. The question now is whether they will finally close ranks, a goal in which they have failed over the years, and whether they will succeed in gaining the backing and support of their brethren in Iraq, something that has never happened before because of the Iraqi Kurds' distinct interests. If these goals remain far off, then the story of the Kurds in Syria may continue to be one of a struggle for survival, and their future will continue to be dependent upon the goodwill of the Syrian regime.

Yet the Syrian government offers no real solutions to the Kurdish problem, apart from assimilation into Syria as part of the fabric of the state. Though Bashar al-Asad was compelled to yield to Kurdish demands and grant Syrian citizenship to many Kurds, it is clear that he did not make this concession because he was favorably disposed toward them. The Syrian opposition movement, for its part, has not shown any particular sympathy for the Kurds either.

And so the Kurds face the very real possibility that the fall of the present Syrian regime will lead to the emergence of a weak and unstable central government in Damascus similar to that which prevailed in the 1940s and 1950s, and that any tolerance shown toward the Kurds will come from a position of weakness. Alternatively, if Bashar al-Asad's regime is able to regain its stability, it is liable to return to the tactics of Hafiz al-Asad, whose policies, while displaying a smiling face to the Kurds, still relentlessly suppressed any manifestations of cultural, ethnic, or nationalist sentiments among them.

Toward a Generational Rupture within the Kurdish Movement in Syria?

JORDI TEJEL

The so-called Arab Spring of 2011 has once more showed that although the political trajectory of Kurdish movements is still determined by the political agenda of the nation in which they exist, Kurds are affected by conditions in other countries with significant Kurdish populations and may at times benefit from what takes place there.[1] The verbal escalation between Syria and Turkey since April 2011 and the threat of a Turkish intervention in Syria, should the Syrian regime attempt to use the "Kurdish card" to destabilize Turkey, illustrate the cross-border character of the Kurdish issue.

The Arab Spring has also opened the door to regional transformations that are not limited to political parties. My main argument in this chapter is that although the protest movements of 2011 may fall short of their most radical goals, they have succeeded in irreversibly changing national and even regional thinking and expectations.[2] The most obvious change that present revolutionary upheavals, including in Syria, have brought about is probably a new beginning for youth seeking to become prominent agents of political change.

The unexpected Middle Eastern revolutions that erupted in December 2010 have propelled the region's youth to the forefront of the political and media stage.[3] It has long been anticipated that young people would emerge as a powerful force, simply because the median age across the Middle East is just twenty-five. Moreover, the Middle East is characterized by the fastest-growing labor force as well as the world's highest regional average of youth unemployment. In the next decade, some 100 million jobs will have to be created in the region to absorb the emerging workforce. The "question of the youth" as a critical object of change was indeed addressed by various international agencies, at least for a while.[4]

But many observers were surprised by the protesters' rejection of traditional opposition leaders. To a certain extent, and as a hypothesis, one could argue that for the first time the youth in the Middle East were trying to make their own revolution, to become the real subjects of change and not just objects or tools of action for the sake of their respective nations, as had been the case in the 1960s and 1970s.[5]

It seems certain that a generation's shared experience and its rejection of the tutelage of "paternal" parties were also in effect in the Middle East; however, the youth movement never reached the point of disowning these parties' conceptions of politics. In other words, throughout the 1960s and 1970s, the radical student movements in Morocco, Egypt, or Turkey were a continuation of the traditional radical politics and social movements, as Arif Dirlik and others have suggested.[6] The students resented the fact that the reformist or left-nationalist parties had not done anything after seizing power, but this did not bring about a radical questioning of the conception of politics held by these parties.

Such a response is partly due to the fact that the state itself played a major role in producing the identity of the "university's youth." The universities were the source from which future ruling elites were to be nurtured. Yet expectations for the universities and the students were not solely those of the state. The forces of the opposition also considered that the students would become the avant-garde within their respective nations. The Middle Eastern students, like their counterparts in other regions of the world, animated the public space and pretended to speak *to* and *in the name of* society as a whole. As time passed, the students and the intelligentsia in general imposed themselves on the wider public as the architects of dissident politics that would extend well beyond their militant circles.

In 2011, however, I would argue that the youth in the Middle East did not wish to sacrifice their collective and individual hopes and expectations (e.g., living standards, job opportunities, personal and collective dignity, and active political participation) "for the sake of the nation." The Kurds had always been an integral part of Middle Eastern societies and as such evolved in a way very similar to that of other Middle Eastern populations. They were also affected by the lack of democracy and by political, social, and economic transformations throughout the second half of the twentieth century: rapid population growth, an increasing proportion of young people, rapid urbanization, rising levels of unemployment, and higher standards of education (especially in urban areas).

Kurdish youngsters now hold social and political expectations that could hardly be met by the Syrian regime. However, traditional Kurdish parties have also failed to offer a comprehensive response to such demands. Instead, they have clung to old strategies (internal divisions, contacts with both the regime and the rest of the Syrian opposition) and cultural framing (e.g., identity politics). The parties' lack of new approaches has led to an increasing gap between them and Kurdish youth.

This chapter considers the complex relationship between young Kurds and the Kurdish political parties over the last three decades. After analyzing Kurdish identity in Syria and its articulation in the political field, a brief discussion is presented on the formation of the Syrian Kurdish political parties and, more specifically, the reasons why the Kurdistan Workers' Party (PKK) filled the vacuum left by previous parties. I suggest that both the engagement of thousands of young Syrian Kurds in the ranks of the PKK throughout the 1990s and the Qamishli revolt of 2004 were signs of more complex dynamics within Kurdish society—namely, the first phase of a generational and political rupture. Finally, I will argue that the "Syrian revolution" of 2011 could lead to a serious widening of this gap between political parties and young Kurds if the Kurdish parties do not take into account the expectations of the younger generation.

The Kurdish Identity in Syria

Most Kurds tend to move back and forth between Kurdish and Arab cultures. Yet despite the fact that the Kurds have been subject to some "linguistic Arabization" and, as Syrian citizens, have come under Arabo-Syrian cultural and political influence through education, television, and the army, Kurdish culture still maintains its vitality. Kurdish ethnic identities in Syria take various forms of group affiliation, such as tribe, locality, or class, depending on the social context in which they are produced and expressed. The geographical fragmentation of the Kurdish enclaves compounds this variety. Nevertheless, there is a shared sense of belonging to a Kurdish community with a common culture and history that articulates the various social and cultural realities of Kurdish life in Syria. The collective emphasis on maintaining certain cultural features, such as the use of the Kurdish language or folklore festivals, aims to mark the ethnic boundaries that define the translocal Kurdish identities.[7]

Although ethnic awareness is an important attribute of the Kurds in Syria, translocal identities have not been conducive to Kurdish national mobilization. A number of approaches could resolve this paradox. The demographic argument, i.e., the relatively small number of Kurds, seems insufficient given that the Alawites, a minority group in Syria, managed to take control of the state apparatus in the mid-1960s. Nor does the geographical distribution of the Kurds in several enclaves in itself explain the political absence of the Kurds in Syria, at least until 2004. Like the Alawites and the Druze, the Kurds took part in the massive exodus from rural areas to Syrian towns and cities, and now populate both rural and urban areas.[8]

A dialectic approach based on the evolution of the Syrian state and of Kurdish communities can, however, provide some explanation for the Kurdish predicament. During the years of the French Mandate (1920–1946), there was no well-defined Kurdish group; this was a direct consequence of their diverse origins, local histories, and the fact that each Kurdish group experienced a different process of integration into their Arab environment. With almost no active involvement by the Syrian state in the country's northern districts, Kurdish peasants and tribesmen there were led by tribal and religious leaders—and this in spite of the Khoybun's efforts to mobilize them around a national Kurdish project.[9] Yet at that time, Kurds were able to live normal lives in the framework of their ethnic identity.

Until 1963, and despite the end of the French Mandate, the Syrian state and its elites possessed neither a clear ideology nor a sufficiently coercive power base to pose a serious threat to Kurdish identity. While the rise to power of the Ba'th led to the imposition of an official ideology, the new regime suffered from internal divisions that prevented it from establishing viable official institutions or even from creating a myth of national integration, which would have given it at least some legitimacy. It was not until Hafiz al-Asad came to power in 1970 that a coherent and dominant power structure was finally established.

The Kurds, along with other ethnic groups lacking an official identity in the Syrian state, were invited to either adhere to the principles of the regime or maintain passive obedience. Like all Syrian citizens, the Kurds were subjected to the state of emergency that came into effect in 1963, with its new norms and restrictions on expression and association. However, some essential principles of the regime, notably that of Arab nationalism, and some laws (including restrictions on Kurdish language and folklore) were direct attacks on the core of Kurdish identity and threatened the survival of Kurdish groups.

The Kurdish Parties at the Margins of the Legal System

The Kurds have resided in four different states since 1925 and therefore fall under the political, economic, and military authority of four distinct jurisdictions. A different mode of action is adopted by the Kurdish nationalist movements in each country in accordance with its political system. It was therefore inevitable that the Kurdish political movements would follow distinctive trajectories in Iran, Iraq, Turkey, and Syria.

An analysis of the history of the Kurdish movement in Syria largely confirms that the Kurdish parties there constitute an exception among oppositional Kurdish nationalist movements. Syrian Kurdish parties never took up arms against the government of Damascus, while armed struggle has long represented the primary mode of opposition for Kurdish movements elsewhere. As a result, Syrian Kurdish parties were unable to put themselves forward as legitimate political actors or to open negotiations with the central government—a step that is normally taken only after a period of armed conflict.

Over the years, political participation has been restricted to such an extent that more often than not the Kurdish parties remained outsiders, marginal actors in the political arena. This was an outcome of an exclusive political system rather than of the nature of the Kurdish movement itself, which had traditionally limited itself to cultural and civic demands such as lifting the ban on the Kurdish language and restoring citizenship to those stateless Kurds affected by the census of 1962.

It was not until the creation in 1957 of the Kurdistan Democratic Party (KDP) in Syria, eventually renamed the Kurdish Democratic Party in Syria (KDPS), that a popular Kurdish national party finally appeared on the Syrian political scene. Even at this point, the party kept a "Syrianized" agenda in that the objectives of the party did not include the liberation of "Syrian Kurdistan." The party did, however, incorporate improved living conditions for the Syrian Kurds. The KDPS's popularity could be assessed effectively for the first time during the legislative elections in December 1961. Although Nur al-Din Zaza and Shaykh Muhammad 'Isa Mahmud, both founding party members of the KDPS, were elected as independent candidates in al-Jazira, the party was unable to develop as a legal political body after Zaza's election was nullified by the government.

The instability of the KDPS was due at least in part to its internal politics. Since its inception, the party had been subjected to internal discord due to generational and ideological differences. Though it succeeded in bringing together the former members of the Khoybun and the Syrian

Communist Party (SCP), this union was not sufficient to neutralize the tensions between its left-wing former SCP members, young students, teachers, and manual laborers and its right-wing notables, religious leaders, and landowners. These differences were exacerbated by the divisions within the Kurdistan Democratic Party of Iraq that separated the partisans of the "progressive" approach of Jalal Talabani and the party's "conservative" followers led by Mustafa Barzani. The internal divisiveness within the KDP also had repercussions for the KDPS, which was divided into three camps: one pro-Barzani, and two contesting parties split between the left ('Uthman Sabri and Muhammad Nayo) and the right ('Abd al-Hamid Hajj Darwish). Even though he was not a leftist, Darwish eventually joined the Marxist camp of his schoolmate Talabani in 1965.

Five years later, Mustafa Barzani attempted to reunify the KDPS by inviting all of the factions to Iraqi Kurdistan. He was unsuccessful in reuniting the contesting factions under his party's banner, however, and a new party was created by Daham Miro, a landowner. Though the new party succeeded in uniting the conservative party members, the "young wolves," led by Nayo and Darwish, were not reintegrated into the KDPS, known henceforth as "the Party" (or "al-Parti"). In fact, the majority of Kurdish parties professed Marxist and anti-imperialist ideologies, following the example of political parties of non-Kurdish regions, and demanded a degree of autonomy and legal rights from the Arab majority. In the face of pointless ideological disputes, many of which were driven by personal differences, many young Kurds left the parties, which were henceforth left in a state of political lethargy.[10]

There is not space here to give a detailed account of the extreme fragmentation of the Kurdish political arena.[11] My main argument is that, divided by personal and ideological quarrels, lacking in human, material, and symbolic resources, and plagued by an (at best) ambiguous relationship with the government, the Kurdish parties in Syria lacked a clear political project ambitious enough to attract the Kurds and inspire them to proclaim their Kurdish identity and their attachment to a nationalist ideal. Drawing a comparison with the evolution of the Kurdistan Workers' Party (PKK) in Syria during al-Asad's presidency based on an analysis of opportunity structures, resource mobilization, and cultural framing might further clarify this issue.[12]

Filling the Gap: The "Success" Story of the PKK

In the 1980s and 1990s, the PKK was the only organization capable of developing into a truly popular party in Syria, and that had the regime's authority to do so. Unlike other Kurdish parties, the PKK could benefit from a favorable political context that facilitated its expansion in Syria. To a large extent, its success can be explained by the complicity of Damascus in its recruitment and propaganda activities. There are, of course, additional reasons behind the engagement of thousands of Kurds in this guerrilla movement.

First of all, the slogan of a united and independent Kurdistan aroused great sympathy across all social classes in the Syrian Kurdish community in the 1980s. As in Turkey, many Syrian Kurds, whether allied with or opposed to the PKK, recognized that the PKK's discourse of the "new Kurd" helped to restore and even reinvent a Kurdish identity on equal footing with Arab identity. The armed struggle led by the PKK also aroused sympathy because it increased the odds of real political achievements, in contrast to the clandestine activities of other Syrian Kurdish parties, which rarely bore fruit. The repressive practices of the Turkish army in Turkish Kurdistan also generated sympathy for the PKK cause.

Second, the role played by Abdullah Öcalan, the charismatic leader of the PKK, should not be underestimated.[13] As he became the embodiment of a political myth, engaging in the PKK's guerrilla movement increasingly meant engaging in Öcalan's army. Following internal purges and the establishment of a rigid hierarchy within the PKK, Öcalan, both loved and feared by his supporters, came to be perceived as an incarnation of Kurdishness.[14]

In addition, in some regions, such as Kurd-Dagh and Jarablus, the PKK filled a vacuum left by Kurdish organizations based mainly in al-Jazira. Well organized and supported by the Syrian government, PKK officials created a highly effective network, which made it possible for them to recruit men for their armed contingent and to accumulate significant financial resources from Kurdish-owned businesses.

Finally, a number of young men from poor border-town areas such as Darbasiyya and Kobane ('Ayn al-'Arab) may have seen military engagement in the PKK as a potential means of economic and social advancement. On the one hand, the complicity of the Syrian authorities with the PKK allowed organized gangs trained by the party to control the illegal traffic in drugs and weapons across the border. On the other hand, their access to weapons and the very fact of belonging to such a gang allowed some young Kurds to emerge as powerful local players, set apart from the older generation in their communities and families. In other words, military engagement offered Kurdish youths an opportunity to challenge the Kurdish social order and to renegotiate their own place within it. On another level, the PKK started promoting gender equality among the Kurdish population in Syria and sought to undermine the tribal and religious allegiances that formed the basis of the traditional Kurdish political elite.

However, the engagement of young Syrian Kurds in the ranks of the PKK and their disengagement from traditional parties did not lead to a distinctive youth agenda separate from the general "nationalist agenda." Their expectations therefore continued to be "sacrificed" for the sake of the nation.

The Qamishli Revolt of 2004

Most media coverage reported that on March 12, 2004, insults between the fans of two football teams, namely the local team of Qamishli and that of Dayr al-Zur, escalated into a riot. The governor of Hasaka ordered the security forces to open fire; the shooting resulted in six dead, all Kurds. This sparked further rioting throughout Qamishli, where youngsters burned grain warehouses and destroyed scores of public buses. New repressive measures sparked Kurdish unrest in all Kurdish enclaves, as well as in Damascus and Aleppo.

The same evening, Kurdish students from the University of Damascus attempted to approach the former United Nations office in a diplomatic quarter of the Syrian capital to protest against the inaction of the United Nations.[15] Later that night, some Kurdish parties—including the Yekîtî Kurd and the PYD (Democratic Union Party, founded in 2003 to replace the PKK)—decided to assemble a protest group by means of placards and portable phones and hold a rally against the actions of the security forces, building on the funeral services for the victims of the clashes.

The next day, Kurdish expectations of a large turnout were greatly surpassed. Thousands of people followed the funeral procession to the cemetery of Qudur Beg, the traditional Kurdish quarter of Qamishli. Security forces, supported by armed militias from Arab tribes, countered this demonstration by firing into the crowd, triggering violent attacks against public buildings and the railroad station, which culminated in the destruction of several statues of Hafiz al-Asad. Rumors of a real massacre quickly circulated, so that thousands of people took to the streets in other Kurdish towns and even in Arab cities with a strong concentration of Kurds, like Hama, Raqqa, Aleppo, and Damascus.

The Qamishli revolt (*serhildan* or *intifada*) signified the beginning of a new era for the Kurds of Syria in a number of ways. First, all players on the Kurdish cultural and political scene immediately abandoned any attempt to conceal the conflict between them and the Syrian government. Both in northern Syria and in Damascus and Aleppo, thousands of Kurds—especially young people—continued to openly defy the Ba'thist regime by mobilizing and initiating collective actions such as marches, demonstrations, commemorations, and cultural festivals.

Furthermore, the Kurdish parties had been courted by other Syrian opposition groups ever since 2004. Abroad, the National Salvation Front (NSF), which was established in early 2006, and the Reform Party of Syria, under the leadership of Farid Ghadri and based in the United States, were about to offer a "democratic" solution to the Kurdish problem in Syria. Within the country, intellectuals, human rights activists, and the secular opposition had already established stable connections with Kurdish organizations. The Syrian regime also issued well-intentioned declarations with respect to the Kurds. And finally, for the first time in history, political parties and population groups from other Kurdish regions expressed their solidarity with the Syrian Kurds by means of public declarations and demonstrations in Diyarbakır (Turkey), Erbil, and Sulaymaniyya (Iraq).

While the identity aspects of the March 2004 mobilization and the irrational dimension of the violence should not be underrated, other factors, socioeconomic ones in particular, facilitated a better understanding of the occurrences at Qamishli.[16] It is true that today the Druze, Isma'ili, and Kurds are still situated at the political, economic, and geographic periphery, with weak representation in government, a fact that is particularly noticeable in upper al-Jazira. These peripheral groups are more likely to use their ethnic or religious identity as a "political resource."[17] Or, to put it differently, although the demands of the Kurdish minority are not limited to economic issues, the inability to satisfy such demands may further radicalize their nationalist agenda.[18]

Certain factors give added weight to this perspective. The rapid urbanization of towns like Qamishli and the migration of Kurdish peasants toward Arab cities like Damascus or Aleppo introduced a new dynamic, namely the marginalization of certain social classes of urban Kurds. In Qamishli, while the traditional Christian and Arab quarters have greatly developed over the last few years, with paved roads, electricity, street lights, and refuse collection, the Kurdish suburbs still resemble large third-world villages suffering from a lack of sewers, potable water, and electricity. In Aleppo, industry had drawn thousands of unskilled Kurdish immigrants from the countryside. These Kurdish immigrants relocated mainly in the working-class neighborhoods of Ashrafiyya, Shaykh Maqsud, and Sh'ar. In Damascus, the Kurdish immigrants, like the thousands of Syrians who had come from all over the country, crowded together in poor neighborhoods, officially called "informal and spontaneous residential zones."

Although the fragility of the Syrian economy affected the entire population of the country, al-Jazira was also affected by an "Arab Belt" policy (i.e., the confiscation of land), by the census of 1962 and its social consequences, by the state's chronic lack of investment, by the mechanization of agriculture (accelerating rural exodus), and by a major drought between 1995 and 1999 that further impoverished thousands of families dependent on the cotton harvest. A dramatic population growth added to the economic strain, as it was far too rapid to be sustainable. The Kurdish population experienced the highest demographic growth in Syria. The 2006 census came to 1 to 1.5 million people, indicating that the population had increased sixfold in half a century, so that the Kurds were now the second-largest minority group, after the Alawites.[19]

In fact, some of the people in the working-class neighborhoods attributed the participation of young Kurds from Damascus in the violence of March 2004 to poverty, coupled with the repression to which the Kurds were subjected.[20] The high level of popular participation in the riots in Qamishli was confirmed by several witnesses.[21]

The Prominent Role of the Youth in the March 2004 Unrests

Their claims notwithstanding, the Kurdish political parties did not play a significant role at the beginning of the uprising. Instead, the revolt sparked as the Kurdish youth took to the streets, storming official buildings and destroying state symbols. Most of the political parties did their best to calm down the demonstrators in the hope that restoring order in the Kurdish enclaves would make it possible for them to obtain at least some concessions from the Syrian government.[22] Reaffirming their loyalty to President Bashar al-Asad, the Kurdish parties—with the exception of Yekîtî Kurd and the PYD/PKK—decided to suspend the festivities of Newroz (the Kurdish National Day, March 21). In return, al-Asad declared amnesty for 312 detainees.

Elsewhere I have argued that a parallel could be established between the aftermath of the Islamic protest following the massacre in Hama in 1982 and the new political equilibrium that followed the Qamishli revolt, namely a new accommodation between the regime and the Kurdish movement in Syria.[23] Aware of the power of the Kurdish movement, the Syrian regime might take a more flexible approach to the public expression of Kurdish identity (language, music, cultural festivals, publications), while the Kurdish movement might at least temporarily abandon its goal of overturning the government of Bashar al-Asad.

This accommodation seemed apparent after the repression of the March 2004 upheavals. The Syrian authorities decreed that the "illegal" Kurdish parties were to cease all political activities and transform themselves into "legal" cultural associations. In addition, at the time of the tenth Regional Congress of the Baʿth Party (June 6–9, 2005) Minister Buthayna Shaʿban made a rare Syrian public statement, proclaiming that "ethnic diversity is a national wealth that should be maintained," though the recognition of diversity should take place under the "umbrella of national interest," which would evidently remain defined solely by the regime.[24]

Yet the accommodation between the regime and the Kurdish movement did not lead to an end of the conflict. The mostly short-term arrests of Kurdish leaders continued, as did the repression of gatherings organized by the PYD (notably in Aleppo) and by the Yekîtî. Furthermore, by 2006 violence between young demonstrators and security forces had become routine during the Newroz festivals and other gatherings.[25]

Kurdish mobilization between 2004 and 2006 created new dynamics in the movement, including the emergence of new actors, particularly women and young people, thereby creating a new brand of public sympathy for the Kurdish parties. However, the decline of collective action, the stabilization of the regime in the international arena before the violent uprising of 2011, and the lengthy process of political unification in the Kurdish movement induced a degree of lassitude within the movement. This social fatigue manifested itself in less public involvement, more criticism directed at the Kurdish parties, more focus on personal development (professional and economic), and more migration toward large Arab cities.

2011—Toward a Generational Rupture?

When the "Syrian revolution" erupted in March 2011, all eyes turned to the Kurds. Would they join the protest movement initiated in the besieged city of Darʿa, or would they maintain the fragile political balance established after 2005? As a matter of fact, the Kurdish areas remained comparatively calm until October 2011, since most of the Kurdish political parties were reluctant to become actively involved in the "Syrian revolution."

There are several complementary explanations as well for the Kurdish response to the Syrian revolution. Some are linked to the present political context. First and foremost, the regime has met two of the main demands put forward by the Kurdish political parties. Given the dangerous context for the Syrian regime, Damascus issued a decree on April 7, 2011, granting Syrian citizenship to tens of thousands of Kurds who, according to the special census of 1962, had been deprived of citizenship for nearly fifty years. At the same time, Decree 49 was repealed on March 26, 2011.[26] However, these concessions were not the result of successful negotiations by the Kurdish parties, but rather seemed to have been granted in order to prevent, or at least minimize, Kurdish participation in the Syrian revolution.

Consequently, the Kurdish parties were buying time to see whether they could obtain more concessions from the regime. One should not forget that the Kurdish leaders, as leaders and not solely as individuals, were invited for the first time by the Syrian government in June 2011 to negotiate more concessions. Yet the government's invitation was eventually declined, mostly due to social pressure (e.g., demonstrations by and meetings with Kurdish youth).

Other more complex factors kept the Kurdish political parties away from protest movements. One factor was that Kurdish parties had not yet made up their minds about the final goals of the struggle. Nearly ten months after anti-government protests started, Syrian Kurdish parties and their leaders still remained divided over whether to participate in the demonstrations and in the broad-based coalition of opposition forces known as the Syrian National Council, established in Istanbul on October 2, 2011.[27] And, more importantly, they still had to agree about essential issues: Did Kurdish parties and leaders want the downfall of the regime? Did they want to implement a regional autonomy in Northern Syria? Or did they want to ask solely for cultural rights?

The existence of seventeen political parties—half of them not really meaningful in terms of numbers and political impact—and the lack of a common and clear agenda paralyzed Kurdish activism until July 2012. This was the main reason why ten Kurdish political parties formed a coalition, the Kurdish National Council, in October 2011, allegedly to support the removal of the regime and the establishment of federalism for Syrian Kurds. Not all parties joined the council. The PYD, arguably one of the few Kurdish mass parties in Syria, did not join but instead demanded that the council oppose any foreign intervention in the country, a condition that clearly targeted Turkey. In the view of the PYD, foreign intervention in Syria would open the door to Turkey, which would take advantage of the situation to eradicate the PKK militants in Syria and establish a puppet Syrian government led by the Muslim Brotherhood.[28]

Another factor at work is that, unlike in most Middle Eastern countries (Palestine is probably the other exception), the Kurdish national question has not yet been solved. Therefore, the "national issue," central to the Kurdish political parties and large sectors of Kurdish society, has persisted. Within the context of a yet incomplete "national" normalization, identity politics have remained prevalent in the Kurdish political field, whereas socioeconomic issues have largely been neglected by the Kurdish parties.

Nevertheless, as mentioned earlier, the Syrian Kurdish parties could hardly meet the expectations or even channel the uncertainty of the politicized and young Kurds, who refused to end a struggle that had finally erupted with the Qamishli revolt. After Qamishli, young activists established their own "cultural centers," with a view to putting forward their own political agenda. In that sense, the 2011 crisis provided the opportunity that dissatisfied youth had been waiting for. From the very beginning, some groups of Kurdish youth in Syria were active in protests against the regime, not only in al-Jazira, but also in Damascus and Aleppo, having received but little backing from the Kurdish political parties. Later on, such developments were publicly acknowledged by Kurdish representatives such as Abdulbasit Hamo, who told al-Jazeera television that "the Kurdish youth organizations and committees are the real Kurdish revolutionaries on the ground. They have been organizing anti-Asad demonstrations since March 2011 and they are the reason behind the unification of the Kurdish political movement in Syria." He added, "We have to learn from those young activists the actual meaning of pro-liberation revolution against suppression and persecution. We have to follow them, in order to be able to represent them."[29]

In Qamishli alone, dozens of Kurdish youth groups were established, among them the Revolutionary Youth, the Jizre Civil Society, the Kurdish Youth, and the Sawa Youth Coalition.[30] As mentioned previously, these groups prevented the leaders of the Kurdish parties from accepting an invitation to an official meeting with Bashar al-Asad and the Syrian government in June 2011. More importantly, three Kurdish parties eventually decided to back the youth movements and participate in the demonstrations. Among them were the Freedom Party (Azadî), the Kurdish Union Party (Yekîtî Kurd), and the Future Movement, of which Mash'al Tammo (who was assassinated on October 8) was the leader. In general, the youth committees were keen to cooperate with the Local Coordination Committees of Syria. In other words, increasing numbers of youngsters were seeking a new beginning within a new framework: a democratic Syria free of sectarian and ethnic strife; a Syria with more job opportunities and a higher living standard.

Another sign of this widening gap between the youth and the political parties became apparent in the last months of 2011. In mid-September the "Army of the Nations," a Kurdish armed group, went public on the Internet, stating its intent to confront the Syrian regime. The founders claimed they had met with a group of military experts and influential Kurdish figures in Qamishli a few weeks previously. Two days after the killing of Mash'al Tammo in October, a video was posted on YouTube by Kurdish men in military uniforms, with flags and maps of Kurdistan in the background, who claimed to be the founders of the Lions of the Kurdish Homeland.[31] They pledged to use arms to protect the Kurds of Syria and encouraged Kurdish soldiers in the Syrian army to defect.

By early 2012, most Kurdish parties were still trying to prevent youths from using force against the regime out of concern that "forming these kinds of groups may bring killings and looting to the Kurdish areas of Syria."[32] Particularly telling was the attitude of the PYD/PKK in Syria. Still influential among the Kurdish youth in 'Afrin, the party decided not to participate in mass demonstrations and seemed to have sealed an alliance with the Syrian government, although this development was denied by its chairman, Salih Muslim Muhammad.[33] The reasons for the alliance with the government, however, are self-evident. PKK activists were under pressure in Iraqi Kurdistan and Turkey,[34] and the party needed a safe haven where militants could find shelter. Ultimately, the PKK hoped that, should the regime not fall, their loyalty would bring about political hegemony in the Kurdish areas.

This chapter takes the view that growing numbers of Kurdish youngsters felt disconnected from the traditional parties, either because they wished to establish bridges with their Syrian counterparts, they sought a more radical solution to the Kurdish issue in Syria (that is, local autonomy), or they strove for both cooperation and autonomy. Consequently, the danger of a generational rupture affected all parties, without exception. In addition, the largest and best-educated generation of Syrian Kurds in history sought new avenues that did not necessarily include a dialogue with the political parties. In that sense, it was suggested that three factors—the PKK's successful buildup of the party in the 1980s and 1990s, the Qamishli revolt of 2004, and the 2011 "Syrian revolution"—eventually distanced Kurdish youth from the traditional political field. The already fragile Kurdish parties thus found themselves at a crossroads where their survival might depend on their willingness to listen to the demands and aspirations of the younger generation.

PART V

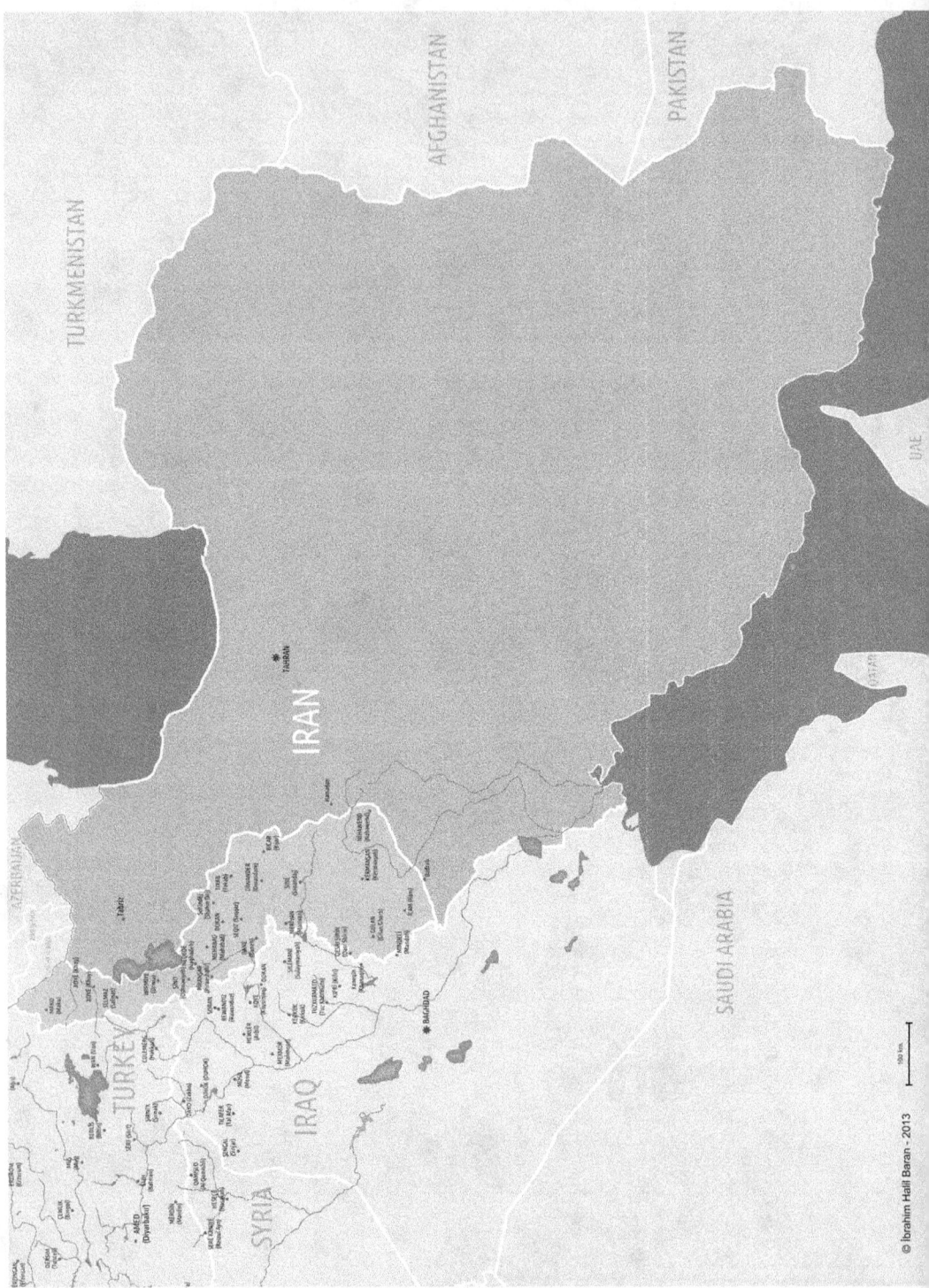

The Kurds in Iran: The Quest for Identity

NADER ENTESSAR

The purpose of this chapter is to examine the place of the Kurds in Iran's sociopolitical mosaic. Are Kurds in a multicultural state like Iran an ethnic group (*qowm*) or a nation (*mellat*)? If we assume that a nation is an ethnic group that seeks political autonomy or independence from the larger entity in which it resides, then how would we categorize the Iranian Kurds? How do they view themselves within the broader context of Iranian nationality and state? What does the oft-repeated term "self-determination" mean when used by politically active Kurdish groups in the country? These are questions that do not lend themselves to easy answers, but they are nevertheless important in terms of understanding Kurdish issues in contemporary Iran. What makes the matter even more problematic is that unlike in the Ottoman Empire, in which the terms *qowm* and *mellat* had distinct meanings, Iranians have for the most part used these terms interchangeably.

The Iranian Kurds, who, like most other Iranian nationalities, are of Indo-European origin, account for roughly six to seven million of Iran's population of seventy-four million. Kurds in Iran have become urbanized at a rapid rate. However, tribal affiliations and tribal organizations have remained strong throughout the process of urbanization. The Kurdish language, which belongs to the Iranic branch of the Indo-European family of languages, is more akin to Persian than to Arabic or Turkish. Although there may not be a Kurdish lingua franca, one should not overemphasize the differences among various Kurdish vernaculars, as they are all related to each other. The main Kurdish dialect in Iran is Sorani, which is widely used in such major cities as Mahabad, Saqqez, Sanandaj, and Marivan. Kurds in Kermanshah use Kermanshahi, which is similar to Lori, an Iranian language spoken by the Lors, an ethnic group living primarily in the neighboring province of Loristan. The Kurds around Paveh and several other towns near the Iran-Iraq border use Hawrami (Gurani).

Three-fifths of the Kurds are Sunni Muslims. However, 1.5 million Iranian Kurds are Shiʿi Muslims, many of whom live in the major cities of Kermanshah and Hamadan, as well as in the Khorasan region. In addition, there are also Kurdish followers of the various Sufi orders and very small communities of Christian Kurds. At times, differences between Shiʿi and Sunni Muslims are exploited by the Iranian government to drive a wedge between the two communities. However, the policy of divide and rule has not been vigorously pursued in Kurdistan as Kurdish ethnonationalism has proved to be a more powerful force than any religious divide that may exist among the Iranian Kurds.

It is beyond the scope of this chapter to review the vast theoretical literature on ethnicity and nationalism.[1] Perhaps, as Hugh Seton-Watson has stated, "no 'scientific definition' of *nation* can be devised; yet the phenomenon has existed and exists."[2] Benedict Anderson has provided an intellectually challenging and interesting approach to the study of nationhood and nationalism. He defines a nation as an "imagined political community . . . Communities are to be distinguished not by their falsity-genuineness, but by the style in which they are imagined."[3] By implication, an ethnic group, like a nation, can be perceived as an imagined political community, irrespective of the strength of the actual primordialist identity or other types of identity that exist among the members of that ethnic community. That is, on the strength of subjective (i.e., imagined) feelings, an ethnic group can transform itself into a nation with rights of sovereignty and self-determination. It is this emotional attachment to an "imagined political community" that has in recent decades fueled an ethnic drive for self-determination throughout the world.

The development of Kurdish nationalism, or at least its politicized variety in Iran, must be seen within the broader context of Iran's journey toward modern, territorially based nationalism. The Russo-Persian War of 1804, which resulted in the loss of vast tracts of land in the Caucasus to czarist Russia, was a defining moment for the development of an Iranian nationalism that was based on a "myth of unity" among the country's constituent parts and groups.[4] Both Iranian officials and intellectuals began to develop a new concept of Iranian identity that moved away from its long-established cultural construct oriented on a land-based, territorially focused, and Persianized concept of nationhood. As Firoozeh Kashani-Sabet has noted, "[t]he Iranian homeland, though still formally the birthplace of Armenians, Kurds, and Baluchis, as well as Farsis and others, increasingly came to represent the *vatan* [country] of Shiʿi Persians through the persistent efforts of the state to extirpate competing cultures."[5] In the same vein, Mostafa Vaziri argues, à la Benedict Anderson, that the modern notion of Iranian nationhood has been an imaginary construct created by Iranian intellectuals and historians to glorify Iran's past and create a fictitious notion of territorial unity.[6] Vaziri, of course, does not deny the existence of a strong sense of Iranian identity and culture. What he contends is that nationalism based on the close identification of a nation with an all-powerful and centrally controlled state dominated by a single ethnic group is an "imagined" nationalism.

This new form of Iranian nationalism was further buttressed after Reza Khan's coronation as the first king of the new Pahlavi dynasty in 1926, as he sought to impose the central government's authority through a series of military ventures in various provinces. Thus, conflict between the increasingly Persian-dominated central government and the non-Persian ethnic groups in Iran intensified at all levels. This was particularly true in the country's Kurdish regions where tribal uprisings had bedeviled the central government's authority for several decades. For example, under the leadership of Ismaʿil Agha Simko, the chief of the Shikak tribe, much of Iranian Kurdistan had defied the authority of the central government in the early part of the twentieth century. Reza Khan's military victory over Simko was indeed a major undertaking that augured similar moves against other rebellions and the ultimate establishment of the central government's authority throughout the country.[7]

The most serious Kurdish challenge to the Iranian government's authority occurred in 1945 when the autonomous Republic of Mahabad was established. Although the Mahabad Republic collapsed after only one year, its ultimate meaning in Iran and elsewhere in the Middle East remains a subject of intense debate among the Kurds. Was Qazi Muhammad, the president of the Mahabad Republic, a Soviet puppet as his critics have claimed, a naïve nationalist, or a patriot whose main objective was to create an autonomous Kurdistan within a democratic and federal Iran? What was the extent of Soviet involvement in supporting the Mahabad Republic and its ill-fated contemporary entity in Iranian Azerbaijan? These and similar questions are important issues for historical research and debate. However, for our purposes, there is little doubt that the rise and fall of the Mahabad Republic was a watershed in politicizing Kurdish ethnic demands in Iran.[8]

The demise of the autonomous republics in Mahabad and Azerbaijan accelerated the process of reintegration of non-Persian ethnic groups into the emerging centralized power structure in Pahlavi Iran. For example, many of the Kurdish tribes that had joined forces with the Mahabad Republic returned to their tribal areas. In the words of General Hassan Arfa, chief of staff of the Iranian army between 1944 and 1946, the Kurds returned to their tribal homelands "not with the bitter and humiliated feelings of a vanquished nation which had lost its dearly won but short-lived independence, but only with the knowledge that this venture, like many others before, had not come off and that for the time being they had better sit quietly and show themselves good citizens."[9] Notwithstanding General Arfa's assessment, the Kurds accelerated their demands for cultural autonomy after the demise of the Mahabad Republic. As people with a common culture and historical experience as well as a distinctive language, the Iranian Kurds have long felt that without cultural autonomy, they cannot attain full citizenship rights in the country. In fact, attachment to the Kurdish language remains perhaps the most important manifestation of contemporary Kurdish identity.[10]

After the Mahabad Republic

After the downfall of the Mahabad Republic, the Iranian government outlawed the Kurdistan Democratic Party (KDP), which had led the revolt against central rule and whose members had been heavily involved in running the Mahabad government. The period immediately following the 1946 Kurdish withdrawal to the tribal areas was marked by nationalistic ferment throughout the country. The issue of nationalization of the Iranian oil industry, which had been championed by the nascent nationalist coalition, the National Front, and its leader, Mohammad Mossadegh, galvanized the entire country. Mossadegh's nationalistic platform, his liberal democratic ideals, and his desire to govern the country through free elections generated enthusiasm among the Iranian Kurds. When Mohammad Reza Shah was compelled, under heavy popular pressure, to appoint Mossadegh as prime minister, the Kurdistan Democratic Party (KDP) resurrected itself and began a campaign in various Kurdish cities and towns. Kurdish support for Mossadegh's government convinced the shah that the Kurds had to be contained at all costs. In a massive display of support for Mossadegh's crusade to force the shah to reign as a constitutional monarch as stipulated in Iran's monarchical constitution, Iranian Kurds voted overwhelmingly in a referendum on August 13, 1953, to limit the shah's power. According to the Kurdish leader Abdul Rahman Ghassemlou, in the city of Mahabad the shah received a meager two votes out of a total of five thousand cast.[11]

After the Anglo American–sponsored coup of August 1953 and Mossadegh's overthrow, the Kurds once again found themselves at the mercy of the shah's regime, and the Iranian army was once again placed in charge of Kurdistan. Although sporadic rebellions continued to occur throughout Kurdistan in the decades after the coup, no sustained Kurdish revolt occurred in Iran from 1953 until the onset of the Iranian revolution in 1978. The shah's success in containing Kurdish nationalism was partly due to the superior forces of the Iranian army and partly a result of his government's successful carrot-and-stick policy. For example, the shah managed to "pacify" Kurdistan through a selective policy of co-opting tribal leaders by offering them political and financial rewards. The powerful Jaf tribal chiefs are a good case in point. The shah's government identified traditional power holders in the tribe and gave them high-level positions in the local and national government apparatus. When he embarked upon his land reform program in the early 1960s, the shah left the large landholdings of the Jaf tribal leaders untouched. Salar Jaf was given a high-level position in the imperial palace bureaucracy, while his brother, Sardar Jaf, became an influential member of the Iranian Parliament.

A large number of Ardalan Kurds rose to prominence during the shah's reign, with many of them reaching the highest military ranks in the shah's armed forces. For example, one of the most loyal supporters of the shah, even after the overthrow of the Pahlavi monarchy, was General Azizollah Palizban, the Kurdish governor general of Kermanshah. Using his knowledge of the topography and geography of Kurdistan and his network of connections in the area, General Palizban remained a thorn in the side of the Islamic Republic, working from his base in Iraqi Kurdistan for many years. The shah sought to stifle overt manifestations of Kurdish ethnicity by enforcing Persian as the sole language not only in governmental communications but also in printed media and books. Although limited radio and television broadcasts in Kurdish were allowed, all primary and secondary teaching was in Persian. To ensure adherence to the shah's linguistic policies, the government sent many non-Kurds to staff educational institutions in the Kurdish regions of the country.

The shah's final policy posture toward the Kurds was precipitated by the Kurdish revolt in neighboring Iraq. The shah viewed the assumption of power by the radical nationalist Ba'th Party in Iraq as a threat to Iran's national security. Therefore, he decided to use the Kurdish revolt in Iraq as a counterforce to weaken the Ba'thi regime in Baghdad. Until 1966, the only significant outside help to the Kurdish guerrillas in Iraq, who were led by the veteran fighter Mulla Mustafa Barzani, had come from the KDP of Iran. However, after 1966, the shah soon recognized the potential for using direct aid to Barzani as a means to further influence and control the direction of the Kurdish national movement. The shah had correctly calculated that by helping Barzani, he could compel him to cease his aid to the Iranian Kurds and even to collaborate with the shah's government in restraining Kurdish activities inside Iran.[12]

As Iranian governmental aid to Barzani increased, so did the shah's influence over his movement's activities. This resulted in Barzani issuing a major policy statement in 1966 regarding the direction of the Kurdish movement in Iran. In his policy directive, Barzani called on Kurdish nationalists to cease their hostile activities against the shah's regime. To do otherwise, the memorandum warned, would result in the cutoff of Iranian support for the Kurdish guerrillas in Iraq and would lead to the certain defeat of the Kurdish uprising against the Ba'thi regime. Barzani further stated that those who refused to obey his directives would be considered enemies of the "Kurdish revolution."[13] Barzani had apparently concluded that his forces stood a better chance of success against the Iraqi government than the Kurds in Iran did against the shah's regime, and that all Kurds would have to sacrifice their own objectives for the more immediate cause of a Kurdish victory in Iraq.

In the final analysis, Barzani's policy of collaborating with the shah's regime proved disastrous for both his own political fortunes and the cause of Kurdish autonomy. Scores of Kurdish militants who had left Iran to join Barzani's forces in the mid-1960s returned home in the early 1970s, disillusioned with his strategy and objectives. The returning Iranian Kurdish fighters soon found themselves surrounded by the Iranian army and with their escape route blocked by Barzani's forces. Some key members of this group, such as Abdullah Moini and Sharif Zadeh, were killed fighting the Iranian army. Abdullah's older brother, Sulayman Moini, was arrested on Barzani's orders and later executed, along with a number of other Iranian Kurds. According to one estimate, some forty Iranian Kurdish militants were either killed by Barzani's forces or handed over to Iranian authorities to face certain death.[14] Barzani himself was victimized by the shah's policy of divide and rule when the shah and Saddam Husayn signed the Algiers Agreement on March 6, 1975, thus abruptly terminating Iran's aid to the Iraqi Kurds and inflicting a severe blow to the cause of Kurdish autonomy in Iraq. This brought to an end the long career of Mulla Mustafa Barzani as the most significant Kurdish leader of his time.[15]

Iran's Revolution and the Kurds: The First Phase

In general, the Kurds enthusiastically supported the Iranian revolution of 1978–1979, and a broad spectrum of the Kurdish population participated in the revolutionary process from the outset. However, the initial Kurdish euphoria over the demise of the Pahlavi monarchy soon gave way to the bitter realization that Kurdish demands for autonomy would go unheeded by the new Islamic government. After the establishment of the Islamic Republic of Iran, it became quite evident that Ayatollah Khomeini's objective of establishing a strong and centralized Islamic state would clash with the goals of autonomy-seeking Kurds. Despite Khomeini's refusal to recognize ethnic differences among Muslims, the Constitution of the Islamic Republic did recognize the existence of linguistic diversity among the Iranian people. In Article 15 of the constitution, Persian is recognized as the official language of the country. All official communications, as well as instructional and educational materials, were required to be in Persian. However, the use of local languages in the media and in the classroom was permitted so long as they were used in conjunction with Persian. (This understanding remains in place today.)[16] The only specific recognition given to the minorities in Iran's Islamic constitution was to non-Islamic religious minorities (namely Christians, Jews, and Zoroastrians), and not to Islamic minorities such as the Kurds. The Kurds were viewed as an integral part of the Islamic *umma*, or community, and hence were not to be treated differently from other Muslim groups in the country.

The Kurds, however, saw an unrivaled window of opportunity, created by the downfall of the monarchy, to push for autonomy and recognition of their cultural rights by the new government in Iran. Abdul Rahman Ghassemlou, who had become the secretary general of the KDP of Iran (KDPI) in 1973 while still living in exile, returned to Iran on the eve of the Iranian revolution after several years of exile in Europe and sought to transform what was then a dormant party into the principal Kurdish political organization in the country. On March 30–31, 1979, the Iranian government conducted a referendum asking the voters to choose whether to maintain the monarchical system or replace it with an Islamic republic. The KDPI, as well as many other secular groups in the country, boycotted the referendum because it only offered two choices to the voters. Given the general antipathy toward the shah's regime at the time and the degree of revolutionary euphoria, it was evident that the majority of voters would opt for an Islamic republic. Khomeini's exhortations for a massive turnout resulted in an overwhelming victory for the new regime, as 98.2

percent of those who participated in the referendum voted to replace the monarchy with an Islamic republic.[17] The Kurds had lost their first political battle with the revolutionary regime in Tehran.

The Kurds then shifted their focus to Iran's new constitution. The proposed constitution was unveiled by the provisional revolutionary government of Mehdi Bazargan, the prime minister, in June 1979. Although the draft contained democratic provisions to safeguard the rights of all Iranians, the Kurds felt that it did not address their autonomy demands adequately. The KDPI joined the many other nationalist and secularist groups in demanding that a constituent assembly consisting of no more than five hundred representatives be elected to debate and revise the draft constitution. Fearing the dilution of the Islamic elements of the draft constitution if a constituent assembly representing different constituencies and interests were to review the document, Ayatollah Khomeini ordered the establishment of a seventy-three-member Assembly of Experts to review the proposed constitution. Kurdish nationalists were not included in this body. Nevertheless, the Kurds continued to articulate their views on the shape of the new constitution in formal and informal gatherings. For example, Sheikh Ezzedin Husseini, the spiritual leader of the Sunni Kurds in Mahabad, argued that since Iran was a multinational state, its constitution must legally recognize the cultural, economic, and sociopolitical rights of all ethnic and religious groups in the country.

Furthermore, many Sunni religious leaders opposed the inclusion of Shi'ism as the official religion of the state in the new constitution. According to Ayatollah Montazeri, the head of the Assembly of Experts at the time of the drafting of the Islamic Republic's constitution, several members of the Assembly expressed conflicting opinions on this issue. The Sunni clerics, as well as some Shi'i members of the Assembly of Experts (e.g., Hassan Azodi) preferred Islam, rather than Shi'i Islam, to be listed in the new constitution as the official religion of the country.[18] Ahmad Moftizadeh, a Sunni Kurdish cleric sympathetic to the Islamic Republic, was also asked to express his views on this topic to the members of the Assembly of Experts. In the final analysis, those favoring the inclusion of Shi'i Islam as the official state religion prevailed. They argued that the overwhelming majority of Iranians are Shi'i Muslims, and that even the monarchical constitution had recognized Shi'i Islam as the official state religion. It would be unthinkable for the Islamic Republic to do less than what the shah had done in this respect. Moreover, they reasoned, the Sunnis would still be able to follow their religious practices, as well as the rulings of their own judges in religious courts.[19] The Kurdish leaders were concerned that the clerical leadership in Tehran would seek to replace Kurdish leaders, both secular and religious, with Shi'i personalities or Sunnis loyal to the Islamic Republic. As evidenced by subsequent developments, the Kurdish fears in this regard were not without foundation.

Acrimonious debates about the draft constitution and Kurdish demands for autonomy conjured up memories of the Mahabad Republic. Furthermore, Ayatollah Khomeini and his supporters within the clergy feared that the foundation of their preferred system of government would be weakened if ethnic demands, especially secular ones, were accommodated in the revised constitution. To make matters worse, tension between the Islamic authorities and Kurds manifested itself in a series of armed clashes between the forces of the KDPI and the newly created Revolutionary Guards (*pasdaran-e enghelab*). To stem the tide of armed conflicts in Kurdistan, Sheikh Mohammad Sadegh Sadeghi Guivi (better known as Sadegh Khalkhali) was dispatched to the region to try to punish those who had taken up arms against the new regime in Tehran. As Khalkhali had been the first judge of the revolutionary courts to condemn scores of high-level officials of the Pahlavi regime to death, his arrival in Kurdistan bode ill for a peaceful resolution of the conflict.

In a series of trials that lacked even the most basic elements of fairness, Khalkhali condemned a large number of Kurdish nationalists to death. He blamed the prime minister, Bazargan, who in the past had tried unsuccessfully to curb Khalkhali's freewheeling dispensation of justice, for the deterioration of conditions in Kurdistan. In particular, Khalkhali accused Bazargan of currying favor with Ghassemlou and other high officials of the KDPI. As Khalkhali put it, by placing "known communists" in key positions in Kurdistan, Bazargan was responsible for the martyrdom of revolutionary guards in the region, and by undermining the authority of the revolutionary courts he "weakened their steadfastness."[20] Continuous armed clashes between the Kurds and the Iranian military and Revolutionary Guards led, inter alia, to the banning of the KDPI at the end of autumn 1979, followed by Ayatollah Khomeini's labeling of Ghassemlou as "one who spreads corruption on earth (*mofsid-e fil arz*, Qur'an 5:64). However, shortly before the complete breakdown of negotiations between the Kurds and the representatives of the Iranian government, Khomeini issued a conciliatory message addressed to the people of Kurdistan. In his message, Khomeini for the first time publicly acknowledged the legitimate grievances of the Kurds. He promised to continue negotiations with religious and nationalist Kurdish leaders until peace was restored in the area. Khomeini further stated that many people in Iran had suffered under the monarchy and the revolutionary government, and advised patience and forbearance. In the last paragraph of the letter, he besought the Kurds to join him in the name of God and Islam to "save our country and to direct our energies against the real enemies of the country, led by the United States."[21] The content and tone of Khomeini's message to the Kurds was profoundly different from his previous message three months earlier, in which he had issued an ultimatum for the Kurds to lay down their arms. It was apparent that Khomeini had feared continuous armed clashes in Kurdistan would rebound to the detriment of the Islamic Republic and might even broaden the conflict, with unforeseen consequences for the integrity of the country.

The banning of the KDPI and damning of its leaders by the Islamic Republic did not put an end to the Kurdish leadership's search for dialogue with the Iranian government. However, Ghassemlou's search for moderate figures within the ruling circles in Tehran caused open dissension within the KDPI. Some on the left in the KDPI accused Ghassemlou and the "Kurdish bourgeoisie" of betraying the Kurdish cause by abandoning the party's ideals in favor of a policy of national conciliation with the "Iranian bourgeoisie" in the Islamic government.[22] This led to a major schism within the KDPI. The ensuing power struggle among the different political factions was carried over into the KDPI's Eighth Congress in 1988, resulting in the expulsion of fifteen prominent leftist members of the party's executive committee. The left then coalesced around the expelled members and established a new movement, the Kurdistan Democratic Party of Iran–Revolutionary Leadership.[23] However, this breakaway party never developed into a broad-based popular organization and eventually withered away as a functioning entity.

The KDPI was dealt a major blow when Ghassemlou was assassinated on July 13, 1989, while meeting with representatives of the Iranian government in a Vienna apartment. Aside from Ghassemlou, Abdullah Ghaderi-Azar, the KDPI's chief representative in Europe, and Fazel Rasul, a member of the Iraqi Patriotic Union of Kurdistan, were also assassinated because, according to both the KDPI and independent sources, they were connected with circles in the Iranian power structure. After Ghassemlou's assassination, the KDPI appointed Sadegh Sharafkandi as the KDPI's new secretary general. In an eerily similar situation to that of Ghassemlou's assassination, Sharafkandi was gunned down in the Mykonos restaurant in Berlin in 1992, along with the European and German representatives of the KDPI and four other Iranian dissident leaders. The Mykonos incident and the subsequent verdict handed down by a German court on April 10, 1997, further strained Kurdish-Iranian relations. The significance of the Mykonos verdict was that a foreign court had, for the first time, implicated the highest echelons of the Iranian government, including the Supreme Guide Ayatollah Ali Khamenei and then-president Ali Akbar Hashemi Rafsanjani, in ordering the killing of the KDPI leader and other dissidents.[24] The KDPI swiftly appointed Mostafa Hejri to replace Sharafkandi. In my judgment, the KDPI has yet to fully recover from the loss of Ghassemlou. He was an adept politician with extensive contacts within a large cross section of Iranian society. Moreover, because of his long residence in Europe, Ghassemlou had established an extended political network in Europe. There is no doubt that he was the most visible political leader, with a wide appeal among the Iranian Kurdish population after the downfall of the Mahabad Republic.

The misfortunes of the KDPI, both before and after Ghassemlou's assassination, made it possible for another Kurdish movement, the Revolutionary Organization of the Kurdish Toilers of Iran (Komala), to emerge as the main contender for leading Kurdish aspirations, especially among urbanized youth. As a Marxist-Leninist movement, the Komala was as critical of the "Kurdish bourgeoisie" (i.e., the KDPI) as it was of the Islamic Republic. It was able to expand its appeal by securing the support of Sheikh Ezzedin Husseini, the popular Sunni religious leader of Mahabad. Unlike the KDPI, the Komala understood the success of the Kurdish struggle in the broader context of a Marxist-Leninist revolution throughout Iran.[25] In other words, the Komala viewed itself as a movement that transcended the ethnic boundaries in the country. As has been the case before with similar ideologically rigid and doctrinaire movements, a faction within the leadership broke away from the Komala and created the Workers' Communist Party of Iran (Hezb-e Kommunist-e Kargari-e Iran). Most of the remaining members of the Komala were eventually reconciled with the KDPI. Today the Komala is but a shell of its former self, and it is unclear whether it still has an effective organization in Iranian Kurdistan. The Workers' Communist Party has remained active outside Iran, with branches in many Western countries, including the United States. Although the party operates an active publication business and is visible in anti-Islamic demonstrations in the West, it is doubtful whether it still has any firm base inside Iranian Kurdistan. In short, despite its organizational setbacks and the personal tragedies suffered by its members, the KDPI still remains the most recognizable and best-organized political movement among the Iranian Kurds.

The Kurds under Islamic Reformism: Phase Two

The election of Mohammad Khatami as Iran's president in May 1997 and the defeat of conservative forces in the February 2000 parliamentary elections generated widespread expectations of political change in Iran. Khatami, a mid-ranking reformist cleric, received some 70 percent of the popular vote, giving him a mandate to reform Iran's political system and allow the emergence of a genuinely pluralistic political culture in the country. As Khatami had stated, "we cannot expect any positive transformations anywhere [in Iran] unless the yearning for freedom is fulfilled. That is the freedom to think and the security to express new thinking."[26] Nevertheless, from the beginning of his presidency he emphasized the notion of inclusiveness, or "Iran for all Iranians" as he called it, and the importance of the rule of law in nurturing and enhancing the foundation of Iran's political system.[27] The Kurds, like many other Iranian citizens, welcomed Khatami's election. The reform movement (the Second of Khordad Movement), which brought Khatami to power and provided him with political backing, proved to be weak. In addition to the constitutional limits imposed on the authority of the president, Khatami and his supporters were challenged in all arenas by their conservative opponents. When challenged, Khatami always conceded. The closing down of the reformist newspapers and organizations, as well as the jailing of supporters of political reform, went largely unchallenged, save in occasional speeches in which he denounced violations of the rule of law.

In Kurdistan the arrest of officials, some of whom identified with Khatami's agenda, intensified during Khatami's two-term presidency. City council elections were nullified by conservative forces, and the credentials of pro-reform or independent Kurdish politicians and candidates were routinely rejected when they sought to run for office in the provinces. In a crackdown on Kurdish officials, Abdullah Ramazanzadeh, the governor general of Kurdistan and a Khatami supporter, was summoned before the Special Court for Public Officials in April 2001 and charged with "dissemination of lies." Ramazanzadeh's "crime" was his objection to the nullification of the votes of two constituencies in the Kurdish cities of Baneh and Saqqez; thus he was accused of making libelous statements against the country's powerful Council of Guardians, which had ordered the nullification of those votes.[28]

Another significant stumbling block between Khatami and the Kurds was the presence of several individuals in the reform movement who had earlier participated in the suppression of Kurdish uprisings. Some Kurds believe that today's reformers were yesterday's "oppressors," and were hence not trustworthy. The case of Hamid Reza Jalaipour is illustrative of this point. In the 1980s, Jalaipour, who became a significant architect of the Second of Khordad reform movement and an editor of *Asr-e Aza-degan*, the now-defunct reformist Tehran daily, spent ten years fighting against Kurdish autonomy demands. As a commander of a *pasdaran* unit and later as the governor of Naqdeh and Mahabad and deputy governor general for political affairs in Kurdistan, Jalaipour was directly or indirectly responsible for some of the worst revolutionary excesses in that region. When asked if he had any remorse about ordering the execution of fifty-nine Kurdish nationalists, Jalaipour refused to offer an apology for his past actions, claiming that he could not be held responsible for actions undertaken when he was a revolutionary in his twenties or that were necessary during wartime and in the interest of saving the nascent Islamic Republic.[29] However, when he was invited to participate in the Berlin Conference organized by the Heinrich Böll Foundation in 2000 to initiate a dialogue between the representatives of the reform movement in Iran and the West, Jalaipour stated that he had been misquoted by the correspondent of *Asr-e Azadegan*, who was a Kurd himself.[30] It is, of course, unfair to single out an individual for actions undertaken under wartime conditions, but the incident highlights the difficulty the reformists have encountered in articulating a coherent nationality policy in Iran.

Iran's ninth presidential election in 2005, which ultimately resulted in the nomination of Mahmoud Ahmadinejad as the country's president, was marked by an open discussion of "nationality issues" by some of the candidates. This was the first time since the establishment of the Islamic Republic that ethnic and nationality issues were recognized as part of a public policy debate, and that several candidates openly sought the votes of Iranian minorities. Mostafa Moin, the main candidate of the reformist camp, made a special effort to woo voters from non-Persian nationalities, turning Iran's multinational character into an important part of his platform. Moin criticized both those who ignored the country's multinational nature and those who sought to divide the country on ethnic, religious, and linguistic grounds. In this vein, Moin promised complete equality for all Iranian citizens, a right that is supposed to be guaranteed under the Iranian constitution. Recognizing discrimination as potentially destabilizing, Moin stated that his administration would include representatives of all nationalities.[31] Echoing Khatami's campaign slogan, Moin also made "Iran for all Iranians" the centerpiece of his presidential campaign. In addition to Moin, several reformist personalities and writers opined that democracy would not take root in Iran unless the rights of all Iranian nationalities were recognized. Furthermore, many reformists welcomed the Kurdish leader Jalal Talabani's election as president of Iraq and viewed his accession to power as a natural progression of the recognition of all nationality rights in the region.[32]

The reformist candidates, including Moin, were defeated in the first round of presidential balloting. Unlike the candidates of the reform bloc, Ahmadinejad, the winner of the presidential race, campaigned on the platform of socioeconomic justice. His main cause was the country's lower classes, whose economic situation had deteriorated under the administration of the outgoing reformist Khatami. Although Ahmadinejad did not make the issue of nationality rights part of his campaign, he was certainly not an unknown figure among the Kurds. In the early years of the postrevolutionary era, he was assigned to the Ramazan base of the Revolutionary Guards, with responsibility for military operations in western Iran, including the Kurdish regions of the country. Ahmadinejad later served in other capacities in western Iran, including a stint as principal adviser to the governor general of the province of Kurdistan.[33]

Given the negative perception of the activities of the Revolutionary Guards in Kurdistan, it was not surprising that the Iranian Kurds participated only minimally in the country's presidential election of 2005. Between the two finalists in the second round of the elections, Ahmadinejad received 17,248,782 votes, while his opponent Ali Akbar Hashemi Rafsanjani garnered 10,460,701 votes.[34] According to figures released by Iran's Ministry of Interior, 62.66 percent of eligible voters participated in the election, with the highest turnout (80.43 percent) in Ilam Province and the lowest rate of participation (37.37 percent) in the province of Kurdistan. West Azerbaijan, which includes the cities of Mahabad and Uromiyah with their large Kurdish populations, recorded the second-lowest participation rate (44.02 percent).[35] By and large, one could say that the Iranian Kurds expressed their dissatisfaction by boycotting the 2005 presidential elections in large numbers.

Moreover, the military confrontation between the Kurds and the Iranian government forces has intensified since 2005. For example, Iranian forces and the guerrillas of the newly formed Free Life Party of Kurdistan (PJAK), an offshoot of Turkey's Kurdistan Workers' Party (PKK), were involved in low-level military confrontations inside Iranian Kurdistan— with mounting casualties on both sides.[36] The involvement of the PJAK and PKK in Kurdish affairs in Iran has added an unpredictable twist to the war of attrition in Iranian Kurdistan. For example, the Komala, which intensified its own low-level warfare inside Iranian Kurdistan,[37] accused the PJAK of undermining the legitimate struggle of the Iranian Kurds with its adventurist tactics.[38]

The most significant development in Iranian Kurdistan in the post-Khatami era was the grassroots uprising in several Kurdish cities throughout the country. The spark that ignited the latest Kurdish challenge to the Iranian government was generated by the July 11, 2005, shooting of Shavaneh Qaderi, a young Kurdish activist from Mahabad. Subsequently, a number of websites posted photographs purporting to show Qaderi's mutilated body, which sparked street demonstrations not only in Mahabad but also in several other Kurdish cities, including Baneh, Bukan, Sanandaj, and Saqqez.[39] In addition, Kurdish groups, including university students in Tehran, issued statements supporting the Mahabad demonstrators and condemning the actions of the Iranian security forces, especially the units of the Revolutionary Guards, in suppressing Kurdish demonstrations.[40] The conditions were further exacerbated by the crackdown on two popular Kurdish-language weeklies, *Ashti* and *Asou*, and the arrest of Roya Tolooi, editor of the monthly *Rasan* and a well-known activist in Iranian and Kurdish women's rights groups.[41] In mid-2008 a number of Kurdish nationalists, including Farzad Kamangar, Farhad Vakili, Ali Heydarian, Anwar Hossein Panahi, Adnan Hassanpour, and Hiwa Butimar, were charged with aiding and abetting terrorism and endangering the security of the Islamic Republic. As a consequence, they received death sentences that were challenged by several Iranian and international human rights organizations. The swiftness of the executions reflected the authorities' concerns that these death sentences might be overturned or commuted to life imprisonment.[42]

Nevertheless, a number of reformist Kurdish groups and civil society organizations have emerged to push for the recognition of Kurdish rights, broadly stated as autonomy for Kurdistan and democracy for Iran within the confines of the existing Iranian sociopolitical system. This trend is reflected in the myriad magazines and newspapers published by the Iranian Kurdish intelligentsia. For example, the weekly *Sirwan* has published sophisticated analytical articles that are a far cry from the bombastic propaganda one finds in almost all of the Kurdish exile publications. Likewise, the biweekly *Hawar* has covered internal developments in Kurdistan in the objective and highly informative manner one does not usually find when reading Iranian Kurdish publications in Europe and North America. Unfortunately, these publications have to fight continuously for their survival. Furthermore, the number of domestically operated Kurdish websites in Iran has declined since 2005. Asoukurd.com, for instance, the best online resource for developments in Iranian Kurdistan, is no longer operational, and the popular political and cultural biweekly *Rojhalat*, which struggled to publish on a regular basis, was ultimately closed down by the government authorities in early January 2009. Notwithstanding the persistence of political and economic hardships in the Kurdish regions, President Ahmadinejad used his rhetorical populism to promise reforms and development planning in Kurdistan. For example, in a highly publicized trip to the region in March 2009, Ahmadinejad touted the passage of 190 government edicts that would result in the establishment of thirty major investment and eight industrial districts in Kurdistan.[43] Similarly, the Ministry of Economic Affairs and Finance has promised major plans for the implementation of investment projects under the country's Foreign Investment Promotion and Protection Act in the Kurdish areas of Iran.[44] The impact of these and similar programs on the region's overall economic development has yet to be realized.

The Green Movement and the Nationality Issues

Iran's presidential election of 2009 and the subsequent upheaval and mass protests against it by a wide spectrum of Iranian citizens augured the emergence of what has now been dubbed the "Green Movement."[45] At the present time, both Mir Hussein Moussavi and Mehdi Karroubi, the Green Movement's putative leaders, are under house arrest, and many other individuals associated with the election protest are either in prison or have been forced out of the country. The Green Movement's manifesto spells out the movement's goals and objectives in some detail, and in lofty terms. It emphasizes the movement's regard for Iran's nationalist (i.e., secular) and Islamic heritage, its endorsement of individual rights and nonviolent mode of political discourse, its pledge to grant justice and liberty to all Iranians and equal rights to men and women, and its rejection of all forms of discrimination.[46]

Iranian nationalities and ethnic groups played an active role in the early formation of the Green Movement. According to Mohammad Ali Tofighi, a Kurdish journalist and former member of the now-banned reformist group Mojahedin of the Islamic Revolution of Iran, the widespread pro-change and democratic sentiments that erupted in support of the Green Movement were influenced by the "ethnic discourse that has sought to liberate diverse Iranian ethnicities from oppression and discrimination."[47] Similarly, Saman Rasoulpoor, a Kurdish human rights activists and journalist, observed that the "unprecedented emphasis of the two reformist presidential candidates" [Moussavi and Karroubi] on minority and ethnic demands had brought ethnic issues to the forefront of contentious political issues in the 2009 presidential election.[48]

Shortly before the June 2009 presidential elections, Mehdi Karroubi, in a frank and wide-ranging interview with Iran's Press TV, addressed the question of endemic ethnic inequality in Iran. In Karroubi's words, the country's constitution clearly states that "all minorities and all followers of different religions are equal. . . . I think our approach should be that all people, regardless of their gender, religion, or ethnicity ought to be able to feel a bond with this government. But no one says the things I am saying."[49] Kurds who supported the reform movement did indeed participate in the Green Movement and in the demonstrations that followed its establishment. The Coordinating Council of Kurdish Reforms (Shoray-e Hamahangi-e Eslahat-e Kurd), which was formed in 2004, issued a strong statement calling for full participation of all Iranians in the February 2011 national march in support of the goals of the Green Movement.[50] Likewise, the council warned the Kurds to refrain from "military adventurism" that would damage the Kurdish cause and provide the excuse for the Iranian government as well as other regional countries to suppress Kurdish demands under the guise of fighting terrorism.[51]

Notwithstanding the support given to the Green Movement by several Iranian ethnic groups and nationalities in the early stages of the movement's existence, the overall support for this latest manifestation of "reformism" in Iran has now lost its earlier appeal. For some Kurds like Tofighi, who had earlier supported the country's reform movement and particularly the Green Movement, this latest manifestation of reformism in Iran ultimately failed to address the root causes of authoritarianism in the country—i.e., *velayat-e faghih*, or the Guardianship of the Jurist with a supreme clerical leader as its guiding light and ultimate source of authority. It thus lost its appeal, not only to a large segment of the Kurds but also to many other democratic activists in Iran.[52] Moreover, no significant figure in the Green Movement adopted measures to establish direct contact with Kurdish political organizations or groups, lest they be accused by their opponents of associating with "separatist groups." When Mostafa Hejri, the leader of the Democratic Party of Iranian Kurdistan, issued a statement in support of the Green Movement's objectives and po-

litical goals, the governing conservative forces in Iran used Hejri's statement as "proof" of the Green Movement's support for a "Kurdish armed
group."[53]

All in all, the inability of President Khatami's reformist government
to address, among other things, ethnic problems in Iran and the lingering suspicion that the reformists were playing the ethnic card as an election tool against their conservative opponents resulted in what can best
be described as benign neglect of the Green Movement by Iran's Kurdish
population.

Conclusion

The Kurds and the Iranian government have had an uneasy relationship
in recent decades. The state's lingering suspicion that the Kurdish demand
for sociocultural autonomy is, in fact, a disguised attempt at secession
interfered with a meaningful dialogue between the Iranian government
(including the reformists who were once in power) and the Kurds. At least
since the establishment of the Islamic Republic, the Kurds have repeatedly stated that they do not aim to weaken Iran. In Ghassemlou's words,
"no political force in Iranian Kurdistan wants to secede from Iran. Our
demands are framed within the context of [the] Iranian state."[54] He also
coined the term "democracy for Iran, autonomy for Kurdistan" as the
motto of the KDPI. This is, of course, akin to the motto of the Kurdistan
Democratic Party of Iraq (KDP). In 2005 the KDPI slogan was changed
to its new motto, "Kurdish national rights within the context of a democratic and federal Iran." This change also reflects the developments in post-
Saddam Iraq and the evolution of a federal structure as demanded by the
Kurdistan Regional Government (KRG). Since Ghassemlou's death,
other prominent KDPI leaders have reiterated this point on numerous
occasions. In other words, the legitimate rights of the Kurds can best
be guaranteed within a democratic Iran that recognizes the rights of its
Kurdish population.

In response, the Iranian authorities have long insisted that the Kurdish leadership, including the leaders of the KDPI, must demonstrate their
loyalty to the state before a meaningful discussion of autonomy can be
undertaken. In the words of Mustafa Chamran, the Islamic Republic's
first defense minister, who was intimately involved in suppressing a Kurdish uprising in early 1979, "we [the state] would give them autonomy—
not only in Kurdistan—and would also ask them to show us how to grant

autonomy and freedom to every ethnic group in the country. However, if they use empty and misleading slogans to hide their intention to harm Islam and our revolution and to serve foreign powers whose interests are diametrically opposed to those of the Iranian people, we will fight them to the end—including the Kurds." Similarly, the prominent reformist Hamid Reza Jalaipour criticized the very notion of autonomy (*khodmokhtari*) proposed by the KDP. He opined that the recipe for Kurdish autonomy was anathema to Iran's national identity and was a foreign concept to most Iranian Kurds. Jalaipour further stated that because Kurdish history in Iran was vastly different from Kurdish experience in Iraq or Turkey, models of autonomy imported from outside are not applicable to Iranian Kurdistan.[55] These reflect some of the underlying problems that have bedeviled Kurdish relations with the state in Iran. However, developments in Iraqi Kurdistan after 2003 have had spillover effects on Iranian Kurdistan. The emergence of a semi-autonomous KRG and its evolving relations with Iran, including with the Kurdish parts of the country, will undoubtedly impact the profile of future developments in Iranian Kurdistan.

The Nostalgic Republic: The Kurdish Republic of 1946 and Its Effect on Kurdish Identity and Nation Building in Iran

HUSSEIN TAHIRI

Kurdistan was divided between the Ottoman and Persian empires for the first time in 1514. From the early nineteenth century onward, there were numerous revolts against the Ottoman Empire and, later, against Turkey and Iraq, nation-states that had inherited Ottoman Kurdistan. Mir Muhammad's uprising against the Ottoman Empire in 1833 was followed by other revolts such as the Badr Khan, Yazdan Sher, Sheikh ʿUbaydullah, Sheikh Mahmud, Sheikh Saʿid, and the Barzani, Khoybun, and Dersim rebellions.

The Kurds did not put up the same level of resistance against the Persian Empire or the Iranian state. The first significant revolt against the Iranian state led by the Kurds of Iran broke out after World War I, when Ismaʿil Agha Shikak, or Simko, attempted to establish a Kurdish state. After the war a power vacuum existed in Iranian Kurdistan, especially in the areas close to the Iran-Ottoman borders. This paved the way for Simko, who was the sole power in the area, to establish his authority in the north of Iranian Kurdistan. From 1918 to 1922 he led a revolt against the Iranian government that was aimed at establishing an independent Kurdistan.[1]

Affected by regional and international events, Simko developed a nationalist worldview. In 1920 he began to promote the idea of an independent Kurdish state.[2] He clashed with government forces on numerous occasions, at times capturing areas near the town of Mahabad, but for a number of reasons was unable to establish a Kurdish state or cultivate a Kurdish national identity. Nor did he manage to gain the support of any external powers or to unite the Kurds. In a tribal and divided Kurdish society, where national identity could not grow, he was considered a tribal rather than a national leader. Simko's nationalist aspirations died with him in 1930, when he was invited by the Iranian government to negotiate in Ushnu, ambushed by the Iranian forces, and assassinated.[3]

The second significant attempt to establish a Kurdish state was made after World War II, when a Kurdish republic was established in Iranian Kurdistan in 1946 with Mahabad as its capital and under the leadership of the Kurdistan Democratic Party of Iran (KDPI).[4]

This chapter will examine the development of Kurdish identity and nationalism prior to the Kurdish Republic of 1946. The impact of the republic on the development of Kurdish identity and nation building will be discussed. The factors that hindered the positive impact of the Kurdish Republic of 1946 on Kurdish identity, nationalism, and nation building will be analyzed.

Kurdish Identity and Nationalism Prior to the Kurdish Republic of 1946

Kurdish identity has been the subject of scholarly controversy for a long time. Although a number of Kurdish principalities were formed, the Kurds have never had an independent empire or state. Consequently, their history has mostly been written by their rulers. At times the Kurds were regarded as Arabs, for instance by Arab historians like Mas'udi.[5] At other times they were regarded as Persians. Wilhelm Gernot states that from 330 BC to AD 224 there was no Persian political entity, but early historians nevertheless referred to the Iranic people, including those living in Anatolia, as Persians.[6] The current ruling states, that is, Turkey, Iran, Iraq, and Syria, have tried to reinvent Kurdish history and identity;[7] the clearest case was Turkey, where the Kurds were named "mountain Turks" after the suppression of the Dersim revolt in 1938.[8]

Nor was the recognition and survival of the Kurdish language beyond controversy. Some claimed that the Kurdish language was a corrupted form of Persian,[9] or influenced by Middle Persian and belonging to the Iranian South-West language group.[10] There were also claims that it was derived from ancient Turkish.[11] In short, the Kurds have been branded Arabs and Persians, as well as Turks.

Despite these controversies, the Kurds have been able to maintain a distinctive identity for centuries. Clear evidence of their unique identity goes back to the late sixteenth century, when Amir Sharafadin Khan of

Bitlis wrote a detailed history of Kurdish nobilities, in which he distinguished the Kurds from neighboring people such as the Turks, Persians, Arabs, Armenians, and Assyrians. In 1696, Ahmed-e Xani criticized the Kurds for their lack of unity, adding that only if they were united would they liberate themselves from the yoke of the Ottomans, Persians, and Arabs.[12]

This expression of Kurdish identity was both rare and elitist, and was not translated into ethnic or national consciousness among the Kurdish masses. The structure of Kurdish society was tribal, and the Kurdish masses were only loyal to their tribes and tribal leaders. All other identities were either nonexistent or took a back seat. In such a society the tribal chief wielded enormous power and established law and order. He acted as the representative of the tribe, and it was he who maintained contact with the outside world. It was virtually impossible to mobilize the tribe without the consent of the tribal chiefs.[13]

From the nineteenth century onward, ambitious tribal leaders rose against the Ottoman or Persian empires to retain their autonomy, or to form a Kurdish state. They became the leaders of embryonic Kurdish national movements. In the Iranian part of Kurdistan, as in the Ottoman part, they occasionally rose against the central government. To centralize the government and consolidate his power, Reza Shah of Iran began to suppress tribal leaders, weakening and undermining their authority. The government followed a policy of forced resettlement. Tribes were forced into a sedentary life: while some settled in villages,[14] others were exiled or forced to live in urban areas. Land registration was introduced in 1926, and individuals were granted land titles. This meant that the tribal leaders, who were the most powerful elements in Kurdish society, acquired land and became landlords.[15] Though the new system of land ownership loosened the ties between the tribal leaders, the new landlords, and former tribesmen who were now peasants, it did not change the tribal structure of Kurdish society. Tribal confederacies simply disintegrated into smaller tribal organizations. Tribes were able to retain their tribal values by shifting their loyalty from the powerful heads of tribal confederacies to new, albeit less powerful, tribal leaders.[16] However, the tribal system did not remain wholly intact. The newly introduced land registration dispossessed tribesmen who had previously held the land in common with other tribesmen. Life became more difficult for them in the villages, so that they had to migrate to the towns. The latter expanded, and with this expansion a new class of Kurdish professionals began to emerge.

This led to the development of a small class of educated Kurds and professionals, particularly in the area of Mahabad. This newly educated Kurdish class formed the nucleus of modern Kurdish nationalism, which paved the way for the establishment of the Kurdish Republic in 1946.

The Rise and Fall of the Kurdish Republic of 1946

During World War II, another opportunity arose for the Kurds of Iran, when the war created a political space allowing for their nationalist aspirations. Iran had already established economic relations with Germany before World War II, and some Iranian officials sympathized with Germany during the war. Iran was an important route for the transport of arms and logistics to the Soviet Union, so that the Allies occupied Iran when Germany attacked the Soviet Union in the summer of 1941.[17]

Like other parts of Iran, Kurdistan was also partitioned into three zones: Saqqez to the south was under the British sphere of influence, the north of Kurdistan was under the control of the Soviet Union, while Mahabad and a few surrounding towns remained as a buffer zone between the British and the Soviets. Still, the Soviets retained their influence over the buffer zone.[18] The power vacuum in the Kurdish buffer zone gave the Kurdish intellectuals in the town of Mahabad an opportunity to form Komalay Jiyanaway Kurdistan (JK), the Committee for the Resurrection of Kurdistan, on September 16, 1942.[19] As its membership increased and to keep up with the pace of developments in the Mahabad region, the JK was transformed into the Kurdistan Democratic Party of Iran, KDPI, on August 16, 1945.[20] The Kurdish Republic of 1946 was established on January 22, 1946, under the leadership of the KDPI and with Qazi Muhammad as its president.[21] On February 11, 1946, Qazi Muhammad formed a cabinet of thirteen ministers, with Haji Baba Sheikh as the prime minister.[22] The ministers were selected from among tribal leaders, religious figures, and Kurdish intellectuals.

There is disagreement regarding whether the Kurdish Republic of 1946 was an independent or an autonomous state. For some, the fact that the Kurds had proclaimed a Kurdish republic, with close relations with the Soviet Union and the Azerbaijan Republic, meant that it was an independent state. Archie Roosevelt Jr., an American intelligence officer, wrote on May 25, 1945, that the main interest of Komala (JK) was to form an independent Kurdish state including the Kurds of Turkey, Iran, and

Iraq.[23] Roosevelt also claimed in his later writings that the republic was an independent state.[24] Hassan Arfa, an Iranian military officer, stated that behind Qazi Muhammad's desk was a huge map of the Middle East on which the frontiers of a prospective greater Kurdistan had been added by hand, indicating that he intended to form a greater Kurdistan and become its leader.[25] The involvement of Kurds from other parts of Kurdistan in the formation and defense of the republic is seen as an additional reason for proclaiming the independence of the Kurdish Republic.

However, the Kurdish Republic of 1946 seemed to be an autonomous Kurdish entity rather than an independent state. The JK had no clearly defined political program, and its successor, the KDPI, did not demand a Kurdish state. The KDPI presented a program that contained eight points, the first of which stated that "the Kurdish people in Iran must manage their own local affairs and be granted autonomy within Iran's frontiers."[26] In an interview with the *Kurdistan* newspaper on January 13, 1946, Qazi Muhammad denied that the Kurds intended to form an independent state and added that they wanted to live autonomously under the Iranian flag.[27] As Abbas Vali stated, Qazi Muhammad clearly left the door open for negotiations with the Iranian government, indicating that regional autonomy was the strategic objective of the Kurdish administration in Mahabad.[28] Consequently, when it became obvious that the Kurds would have to submit to the Iranian government, the Kurdish representative and the Iranian prime minister, Ahmad Qavam (Qavam as-Saltaneh), agreed on the following points: the Kurdish language was to be used in education; there was to be political freedom for democratic organizations in general and Kurdish organizations in particular; Persian forces were to withdraw from all the areas in which the Kurds lived; Kurdish publications were to be allowed; and autonomous status for the Kurds was to be recognized.[29] However, the terms and conditions agreed on by the Iranian government with the Kurdish Republic merely proved to be tactics devised by Qavam to get the Soviets out of Iran and to break Kurdish resistance. On December 16, 1946, Qazi Muhammad went to Miandoab to facilitate the surrender of the Kurdish Republic, and on December 17, 1946, Mahabad was officially handed over to the Iranian forces without any resistance.[30]

Irrespective of its status, the short-lived Kurdish Republic did institutionalize Kurdish identity and nationalism, leaving a legacy future generations could aspire to.

Kurdish Identity and Nationalism:
The Legacy of the Kurdish Republic of 1946

One of the main achievements of the Kurdish Republic was to institu-tionalize Kurdish identity and the process of nation building. Through-out their long history of struggle, the Kurds had never been able to form a unified Kurdish entity until the establishment of the Kurdish Republic of 1946, which was their first opportunity to create a modern Kurdish entity built on a Kurdish identity. Thus, the leaders of the Kurdish Repub-lic immediately started the process of nation building: for the first time, Kurdish schools were opened and the Kurdish language became the offi-cial teaching language; Kurdish books, newspapers, and magazines were printed; Kurdish literature and theater were promoted; officials were re-cruited from among the Kurds; youth and women organizations were formed, and women participated in political, cultural, and social events; hospitals and medical centers were built; a Kurdish radio program was opened and started broadcasting in Kurdish and other languages; the Kurdish flag was hoisted and the Kurdish national anthem played for the first time; and the new Kurdish Republic established relations with the Soviet Union and the Azerbaijan Republic.[31]

The Kurdish administration started building the nucleus of a Kurdish army, which consisted of seventy officers, forty noncommissioned offi-cers, and twelve hundred soldiers. The Soviet Union supplied arms and military logistics. A Soviet captain was sent to train the Kurdish army alongside the Kurdish officers who had joined Mulla Mustafa Barzani's revolt in Iraq and went with him to support the Mahabad Republic. The Kurdish Republic gained a semi-legal status as it was recognized by the Soviet Union and the Azerbaijan Republic.

As noted, the Kurdish Republic laid the foundation of pan-Kurdish nationalism. From the start of the JK, contacts were established between the Kurds of Iran and Iraq. Before its formation, the founders of Komala asked the Heva Party in Iraq to help them form an organization since they did not have enough experience. A member of the Heva Party attended the inception meeting of the JK.[32] On October 11, 1945, Barzani and his armed forces, which had been attacked by Iraqi units and the British air force, crossed the border into Iranian Kurdistan. Barzani's brother, Sheikh Ahmad, and one thousand Barzani forces (according to another account the number was three thousand) accompanied him with their families. They joined the Kurdish Republic, forming its military backbone.[33] Kurd-ish representatives from Turkey and Syria also visited the republic.[34]

The following dialogue between General Fazlulah Homayouni, commander of the Iranian forces, and Mustafa Barzani highlights the significance of the Kurdish Republic in the development of pan-Kurdish nationalism. After the collapse of the republic and his arrival in Mahabad, Homayouni negotiated the disarmament of Barzani and his men. Homayouni asked Barzani, "You are an Iraqi tribal leader; why did you come to Iran?" Barzani responded, "Firstly, this is Kurdistan and it is the land of my fathers. Secondly, you are an Iranian, why did you come to Kurdistan and occupy it by force?"[35]

However, the Kurdish Republic was too short-lived to allow nation building to be completed or even to make any substantial progress. Effective nation building would have required a long process. In a tribal society, like that of the Kurds, nation building also implies generational change:

Nation building stresses the cultural aspect of political development. It involves a process where a population transfers its commitment and loyalty from smaller units such as tribe and village to a larger, centralized political system.[36]

Despite the development of a new middle stratum of Kurdish intellectuals, professionals, and leaders, loyalty among the Kurdish masses did not extend significantly beyond tribal allegiances, so that nation building could not have a significant impact.

Furthermore, soon after the defeat of the Kurdish Republic of 1946, the Iranian government tried to eradicate all signs of the republic and undermine the process of nation building. Qazi Muhammad and some other Kurdish leaders were arrested, tried in a martial court, and condemned to death. On March 30, 1947, Qazi Muhammad, his cousin Seif Qazi, and his brother Sadr Qazi were hanged in Chwar Chira Square, at the very spot where the republic had been proclaimed.[37] The Kurdish publishing press was closed, Kurdish publications banned, Kurdish books burnt, and teaching in the Kurdish language prohibited.[38] Thus, no institution or initiatives by the Kurdish Republic survived, and it became difficult for those who had escaped persecution to continue the process of nation building in Iranian Kurdistan. Kurdish aspirations for self-rule were once again dashed.

Nevertheless, the Kurdish Republic of 1946 has continued to inspire Kurdish nationalism. The KDPI in particular still sees its golden age embodied in the Kurdish Republic and looks back at it with nostalgia. It still aims to achieve what the Kurdish Republic attained over sixty years ago.

On the fifty-fifth anniversary of the Kurdish Republic, KDPI Secretary General Mostafa Hejri stated:

> In a short period of time, and despite the fact that it controlled only a small part of Kurdistan, the Kurdistan Republic, which was established after the collapse of Reza Shah's dictatorship, took many valuable steps toward achieving the goals of the Kurdish people and draw the Kurds from other parts of Kurdistan. It became the center of attraction for Kurdish patriots and had a significant role in reviving Kurdish nationalist sentiments. It also tried to establish a common struggle with advocates of freedom throughout Iran. It was a positive model of a democratic republic. Unfortunately, it only lasted for eleven months and became the victim of international conspiracy. Nevertheless, it had a positive impact on the Kurdish people. The enemies of freedom thought that, with the destruction of the Kurdish Republic, they would destroy Kurdish nationalist sentiments, but the Kurdish struggle in particular and the spread of civilization in the world in general show how legitimate the Kurdish achievements of January 22, 1946, and the Kurdish Republic had been. The continuation of Kurdish struggle to achieve those goals is a source of pride to all of us.[39]

The formation of the Kurdish Republic is commemorated every year in various parts of Kurdistan, as well as in the diaspora. Kurds celebrate this occasion in different Kurdish cities in Iran. The Iranian government considers such celebrations seditious as they represent Kurdish nationalist aspirations, and those who are involved face extreme retribution. Celebrations are therefore held in secret and are mainly confined to the distribution of leaflets and writing of slogans on the walls. The Kurds in the diaspora, too, particularly in Western countries such as Sweden, France, Germany, the United Kingdom, the United States, Canada, and as far as Australia celebrate the republic's formation every year. It is an opportunity to remember its achievements and boost their nationalist sentiments.

Recollection of the Kurdish Republic of 1946 is also used to create unity among Kurds from different parts of Kurdistan. On February 19, 2012, a ceremony was held to mark the sixty-sixth anniversary of the Kurdish Republic. Kurds from Iraq, Iran, Turkey, and Syria attended the ceremony. The president of the Kurdistan Region of Iraq, Masʿud Barzani, the prime minister, Dr. Barham Salih, members of Kurdistan Regional Parliament, and the Erbil governor were present.[40] In addition, Selahattin Demirtaş, the chairman of the Peace and Democracy Party (BDP), whose base is in

Turkey, attended the ceremony and called upon Kurdish political parties to unite.[41] He said, "After centuries, a gate for freedom has been opened for the Kurdish people. And we must make a decision. . . . Today is a chance to learn a lesson from the collapse of the Republic of Mahabad to create this national unity."[42] Leyla Zana, a prominent Kurdish political activist from Turkey who also attended the ceremony, called on the Kurds from Iraq, Iran, Turkey, and Syria to unite for a common cause.[43]

The ceremony also brought together the two rival KDPI parties, which had split in 2006. Both Hassan Sharafi, the deputy leader of one KDPI party, and Khalid Azizi, secretary general of the other KDPI party, attended the ceremony.[44] Abdullah Hassanzadah, former secretary general of the KDPI, stated that such occasions would help foster unity between Iranian Kurdish political parties.[45] Thus the Kurdish Republic of 1946 is not just an inspiration; it has become a symbol of unity among the disparate and divided Kurdish political parties, as have the flag and the national anthem of the Kurdish Republic of 1946, which have now been officially adopted by the Kurdistan Regional Government in Iraq. It is also the flag and national anthem of the Kurds in Iran and Syria.[46] In fact, the Kurdish Republic and its leaders have always been of symbolic significance to the Kurds. *Lvin Magazine* conducted an opinion poll on Facebook, asking people to choose symbols of Kurdish nationhood among ten Kurdish leaders. About twenty-seven thousand people participated in the opinion poll. Qazi Muhammad was voted as the foremost symbol of Kurdish nationhood, followed by Mulla Mustafa Barzani.[47]

There is no doubt that the Kurdish Republic has had a significant impact on the revival of Kurdish nationalism and has played an important, albeit symbolic, role in developing Kurdish national unity. However, for a number of reasons that will be discussed later, Kurdish nationalist inspirations did not suffice to create a separate Kurdish identity and develop pan-Kurdish nationalism in Iranian Kurdistan.

Dual Identities Impeded Kurdish Nationalism in Iran

Socioeconomic changes in the 1960s and 1970s, agrarian reforms in particular, improved communication both within Iranian Kurdistan and between it and other parts of Kurdistan. In addition, migration to towns and cities have considerably weakened the tribal structure of Kurdish society and paved the way for Kurdish ethnicity to become a central, cohesive factor in Iranian Kurdish identity.[48] Kurdish satellite TV channels have added another dimension to the promotion of Kurdish ethnicity. A significant number of Kurds from Iran in the diaspora are in close contact with Kurds from other parts of Kurdistan and no longer subjected to Iranian assimilation policies. They strongly promote Kurdish nationalism. Furthermore, developments in Iraqi Kurdistan have further heightened Kurdish national consciousness. These developments should have given the Kurds in Iran an opportunity to develop a distinctive Kurdish identity and paved the way for the growth of pan-Kurdish nationalism. However, the Kurds of Iran have not yet been able to develop a separate Kurdish identity distinct from their Iranian identity. Perceived historical affiliation between Kurds and Persians, Iran's assimilation policies, and the policies of Kurdish political parties have contributed to this dual identity.

Historical records show that the Kurds and Persians who migrated to what is now known as Iran and Kurdistan[49] in the same period shared the same Aryan ancestry.[50] However, despite some affinity between them, history also shows that they were very distinct from each other. There is a belief among many Persians and Kurds that the pre-Islamic religion they shared was Zoroastrianism. Many Kurdish nationalists, disenchanted with Islam, still try to revive Zoroastrianism, which they, too, view as the ancient Kurdish religion. Although Zoroaster is believed to have been born in Kurdistan and to have proclaimed his mission there, his religion did not get a foothold in Kurdistan. It is claimed that he preached his religion for ten years and during this period only one person converted to his religion. He then had to migrate to eastern Persia (currently called Khorasan), where he converted three members of the ruler's court and thus expanded his religion.[51]

Persian Zoroastrians continue to reside in different parts of Iran, especially in Yazd. Some escaped persecution and sought refuge in India, where they are known as Parsi. However, there are no known Kurdish Zoroastrians, either in Kurdistan or in any other part of the world.[52] If the Kurds were originally Zoroastrians, then there would still be some Kurdish adherents of this religion. There are significant numbers of Kurds who follow Ēzidism (Yezidism)[53] and other religions believed to be pre-Islamic Kurdish religions. In short, the claim that the Persians and Kurds shared the same religion in pre-Islamic Iran has not been substantiated.

The Kurds and Persians also have distinct languages. The Kurdish language belongs to the northwestern branch of Indo-European language groups,[54] while the Persian language belongs to the southwestern branch.[55] Although Persian and Kurdish share some vocabulary, the speakers of these languages cannot understand each other.

Anyone who is familiar with Kurdish and Persian cultures can see a clear distinction between the two. Their family and kinship relationships and their wedding and mourning rituals, for instance, are quite different. Nevertheless, successive Iranian rulers have tried to exploit this perceived historical affinity between Kurds and Persians to show that the Kurds are an inseparable, integral part of Iran. In this way, they hope to prevent the emergence of a distinct Kurdish identity and the development of Kurdish nationalism. On May 1, 1936, the American chargé d'affaires in Tehran wrote to the U.S. Secretary of State:

> Iran . . . has done and is doing everything possible to prevent this [Kurdish nationalism] from happening in Iranian territory . . . Iranian Government seeks to disestablish contact between the Kurds of Iran and those of Iraq and Turkey, to make them forget that they are Kurds and to [sic] realize that they are primarily Iranians—in a word, to wear down and finally to obliterate the differences between the Kurds and the Iranians . . .[56]

From the 1920s to 1979, the Pahlavi shahs' policies aimed to encourage the Kurds to assimilate into mainstream society.[57] In fact, successive Iranian rulers promoted Persian nationalism at the expense of other nationalities.

There have been two planks in the Iranian rulers' approach to nationalism: Iran's pre-Islamic history, which was promoted by the Iranian shahs, and Shi'ism, which has been actively promoted by the Islamic Republic of Iran. As to the first plank, the shahs and secular intellectuals resorted to emphasizing pre-Islamic history and giving prominence to the Aryan roots of Persian identity in their attempt to centralize state power, weaken the influence of religion, and undermine the power of the clergy.[58] Reza Shah promoted the union of all Iranian people, based on a pan-Iranian identity.[59] The shah claimed that the Kurds were Aryans and that all the Aryans were "pure" Iranians.[60]

As ancient history of the Kurds was willfully merged with that of the Persians and there was little opportunity or effort by Kurdish historians or intellectuals to extract Kurdish from Iranian history, the Kurds came to identify themselves as Iranians. In fact, Kurdish historians such as Rashid Yassami tried to prove that the Kurds are of Iranian origin and have a strong historical affinity with the Persians. Sunni Kurds, even when in opposition to the Shi'is, had no problem identifying themselves with pre-Islamic Iranian history, at the expense of pan-Kurdish nationalism. Historically, there has long been a deep divide between the Sunnis and the Shi‘is. The Kurds of Iran belong to both the Sunni and the Shi‘i branches of Islam. Although the Shi‘i Kurds have felt a part of Iranian Shi‘ism, the Sunni Kurds have always felt discriminated against by the Shi‘i Iranians. Yet Sunni Kurds have had no problem sharing a common history with the Persians when a pre-Islamic Iranian identity was evoked.

The second plank in Iranian nationalism has been Shi‘ism. Since the Safavid rule (1502–1736), Iranian nationalism has been intertwined with Shi‘i Islam. Shi‘ism has become part of a uniquely Iranian identity, which distinguishes the Iranians from their Arab and Turkish neighbors and also, at times, from their foes.[61] As Nikki Keddie points out, it is often difficult "to say if a trend or identification is Iranian national or Shi‘i."[62]

The Islamic regime of Iran has been using pan-Islamic ideology to foster Persian nationalism. When the Kurds put their national demands to the Islamic Republic of Iran, which had come into power in 1979, they were frequently told that all Iranians were Muslims and that ethnic identification was not to be emphasized because all Muslims were brothers. In the final draft of the Islamic constitution, which was approved by the Majlis-e-Khobragan (Assembly of Experts) in 1979, there was no mention of the equality of ethnic groups in Iran, though the phrase "using vernacular languages besides Persian" was retained. For Ayatollah Khomeini, the term "minority" could only be applied to non-Muslim religious groups. Khomeini stated:

> Sometimes the word minority is used to refer to people such as the Kurds, Lurs, Turks, Persians, Balouchis, and such. These people should not be called minorities, because this term assumes that there is a difference between these brothers [*sic*]. In Islam, such a difference has no place at all. There is no difference between Muslims who speak different languages, for instance, the Arabs or the Persians. It is very probable that such problems have been created by those who do not wish the Muslim countries to be united. . . . They create the issues of nationalism, of pan-Arabism, pan-Turkism, and such -isms, which are contrary to Islamic doctrines. Their plan is to destroy Islam and the Islamic philosophy.[63]

However, in reality the Islamic Republic of Iran has often put Iranian nationalism above all other interests. When the Kurds were negotiating with the Islamic regime, the government refused to recognize the Kermanshah and Ilam provinces as part of Kurdistan, claiming that they were Shi‘i and that religious identity should override ethnicity.[64] Yet when it comes to Persian nationalism and Iranian territorial integrity, Persian nationalism takes primacy over Islam. For example, after the collapse of the Soviet Union, Iran felt threatened by the influence of the Azerbaijan Republic on its own Azeri population, which constituted an estimated one-third of the Iranian population. When war broke out between Armenia and Azerbaijan over Nagorno and Karabakh in 1992, Iran supported Christian Armenia against Shi'i Muslim Azerbaijan.[65] As Barry Rubin states, "In a sense, it could also be said that Khomeini's revolution encompassed nationalism even while rejecting it explicitly . . . he did offer an implicit Iranian nationalism."[66]

Also implicit in the pursuit of Persian nationalism has been a subtle assimilation policy by successive Iranian governments. The Special Representative of the UN Commission on Human Rights reported that there were claims of a tacit governmental policy of assimilation of ethnic minorities in the Islamic Republic of Iran, a policy that was first started by Reza Shah.[67]

If Iranian ethnic minorities, especially the Kurds, persist in the belief that the assimilation policies initiated by Reza Khan and continued by the Islamic Republic of Iran may cease if a new regime comes to power, they could be disappointed. The Kurds were hopeful that after the overthrow of the shah, the new regime would grant them their rights. However, the Islamic Republic of Iran has continued the shah's policies, though under a different guise. The Iranian opposition does not seem to offer much hope either. Generally, there is unease among the Persian population when it comes to Kurdish autonomy. It is feared that the idea of Kurdish autonomy would incite other ethnic groups in Iran, such as the Azeris, Arabs, and Baluchis. The Kurdish demand for autonomy is seen as potentially leading to the partition of Iran. The royalists oppose any territorial or ethnic rights for the peoples of Iran. They follow the same policy as that of the shah. The other nationalist groups, such as the National Front of Iran, also oppose autonomy for the Kurds. The National Front of Iran in a letter to the KDPI leadership accused them of separatism for demanding autonomy.[68]

Even among the groups that were regarded by the KDPI as "progressive," there was a deep distrust of Kurdish demands. The National Republicans of Iran stated that it would not accept the idea that Iran was a multinational country. They argued that such an idea was incompatible with the structure of Iranian society and might result in the partition of Iran.[69]

Nevertheless, unlike in Turkey, neither the Iranian rulers nor the opposition for that matter have denied the existence of the Kurds. On occasion they have tolerated the expression of Kurdish culture when it was manifested in cultural terms within the broader concept of Iranian identity. They have always considered the Kurds as an integral part of Iran. Had they denied the existence of the Kurds or denied their limited cultural expression, a more violent and highly ethnicized expression of Kurdish nationalism might have ensued, which could have paved the way for a more distinctive Kurdish identity.[70] This inclusive approach by the Iranian state and the opposition, in conjunction with the factors outlined above, has affected the way the Kurdish nationalist movements themselves express their identity.

Instead of promoting a distinct Kurdish identity, Kurdish political parties in Iran have advocated a dual identity: Kurdish and Iranian. The Komala, though based in Kurdistan, considered a more explicit manifestation of Kurdish identity as a narrow form of nationalism that would impede the union of the Iranian proletariat. In its program Komala defined itself as a political organization of "workers and toilers" of Kurdistan, striving for the establishment of a Revolutionary Democratic Republic in Iran based on socialism. In such a republic the Kurds would be free to determine their own future. Komala, however, also emphasized a voluntary union of the Kurds with the other peoples of Iran.[71]

The Parti Jiyani Azadi Kurdistan (Free Life Party of Kurdistan or PJAK) was established on April 4, 2004, and is considered to be the Iranian front of the Kurdistan Workers' Party, PKK, though it has denied this. In its constitution, the PJAK stated that it would create a Kurdish society in accordance with the philosophical and ideological views of Apo (Abdullah Öcalan) and within a democratic framework.[72] Although the PKK's goal until at least the early 1990s was the formation of an independent Greater Kurdistan, the PJAK aimed to resolve the Kurdish question within a democratic confederation without changing the current political borders.[73] In effect, like the Komala and the KDPI, the PJAK wanted to tackle the problem within the framework of Iranian territorial integrity. However, the KDPI does not accept the PJAK as an Iranian Kurdish political party. It sees the PJAK as the Iranian branch of the PKK, with its main area of conflict in Turkey's Kurdistan.[74]

The KDPI, while representing a Kurdish nationalist agenda, views the Kurds as an integral part of Iran. Dr. Abdurahman Qasimlo, former secretary general of the Kurdistan Democratic Party of Iran, who was assassinated by the Islamic regime of Iran, used to say that no one had the right to consider themselves as more Iranian than the Kurds. He argued that "Iran was his motherland and that from the point of view of history, language, and culture, Kurds had Iranian roots."[75] He further emphasized that no political force in Iranian Kurdistan wanted to secede from Iran, and that they therefore framed their demands within the context of the Iranian state.[76] Until the fourteenth congress in 2008, the KDPI's slogan was "democracy for Iran and autonomy for Kurdistan." Since then, it has changed its demands to a claim for a federal Iran, in which the Kurds would have their own state. Indeed, ever since the Kurdish Republic of 1946, there have been no significant changes in KDPI policies. Therefore, it would be difficult for a distinct Kurdish identity and for pan-Kurdish nationalism to emerge when Kurdish nationalist movements continue to contribute to the reinforcement of dual identities among the Kurds of Iran.

Conclusion

Compared to other parts of Kurdistan, there have been fewer uprisings among the Kurds of Iran against the Persian Empire or the Iranian state, for a number of reasons. First, the Persian part of Kurdistan was smaller in area and population size than was Ottoman Kurdistan. Second, the Iranian authorities have often been more accommodating to Kurdish identity when such an identity did not threaten state sovereignty. Third, and more importantly, there was a perceived historical kinship between the Kurds and Persians. The Iranian rulers used this relationship to assimilate the Kurds, or at least to break their resistance toward the Iranian state. The Kurds of Iran also came to accept this perceived historical kinship so that the majority of the Kurds now consider themselves Iranians. This has hindered the development of a distinct Kurdish identity and limited the development of Kurdish nationalism. Nevertheless, within this limitation, the Kurds of Iran were able to establish an autonomous, though short-lived, Kurdish state in 1946.

The Kurdish Republic of 1946 was the first modern political entity the Kurds had ever been able to establish in their ongoing struggle with Iran. It institutionalized Kurdish identity and aspirations for nationhood and set about the process of nation building, and has therefore become a symbol of Kurdish nationalism. Every year the Kurds in various parts of Kurdistan commemorate the republic's establishment. Kurdish nationalist movements refer to and evoke the memory of the republic to prove their nationalist credentials and recruit Kurds.

Alas, commemoration has never been about the lessons to be learned.

Since the collapse of the republic, the structure of Kurdish society has changed substantially, paving the way for a distinct Kurdish mass nationalism. Advances in communication technology and increasing globalization have further prepared the ground for pan-Kurdish nationalism. Nevertheless, the KDPI has still not been able to extend its authority beyond the borders of the Kurdish Republic of 1946. Nor has it gained widespread support among the Kurds in Kurdistan province, particularly in Sanandaj. As was the case in the Kurdish Republic, the KDPI has not been able to mobilize the Kurds in Kermanshah and Ilam provinces, where they still feel greater affinity with Shi'ism than with Kurdish nationalism. Nor did they join the Kurdish national struggle during the Simko revolt and the Kurdistan Republic of 1946, and they still are not a part of it. The religious bond between the Shi'i Kurds and the Shi'i government of Iran even made it possible for the government to recruit Kurdish Shi'is to fight the KDPI and Komala.[77]

In the Kurdish Republic of 1946, Kurdish masses were loyal to their tribes, and their Kurdish ethnic or Iranian identity was not a significant issue. Since then, and as a result of the efforts by successive Iranian governments and Kurdish political movements, the Kurds have developed a dual identity, both Kurdish and Iranian. One would expect the Kurdish Republic of 1946 to have become a focal point for Kurdish nationalism. However, the Kurdish political movements were unable to foster such a development. On the contrary, they helped to ingrain an Iranian identity into the Kurdish psyche, resulting in the widespread containment of Kurdish nationalism.

Since the collapse of the Kurdish Republic in 1946, the KDPI's position has not changed significantly. The Kurdish leadership has alternately claimed to be socialist, social democratic, and at times even revolutionary. Their approach to the Kurdish question has nevertheless been very conservative. In fact, the KDPI was more progressive in its outlook in 1946 than it is today. The majority of Kurds in Iran thus look back at the Kurdish Republic with nostalgia. It was a great opportunity and experience, though very brief, and one that might not recur in the foreseeable future.[78]

Conclusion: The Kurdish Momentum

OFRA BENGIO

For the greater part of the twentieth century the state-centric literature on the Middle East tended to either belittle the role of the Kurds or disregard them altogether.[1] However, things began to change owing to a variety of interrelated factors: political developments on the ground, the growth of a young generation of Kurds that began to present a Kurdish narrative based on Kurdish sources, the role of the diaspora, and the new media. These developments impacted the literature on the Kurds, making them the focus of many new studies.

Meanwhile, a new discourse developed, not only among the Kurds themselves but also in what used to be the state's hegemonic discourse. A book published in early 2013 in Turkey, *Yeni Komşumuz Kürdistan* (Our New Neighbor Kurdistan), clearly illustrates this transformation.[2] The title alone speaks volumes. First of all, the Turkish author, Simla Yerlikaya, was not reluctant to use the term "Kurdistan," which only a few years earlier could have sent her to prison in Turkey. Second, referring to Kurdistan—namely the Kurdistan Regional Government (KRG)—as a neighbor implied that the neighbor was no longer the Iraqi state, but the Kurdistan entity in Iraq. As such, it no longer seemed to pose a threat to Turkey, but rather to open up new opportunities.

Changing Paradigms of the Nation-State

Yerlikaya's book reflects in a nutshell the geopolitical transformations that have taken place in the region in the last few years, as clearly demonstrated in the chapters of this volume. The Iraqi war of 2003, the "Arab Spring"—which was ignited at the end of 2010 and engulfed Tunisia, Egypt, Yemen,

Libya, and Syria—and the withdrawal of the American forces from Iraq at the end of 2011 all combined to weaken the state system while empowering what one might call the Kurdish subsystem.

Historically, the four states that share the Kurdish "problem" managed to contain the Kurds through cooperation and mutual alliances. At any given time two or more states formed an alliance to that end. For example, the Saadbad Pact of 1937 and the Baghdad Pact of 1955, which included Turkey, Iran, and Iraq, were said to have had as one of their targets the curbing of Kurdish uprisings.[3] More recently, Turkey and Iraq cooperated against the PKK during the Iran-Iraq war from 1980 to 1988, and even the erstwhile enemies Turkey and Syria cooperated against the PKK for an entire decade from 2000 to 2010. It is quite puzzling how dangerous the Kurds were perceived to be by the infinitely stronger political establishments of these states and how far these establishments were willing to go to avert that danger. Indeed, this threat perception was a major motive for anti-Kurdish alliances.

However, in the last few years such alliances have seemed unattainable due to the fundamental transformations in the geopolitical arena in general and the Kurdish subsystem in particular. The states were weakened on two levels. Domestically, all of them lost some of their hegemonic clout. Externally, they lost the glue that cemented their alliances against the Kurds. In some cases, like in Syria, the system went bankrupt. In contrast, the Kurdish subsystem was strengthened significantly, both internally and in its transborder relations.

As to their policies, each of the four countries was pulling in a different direction regarding the Kurdish issue. In Iraq, the central government lost control of the Kurdistan region. Hence for all practical purposes Baghdad no longer commanded the long border with Turkey, nor could it forge alliances with Ankara with a view to containing either the PKK or the KRG.

The transformation in Turkey's policies and orientation were no less dramatic. Turkey allied itself more and more with Erbil, the capital of the KRG, while distancing itself from Baghdad, a move which would not have been conceivable even five years earlier. One of the recent examples of this change was when Ankara invited the president of the KRG, Masʿud Barzani, and not Iraq's prime minister, Nuri al-Maliki, to deliver a speech at the AKP congress in September 2012. Similarly, in March 2013 Turkey's prime minister Recep Tayyip Erdoğan held talks in Ankara with the prime minister of the KRG, Neçirvan Barzani, on a number of political, economic, and cultural issues that concerned the two parties.[4] Ankara's increasing policy of bypassing Baghdad on various issues with regard to the KRG deviated from its traditional position of standing solidly behind the territorial integrity of Iraq. This policy also put Ankara at loggerheads with the United States, which grew fearful that it would expedite the disintegration of Iraq. This was another ironic twist, since until very recently it was the United States that had to smooth out the relationship between Ankara and Erbil.

The growing alienation between Ankara and Baghdad was due, among other things, to the Sunni-Shiʻi divide, which surfaced after the Shiʻi-based government came to power in Baghdad, and to the economic advantages of doing business with Erbil, especially in the field of oil and gas. Another rarely discussed matter was Ankara's aspiration to return to the *vilayet* of Mosul, which it had lost to Iraq in 1925. This it hoped to achieve by means of soft power and in fulfillment of AKP's so-called neo-Ottoman vision, in which a policy of "zero problems with the neighbors" would be realized. Ironically, one can say that the only place where Turkey's foreign policy vision could become a reality was in the KRG area. The big change in Turkey's conceptualization of the KRG may be described as follows: While in the past Erbil was perceived as part of Turkey's internal Kurdish problem, it is now perceived as part of a viable solution. At the same time, Ankara came to the conclusion that Baghdad was a partner neither for the containment of the Kurds nor for a solution to the Kurdish problem.

The perception of the KRG's role as pivotal had to do with the chain of reactions spurred by the upheavals in the Middle East, most importantly the uprising in Syria. The Kurds of Syria took control of the Kurdish region and established an autonomous region there, very much like the KRG had in Iraq in the 1990s. At the same time, a decade of cooperation between Turkey and Syria vanished as the two states were now at opposite poles. Syria was no longer a partner for anti-Kurdish alliance or coordination because, like Iraq, it had lost its control over the Kurdish region. There were a number of reasons for this: Damascus was willing to use the Kurdish card against Turkey once again, as it had in the 1980s and 1990s and, most importantly, Turkey had turned itself into the enemy par excellence of the Baʻthi regime in Damascus.[5]

As with Iraq and Syria, Turkey found it increasingly difficult to cooperate with Iran on the Kurdish issue. Iran was completely opposed to Turkey's Kurdish policy and was becoming especially resentful of Turkey's growing rapprochement with the KRG, against which it kept warning Erbil. In fact, the two countries were vying for influence in the region. Furthermore, Iran was apprehensive that Turkish backing of the KRG would end up splitting Iraq. Iran's backing of Nuri al-Maliki's Shiʻi-based government was another cause for the growing hostility between Ankara and Tehran. Iran was also suspicious of a possible solution to the Kurdish domestic issue in Turkey, which could result in its granting autonomy to the Kurds, thus indirectly affecting the Iranian Kurds. In fact, this had been Iran's reaction to the 1970 agreement between Barzani and the Baʻth, which gave autonomy to the Kurds of Iraq. Accordingly, Iran was reportedly trying to revive the PKK card against Turkey.

In evaluating these tectonic changes, one could argue not only that the states were unable to forge alliances against the Kurds but also that the "inspiration" they drew from each other against the Kurds had become unworkable. In the twentieth century all four states adopted similar policies against the Kurds, including the suppression of Kurdish identity in all its forms, prevention of political activities by military means, destruction of the Kurdish habitat, and forced resettlement, which drove millions of Kurds either to other regions in Greater Kurdistan or abroad to establish a Kurdish diaspora.[6] However, different sociopolitical and geopolitical developments at the turn of the century made it difficult for any one state to mirror the policies of the other. This, together with the weakening of the ethos of the nation-state, opened a window of opportunity for the Kurds to reassert themselves.

The Kurdish Revival

Seen from the Kurdish point of view, the turn of the twenty-first century ushered in an era of Kurdish awakening in Greater Kurdistan similar to the one that the Arabs had experienced one century earlier. Moreover, and interestingly enough, the Kurdish awakening took place against the background and in conjunction with the "Arab Spring," or what one could call the second Arab awakening at the beginning of the twenty-first century. One could therefore say that the Middle East has witnessed a Kurdish revolution within an Arab revolution.

However, the concurrence of the Arab and Kurdish revolutions blurred the fundamental differences between them. A comparison between the two will indeed help to illustrate the huge strides made by the Kurds at the turn of the century. While the Arab revolutions challenged the regimes, the Kurds were perceived as challenging the very territorial integrity of the state, its national identity, and the idea of the nation-state. On the whole, the idea of the nation-state, which took root in Europe in the nineteenth century, was adopted wholeheartedly in the twentieth century by the new states in the Middle East. However, these centralized and homogenizing states failed to accommodate the demands of ethnonationalism.[7] Consequently, with the emergence of notions such as multiculturalism, pluralism, and participatory democracy,[8] the ethos of the nation-state began to lose its monopoly as a guideline for the building of a state system.

This is true especially for Iraq and for its Kurdish entity, but it is becoming more and more relevant to the Kurds in Syria and, though to a lesser extent, in Turkey and Iran. For the Kurds the nation-state signified the effacing of their identity and political rights for the greater part of the twentieth century—hence the backlash. The weakening of the state versus the society as it occurred in most of the countries of the region, especially the countries that experienced a revolution, also played into the hands of the Kurds.

Another difference between the Arab and Kurdish cases is that while the Arab revolutions brought to the surface cracks and divisions within the Arab societies, in the Kurdish case we notice a growing tendency toward transborder cooperation and unity. Thus, if the beginning of the twentieth century witnessed the division of Kurdish territories between four states so that ties among the different communities could only be maintained randomly,[9] the beginning of the twenty-first century, and especially its latest upheavals, brought them closer together. Furthermore, it opened the way for some degree of pan-Kurdism and somehow mitigated the chronic tendency toward tribalism, internal wars, and factionalism.

Despite the fact that the Kurds reside in four different countries, there are mutual influences and synergetic effects among them.[10] The transnational movement has gathered momentum thanks to the geopolitical changes in the region, the growing assertiveness of the Kurds, the crucial role of the diaspora, the new media, and, most importantly, the Kurdistan Regional Government (KRG), that is, a de facto state that has become the magnet and role model for all the Kurds. Indeed, the act of imagining Kurdistan underwent important transformations. While localism and particularism in each of the four parts of Kurdistan used to be the order of the day,[11] Greater Kurdistan has now become an integral part of the new Kurdish discourse, especially in the diaspora. This new discourse, which gradually replaced the hegemonic one, put a growing emphasis on the Kurdish language, culture, and public space. In most parts of Kurdistan, Kurdish heroes or symbols were thus substituted step by step for the heroes and symbols of the hegemonic culture.[12] Likewise, the Kurdish narrative, which had been subdued for most of the twentieth century, began asserting itself toward the end of the century.

The democratization process of the Kurdish and Arab societies was quite different. Although the postrevolutionary regimes in the Arab states did declare their commitment to democracy, the results so far have been quite disappointing. While they have put in place a framework of democratic institutions, beginning with post-Saddam Iraq, the democratic norms have not yet taken root. The new regimes have tended to become authoritarian and Islamist, as noted by one observer, who described the postrevolutionary regime in Egypt under the Muslim Brotherhood as a "phony democracy."[13]

By contrast, democracy is an existential matter for the Kurds. As Cengiz Gunes suggested, "democracy is seen as the central component of a lasting solution to the Kurdish question."[14] For one thing, the Kurds were subjected to the worst repressions under the dictatorial, authoritarian, or Islamist regimes, so that only a truly democratic state could hold out the Kurds' hope of preserving their identity and gaining their rights.[15] Little wonder then that the major Kurdish parties in all four parts of Kurdistan add the term "democracy" to their name as a kind of declaration of faith. Thus, there are parties with the name "Kurdistan Democratic Party" in Iran, Iraq, Syria, and Turkey. Interestingly, all parties active in Turkey after 1990 also included "democracy" in their names. Even the leading Kurdish organization in Turkey, Partiya Karkerên Kurdistan (PKK), which initially adopted a Marxist-Leninist ideology and demanded independence for Kurdistan, switched to a democratic discourse in the 1990s.[16] Later on, in July 2011, the PKK announced its plan for "democratic autonomy" in Turkey, which seemed to be a substitute for the goal of independence.[17] Likewise, the Kurdish party in Syria, which has become dominant in the aftermath of the upheavals in that country, is called Democratic Union Party (PYD).

In the case of the KRG, democracy is a condition sine qua non for gaining world support should it decide to cross the Rubicon and declare independence. Thus, since the establishment of the KRG in 1992, and especially from the late 1990s onward, fratricidal infighting has practically disappeared and elections in the region and transfers of power from one government to another have gone quite smoothly, so that there has been relative freedom of expression and organization. This is not to say, however, that corruption, fraud, and nepotism have been uprooted. In fact, they are still quite widespread, but there are certain checks and balances that help contain these negative phenomena.

Another major difference between the Arab and Kurdish revolutions has to do with political Islam. Even though the Islamists did not play a key role in any of the Arab uprisings, they have received the highest number of votes "in most elections held after the uprisings."[18] By contrast, in the Kurdish case, political Islam has not gained any moral or political ground. In the July 2009 elections for the Kurdistan Regional Government (KRG) in Iraq, for instance, the two Islamist parties won a mere 14 percent of the vote.[19] The same picture repeated itself in the September 2013 elections. Another facet of this issue is the growing identification of Kurdish Islamists in the KRG and in Turkey with Kurdish nationalism. Blaming the AKP for promoting "religious assimilation," a group of Kurdish imams and Islamic scholars in Turkey went so far as to launch a boycott against state-controlled mosques.[20]

The approach to the thorny problem of minorities has also been different in Arab and Kurdish societies. While persecution of Christians escalated significantly in the democratizing Arab states, such as in post-Saddam Iraq or in post-Mubarak Egypt, the KRG became a kind of safe haven for Christians fleeing Arab Iraq. According to a French report, "in the last decade it [the KRG] has also welcomed Christians from the rest of Iraq who were persecuted for their religious beliefs."[21] It is indeed ironic that under the watchful eyes of the American military forces, the harassment of indigenous Christians and other religious minorities reached its peak in Iraq.[22] Nor was the situation of the Copts in post-Mubarak Egypt any more enviable.[23]

There is also an important difference with regard to the role of women in the societies and polities of Arabs and Kurds. A study on the democratizing Arab countries showed that there were in fact fewer women in the parliaments after the Arab Spring. The most glaring example is Egypt, where the percentage of women in parliament fell from 12 percent under Husni Mubarak to a mere 2 percent under the Muslim Brothers' government that followed it.[24] However, in some of the Kurdish societies we notice a different approach, explained as follows in the KRG case: "as our friendship and alliance with the United States continues to grow, we are eager to showcase to the world, the vital contribution of Kurdish women, in all aspects of life."[25]

As to the participation of Kurdish women in the social and political sphere, the most advanced are the Kurdish women in Turkey. Cengiz Gunes maintains that "from the 1980s onwards . . . more and more Kurdish women started to engage in politics," taking on active roles both in the legal parties and in the PKK.[26] Women were integrated into the guerrilla organization early on, so that in 2012 a quarter of the fifty-five hundred PKK militants were said to be women.[27] In the BDP and other Kurdish organizations, females fulfilled the post of co-chairs with males, something unique to the Kurds.

In the Kurdish "liberated area" in Syria, new laws were passed forbidding polygamy, marriage at a young age, and unilateral divorce.[28] The PYD, the leading Kurdish party in Syria, followed in the footsteps of the BDP by accepting a woman as co-chair of the party. Indeed, in conjunction with the younger generation, women are now important pillars of the "democratic autonomy," which includes equal representation for women in the decision-making process.[29] Asked about the role of women in the Kurdish takeover of power in Syria, Asya ʿAbdullah, co-chair of the PYD (together with Salih Muslim), stated that "the revolution in West Kurdistan [Kurdistan of Syria], where self-government is in place since some areas were liberated, is led by women."[30]

Another point of comparison is the role of the diaspora. Unlike in the Arab case, the Kurdish diaspora has played a crucial role in national mobilization, and hence in the latest developments in Kurdistan. Especially important are the networks that were established in the European Union and its capital, Brussels. In fact the diaspora has played a threefold role: mobilizing the Kurds in the diaspora for the Kurdish national cause; keeping relations with the homeland alive so as to influence developments there; and lobbying governments in Europe and bringing pressure to bear on them to recognize the Kurdish plight. The main organization directing these activities is the Kurdistan National Congress (KNK), which is based in Brussels but also has offices in other major cities in Europe. The KNK has brought together Kurdish activists from all parts of Europe, as well as from the Kurdish region itself.

Finally, while the new media have played an important part in the Arab uprisings, their role has been even more crucial in the Kurdish case. The new Kurdish media were able to overcome the barriers put up by the states against the use of the Kurdish language and against cross-border communication between the different Kurdish communities. The new media enabled the transmission of new ideas from the diaspora to the different parts of Kurdistan, and vice versa. As it was suggested, "the Internet has become the weapon of choice for diasporic communities."[31] Similarly, the Internet, Twitter, and Facebook have become effective tools for quickly mobilizing Kurdish youths who had been silenced for generations.

The Synergic Effects in Greater Kurdistan

The repercussions of geopolitical transformations in the Middle East on the KRG are far-reaching, as they catapulted it to the position of actual leader of Greater Kurdistan. They also transformed it into an "unrecognized state" par excellence.[32] The fact that the KRG remained an island of stability and prosperity won it growing legitimacy in the international arena, all the more so as it was set against the background of instability in Iraq and tectonic changes in the region. The oil and gas assets contributed their own share to the region's attractiveness to the outside world. One indication thereof was that no fewer than twenty-five consulates and representations from various world countries were opened in Erbil,[33] performing as embassies in all but name.

The deteriorating situation in Syria and the marriage of convenience between the KRG and Turkey increased Erbil's political maneuverability in the region and emboldened it in its relations with Baghdad. Indeed, since the beginning of the upheavals in the region, Erbil has felt strong enough to challenge Baghdad on various domestic and foreign issues. The boldest move was taken in early April 2013, when the KRG government decided to pull its ministers and parliament members from the central government in Baghdad and to consider the possibility of establishing an independent Kurdish state.[34] At the time of this writing, no final decision has yet been taken regarding independence, but it is clearly a critical moment for the entire Kurdish people.

No less revolutionary were developments among the Kurds of Syria, who until recently were a silent minority insulated from the rest of the world. Many analysts doubted that such a community, which was fragmented both politically and geographically and lacked the bonus of living in impregnable mountains, could play a significant role on the Kurdish scene. For a long time even the studies on the Kurds tended to ignore the Kurds of Syria.[35] Yet within a short span of time, the Kurds emerged as a player to be reckoned with in Syria.

With a force of some ten thousand fighters,[36] the Kurds managed to take control of ten cities as well as of part of Aleppo, which then had a population of about six hundred thousand. They established what they termed "democratic autonomy," including city councils, police, and a military force, and also enacted a new constitution.[37] Furthermore, in January 2013 they took control of the oil-rich region of Rimelan (Girkê Legê), which would give them additional political and economic leverage if they managed to hold on to it.[38]

The developments in Kurdistan in Syria had an immediate impact on the KRG, opening new horizons never before dreamt of, namely the possibility of reaching out to the Mediterranean Sea via Kurdistan in Syria and Turkey. For a landlocked region, this could be an important step toward independence. The borders are usually open between these three parts now, and the KRG is providing a kind of strategic backing for the Kurdish regions in both Turkey and Syria.

The Kurdish national movement in Turkey, too, was given a further boost by the far-reaching effect of the Kurdish uprising in Syria. Unbelievable as this may seem, the far smaller and weaker Kurdish community in Syria has become a source of inspiration for the Kurds of Turkey. The fact that the border between Turkish and Syrian Kurds became porous further strengthened cross-border influences between the two communities.

Following the takeover of the Kurdish region in Syria, the PKK significantly escalated its strikes against Turkish targets. Concurrently, a wave of Gandhi-style popular resistance led by the PKK and the (lawful) BDP became widespread. These protest activities included sit-in demonstrations by mothers whose sons had disappeared; "democratic solution tents" set up to draw attention to the political stalemate;[39] civic Friday prayers conducted in the open in Kurdish; the boycott of parliamentary sessions and government mosques; and hunger strikes by Kurdish prisoners.

At the same time, another important change took place in the Turkish discourse. While the Kurdish issue had been taboo for decades, in recent months it has become the most debated issue in public life. Many intellectuals and journalists now talk of the need to solve the Kurdish problem peacefully to pull the rug from under the PKK.

For the AKP government, these developments formed a sobering experience, leading it to conclude that it needed to make its peace with its own Kurds in order to contain the long-term impact of the Kurds in Syria.[40] Accordingly, at the beginning of 2013 the AKP initiated a second peace process, following the failed one of 2009. This process is now in midcourse, but however it ends, it will be crucial for the Kurds' relationship with the state.

As for the Kurds of Iran, it appears that the upheavals in the region have bypassed them. In fact, since the brutal suppression of their uprising in the early years of the Islamic Republic, the Kurds of Iran have continued to oppose the Iranian regimes in various periods and in varying intensity.[41] Although they appear to have been politically dormant over the last few years, they still have the potential to become a dynamo for change in Iran itself, as well as in the entire Kurdish region.

For one thing, the Kurds of Iran, who are mostly Sunni Muslims, have been oppressed by the Shiʻi Islamic Republic of Iran on both religious and ethnic grounds. In addition, the government sought to weaken the Kurds, among others, by appealing to the Shiʻi part of the Kurdish community, which amounts to 30 percent of the total Kurdish population. Historically, the Shiʻi Kurds kept aloof from the Kurdish national movement for a number of reasons: their religious affinities with the different Persian rulers; their residence in the geographical periphery of the movement; and the propensity of Sunni Kurds to exclude the Shiʻi Kurds from the movement. For their part, the Iranian governments managed to distance the Shiʻi Kurds from the Kurdish national movement by harping on their religious affinity to Shiʻism and employing the infamous strategy of divide and rule.

However, the situation has begun to change in recent years, with Shiʻi Kurds joining the movement, as evidenced by the role they played in the green uprising against the Iranian regime in 2009.[42] The change stems from the economic crisis in Iran, which has weakened the government's ability to buy the goodwill of the Shiʻi Kurds by economic patronage. Furthermore, the electronic media, which strengthened the mounting wave of Kurdish nationalism in other parts of Kurdistan, especially in Syria, inspired the younger generation in Iran as well.

One more factor to bear in mind is that the Kurds of Iran outnumber those in Iraq and vastly outnumber those in Syria. Their historical record in the Kurdish movement is also much richer than that of the Syrian Kurds, for example. It was in the Republic of Mahabad, where for the first time in modern times a sense of pan-Kurdish solidarity was forged, when a substantial number of Iraqi Kurds headed by Mulla Mustafa Barzani crossed the Iraqi borders into Iran to support the Kurdish republic, which was in dire straits.

This trend of pan-Kurdish activity has been reversed. In the last decade it was the KRG that provided asylum to Kurdish refugees from Iran, as well as to various Kurdish Iranian groups such as Komala and the Democratic Party of Iranian Kurdistan, which had established their own bases in Iraq, benefiting from the experience of their brethren there. The most efficient of these groups is perhaps the Free Life Party of Kurdistan, known by its initials PJAK. In fact, the Kurds in Iran have been waiting for some event inside that country to trigger their entry into the rising wave of Kurdish nationalism.

Prospects for the Twenty-first Century

Writing in the aftermath of the 1990 Gulf War about the Kurds of Iraq, Turkey, and Iran, the Kurdish expert David McDowall was quite pessimistic about the prospects of Kurdish nationalism. In his view, "one must doubt whether Kurdish nationalism can ever prevail against three hostile governments willing to apply ruthless methods to contain the challenge."[43] Another scholar, Munir Morad, wrote in a similar vein that "for a long time, the Kurdish question has failed to feature in world affairs. Apart from occasional press attention, world opinion has been given little opportunity to reflect on the plight of the Kurdish nation." Morad put the main blame for this state of affairs on "inept Kurdish politicians."[44] Seen from the vantage point of the late twentieth century, a vivid imagination was needed for one to believe that only two decades later this picture would be altered dramatically.

The assumptions of the two scholars were built on the realities of the twentieth century, which was indeed one of the worst periods in Kurdish history. But the turn of the twenty-first century heralded new and better beginnings. The convergence of regional and international transformations, together with the crystallization of a strong national movement in Greater Kurdistan, marked the crucial difference between the two eras. The Kurds regained their voice, identity, and visibility in the region, as well as in the international arena. The very discourse of the Kurds changed from victimhood to that of assertive actors capable of changing their fate and image.

Furthermore, the upheavals in the Arab world catapulted them into playing an important role in reshaping the geopolitical map of the region. An important explanation for the improved status of the Kurds, as already mentioned, was the weakening of the nation-states and their inability to forge alliances against the Kurds. Another explanation involves the growing cohesiveness between the Kurds themselves and their greater sense of unity and purpose. Unlike in the twentieth century, there are fewer tendencies now among the Kurds of one state to cooperate against their brethren in a neighboring state. Quite to the contrary, the role of mutual influence and, at times, coordination and support between the Kurdish areas is impressive—with the Kurdish diaspora serving as a kind of glue. If we add to this the fact that in the twenty-first century the "sanctity" of the nation-state has lost some of its appeal, then we may realize that the Kurds now have a window of opportunity for redressing some of the evils resulting from World War I.

While at the end of that war the British and French powers helped dismember the Kurdish homeland, the United States unleashed a momentum after the two Gulf wars that moved the Kurds in the opposite direction. The wars of 1991 and 2003 set in motion dynamics that changed the situation of the Kurds in Iraq and reverberated in other parts of Kurdistan. Although the United States now upholds the territorial integrity of Iraq, it cannot actually stop the Kurds from distancing themselves from Baghdad. Similarly, while the prospects of finding oil in the Kurdistan area prompted the British to annex the oil-rich Kurdish region to Iraq at the end of World War I, the attraction of this same oil for companies worldwide helped the Kurds to disengage from Iraq in the twenty-first century.

What then is the geopolitical map that is emerging from the Kurdish awakening? Although the region is in a constant state of flux, a few conclusions can be drawn. The close relationship between Ankara and Erbil against Baghdad is a historical turning point, casting the KRG in the role of game changer in the region. The Ankara-Erbil axis, at times even against the Americans' best advice, may tip the balance toward the formation of a new state in Iraq: Kurdistan.[45] The autonomous Kurdish region in Syria is becoming another game changer. Whatever the results of the upheavals in that country, it is highly unlikely that the situation of the Kurds will revert to that of the pre-2012 period. Likewise, the role of the Kurds in Syria as energizers of the whole Kurdish scene is here to stay. The Turkish-Kurdish peace process is opening new vistas for the Kurds, all of which promise to influence the Kurds of Iran. Nor are the borders that separated the Kurdish communities from each other likely to be closed tightly once again. The vibrant Kurdish national movement has turned the imagined Greater Kurdistan into a kind of subsystem that is functioning underneath the regional state system and eroding it.

The Turkish sociologist Ismail Beşikçi, who dared write on the Kurdish issue during the Kemalist era and as a result spent seventeen years in prison, opined that the twenty-first century would be the century of the Kurds.[46] Whether this prophecy will come true or not, it is quite certain that the Sykes-Picot map is changing rapidly and that the Kurds stand to benefit from these changes. Certainly, there are many challenges and dangers, but the general trend seems more promising for the Kurds than ever before.

Notes

Introduction

1. This volume will compile these various studies into a collection.

2. Their complex relationship resembles in some ways that among Arab countries.

3. Abel Polese, "Language and Identity in Ukraine: Was It Really Nation-Building?" *Studies of Transition States and Societies* 3, no. 3 (November 2011): 40.

4. Ibid., 38.

5. In this sense the Kurds somewhat resemble the Jews, although the process of divesting the Jews of their identity was much more prolonged and intense.

6. This is not unique to the Kurds as it is, generally speaking, believed that the modern nation-states have had a negative impact on ethnic minority languages. For a study on the "linguicide" of the Kurdish language, see Amir Hassanpour, *Nationalism and Language in Kurdistan, 1918–1985* (San Francisco: Mellen Research University Press, 1992).

7. Kurdish politician Mahmut Alinak wrote a letter to Prime Minister Recep Tayyip Erdoğan in Kurdish, using the three forbidden letters. He consequently received an eighteen-month prison sentence. *The World*, November 25, 2009. http://www.theworld.org/2009/11/illegal-letters-in-turkey.

8. The establishment of the Republic of Mahabad was mainly a Sunni affair.

9. For the history of these *tariqas*, see Martin van Bruinessen, "The Naqshbandi Order in Seventeenth-Century Kurdistan," http://www.hum.uu.nl/medewerkers/m.vanbruinessen/publications/Bruinessen_Naqshbandi_order_17th_c_Kurdistan.pdf; van Bruinessen, "The Qadiriyya and the Lineages of Qadiri Shaikhs in Kurdistan," http://www.hum.uu.nl/medewerkers/m.vanbruinessen/publications/Bruinessen_Qadiriyya_in_Kurdistan.pdf.

10. The fifth was in the former Soviet Union, which is not included in this study.

11. There has been an upturn in the use of Kurdish in spite of the fact that so far there has been no real progress in standardizing the language.

12. According to the Kurdish Academy of Language, "in the age of computer-

ized communication networks, Kurds are beginning a new chapter of the history of their language that may enable them to mobilize nationally to ensure that Kurdish is the primary language used by their children." http://www.kurdishacademy .org/?q=node/2.

13. As a rule, Kurdish activists in the diaspora tend to hold more radical views than those on the ground, who have had to be more pragmatic.

14. The Kurdish case may be empowered by a quest for separatism by various communities, even in Western states such as Spain, Belgium, and Canada.

Kurdish Nationalism in Comparative Perspective

1. Anthony D. Smith, *The Ethnic Origins of Nations*, 84.
2. See Clifford Geertz, "The Integrative Revolution," 117–118.
3. Walker Connor, *Ethnonationalism: The Quest for Understanding*, 4.
4. Milton Esman, *Ethnic Politics*, 217.
5. Anthony D. Smith, *Theories of Nationalism*; Peter Alter, *Nationalism*.
6. Donald Horowitz, *Ethnic Groups in Conflict*.
7. Denise Natali, *The Kurds and the State*, 34.
8. Smith, *Ethnic Origins*, 34, 129, 142.
9. Joseph Rothschild, *Ethnopolitics: A Conceptual Framework*.
10. Ofra Bengio, *Saddam's Iraq: Political Discourse and the Language of Power*, 144; Romano, *The Kurdish National Movement*, 7.
11. Horowitz, *Ethnic Groups in Conflict*, 544.
12. Bengio, *Saddam's Iraq*, 144, 147; Romano, *The Kurdish National Movement*, 216.
13. Natali, *The Kurds and the State*, 37.
14. Ernest Renan, in an 1882 Sorbonne lecture, and in *Qu'est-ce Qu'une nation? Et autres écrits politiques*, 15.
15. Ernest Renan, as quoted in Philip Spencer and Howard Wollman, *Nationalism: A Critical Introduction*, 42.
16. Maurice Barrès, *Scènes et doctrines du nationalisme*; see also Carlton Hayes, *Historical Evolution of Modern Nationalism*, 194.
17. Boyd C. Shafer, *Nationalism: Myth and Reality*; Shafer, *Faces of Nationalism: New Realities and Old Myths*.
18. Johann Gottfried von Herder, *Ideen zur Philosophie der Geschichte der Menschheit*.
19. Benedict Anderson, *Imagined Communities: Reflections on the Origin and Spread of Nationalism*; Ernest Gellner, *Nations and Nationalism*.
20. Natali, *The Kurds and the State*, 74.
21. Amir Hassanpour, as quoted in Romano, *The Kurdish Nationalist Movement*, 13.
22. Romano, *The Kurdish Nationalist Movement*, 220.
23. Smith, *Ethnic Origins*, 163–164.
24. Romano, *The Kurdish Nationalist Movement*, 3.
25. Ibid., 131.
26. Renan, *Qu'est-ce Qu'une nation?*, 32.

27. Smith, *Theories of Nationalism*, 169.

28. Romano, *The Kurdish Nationalist Movement*, 133–134.

29. Hans Kohn, "Western and Eastern Nationalisms," 162–165.

30. On the varieties of nationalism, see Smith, *Theories of Nationalism*, 211–229.

31. Michael Hechter, Tuna Kuyucu, and Audrey Sacks, "Nationalism and Direct Rule," 84–93.

32. Hedva Ben Israel, *In the Name of the Nation: Studies in Nationalism and Zionism*, 3–31.

33. Robert Melson and Howard Wolpe, "Modernization and the Politics of Communalism," 1012–1030.

34. Charles Tilly, "States and Nationalism in Europe 1492–1992."

35. Connor, *Ethnonationalism*, 77.

36. Romano, *The Kurdish Nationalist Movement*, 224. See also Nader Entessar, *Kurdish Ethnonationalism*, 7.

37. Smith, *Ethnic Origins*, 164.

38. Lee C. Buchheit, *Secession: The Legitimacy of Self-Determination*, 155; David McDowall, *A Modern History of the Kurds*, 115.

39. McDowall, *Modern History of the Kurds*, 450.

40. Romano, *The Kurdish Nationalist Movement*, 146.

41. Horowitz, *Ethnic Groups in Conflict*, 229–288.

42. Natali, *The Kurds and the State*, 97, 128; Romano, *The Kurdish Nationalist Movement*, 89; Eva Savelsberg and Siamend Hajö, "Ten Years of Bashar Al-Asad and No Compromise with the Kurds."

43. McDowall, *Modern History of the Kurds*, 188.

44. Henry Kissinger, as quoted by William Daugherty, *Executive Secrets: Covert Action and the Presidency*, 176.

45. McDowall, *Modern History of the Kurds*, 299–300.

46. Ofra Bengio, "Kurdistan Reaches toward the Sea," *Haaretz*, August 3, 2012.

Historical Setting: The Roots of Modern Kurdish Nationalism

1. Robert Olson, *The Emergence of Kurdish Nationalism and the Sheikh Said Rebellion, 1880–1925*, 1–25; Hakan Ozoglu, *Kurdish Notables and the Ottoman State: Evolving Identities, Competing Loyalties, and Shifting Boundaries*, 72–78; Wadie Jwaideh, *The Kurdish National Movement: Its Origins and Development*, 75–102; Sulayman Asad Aslan, "Clashes of Agencies Formation and Failure of Early Kurdish Nationalism 1918–1922," 59–65.

2. Amir Hassanpour, "The Making of Kurdish Identity: Pre-20th Century Historical and Literary Discourses," 106–161; Martin van Bruinessen, "Ehmedi Xani's *Mam U Zin* and Its Role in the Emergence of Kurdish National Awareness," 40–57; Ferhad Shakely, *Kurdish Nationalism in* Mam U Zin *of Ahmad-I Khani*.

3. On the importance of a "collective name" or signifiers of the premodern *ethnie* or ethnic group, see Anthony Smith, *The Ethnic Origins of Nations*, 22–23.

4. The term "protonationalism" is used in the context of the present article in the sense of social and cultural characteristics, collective identities, and perceptions in a premodern, prenationalist era that resemble or are precursors of their counterparts in modern nations and nationalisms.

5. Ahmad bin Yahya bin Jabbar al-Baladhuri, *Futuh al-Buldan*, 464, 467, 538, 548.

6. Tabari, *History of Tabari (Ta'rikh al-rusul wa-al-muluk)*, vol. 15, *The Crisis of the Early Caliphate*, trans. R. Stephen Humphreys, 34.

7. Tabari, ibid., vol. 14, *The Conquest of Iran*, trans. G. Rex Smith, 73, 78–79.

8. J. Kurdo [pseud.], *Kurdistan: The Origins of Kurdish Civilization*, 55.

9. On the crucial role of language in the development of national identity and national consciousness, see Amir Hassanpour, *Nationalism and Language in Kurdistan: 1918–1958*.

10. According to Ibn Khaldun: Rizankas. Ibn Khaldun *Ta'rikh al-ʿalamat*, vol. 4, 1093. See also Muhammad Zaki Amin, *Khulasat ta'rikh al- Kurd wa Kurdistan Ta'rikh al-duwal wa al-imarat al-Kurdiyyah fi ʿahd al-Islami*, vol. 2, 66–89.

11. Vladimir Minorsky, "Annazids," *EI*, New Edition (Leiden: E. J. Brill, 1954–2003), vol. 1, 512–513.

12. See the classic study of Shaddadids: Vladimir Minorsky, *Studies in Caucasian History*, 33–78. See also Zaki Amin, *Khulasat Ta'arikh Kurd wa Kurdistan*, 90–94.

13. On the Marwanid dynasty, see Ibn Khaldun, *Ta'rikh al-ʿalamat*, vol. 4, 674–686; and H. F. Amedroz, "The Marwanid Dynasty at Mayyafariqin in the Tenth and Eleventh Centuries A.D.," 123–154. See also Zaki Amin, *Khulasat ta'rikh al-Kurd wa Kurdistan*, vol. 2, 95–135.

14. Amedroz, "The Marwanid Dynasty," 131.

15. ʿIzz al-Din Ibn al-Athir, *Al-kamil fi al- ta'rikh*, vol. 9, 384–386.

16. Ibid., 598–599.

17. Ibid., vol. 10, 65–67.

18. Ibid., 144.

19. Ibid., 604. See also the English translation: ʿIzz al-Din Ibn al-Athir, *The Chronicle of Ibn al-Athir for the Crusading Period from al-kamil fi al- ta'rikh, Part 1: The Years 491–541/1097–1146, The Coming of the Franks and the Muslim Response*, trans. D. S. Richards, 240, 307, 367; ʿIzz al-Din Ibn al-Athir, *The Annals of the Saljuq Turks: Selections from al-kamil fi al- ta'rikh of ʿIzz al-Din Ibn al-Athir*, trans. D. S. Richards, 15, 19, 45, 58, 60–62, 86, 91–92, 97, 156, 181, 208.

20. Minorsky, *Caucasian History*, 116–139, 146–157.

21. Ibid., 138.

22. For an in-depth discussion of the different social aspects and patterns of Kurdish society and Kurdish identity, see Martin van Bruinessen, *Agha, Shaikh and State: The Social and Political Structures of Kurdistan*, 50–132. For a discussion of the issue of the meaning behind the signifier *kurd* in the sixteenth and seventeenth centuries, see van Bruinessen, "Kurdish Society, Ethnicity, Nationalism and Refugee Problems," 33–67.

23. On the Kurdish tribes and emirates under Qaraqoyunlu and Aqqoyunlu, especially the emirates Hasankeyf (between Amid [Diyarbakır] and Cizre), Hakkari, and Chemishkezek (in Dersim, Turkish Tunceli region in Western Kurdi-

stan), see van Bruinessen, *Agha, Shaikh and State*, 137, 145–151. On Aqqoyunlu, see John E. Woods, *The Aqqoyunlu Clan, Confederation, Empire*.

24. Martin van Bruinessen and Hendrik Boeschoten, eds., *Evliya Celebi in Diyarbekir: The Relevant Section of The Seyahatname*, 13–15.

25. Ozoglu, *Kurdish Notables*, 50.

26. Jwaideh, *The Kurdish National Movement*, 23.

27. Martin van Bruinessen, "Kurdistan in the Sixteenth and Seventeenth Centuries as Reflected in Evliya Celebi's *Seyahatname*," 1–11; van Bruinessen and Boeschoten, *Celebi in Diyarbekir*; Robert Dankoff, ed., *Evliya Celebi in Bitlis*; Ozoglu, *Kurdish Notables*, 33–35.

28. Dankoff, *Celebi in Bitlis*, 92–107.

29. Ibid., 283–295; van Bruinessen, *Agha, Shaikh and State*, 162–170.

30. Shakely, *Kurdish Nationalism*. For an in-depth discussion of the poem, see Amir Hassanpour, "The Making of Kurdish Identity," especially pp. 106–131.

31. As translated in Hassanpour, "The Making of Kurdish Identity," 118–119.

32. As translated in ibid., 109.

33. As translated by Shakely in *Kurdish Nationalism*, 71.

34. Ibid., 74.

35. On the use of *Mem u Zin* by the modern Kurdish national movement, see Hassanpour, "The Making of Kurdish Identity," 129–142. Van Bruinessen, "Ehmedi Xani's *Mam U Zin*," 40–57.

36. Sharaf al-Din Khan Bidlisi, *Sharafnameh, Fi Ta'rikh al-Duwal wal-Imarat al-Kurdiyya*. For an English translation, see Prince Sharaf al-Din Bidlisi, *The Sharafnama or the History of the Kurdish Nation*, trans. M. R. Izady.

37. Michael Eppel, "The Demise of the Kurdish Emirates: The Impact of Ottoman Reforms and International Relations on Kurdistan during the First Half of the Nineteenth Century," 244–246.

38. Claudius J. Rich, *Narrative of a Residence in Koordistan*, vol. 1.

39. Ibid., 96–97; T. Nieuwenhuis, *Politics and Society in Early Modern Iraq: Mamluk Pashas, Tribal Shayks and Local Rule between 1802–1831*, 97.

40. Djalile Djalil, *Kurdi Ocmanskoi Imperii Pervoy Polovine 19 Beka* [The Kurds of the Ottoman Empire in the First Half of the Nineteenth Century], 96; James Bailie Fraser, *Travels in Koordistan, Mesopotamia & Including an Account of Parts of those Countries Hitherto Unvisited by Europeans: with Sketches of the Character and Manners of the Koordish and Arab Tribes*, 64.

41. Djalil, *Kurdi Ocmanskoi Imperii Pervoy Polovine 19 Beka*, 55.

42. A general description of the growth of Mohammad Kor's power may be found in Jwaideh, *The Kurdish National Movement*, 55–56. For a more detailed though somewhat incomplete portrayal, see Fraser, *Travels*, vol. 1, 102. H. C. Rawlison, "Notes on a Journey from Tabriz, Through Persian Kurdistan, to the Ruins of Takhti-Soleiman," 32. Muhammad Zaki Amin, *Khulasat ta'rikh al-Kurd wa Kurdistan min aqdam al-ʿusur hatta al-ʿan*, 243.

43. Jwaideh, *The Kurdish National Movement*, 59; Zaki Amin, *Khulasat*, 245.

44. For a detailed discussion of the fall of Muhammad Kor, see Djalil, *Kurdi Ocmanskoi Imperii Pervoy Polovine 19 Beka*, 100–122.

45. A. B. Cunningham, ed., *The Early Correspondence of Richard Wood, 1831–1841*, 97. This attempt by Wood to achieve a compromise that would leave Mo-

hammad Kor in charge of Rawanduz but subordinate to the Ottomans is also discussed by the British traveler W. F. Ainsworth in *Travels and Researches in Asia Minor, Mesopotamia, Chaldea and Armenia*, 323.

46. Zaki Amin, *Khulasat*, 247; Fraser, *Travels*, vol. 1, 81–82; Jwaideh, *The Kurdish National Movement*, 60, 319.

47. Ainsworth, *Travels*, vol. 1, 323; Jwaideh, *The Kurdish National Movement*, 60.

48. The missionary activity, the Nestorian sect, and the events set forth here are discussed in a series of primary sources and studies that reflect the viewpoints of missionaries and local Christians. See Kamal Salibi and Yusuf K. Khoury, eds., *The Missionary Herald, Reports from Northern Iraq 1833–1847*. A more balanced account may be found in the books by the British traveler and archaeologist Sir Austen Henry Layard: *Discoveries in the Ruins of Nineveh and Babylon: With Travels in Armenia and Kurdistan, and the Desert* and *Popular Account of Discoveries at Nineveh*, 122–170. See also John Joseph, *The Nestorians and their Neighbors*; Gordon Taylor, *Fever and Thirst: Dr. Grant and the Christian Tribes of Kurdistan*.

49. E. B. Soane, *To Mesopotamia and Kurdistan in Disguise*, 156; Jwaideh, *The Kurdish National Movement*, 69; van Bruinessen, *Agha, Shaikh and State*, 292.

50. Austen Henry Layard, *Nineveh and Its Remains*, vol. 1, 173; Jwaideh, *The Kurdish National Movement*, 72, 322.

51. Ainsworth, *Travels*, 271, 281.

52. *Salibi and Khoury, Missionary Herald*, 474, 483.

53. Layard, *Discoveries*, 122.

54. Nezan, "The Kurds under the Ottoman Empire," in *A People without Country: Kurds and Kurdistan*, ed. G. Chailand, 24. Although the Bedir Khan family was integrated in the establishment of the Ottoman state, family members continued to strive for the revival of the Botan Emirate, and from the end of the nineteenth century played a central role in the growth and dissemination of Kurdish nationalism. Othman Pasha Bedir Khan tried to revive the emirate of Botan in 1879 and to unify the Kurds under his leadership. Other members of the Bedir Khan family tried to advance Kurdish autonomy after the Young Turks revolution in 1908 until the beginning of World War I. In 1909 'Abd al-Razzaq Bedir Khan tried to convince Russia to support the establishment of a Kurdish state. During World War I, 'Abd al-Razzaq and Kamil Bedir Khan cooperated with Russia. See David McDowall, *A Modern History of the Kurds*, 99–100. Jwaideh, *The Kurdish National Movement*, 121.

55. The revolt of Yezdansher has been studied quite infrequently. Only Candan Badem's book on the Crimean War provides a survey, primarily of those aspects involved in the relations between the Ottoman Empire and Britain and the overview of the Crimean War; see *The Ottoman Crimean War (1853–1856)*, 360–377. An important source, which contains a reference to the war from the Russian point of view, is a book by an intelligence officer in the staff of the Russian Army in the Caucasus: Captain L. I. Averyanov, *Kurdi w woynakh Rosii c Perciej i Turcej w teczenie 19 ctoletia* [Kurds in the wars of Russia with Persia and Turkey in the 19th century]. It includes important documents and a historical review of the relations between Russia and the Kurds throughout the nineteenth century.

56. Badem, The Ottoman Crimean War, 366; Averyanov, *Kurdi w woynakh Rosii c Perciej i Turcej w teczenie 19 ctoletia*, 93.

57. Bedem, The Ottoman Crimean War, 373.

58. The details of the British involvement are discussed in the memoirs of the British doctor Humphrey Sandwith, who was in charge of the British medical detachment in the Ottoman forces in the area. Sandwith, *A Narrative: The Siege of Kars*, 212–215.

59. Ferhad Shakely, "Haji Qadir Koyi," *Kurdish Globe* (Erbil-Hewler), February 7, 2010.

60. Aslan, "Clashes," 311, also exemplified in chapter 2 of his research, 101–103, 150–159.

The Dual Relationship between Kurdish Tribalism and Nationalism

1. Martin van Bruinessen, *Agha, Shaikh and State*, 220–224, 267–269.

2. Kendal Nezan, "The Kurds under the Ottoman Empire"; Hussein Tahiri, *The Structure of Kurdish Society and the Struggle for a Kurdish State*.

3. Sociologists, anthropologists, and political experts define "tribe" in different ways, so that there is no one generally accepted definition. The definitions range from "primitive isolated communities" to a framework of solidarity, which can subsist in non-isolated and even modern societies. For a variety of definitions of the term, see Roger M. Keesing, *Cultural Anthropology*, 118–119; David E. Hunter and Philip Whitten, *Encyclopedia of Anthropology* (New York: Harper and Row, 1976), 393–394; William A. Haviland, *Cultural Anthropology*, 314–315; Patricia Crone, "The Tribe and the State," 48–77; John H. Bodley, *Cultural Anthropology, Tribes, States and the Global System*, 30; Jules Henry, *Jungle People, A Kaingang Tribe of the Highlands of Brazil*; Paula Brown, *Highland Peoples of New Guinea*.

4. Ernest Gellner, *Muslim Society*, 56–58; Ernest Gellner, "Tribalism and the State in the Middle East."

5. Joseph Kostiner, "Transforming Dualities: Tribes and State Formation in Saudi Arabia."

6. Bassam Tibi, "The Simultaneity of the Unsimultaneous: Old Tribes and Imposed Nation-States in the Modern Middle East."

7. Anthony Smith, *The Ethnic Origins of Nations*, 2–15, 133–147.

8. Amir Hassanpour, "Ferment and Fetters in the Study of Kurdish Nationalism."

9. Hamit Bozarslam, "Tribal Asabiyya and Kurdish Politics: A Socio-Historical Perspective."

10. Ibid.

11. Hakan Ozoglu, "State-Tribe Relations: Kurdish Tribalism in the 16th and 17th Century Ottoman Empire."

12. David McDowall, *A Modern History of The Kurds*, 5–6.

13. Nader Entessar, *Kurdish Ethnonationalism*, 3; van Bruinessen, *Agha, Shaikh and State*, 147–165.

14. McDowall, *A Modern History of the Kurds*, 38–47; Nezan, "The Kurds under the Ottoman Empire;" Hanna Batatu, *The Old Social Classes and the Revolutionary Movements of Iraq*, 44–45, 59, 214–215; van Bruinessen, *Agha, Shaikh and State*, 175–181.

15. Van Bruinessen, *Agha, Shaikh and State*, 210–221; McDowall, *A Modern History of the Kurds*, 50–52.

16. Mah'mud al-Durra, *Al-Qad'iyya al-Kurdiyya*, 194.

17. William Eagleton, *The Kurdish Republic of 1946*, 47.

18. Nezan, "The Kurds under the Ottoman Empire," 26–27; van Bruinessen, *Agha, Shaikh and State*, 275; Entessar, *Kurdish Ethnonationalism*, 49. Entessar mentions the Kurdish poet Haji Qadir as one of the few who promoted Kurdish nationalism by writing poems that call for Kurdish independence.

19. Hassan Arfa, *The Kurds: An Historical and Political Study*, 24; Nezan, "The Kurds under the Ottoman Empire," 17–23; Martin van Bruinessen, "The Sadate Nehri or Gilanizade of Central Kurdistan."

20. Robert Speer, *The Foreign Doctor*, 74–94.

21. Robert Olson, *The Emergence of Kurdish Nationalism and the Sheikh Said Rebellion, 1880-1925*, 1–3; Speer, *The Foreign Doctor*, 74–94; al-Durra, *Al-Qad iyya al-Kurdiyya*, 91; McDowall, *A Modern History of the Kurds*, 53–59; Nezan, "The Kurds under the Ottoman Empire," 23–24; Arfa, *The Kurds*, 24.

22. Van Bruinessen, "The Sadate Nehri," 4; McDowall, *A Modern History of the Kurds*, 53–59.

23. McDowall, *A Modern History of the Kurds*.

24. Arfa, *The Kurds*, 24.

25. McDowall, *A Modern History of the Kurds*, 57–59.

26. Ibid.

27. Arnold Wilson, *Loyalties, Mesopotamia 1917–1920*, 86–87; Walid Hamdi, *Al-Kurd wa Kurdistan fi al-Watha'iq al-Britaniyya* (London: Matabiʿ Sijil al-ʿArab, 1991), 71; Wadie Jwaideh, *The Kurdish National Movement: Its Origins and Development*, 160–161; British Foreign Office, F.O. 371/4192.

28. Wilson, *Loyalties*, 129–130.

29. Jwaideh, *The Kurdish National Movement*, 169; McDowall, *A Modern History of the Kurds*, 156; Wilson, *Loyalties*, 126–128; Gertrude Bell, *Review of the Civil Administration of Mesopotamia*, 60.

30. McDowall, *A Modern History of the Kurds*, 157–158; Wilson, *Loyalties*, 136–138.

31. Wilson, *Loyalties*, 136–138; McDowall, *A Modern History of the Kurds*, 157–158; C. J. Edmonds, *Kurds, Turks and Arabs*, 30.

32. McDowall, *A Modern History of the Kurds*, 158.

33. Ibid., 159–163; Charles Tripp, *A History of Iraq*, 54–55; Jwaideh, *The Kurdish National Movement*, 185–202; Air 23/2, August 22, 1922; British Foreign Office, F.O. 371/52404, November 25, 1946.

34. Martin van Bruinessen, "Kurdish Tribes and the State of Iran: The Case of Simko's Revolt," in Martin van Bruinessen, *Kurdish Ethno-Nationalism Versus Nation-Building States*, 125–155; McDowall, *A Modern History of the Kurds*, 214–216; Nader Entessar, *Kurdish Politics in the Middle East*, 16–17.

35. Van Bruinessen, "Kurdish Tribes and the State of Iran," 125–155; Arfa,

The Kurds, 59; Edmonds, *Kurds, Turks and Arabs*, 305–307; A. R. Ghassemlou, "Kurdistan in Iran," 117; McDowall, *A Modern History of the Kurds*, 216–222; Jwaideh, *The Kurdish National Movement*, 410–413.

36. Entessar, *Kurdish Politics in the Middle East*, 16–17; McDowall, *A Modern History of the Kurds*, 221–222; van Bruinessen, "Kurdish Tribes and the State of Iran," 147.

37. Van Bruinessen, *Agha, Shaikh and State*, 265–299; McDowall, *A Modern History of the Kurds*, 192–211; Jwaideh, *The Kurdish National Movement*, 203–218.

38. Van Bruinessen, *Agha, Shaikh and State*, 265–299; McDowall, *A Modern History of the Kurds*, 192–211; Jwaideh, *The Kurdish National Movement*, 203–218.

39. McDowall, *A Modern History of the Kurds*, 194, 209.

40. Edmonds, *Kurds, Turks and Arabs*, 12–14; Phebe Marr, *The Modern History of Iraq*, 9; Air 23/671, March 31, 1939; See also British Foreign Office, F.O. 371/128041, July 31, 1957.

41. The Kurdish name Mulla (the pronunciation is "mala") means clergyman, like in Arabic. However, when prefixed to male names, the word does not always imply that the person is a religious dignitary. See Massoud Barzani and Ahmed Ferhadi, *Mustafa Barzani and the Kurdish Liberation Movement, 1931-1961* (New York: Palgrave Macmillan, 2003), 5.

42. McDowall, *A Modern History of the Kurds*, 290; Saad Jawad, *Iraq and the Kurdish Question, 1958-1970*, 15, 32; al-Durra, *Al-Qad'iyya al-Kurdiyya*, 206–207; British Foreign Office, F.O. 371/45341, E6723, September 26, 1945.

43. Jawad, *Iraq and the Kurdish Question*, 15–16, 32–33; Stephen Longrigg, *Iraq, 1900 to 1950*, 325–326; Gareth Stansfield, *Iraqi Kurdistan, Political Development and Emergence of Democracy*, 62–63; Edmund Ghareeb, *The Kurdish Question in Iraq*, 33; British Foreign Office, F.O. 371/40038, January 3, 1943; F.O. 371/40041, E519/37/93, January 24, 1944; F.O. 371/40041, March 23, 1944.

44. McDowall, *A Modern History of the Kurds*, 291–292; Eagleton, *The Kurdish Republic of 1946*, 53–54; Sami al-Ghamrawi, *Qissat al-Akrad fi Shimal al-'Iraq*, 223–224.

45. Jawad, *Iraq and the Kurdish Question*, 16; al-Durra, *Al-Qad iyya al-Kurdiyya*, 213; al-Ghamrawi, *Qissat al-Akrad fi Shimal al-'Iraq*, 224–225; British Foreign Office, F.O. 371/45311, August 15, 1945; F.O. 371/45323, August 7, 1945; F.O. 371/52369, January 18, 1946.

46. British Foreign Office, F.O. 371/40041, March 23, 1944; McDowall, *A Modern History of the Kurds*, 231–240.

47. Eagleton, *The Kurdish Republic of 1946*, 56, 86; McDowall, *A Modern History of the Kurds*, 241; British Foreign Office, F.O. 371/40039, August 23, 1944.

48. McDowall, *A Modern History of the Kurds*, 242–244; Eagleton, *The Kurdish Republic of 1946*, 83; Jwaideh, *The Kurdish National Movement*, 243–261. At the time, thirteen newspapers were published in the Kurdish language throughout the whole of Kurdistan, and leaflets were distributed in Kurdish; see British Foreign Office, F.O. 371/52369, May 1, 1946.

49. McDowall, *A Modern History of the Kurds*, 296–297; Stansfield, *Iraqi Kurdistan*, 61, 65.

50. McDowall, *A Modern History of the Kurds*, 296–297; Ofra Bengio, *The Kurdish Revolt in Iraq*, 19; Stansfield, *Iraqi Kurdistan*, 61, 65.

51. Ghareeb, *The Kurdish Question in Iraq*, 34; McDowall, *A Modern History of the Kurds*, 245–246; al-Durra, *Al-Qad iyya al-Kurdiyya*, 215.

Kurdish Integration in Iraq:
The Paradoxes of Nation Formation and Nation Building

1. Clifford Geertz, "The Integrative Revolution: Primordial Sentiments and Civil Politics in the New States," 3–6.

2. Benedict R. Anderson, *Imagined Communities: Reflections on the Origin and Spread of Nationalism*, 5–7.

3. Ernest Gellner, *Nations and Nationalism*, 5–7; See also Gellner, "Nationalism and Modernization"; and Gellner, "Adam's Navel: 'Primordialists' versus 'Modernists.'"

4. Anthony D. Smith, "The Nation: Real or Imagined"; Smith, "When Is a Nation?," 8–9.

5. See Anthony D. Smith, *The Ethnic Origins of Nations*, 154; John Hutchinson, "Ethnicity and Modern Nations," 654.

6. Anthony D. Smith, *Theories of Nationalism*, 22; Smith, "The Nation: Real or Imagined," 41–42.

7. Montserrat Guibernau, "Anthony D. Smith on Nations and National Identity: A Critical Assessment," 132; and Anthony D. Smith, *Ethnosymbolism and Nationalism: A Cultural Approach*, 49.

8. Amatzia Baram, *Culture, History and Ideology in the Formation of Ba'thist Iraq, 1968–89*; Ofra Bengio, *Saddam's Word: Political Discourse in Iraq*; Bengio, "Nation Building in Multiethnic Societies: The Case of Iraq"; Charles Tripp, *A History of Iraq*; Phebe Marr, *The Modern History of Iraq*; Sherko Kirmanj, "The Construction of the Iraqi State and the Question of National Identity."

9. U.S. Department of Defense, *Measuring Stability and Security in Iraq: March 2009 Report to Congress*, 1–2; U.S. Department of Defense, *Measuring Stability and Security in Iraq: September 2009 Report to Congress*, iv.

10. "Turnout for Iraq Election Solid at 62 pct.," Reuters, March 8, 2010.

11. Kirmanj, "Construction of the Iraqi State."

12. Eric Davis, "Democracy's Prospects in Iraq"; Thomas E. Ricks, *Fiasco: The American Military Adventure in Iraq*; Kenneth M. Pollack, "The Seven Deadly Sins of Failure in Iraq: A Retrospective Analysis of the Reconstruction."

13. Maia Hallward, "Who Is Iraqi? The Changing Boundaries of Identity in Contemporary Iraq," 13.

14. The textbooks (which are currently under review) were written from a Sunni perspective, since the Sunnis dominated the Iraqi state institutions from 1921 to 2003.

15. *Al-Tarikh al-Hadith wa al-Mu'asir lil-Watan al-'Arabi lil-Saf al-Thalith al-Mutawassit* [The modern and contemporary history of the Arab homeland for grade three intermediate], 90–93; *Al-Tarikh al-Hadith wa al-Mu'asir lil-Watan al-'Arabi lil-Saf al-Sadis al-Adabi* [The modern and contemporary history of the Arab homeland for grade six humanities], 2009, 179–188; *Al-Tarikh al-Hadith wa al-Mu'asir lil-Watan al-'Arabi lil-Saf al-Sadis al-Adabi*, 188–193; *Mejuy Nwe w*

Hawcharkh Poli Dwazdahami Amadayi Wejayi [New and modern history for grade twelve high school—humanities], 176–184.

16. *Al-Tarikh al-Hadith lil-Watan al-Arabi lil-Saf al-Sadis al-Ibtidai* [The modern history of the Arab homeland for grade six primary school], 59–65; *Al-Tarikh al-Hadith wa al-Muʿasir lil-Watan al-ʿArabi lil-Saf al-Sadis al-Adabi,* 2001, 183–188.

17. *Mejuy Nwe w Hawcharkh Poli Dwazdahami Amadayi Wejayi,* 156–157.

18. The *Anfal* operations were genocidal campaigns against the Kurdish people and many other ethnic groups in areas of Iraq within Kurdistan, conducted by the Iraqi regime in 1988.

19. *Al-Tarikh al-Hadith wa al-Muʿasir lil-Watan al-ʿArabi lil-Saf al-Sadis al-Adabi,* 2001, 302–303; ʿAli al-Kash, *Al-Dawr al-Takhribi al-Irani fi al-ʿIraq: Intifada Shaʿbaniyya am Safhat al-Ghadr wa al-Khiyana* [The Iranian role of destruction in Iraq].

20. Muhammad Amin Zaki Beg, *Khulasat Tarikh Kurd wa Kurdistan* [A brief history of the Kurds and Kurdistan], vols. 1–2 (Beirut: al-Jamʿiyya al-Kurdiyya al-Lubnaniyya al-Khayriyya, 2003); Ihsan Nuri Pasha, *Mejuy Rishay Nazhadi Kurd* [The history of Kurdish origin]; Jawad Mella, *Kurdistan and The Kurds: A Divided Homeland and a Nation without State.*

21. Cyaxares (625–585 BC) was the first King of the Medes.

22. The Kurdish national anthem was written by the Kurdish poet Dildar in 1938. See Ala al-Din, Abdul Khaliq, ed., *Dildar: Shaʿiri Shorshgeri Kurd* [Dildar: A Kurdish revolutionary poet], 174.

23. *Babaten Komalayati Pola Penje Saratayi* [Societal issues for grade five primary school], 68; Sherko Bekas, *Diwani Sherko Bekas Bargi Seyam 1971–1993* [Poetical works of Sherko Bekas, third volume, 1971–1993], 31–217.

24. *Babaten Komalayati Pola Penje Saratayi* [Societal issues for grade five primary school], 66–69, 71–78; Bekas, *Diwani Sherko Bekas Bargi Seyam 1971–1993,* 3, 21, 28; *Mejuy Nwe w Hawcharkh Poli Dwazdahami Amadayi Wejayi,* 53–89.

25. *Al-Tarikh al-Qadim Lil-Watan al-ʿArabi lil-Saf al-Awwal al-Mutawassit* [The ancient history of the Arab homeland for grade one intermediate school], 38–57.

26. Nawshirwan Mustafa Amin, *Mirayati Baban la newan Bardashi Rom u Ajamda* [The Emirate of Baban between the grindstones of Turks and Persians], 261–295; Rebwar Siwayli, *Ktebi Nali* [The book of Nali], 39–45; Bekas, *Diwani Sherko Bekas Bargi Seyam 1971–1993,* 332–356.

27. *Mejuy Nwe w Hawcharkh Poli Dwazdahami Amadayi Wejayi,* 118–126, 141–168.

28. Irredentist nationalism attempts to extend the existing boundaries of a state by incorporating territories of an adjacent state occupied principally by co-nationals. Unification or pan-nationalism involves the merger of a politically divided but culturally homogeneous territory into one state.

29. Ibrahim Al-Jaʿfari, "A New Marshall Plan for Iraq," *Times* (London), June 27, 2005; Wifaq, *Aladhi yahsul al-Aan fi al-Iraq min Tahmish wa Tamyiz Muʾlim jidan* [What is happening in Iraq at the moment, when marginalization and discrimination are very painful], Iraqi National Accord; "Al-Maliki's Description of Iraq as Arab Country rankles Kurds," accessed March 31, 2009.

30. Anderson, *Imagined Communities*.

31. David McDowall, *A Modern History of the Kurds*, 3.

32. *Tanzimat* were series of reforms promulgated in the Ottoman Empire between 1839 and 1876.

33. Turanism was a movement that aspired to unite politically and culturally all the Turkic, Tatar, and Uralic peoples living in Turkey and across Eurasia from Hungary to the Pacific. See Bassam Tibi, *Arab Nationalism: A Critical Enquiry*, trans. Marion Farouk-Sluglett and Peter Sluglett, 106–109.

34. Robert Olson, *The Emergence of Kurdish Nationalism and the Sheikh Said Rebellion, 1880–1925*, 4.

35. Tibi, *Arab Nationalism*, 109.

36. Ibid., 112–115.

37. Ibid., 148.

38. Ahmedi Khani, *Mem u Zin*, 33–48.

39. Al-Amir Sharaf Khan Al-Bitlisi, *Sharafnama*, trans. Muhammad Jamil Al-Rojbayani, 50–51.

40. Khani, *Mem u Zin*, 17–20; Giwi Mukiryani, ed., *Diwani Haji Qadiri Koyi* [Collected works of Haji Qadiri Koyi], 54; Martin van Bruinessen, *Agha, Shaikh and State: The Social and Political Structures of Kurdistan*, 34; Amir Hassanpour, *Nationalism and Language in Kurdistan: 1918–1985*, 42.

41. It has to be mentioned that Kurdish journalism came much later, after Arab journalism, and even then it was just a trickle.

42. Olson, *The Emergence of Kurdish Nationalism*, 2, 153; Bruinessen, *Agha, Shaikh and State*, 405.

43. Olson, *The Emergence of Kurdish Nationalism*, 15; Abdullah Zangana, ed., *Roji Kurd: Govari Jivati Hevi Qutabiyani Kurd 1913—Astamul* [The sun of Kurd: The journal of Kurdish students' Hope Society 1913—Istanbul], 67–76.

44. *Al-Tarikh al-Hadith wa al-Muʿasir lil-Watan al-ʿArabi lil-Saf al-Sadis al-Adabi*, 2001; *Mejuy Nwe w Hawcharkh Poli Dwazdahami Amadayi Wejayi*. See also Figures 1 and 2.

45. *Al-Tarikh al-Hadith wa al-Muʿasir lil-Watan al-ʿArabi lil-Saf al-Thalith al-Mutawassit*; *Al-Tarikh al-Hadith wa al-Muʿasir lil-Watan al-ʿArabi lil-Saf al-Sadis al-Adabi*.

46. Woodrow Wilson delivered his famous Fourteen Points on January 8, 1918. See *World War I Document Archive*, accessed July 17, 2008, http://wwi.lib.byu.edu/index.php/President_Wilson%27s_Fourteen_Points.

47. The Anglo-French declaration was signed on November 7, 1918. Great Britain and France agreed to complete the "final liberation of the peoples who have for so long been oppressed by the Turks, and the setting up of national governments and administrations that shall derive their authority from the free exercise of the initiative and choice of the indigenous populations." See *Documents of Western Betrayal and Arab Opposition 1915–1919*, accessed July 19, 2008, http://sitemaker.umich.edu/emes/sourcebook/da.data/82633/FileSource/1938_anto nius.pdf.

48. Jamal Baban, *Handek Dadwari Banawbang* [Several Famous Trials], 113–114; Abdul Rahman Idris Al-Bayyati, *Sheikh Mahmud al-Hafid wa al-Nufuz al-*

Britani fi Kurdistan al-ʿIraq hatta ʿam 1925 [Sheikh Mahmud al-Hafid and the British influence in Iraqi Kurdistan until 1925], 160–163.

49. Rafiq Hilmi, *Yaddasht* [Memoirs], 114–117; McDowall, *Modern History of the Kurds*, 158.

50. ʿAli Kashif Al-Ghita, *Saʿd Salih wa Mawaqifihi al-Wataniyya 1920–1950* [Saʿad Salih and his national views 1920–1950], 78.

51. Marvin E. Gettleman and Stuart Schaar, *The Middle East and Islamic World Reader*, 114–116.

52. For the text of the letter, see *Memorandum Submitted to the Conference of Allied Powers at the House of Commons*, accessed August 15, 2009, http://domino .un.org/UNISPAL.NSF/b9bd5f5d9be9a82c8525718b0058040e/14f06fe1edd5 0616852570c00058e77e?OpenDocument.

53. Denise Natali, "Manufacturing Identity and Managing Kurds in Iraq, Turkey, and Iran: A Study in the Evolution of Nationalism," 66.

54. Quoted from *Tegayishtini Rasti* 17 (February 23, 1918) and 19 (March 5, 1918), cited in Kamal Mudhir Ahmad, *Kirkuk wa Tawabiʿuha: Hukm al-Taʾrikh wa al-Damir: Dirasa Wathaiʾqiyya ʿan al-Qadiyya al-Kurdiyya fi al-ʿIraq* [Kirkuk and surroundings: the verdict of the history and conscience: A documentary study on the Kurdish issue in Iraq], vol. 1, 98.

55. Feisal Amin Rasoul Al-Istrabadi, "Rebuilding a Nation: Myths, Realities, and Solutions in Iraq."

56. Magnus Thorkell Bernhardsson, *Reclaiming a Plundered Past: Archaeology and Nation-building in Modern Iraq*, 97–98; Alastair Northedge, "Al-Iraq al-Arabi: Iraq's Greatest Region in the Pre-Modern Period," in *An Iraq of Its Regions: Cornerstones of a Federal Democracy?*, 151–166; Liora Lukitz, "Nationalism in Post-Imperial Iraq: The Complexities of Collective Identity," 9; Brendan O'Leary, *How to Get Out of Iraq with Integrity*, 237–238.

57. Fadil Husayn, *Mushkilat al-Mosul* [The Mosul problem], 78.

58. Salim Matar, *Al-dhat al-Jariha* [The wounded self]; Salim Matar, *Jadal al-Hawiyat* [Argumentation of identities].

59. *Ustan* means land, place, or state. The Seljuks used it to label the autonomous regions that they administered.

60. Ferhad Pirbal, "When Did the Word Kurdistan Appear?," 14.

61. Amin Qadir Mina, *Amni Stratiji Iraq w Sekuchkay Baʿsiyan: Tarhil, Taʿrib, Tabʿith* [Iraq's security strategy and the Baʿthists tripod: Displacement, Arabization, and Baʿthification], 135; Rafiq Sabir, *Iraq: Dimokratizakirdin yan Halwashandinawa* [Iraq: democratization or disassembly], 7.

62. The Shiʿas normally take the bodies of their dead family members to Wadi al-Salam in Najaf for burial, but most of the Arab settlers in the areas visited by the author were Sunnis from central parts of Iraq.

63. The author visited the villages of Palkana, Sarbashakh, Shanagha, Gabalaka, and Dirka, among others in the district of Dibs (in the province of Kirkuk) in March 2005 and April 2007. He visited the cemeteries of many villages in the area and talked to a few Arab settlers who were still living in the region. The same pattern of behavior was also confirmed to the author by local people from the Khanaqin area. Dr. Nawzad Rasheed and Ahmed Jaf reported that the Arab settlers from

the villages of Kanasur, Alwash, Suleiman, and Baplawi had not buried their dead in these villages but took them back to where they were originally from.

64. Anthony D. Smith, *National Identity*, 16.

65. This figure perhaps reflects an accurate account of the numbers of minorities and refugees from elsewhere residing in Kurdistan.

66. KIPI, Kurdistan Institute for Political Issues, *Rapirsi lasar Pirsi Ziman u Nasnama la Kurdistan* [A survey on the question of language and identity in Kurdistan].

67. KIPI, Kurdistan Institute for Political Issues, *La Hawlatiyawa bo Dasalat* [From citizens to the authority], 49.

68. See Leila Fadel and Hussein Kadhim, "Some Sunni Muslims Won't Salute Iraq's New Flag." See also *Ahl al-Iraq* official website, accessed September 10, 2009, http://ahlaliraq.com/.

69. Eric J. Hobsbawm, "The Nation as Invented Tradition," 77.

70. Daniel L. Byman and Kenneth M. Pollack, "Democracy in Iraq?"; Peter Sluglett, "Is Democracy the Problem?," Carnegie Endowment website, accessed June 14, 2010, http://carnegieendowment.org/publications/?fa=view&id=20640.

The Evolution of National Identity and the Constitution-Drafting Process in the Kurdistan-Iraq Region

This chapter employs the term "Kurdistan-Iraq" to refer to what is commonly named "Iraqi Kurdistan," exclusively because it is the official title used by the Kurdistan Regional Government itself to refer to its polity. The Kurdistan-Iraq Region, or Kurdistan-Iraq for short, will be employed throughout the chapter for the sake of clarity, even at the risk of describing the polity anachronistically. Robert Olson has used the term "Kurdistan-Iraq" to represent what he considers to be "the degree of governmental control which the Kurdistan Democratic Party (KDP) and Patriotic Union of Kurdistan (PUK) exercised over the territories they controlled after the establishment of the Kurdistan Regional Government (KRG)." For him it indicates his awareness that "regions controlled by KDP and PUK are not fully sovereign." Olson, *The Goat and the Butcher: Nationalism and State Formation in Kurdistan Iraq Since the Iraqi War*, 1–2.

I sincerely thank Professor Ofra Bengio for her support and guidance in writing this chapter. Of course, any errors are mine.

1. Nathan Brown observed that in Middle Eastern states, constitutions have been written mainly for three purposes: 1) to enable authority, and organize power, without limiting it; 2) to express national sovereignty symbolically; and 3) to promulgate ideology. See Nathan Brown, *Constitutions in a Nonconstitutional World: Arab Basic Laws and the Prospects for Accountable Government*.

2. See, for example, Ashley S. Deeks and Matthew D Burton, "Iraq's Constitution: A Drafting History," 1–87; Humam Hamoudi, "My Perceptions on the Iraqi Constitutional Process"; Michael J. Kelly, "The Kurdish Regional Constitution within the Framework of the Iraqi Federal Constitution: A Struggle for Oil, Sovereignty and Ethnic Identity," ExpressO, 2009, available at http://works .bepress.com/michael_kelly/5; Haider Ala Hamoudi, "Ornamental Repugnancy:

Identitarian Islam and the Iraqi Constitution"; and see Haider Ala Hamoudi's forthcoming book, *Negotiating in Civil Conflict: Constitutional Construction and Imperfect Bargaining in Iraq*.

3. Kelly, "The Kurdish Regional Constitution." Kelly's article betrays his pro-Kurdish leanings, which are also prevalent in his overt advocacy for activist scholarship. In an interview with a Kurdish journalist and researcher, he states that the KRG should ". . . fund lawyers and academics to write books and articles about the genocide and publish these in the Asian and Western presses so that support can be built for the Kurds internationally." Interview with Michael J. Kelly, *Independent Kurdish Journalist*, March 18, 2010, accessed July 8, 2010, http://kurdishjournalist.blogspot.com/2010/03/interview-with-michael-j-kelly.html.

4. Said Arjomand, "Constitutions and the Struggle for Political Order: A Study in the Modernization of Political Traditions," 39.

5. See, for example, Elzbieta Halas, "Constructing the Identity of a Nation-State: Symbolic Conflict over the Preamble to the Constitution of the Third Republic of Poland."

6. In March 2009 the Kurdistan Election Law was passed and the Kurdistan National Assembly was henceforth called the Kurdistan Parliament.

7. See the Kurdistan Regional Government Unification Agreement at http://www.krg.org/articles/detail.asp?rnr=223&lngnr=12&anr=8891&smap=02010100.

8. The topic of Kurdish nationalism and national identity is complex and multifaceted. In scholarly debates, "the Kurdish question" in the Middle East has often led to investigations into pan-Kurdish nationalism and identity, Kurdayeti, or into the particularist manifestations of Kurdish nationalism and identity in the main countries where Kurds reside. Scholars have asked: Why has Kurdish identity formation lagged behind that of other peoples? Where should the origins of Kurdish nationalism be located? Is there a Kurdish nationality with a highly developed national consciousness and distinctive characteristics that warrants discussion of a modern Kurdish national movement? See, for example, Wadie Jwaideh, *The Kurdish National Movement: Its Origins and Development*, xvi.

9. Abbas Vali, "The Kurds and Their 'Others': Fragmented Identity and Fragmented Politics." Vali argues that the diversity and violence of the Kurds' "other," combined with the chronic weakness of civil society in Kurdistan, have created a scenario in which there are Kurdish nationalists without Kurdish nationalism.

10. Abbas Vali, "Genealogies of the Kurds: Construction of Nation and National Identity in Kurdish Historical Writing," 68–69.

11. Denise Natali, *The Kurds and the State: Evolving National Identity in Iraq, Turkey, and Iran*, xviii.

12. If not noted otherwise, each reference to the Draft Constitution of the Kurdistan-Iraq Region refers to the original Arabic-language 2009 version. Preamble, The Draft Constitution of the Kurdistan-Iraq Region, Arabic version available at the KRG official website: http://www.krg.org/articles/detail.asp?lngnr=14&smap=0403000&rnr=114&anr=30154; English version available at http://www.mpil.de/ww/en/pub/research/details/know_transfer/iraq/legal_documents/constitution.cfm.

13. The KRG has referred to its polity as the "Kurdistan-Iraq Region" at least

since July 2006. For the text of the Arabic-language Kurdistan-Iraq Region Investment Law, see the official KRG website: http://www.krg.org/articles/detail .asp?lngnr=12&smap=04030000&rnr=107&anr=12626, accessed October 3, 2011.

14. Ofra Bengio, *Saddam's Word: Political Discourse in Iraq*, 116–117.

15. Ibid., 116.

16. For a more extensive explanation, see A. F. L. Beeston, "Sha'b," in *Encyclopaedia of Islam*, ed. P. Bearman et al., Brill Online, accessed September 20, 2011, http://www.brillonline.nl/subscriber/entry?entry=islam_COM-1017.

17. The word *watan* is most commonly translated as homeland or fatherland. It denotes patriotism and affinity to one's homeland. *Wataniyya* describes the notion of territorial nationalism. For a more extensive explanation of the usage of *watan* and *wataniyya*, see J. Couland, "Wataniyya (a.)," in *Encyclopaedia of Islam*.

18. Preamble, Draft Constitution of the Kurdistan-Iraq Region.

19. For a broader explanation of the term, see P. J. Vatikiotis et al., "Kawmiyya," in *Encyclopaedia of Islam*.

20. Note that Iraqi president and Kurdish leader Jalal Talabani employed the term *qawmiyya* in his seminal work, *Kurdistan wa al-Haraka al-Qawmiyya al-Kurdiyya* [Kurdistan and the Kurdish National Movement], which has been lauded as one of the best works on the history of broader Kurdish nationalism in the twentieth century.

21. Michael Gunter, "Federalism and the Kurds of Iraq: The Solution or the Problem?," 234.

22. See Articles 62–64 of the Treaty of Sèvres. The 1923 Treaty of Lausanne, which provided for international recognition of the Turkish Republic, effectively abrogated the treaty.

23. Mohammad M. A. Ahmed, "Laying the Foundation for a Kurdistani State," 165.

24. Hussein Tahiri, *The Structure of Kurdish Society and the Struggle for a Kurdish State*, 330–331.

25. Article 2, Draft Constitution of the Kurdistan-Iraq Region.

26. Article 2, 2008 Draft Constitution of the Iraqi Kurdistan Region.

27. Draft provided by Nouri Talabani, Appendix 1 in Charles G. MacDonald and Carole A. O'Leary, eds., *Kurdish Identity: Human Rights and Political Status*, 26.

28. Vali, "The Kurds and Their 'Others,'" 49.

29. Ofra Bengio, "Iraqi Kurds: Hour of Power?"

30. See the 2002 draft, which marked the first time that the 1992 draft was amended. Official website of Unrepresented Nations and Peoples Organization, http://www.unpo.org/article/538.

31. Article 6, Draft Constitution of the Kurdistan-Iraq Region.

32. Article 21, Draft Constitution of the Kurdistan-Iraq Region.

33. Article 19, Draft Constitution of the Kurdistan-Iraq Region.

34. Natali, *The Kurds and the State*, 166.

35. This grievance has been raised most recently in the context of the KRG's response to popular citizen protests in Kurdistan-Iraq, which were spawned in part

by the fall of authoritarian regimes in the spring and winter of 2011. However, for a positive appraisal of the KRG's democratic merits, see Gareth Stansfield, *Iraqi Kurdistan: Political Development and Emergent Democracy*, 2003.

36. David McDowall, *A Modern History of the Kurds*, 299.

37. Tahiri, *The Structure of Kurdish Society and the Struggle for a Kurdish State*, 171.

38. Mas'ud Barzani, "Kurdistan Is a Model for Iraq."

39. Article 7, Draft Constitution of the Kurdistan-Iraq Region.

40. Article 6, Draft Constitution of the Kurdistan-Iraq Region.

41. The 2002 draft also noted that both Kurdish and Arabic should be used in official correspondence with the federal and regional authorities. It also designated the Turkmen language as the "language of education culture for the Turkmen" and Syriac for "those who speak it in addition to the Kurdish language." Article 7, 2002 Draft, official website of Unrepresented Nations and Peoples Organization, http://www.unpo.org.article/538.

42. It seems as though the addition of the Turkmen language is meant to be viewed in contrast to Turkey's obdurate stance concerning the national language issue. This idea was brought to my attention by Ofra Bengio. Article 14, 2008 Draft, official website of Global Justice Project of Iraq, http://gjpi.org/2009/06/24/draft-kurdish-constitution/; Article 14, Draft Constitution of the Kurdistan-Iraq Region.

43. Article 4, 2002 Draft, official website of Unrepresented Nations and Peoples Organization, http://www.unpo.org/article/538.

44. In subsequent drafts, the "national" was omitted from this article, and the phrasing was modified to simply depict the reality in which "the people of the Kurdistan Region are composed of Kurds, Turkmens, Arabs, Chaldo-Assyrian-Syriacs, Armenians and others who are citizens of Kurdistan." It goes on to state that the constitution "upholds and respects all religious rights of the Christians, Yezidis, and others, and guarantees to every individual in the region freedom of belief and the freedom to practice their religious rites and rituals." Article 6, Draft Constitution of the Kurdistan-Iraq Region.

45. Shafiq Qazzaz, "Perspective of Shafiq Qazzaz, Minister of Humanitarian Assistance and Cooperation, Kurdistan Regional Government," in MacDonald and O'Leary, *Kurdish Identity*, 25.

46. Preamble, Draft Constitution of the Kurdistan-Iraq Region.

47. The article stipulates that it is not applicable to the process of reversing Arabization policies. This is the case because some Kurdish politicians believe that Iraqi Arabs who settled in strategic areas such as Kirkuk in order to reduce Kurdish presence should be resettled elsewhere. Article 32, Draft Constitution of the Kurdistan-Iraq Region.

48. Article 7, Draft Constitution of the Kurdistan-Iraq Region.

49. Draft provided by Nouri Talabani for Michael Gunter in Gunter, "Federalism and the Kurds of Iraq," 234–235; Preamble, 2002 Draft.

50. Nouri Talabani, "Concerning the Proposed Constitution for Iraqi Kurdistan," Appendix 1 in MacDonald and O'Leary, *Kurdish Identity*, 265–266.

51. Ibid., 279–280.

52. Article 75, the 2002 Draft.

53. Michael Gunter wrote of this article that it "of course, means the right to become an independent state." Gunter, "Federalism and the Kurds of Iraq," 238.

54. Dr. Kamal Mirawdeli, "South Kurdistan's Case for Self-determination," *KurdishMedia.com*, January 3, 2005, accessed from ahwazstudies.org, September 10, 2011, http://www.ahwazstudies.org/index.php?option=com_content&view =article&id=385&Itemid=53&lang=en.

55. Referendum Campaign, "Al-Yawar's chauvinistic proclamation must be vehemently condemned," October 14, 2004, accessed from www.ekurd.net, September 10, 2011, http://www.ekurd.net/mismas/articles/misc/yawarschauvinistic .htm.

56. Tahiri, *The Structure of Kurdish Society and the Struggle for a Kurdish State*, 325–327.

57. Gregory Gause, "Can Democracy Stop Terrorism?" *Foreign Affairs* 84 (September–October 2005): 74.

58. As quoted by Olson, *The Goat and the Butcher*, 219–220.

59. Ahmed and Gunter, *The Evolution of Kurdish Nationalism*, 173–174.

60. See Denise Natali, "The Kirkuk Conundrum."

61. Denise Natali, *The Kurdish Quasi-State: Development and Dependency in Post-Gulf War Iraq*, xiv.

62. See Ofra Bengio, "A Kurdish Call for Self-Determination: Crossing the Rubicon?," *Tel Aviv Notes* 4, no. 18 (December 26, 2010).

63. Qazzaz, "Perspective of Shafiq Qazzaz," 28–29.

Forging Iraqi-Kurdish Identity:
A Case Study of Kurdish Novelists Writing in Arabic

1. Benedict Anderson, *Imagined Communities: Reflections on the Origin and Spread of Nationalism*. The concept of national identity appears throughout the book; see pp. 9–36.

2. Hashim Ahmadzade, *Nation and Novel: A Study of Kurdish and Persian Narrative Discourse*. Also helpful is Ofra Bengio's "The Muses Do Not Remain Silent: A Love Story in the Service of Kurdish Nation-Building."

3. Bengio, "The Muses."

4. Khalid ʿAbd al-Majid Lutfi, "*Fi al-Dhikra al-Miʾawiyya limiladihi . . . al-Adib wal-Mufakkir al-ʿIraqi al-Kurdi ʿAbd al-Majid Lutfi*," accessed April 12, 2011, www.aliraqi.org/forums/archive/index.

5. www.PUKmedia.com, October 23, 2009.

6. www.aknews.com/ar/aknews/1/176468, accessed April 14, 2011.

7. On the Kurdish struggle in the 1920s to gain an official status for their language, see Liora Lukitz, *Iraq: The Search for National Identity*.

8. For an article that shows how the choice of language affects the target audience, see Ronen Zeidel, "A Question of Language and Audience: On the Possibility of 'Iraqi Novels' in Hebrew."

9. Azad al-Ayyubi, *Efin . . . Wa Intizar al-Fajr*.

10. Zuhdi al-Dahoodi, *Tahawwulat*.

11. Haval Amin, *al-Bum wal-Miqqas*.

12. Burhan Shawi, *al-Jahim al-Muqaddas*.

13. Al-Ayyubi, *Efin*, 187–188.

14. Al-Dahoodi, *Tahawwulat*, 299.

15. Amin, *al-Bum wal-Miqqas*; see the book jacket.

16. Saʿd Sallum, "*Burhan Shawi bil-Ahmar wal-Aswad*."

17. On one such family, see Fuʾad al-Takarli, *al-Masarrat wal Awjaʿ* (Damascus: al-Mada, 1998).

18. Hanna Batatu, *The Old Social Classes and the Revolutionary Movements of Iraq*, 964.

19. For the best account of the history of the ICP, see ibid., particularly pp. 659–709.

20. Zuheir al-Jazaʾiri, *Mudun Fadhila* (Damascus: al-Ahali, 1992).

21. Lutfi, "*Fi al-Dhikra al-Miʾawiyya limiladihi . . .*"

22. Zuhayr al-Jazaʾiri, who at one point even joined the Kurdish Peshmerga, describes his meetings with his comrades in arms when he returned to Kurdistan after 2003. Zuhayr al-Jazaʾiri, *Harb al-ʿAjiz*, 253–275.

23. On the Fayli Kurds, see Saʿd B. Eskander, "The Fayli Kurds of Baghdad and the Baath Regime." Over the past decade, the Arab novel in Iraq has rediscovered the Fayli Kurds, who appear in some modern novels. Iraqi Shiʿi novelists put them in Shiʿi environments and present them as illustrations of the feasibility of a metaphorical Shiʿi and Kurdish merging. Ronen Zeidel, "The Iraqi Novel and the Kurds."

24. Lutfi, "*Fi al-Dhikra al-Miʾawiyya limiladihi . . .*"; Sallum, "*Burhan Shawi bil-Ahmar wal-Aswad*."

25. Al-Hajj later collaborated with the Baʿth and even served as Iraqi envoy in the UN headquarters in Geneva.

26. Amin, *al-Bum wal-Miqqas*, 155.

27. Al-Dahoodi, *Tahawwulat*, 296.

28. Sallum, "*Burhan Shawi bil-Ahmar wal-Aswad*."

29. Al-Ayyubi, *Efin*, 223.

30. For more on *Mem u Zin*, see Bengio, "The Muses."

31. Amin, *al-Bum wal-Miqqas*, 155.

32. Burhan al-Khatib, *Shaqqa fi Shariʿ Abi Nuwwas*. For an attempt to fit this novel into a more general view of Iraqi attitudes toward the Kurds, as reflected in the Iraqi novel, see Zeidel, "The Iraqi Novel and the Kurds."

33. Shawi, *al-Jahim al-Muqaddas*, 4, 36.

34. Ibid., 95.

35. A discussion of this subject is found in Zeidel, "The Iraqi Novel and the Kurds."

36. The case of Muhyi al-Din Zangane seems more complicated.

37. The book is Muhammad al-Mulla ʿAbd al-Karim, *Hisad al-Aʿwam min Baʿd Suqut Saddam* (Erbil: Yaras, 2006). It is a collection of essays by a Kurdish journalist. I am indebted to Kara Francis for her help and support, and for the concluding story.

A Tale of Political Consciousness:
The Rise of a Nonviolent Kurdish Political Movement in Turkey

1. "Türk: Haykırışımız Mısır ve Libya'dan büyük olacak" [Türk: Our cry will be greater than than that of Egypt and Libya], *Radikal*, March 28, 2011.

2. Treaty of Sèvres, Articles 62, 63, 64, accessed July 9, 2009, http://wwi.lib .byu.edu/index.php/Section_I,_Articles_1_-_260.

3. William Hale, *Turkish Foreign Policy 1774–2000*, 45.

4. Lausanne Treaty, Articles 37–42, accessed July 12, 2009, http://wwi.lib .byu.edu/index.php/Treaty_of_Lausanne.

5. Adem Çaylak and Adem Çelik, "Osmanlı ve Cumhuriyet Modernleş (tir) mesinde tarih din ve etnisite algısı" [The perception of history, religion and ethnicity in the (making of the) Ottoman and Republican modernization, Turkey's political history from the Ottoman Empire to the year 2000], 125.

6. Hale, *Turkish Foreign Policy 1774–2000*, 56–57.

7. Kemal Kirisci and Gareth Winrow, *The Kurdish Question and Turkey*, 91–103.

8. Ziya Gökalp, *Türkçülüğün Esasları* [The principles of Turkism], 15–27.

9. Paul White, *Primitive Rebels or Revolutionary Modernizers? The Kurdish National Movement in Turkey*, 79.

10. Ibid., 82–83.

11. A. Osman Ölmez, *Türkiye Siyasetinde DEP Depremi* [The DEP earthquake in the politics of Turkey], 38–45.

12. Chris Kutschera, "Mad Dreams of Independence: The Kurds of Turkey and the PKK," 13.

13. David McDowall, *A Modern History of the Kurds*, 409.

14. White, *Primitive Rebels or Revolutionary Modernizers?*, 132–133.

15. Ibid.

16. Ibid.

17. Kirisci and Winrow, *The Kurdish Question and Turkey*, 108–109.

18. White, *Primitive Rebels or Revolutionary Modernizers?*, 129.

19. Martin van Bruinessen, "The Kurds in Turkey," 8.

20. Michael M. Gunter, *Historical Dictionary of the Kurds*, 44–45.

21. Van Bruinessen, "The Kurds in Turkey," 8.

22. Trial Records Öcalan, Preamble, May 31, 1999–November 25, 1999, İmralı Island, Mudanya, Turkey.

23. Ömer Taşpınar, *Kurdish Nationalism and Political Islam in Turkey*, 100–101.

24. Martin van Bruinessen, "Between Guerilla War and Political Murder: The Workers' Party of Kurdistan," 45.

25. Ibid., 45.

26. Michael M. Gunter, "The Changing Kurdish Problem in Turkey," 4.

27. McDowall, *A Modern History of the Kurds*, 426.

28. Gunter, "The Changing Kurdish Problem in Turkey," 5.

29. Nicole F. Watts, "Allies and Enemies: Pro-Kurdish Parties in Turkish Politics, 1990–1994," 636.

30. Ölmez, *Türkiye Siyasetinde DEP Depremi*, 112–125.

31. Aliza Marcus, *Blood and Belief: The PKK and the Kurdish Fight for Independence*, 208.

32. Ölmez, *Türkiye Siyasetinde DEP Depremi*, 126–135.

33. Faili Meçhuller devlet politikasıydı [Mysterious killings were state policy], CNN Türk, http://www.cnnturk.com/2010/turkiye/08/05/faili.mechuller.devlet.politikasiydi/585697.0/index.html 07.02.2012.

34. Gunter, "The Changing Kurdish Problem in Turkey," 10.

35. Genelkurmay'dan JİTEM açıklaması [Statement of the chief of staff concerning JİTEM], http://www.ntvmsnbc.com/id/25037923/ 24.3.2011.

36. İsmet İmset, *PKK Ayrılıkçı Şiddetin 20 Yılı (1973-1992)* [The PKK: 20 years of separatist violence (1973–1992)], 376.

37. Watts, "Allies and Enemies," 637–638.

38. Ölmez, *Türkiye Siyasetinde DEP Depremi*, 160–168.

39. Siyasi Partiler Kanunu [The law of political parties], accessed October 20, 2013, http://www.mevzuat.gov.tr/MevzuatMetin/1.5.2820.pdf.

40. Marcus, *Blood and Belief*, 226.

41. Ibid., 227.

42. White, *Primitive Rebels or Revolutionary Modernizers?*, 170.

43. Ali Çarkoğlu and William Hale, eds., *The Politics of Modern Turkey*, 269.

44. Ömer Taşpınar, *Kurdish Nationalism and Political Islam in Turkey*, 112.

45. Çarkoğlu and Hale, *The Politics of Modern Turkey*, 267.

46. Oktay Pirim and Süha Örtülü, *PKK'nın 20 Yıllık Öyküsü* [The PKK 20-year story], 79–98.

47. Watts, "Allies and Enemies," 649–650.

48. Çarkoğlu and Hale, *The Politics of Modern Turkey*, 272–274.

49. Gürbüz Evren, *Avrupa Birliği Sürecinde Kürtçülük* [Kurdishness in the European Union process (i.e., Turkey's accession to the EU)], 128–129.

50. Taşpınar, *Kurdish Nationalism and Political Islam in Turkey*, 113.

51. Ibid.

52. DTP Official Website, accessed November 22, 2007, www.dtpgm.org.tr.

53. DTP Party Program, accessed June 4, 2008, http://www.dtp.org.tr/?sf=icerik&icerikid=226.

54. "DTP Political Stance Document," *Hürriyet*, November 9, 2007.

55. Evren, *Avrupa Birliği Sürecinde Kürtçülük*, 130.

56. "Bahçeli: DTP Kandil'in Ankara Şubesi," *Hürriyet*, November 20, 2007.

57. Gareth Jenkins, "DTP Presents Final Defense in Closure Case."

58. Ibid.

59. *Hürriyet*, November 25, 2007.

60. Saygı Öztürk, "Genelkurmay Yetki Arttırımı İstiyor," *Hürriyet*, October 5, 2008.

61. "İşte Karar," *Hürriyet*, October 15, 2008.

62. Sefa Mutlu, "PKK'da Yeni Açılımlar" [New openings in the PKK], April 30, 2009.

63. "DTP kürsüden Kürtçe konuşacak" [The DTP will speak Kurdish from the podium], *Milliyet*, September 11, 2008.

64. "PKK'dan emir mi alıyorsunuz?" [Are you getting orders from the PKK?], *Vatan*, May 26, 2009.

65. Erhan Akdemir, "Avrupa Parlamentosu Türkiye Raporu'un Değerlendirilmesi" [Analysis of the European Parliament's Turkey Report], May 23, 2008.

66. "Karayılan: Katalonya statüsü silah bıraktırır" [Karayılan: Catalonia model will cause handing over the guns], accessed October 20, 2013, www.radikal.com .tr/turkiye/karayilan_katalonya_statusu_silah_biraktirir-1018720.

67. İhsan Bal, "The Democratic Initiative Knocked over the KCK."

68. Mümtazer Türköne, "What Sort of Organization Is the KCK?" *Today's Zaman*, August 25, 2011, http://www.todayszaman.com/columnists-225126-what -sort-of-organization-is-the-kck.html.

69. Human Rights Foundation Turkey—Democratic Turkey Forum, "Arrests and Court Cases against KCK," August 25, 2011, http://www.tuerkeiforum.net /enw/index.php/Arrests_and_court_cases_against_KCK/TM.

70. David Romano, "Turkey Addresses PKK Challenge with Kurdish Language Reforms."

71. Emrullah Uslu, "Turkey's Kurdish Question: Irony within Irony."

72. *DTP Kapatıldı*, Sabah, December 11, 2009.

73. Jenkins, "DTP Presents Final Defense in Closure Case," Eurasia Daily Monitor 5:177 (September 5, 2008).

74. BDP Party Program, www.bdp.org.tr/hakkimizda/program.html, accessed March 30, 2011.

75. *Türkiye'nin Demokratikleşmesi ve Kürt Sorununda Çözüme Dair Siyasi Tutum Belgesi* [The Political Stance Document regarding Turkey's democratization process, and solution to the Kurdish question], accessed March 30, 2011, www.bdp .org.tr/yayinlarimiz/demokratik-ozerklik/demokratik-ozerklik.html.

76. "BDP'den yarından itibaren eylem kararı" [Tomorrow the BDP will implement its decision to demonstrate], *Hürriyet*, March 23, 2011.

77. "Başbakan kabul ederse seçime girmeyecekler!" [If the prime minister approves, they will not run for election!], *Habertürk*, March 28, 2011.

78. "YSK'dan 12 vekil adayına veto" [12 Parliament member (YSK)], *Hürriyet*, April 18, 2011.

79. "Bu Türkiye'yi kaosa sürükleme projesidir" [This is the project that will throw Turkey into chaos], *Hürriyet*, April 18, 2011.

80. "Bismil'de olaylar çıktı" [Unrest in Bismil], *Hürriyet*, April 20, 2011.

81. "YSK'dan BDP destekli 6 adaya vize" [The High Election Authority granted visas to 6 BDP affiliated candidates], *Hürriyet*, April 21, 2011.

82. "2011 Genel Seçim Sonuçları" [General election results], *Hürriyet*, August 21, 2011, http://www.hurriyet.com.tr/secim2011/default.html.

83. "YSK: Hatip Dicle milletvekili olamaz" [The High Election Authority: Hatip Dicle cannot become a member of Parliament], *CNN Türk*, August 21, 2011, http://www.cnnturk.com/2011/turkiye/06/21/ysk.hatip.dicle.milletvekili.ola maz/620827.0/.

84. Turkish Constitution, Article 76.

85. "BDP'li bağımsız vekiller meclise girmeyecek" [The independent Parliament members that are affiliated with the BDP will not enter Parliament], *Radikal*,

August 21, 2011, http://www.radikal.com.tr/Default.aspx?aType=RadikalDetay
V3&Date=&ArticleID=1053820&CategoryID=78.

86. "Dicle'nin yerine AK Partili Oya Eronat mazbata aldı" [Oya Eronat of the
AKP received a parliamentary membership document, instead of Dicle], *Hürriyet*,
August 21, 2011, http://www.hurriyet.com.tr/gundem/18087033.asp.

87. "Demokratik özerklik ilan edildi" [Democratic autonomy has been de-
clared], *Radikal*, July 14, 2011.

88. Fikret Bila, "Erdoğan'ın özerkliğe çektiği set" [The wall erected by Erdoğan against autonomy], *Milliyet*, August 23, 2011, http://siyaset.milliyet.com.tr
/erdogan-in-ozerkligecektigiset/siyaset/siyasetyazardetay/16.08.2011/1427183
/default.htm.

89. "BDP'li Demirtaş'tan Burkay'a çağrı" [BDP's Demirtaş's call to Burkay],
Radikal, August 5, 2011.

90. "Burkay: Devlet Projesi değilim" [Burkay: I am not the state's project],
Radikal, August 6, 2011.

91. Murat Aksoy, "BDP-PKK-Öcalan ilişkisinin zihniyet analizi" [Mentality
analysis of the relationship between the BDP-PKK and Öcalan], *Yeni Şafak*, June
30, 2010.

92. Ibid.

93. "BDP PKK'nın sözcüsü oldu," *Vatan*, March 3, 2011.

94. "Kimlik tartışmasını Erdoğan başlattı" [Erdoğan has started an identity
dispute], *Radikal*, April 15, 2009.

95. Ibid.

96. "İşte Kılıçdaroğlu'nun Diyarbakır mesajları" [Kılıçdaroğlu's Diyarbakır
messages], CNN Türk, May 31, 2011, http://www.cnnturk.com/2011/turkiye/05
/31/iste.kilicdaroglunun.diyarbakir.mesajlari/618505.0/index.html.

97. "Kılıçdaroğlu Diyarbakır'da konuştu" [Kılıçdaroğlu spoke in Diyarbakır],
Hürriyet, May 31, 2011.

98. "Bahçeli Diyarbakır'da: Ana dilde eğitim karnınızı mı doyuracak?" [Bah-
çeli in Diyarbakır: will you be sated by education in the mother tongue?], *Zaman*,
June 6, 2011.

99. "Sandık Sonuçları Barometresi" [Barometer of the election results], Konda
Araştırma ve Danışmanlık [Konda research and consultancy], October 26, 2011,
http://www.konda.com.tr/download.php?tok=cea69985e0e13a9be9989ea0be5
923c9&ln=tr.

The Role of Language in the Evolution of Kurdish National Identity in Turkey

1. Mesut Yeğen, *Müstakbel Türk'ten Sözde Vatandaşa: Cumhuriyet ve Kürtler*, 13.

2. Fernand de Varennes, *Language, Minorities, and Human Rights*, 5.

3. Hans Kohn, *Prelude to Nation-States: The French and German Experience,
1789–1815*, 239.

4. Elie Kedourie, *Nationalism*, 79.

5. Anthony D. Smith, *Theories of Nationalism*, 143.

6. Ibid.

7. Ernest Gellner, *Nations and Nationalism*, 61.

8. Benedict Anderson, *Imagined Communities: Reflections on the Origin and Spread of Nationalism*, 44.

9. Ayşe Betül Çelik, "Transnationalization of Human Rights Norms and Its Impact on Internally Displaced Kurds," 969–997.

10. Stephen May, "Language Policy and Minority Rights," 267.

11. Tove Skutnabb-Kangas, "Language Policy and Linguistic Human Rights," 285. See also Tove Skutnabb-Kangas and Robert Phillipson, eds., *Linguistic Human Rights: Overcoming Linguistic Discrimination* (Berlin, New York: Mounton de Gruyter, 1994).

12. Geoffrey Haig, "The Invisibilisation of Kurdish: The Other Side of Language Planning in Turkey," 3.

13. Mesut Yeğen, "Banditry to Disloyalty: The Kurdish Question in Turkey," accessed June 5, 2011, http://www.setav.org/public/BilgiBelge.aspx?Dil=tr.

14. Lausanne Treaty: Part 1, accessed May 20, 2011, www.hri.org/docs/lausanne/part1.html.

15. Yeğen, *Müstakbel Türk'ten Sözde Vatandaşa: Cumhuriyet ve Kürtler*, 53.

16. Propounded for the first time at the First Turkish History Congress in 1932, the Turkish History Thesis was an attempt to establish a history of the Turkish people that would reach beyond their Islamic past and in so doing place them on an equal pedestal with the civilizations of the West. The thesis traces the origin of all the great civilizations of the world to a prehistoric civilization in Central Asia, which later spread to the other parts of the world through migration. It establishes the Turks as the direct descendants of the inhabitants of this Central Asian civilization.

17. Kemal Kirisci and Gareth M. Winrow, *The Kurdish Question and Turkey: An Example of a Trans-State Ethnic Conflict*, 102.

18. İlker Aytürk, "Turkish Linguists against the West: The Origins of Linguistic Nationalism in Ataturk's Turkey," 2.

19. Yılmaz Çolak, "Language Policy and Official Ideology in Early Republican Turkey," 85.

20. David McDowall, *A Modern History of the Kurds*, 207.

21. Mary Lou O'Neil, "Linguistic Human Rights and the Rights of the Kurds," 76.

22. Mesut Yeğen, *Son Kürt İsyanı*, 31.

23. Haig, "The Invisibilisation of Kurdish," 8.

24. Michael M. Gunter, *The Kurds in Turkey: A Political Dilemma*, 16.

25. Nesrin Uçarlar, *Between Majority Power and Minority Resistance: Kurdish Linguistic Rights in Turkey*, 129.

26. Henri J. Barkey and Graham E. Fuller, *Turkey's Kurdish Question*, 14.

27. Yeğen, *Son Kürt İsyanı*, 32.

28. Amir Hassanpour, *Nationalism and Language in Kurdistan: 1918–1985*, 136.

29. Binnaz Toprak, "The State, Politics, and Religion in Turkey," 126.

30. M. Hakan Yavuz, "A Preamble to the Kurdish Question: The Politics of Kurdish Identity," 14.

31. Uçarlar, *Between Majority Power and Minority Resistance*, 134.

32. This refers to devaluation of a language "by denying it a variety of positive attributes." Haig, "The Invisibilisation of Kurdish," 14.

33. Uçarlar, *Between Majority Power and Minority Resistance*, 134.

34. Senem Aslan, "Incoherent State: Controversy over Kurdish Naming in Turkey," 5.

35. M. Hakan Yavuz, "Five Stages of the Construction of Kurdish Nationalism in Turkey," 12.

36. Metin Heper, *The State and Kurds in Turkey: The Question of Assimilation*, 135–136.

37. Hassanpour, *Nationalism and Language in Kurdistan*, 136.

38. For a more detailed analysis, see Kerim Yildiz, *The Kurds in Turkey: EU Accession and Human Rights*.

39. "Conditions for Membership," European Commission, accessed November 19, 2011, http://ec.europa.eu/enlargement/policy/conditions-membership/index_en.htm.

40. Yaşar Salihpaşaoğlu, "Türkiye'nin Dil Politikaları ve TRT 6," 1043.

41. "Opened with a Flourish, Turkey's Kurdish-Language Schools Fold," *Christian Science Monitor*, October 5, 2005.

42. "Soruları ve Cevaplarıyla Demokratik Açılım Süreci: Milli Birlik ve Kardeşlik Projesi," AK Parti Tanıtım ve Medya Başkanlığı, Ocak 2010.

43. Ibid., 20.

44. "TRT'nin Kürtçe Kanalı TRT 6 Yayına Başladı," *Zaman*, January 1, 2009.

45. "Erdoğan: Kürtçe TV Başka Adımlara da Vesile Olacak," *Radikal*, January 2, 2009.

46. "Üniversitede Kürt Dili ve Edebiyatı Bölümüne YÖK'ten Onay Çıktı," *Radikal*, March 1, 2011.

47. "YÖK'ten Kürtçe Lisans Bölümüne Onay Çıktı," *Radikal*, September 23, 2011.

48. Hüseyin Yayman, *Şark Meselesinden Demokratik Açılıma Türkiye'nin Kürt Sorunu Hafızası*, 61.

49. "Kürtçe Siyasi Propagandaya 'Sözde' Serbestlik Geliyor," *Bianet*, March 26, 2010.

50. "Soruları ve Cevaplarıyla Demokratik Açılım Süreci: Milli Birlik ve Kardeşlik Projesi," 21–22.

51. "Labor, Democracy and Freedom Block Elections Manifesto," *Fırat News Agency*, May 10, 2011.

52. Halil M. Karaveli, "Reconciling Statism with Freedom: Turkey's Kurdish Opening," 19.

53. "Civil Disobedience Call for Kurdish Issue," *Hürriyet Daily News*, March 23, 2011.

54. "Second Democratic Solution Tent in Istanbul," *Dicle News Agency*, March 26, 2011.

55. "BDP's Civil Disobedience Campaign Followed by Adhan in Kurdish," *Today's Zaman*, June 7, 2011.

56. "BDP Lideri Demirtaş: AK Parti İmamlar Ordusu Kuruyor," *Milliyet*, April 6, 2011.

57. "Turkey's Kurds Protest for Religious Rights Ahead of Elections," *Ekurd*, June 9, 2011.

58. "KCK Davasında 'Bilinmeyen Dil' Krizi," *Radikal*, November 4, 2010.

59. "KCK'ye Avukatlardan Boykot," *Birgün*, April 27, 2011.

60. "Diyarbakır'da Yol Levhaları Artık Kürtçe," *Radikal*, November 26, 2009.

61. "Belediyeden İki Dilli Levhalar," *Ergani Gündem*, December 28, 2010.

62. "Kürtçe Serbest Mumu Seçime Kadar Yandı," *Özgür Gündem*, July 2, 2011.

63. "Anadil İçin Kalem Kırıldı," *Diyarbakır Haber*, January 4, 2011.

64. "BDP Eşbaşkan Vekillleri 15 Mayıs Kürt Dil Bayramı Nedeniyle Bir Kutlama Mesajı Yayımladı," *İnternet Haber*, May 14, 2011.

65. Muhsin Kızılkaya, *Bir Dil Niye Kanar?*, 16.

66. "Eğitimde Anadilinin Kullanımı ve Çiftdilli Eğitim: Halkın Tutum ve Görüşleri, Türkiye Taraması 2010," Eğitim-Sen, February 21, 2011.

67. Seyfettin Gürsel, Gökçe Uysal-Kolaşin, and Onur Altındağ, "Anadili Türkçe Olan Nüfus ile Kürtçe Olan Nüfus Arası Eğitim Uçurumu Var," *BETAM Araştırma Notu* 9, no. 49 (October 13, 2009).

68. Müge Ayan Ceyhan and Dilara Koçbaş, *Çift Dillilik ve Eğitim*, 7.

69. Fatoş Gökşen, Zeynep Cemalcılar, and Can Fuat Gürlesel, "Türkiye'de İlköğretim Okullarında Okulu Terk ve İzlenmesi ile Önlenmesine Yönelik Politikalar," Eğitim Reformu Girişimi, Haziran 2008.

70. Vahap Coşkun, M. Şerif Derince, and Nesrin Uçarlar, *Dil Yarası: Türkiye'de Eğitimde Anadilinin Kullanılamaması Sorunu ve Kürt Öğrencilerin Deneyimleri*, 41.

71. Ibid., 122–123.

72. Mesut Yeğen, "Turkish Nationalism and the Kurdish Question," 119.

The Kurdish Women in Turkey: Nation Building and the Struggle for Gender Parity

1. Human Rights Watch, "He Loves You, He Beats You: Family Violence in Turkey and Access to Protection," 5.

2. "72 Women Killed in the Past Year in South East Turkey," *Rojwomen.com*.

3. Metin Yüksel, "The Encounter of Kurdish women with Nationalism in Turkey," 779.

4. Eda S., "We Can Change . . ."

5. Martin van Bruinessen, "From Adela Khanum to Leyla Zana: Women as Political Leaders in Kurdish History," in *Women of a Non-State Nation: The Kurds*, ed. Shahrzad Mojab (Costa Mesa, CA: Mazda Publishers, Inc., 2001), 98.

6. Ibid., 99.

7. Ibid.

8. Ibid.

9. Mirella Galletti, "Western Images of the Woman's Role in Kurdish Society," in *Women of a Non-State Nation*, 215.

10. Rohat Alakom, "Kurdish Women in Constantinople at the Beginning of the Twentieth Century," in *Women of a Non-State Nation*, 54–55.

11. E. B. Soane, *To Mesopotamia and Kurdistan in Disguise*, 216.

12. Ibid., 219.

13. Janet Klein, "En-Gendering Nationalism: The 'Woman Question' in Kurdish Nationalist Discourse of the Late Ottoman Period," in *Women of a Non-State Nation*, 25.

14. Ibid., 28–29.

15. Alakom, "Kurdish Women in Constantinople," 58.

16. Ibid.

17. Klein, "En-Gendering Nationalism," 32.

18. Alakom, "Kurdish Women in Constantinople," 63.

19. Klein, "En-Gendering Nationalism," 25–26.

20. Treaty of Sèvres, 1920, Section III, Articles 62–64, from *The Treaties of Peace 1919–1923, Vol. 2* (New York: Carnegie Endowment for Peace, 1924), accessed October 1, 2011, http://wwi.lib.byu.edu/index.php/Section_I,_Articles_1_-_260.

21. Bernard Lewis, *The Emergence of Modern Turkey*, 255.

22. Ibid., 275.

23. Shahrzad Mojab, "Nationalism and Feminism: The Case of Kurdistan," 70.

24. Christine Allison, "Folklore and Fantasy: The Presentation of Women in Kurdish Oral Tradition," in *Women of a Non-State Nation*, 185–186.

25. Aliza Marcus, *Blood and Belief: the PKK and the Kurdish Fight for Independence*, 18.

26. Ali Kemal Özcan, *Turkey's Kurds: A Theoretical Analysis of the PKK and Abdullah Öcalan*, 60.

27. Marcus, *Blood and Belief*, 7.

28. Ibid., 1.

29. Nicole F. Watts, "Allies and Enemies: Pro-Kurdish Parties in Turkish Politics, 1990–1994," 635.

30. International Free Women's Foundation, *Psychological Consequences of Trauma Experiences*, 29.

31. Marcus, *Blood and Belief*, 52.

32. Nihat Ali Özcan, "PKK Recruitment of Female Operatives."

33. Ali Kemal Özcan, *Turkey's Kurds*, 3.

34. Ibid., 170.

35. "Patriarchy—The Enslavement of Women," from "All Articles" on the *Partiya Karkerên Kurdistan (PKK)* website in English, accessed August 2011, http://www.pkkonline.com/en/index.php?sys=article&artID=56.

36. Margaret Gonzalez-Perez, *Women and Terrorism: Female Activity in Domestic and International Terror Groups* (New York: Routledge, 2008), 87.

37. David Romano, *The Kurdish Nationalist Movement: Opportunity, Mobilization, and Identity*, 77.

38. Nihat Ali Özcan, "PKK Recruitment of Female Operatives."

39. Romano, *Kurdish Nationalist Movement*, 78.

40. Shahrzad Mojab, "Women and Nationalism in the Kurdish Republic of 1946," in *Women of a Non-State Nation*, 87.

41. Nihat Ali Özcan, "PKK Recruitment of Female Operatives."

42. Mojab, "Women and Nationalism," 87.

43. Gonzalez-Perez, *Women and Terrorism*, 88.

44. Kevin McKiernan, *The Kurds: A People in Search of Their Homeland*, 143.

45. Ibid., 158–159.

46. Nazand Bagikhani, "Kurdish Women and National Identity."

47. Susan McDonald, "Kurdish Women and Self-Determination: A Feminist Approach to International Law," in *Women of a Non-State Nation*, 150.

48. Ibid., 148; Nihat Ali Özcan, "PKK Recruitment of Female Operatives."

49. Van Bruinessen, "From Adela Khanum to Leyla Zana," 105–106.

50. Anna Secor, "'There Is an Istanbul that Belongs to Me': Citizenship, Space and Identity in the City," 356.

51. Yüksel, "Encounter of Kurdish Women," 780.

52. Van Bruinessen, "From Adela Khanum to Leyla Zana," 106.

53. Yüksel, "Encounter of Kurdish Women," 781.

54. Steven Argue, "Kurdish Culture, Repression, Women's Rights, and Resistance," June 12, 2007, accessed April 30 2011, http://www.indybay.org/news items/2007/06/12/18426957.php.

55. Deborah Haynes, "The Kurdish Women Rebels Who Are Ready to Fight and Die for the Kurdish Cause."

56. Bagikhani, "Kurdish Women and National Identity."

57. Secor, "There Is an Istanbul," 364. According to the author, some women hesitated to acknowledge the role of the PKK in this transformation for fear that they would be accused of being terrorists or sympathizers with a terrorist group.

58. Nihat Ali Özcan, "PKK Recruitment of Female Operatives."

59. Boris Kalnoky, "Feminists and Terrorists? Women and the PKK."

60. Paul Schemm, "Kurdish Fighters Offer Guerilla Feminism."

61. Haynes, "Kurdish Women Rebels."

62. Kalnoky, "Feminists and Terrorists?"

63. Arwa Damon, "Female Fighters: We Won't Stand for Male Dominance."

64. Chris Kutschera, "A Silent Scream," 33–35.

65. Leyla Zana, *Writings from Prison*, 56.

66. "12 Haziran'da seçilen kadın milletvekilleri 'rekor' kırdı" ["On June 12 the Record for Elected Women MPs is Broken"].

67. "Yine Vekil" ("Representative Wants More"), *Radikal*, October 1, 2011, accessed October 2, 2011, http://www.radikal.com.tr/Radikal.aspx?aType=Radikal DetayV3&ArticleID=1065034&Date=01.10.2011&CategoryID=78.

68. Kutschera, "A Silent Scream," 34.

69. Yüksel, "Encounter of Kurdish Women," 780.

70. "About Us," *Roj Women: Kurdish and Turkish Women's Rights*, accessed June 3, 2011, http://rojwomn.com/about/.

71. "About," Kurdish Women against Honour Killing (KWAHK), accessed August 27, 2011, http://www.kwrw.org/kwahk/.

72. Ibid. For more information about the Kurdish Women's Rights Watch (KWRW), see the organization's website, http://www.kwrw.org/.

73. Secor, "There Is an Istanbul," 365.

74. *Hürriyet Daily News*, "Kurdish Women Fight for Rights of Both Groups, Istanbul Deputy Says."

75. "BDP's Second Congress: Is the Destination Ankara or Is It Kurdistan?," *Kurdish Globe*, September 10, 2011, accessed October 1, 2011, http://www .kurdishglobe.net/display-article.html?id=C301773E51DFD77C897D64EF67 81803C.

76. *Hürriyet Daily News*, "Kurdish Women Fight."

77. *Hürriyet Daily News*, "Kurdish Women in Southeast Turkey Grow Strong Support Networks."

78. "12 Haziran'da seçilen kadın milletvekilleri 'rekor' kırdı."

79. Soner Çağaptay, "Women 'appear' in Turkey's Parliament."

80. Mojab, "Women and Nationalism," 75.

81. Shahrzad Mojab, "Introduction: The Solitude of the Stateless: Kurdish Women at the Margins of Feminist Knowledge," in *Women of a Non-State Nation*, 12.

82. Secor, "There Is an Istanbul," 352.

83. Mojab, "Introduction," 12.

84. Zana, *Writings from Prison*, 7.

The Kurds in Syria: Caught between the Struggle for Civil Equality and the Search for National Identity

1. Philip S. Khoury, *Syria and the French Mandate: The Politics of Arab Nationalism 1920–1945*, 12, 15. See also C. Vanly, "The Kurds in Syria and Lebanon," 151–155. Hanna Batatu, *Syria's Peasantry, the Descendants of Its Lesser Rural Notables, and Their Politics*, 119–120; Eyal Zisser, *Asad's Legacy: Syria in Transition*, 1–3, 179–182. See also *al-Hayat* (London), March 26, 2011.

2. Jordi Tejel, *Syria's Kurds: History, Politics and Society*, 1–6.

3. For more see Claude Cahen, *Der Islam I: vom Ursprung bis zu den Anfängen des Osmanenreiches*; *HaIslam miLedato vead Techilat HaImperia HaOthmanit*, 347–397. See also Hakan Özoğlu, *Kurdish Notables and the Ottoman State*; Dick Douwes, *The Ottomans in Syria: A History of Justice and Oppression*.

4. See Ross Burns, *Damascus: A History*, 158–186; Khoury, *Syria and the French Mandate*, 292, 309.

5. Philip S. Khoury, *Urban Notables and Arab Nationalism: The Politics of Damascus, 1860–1929*.

6. Sami Moubayed, *Steel and Silk: Men and Women Who Shaped Syria, 1900–2000*, 194, 336, 350. See also Tareq Y. Ismael and Jacqueline S. Ismael, *The Communist Movement in Syria and Lebanon*.

7. Khoury, *Syria and the French Mandate*, 525–531; see also Tejel, *Syria's Kurds*, 8–38.

8. Khoury, *Syria and the French Mandate*, 531–532.

9. Tejel, *Syria's Kurds*, 42, 89; see also Patrick Seale, *The Struggle for Power for Syria, A Study of Post-War Arab Politics, 1945–1958*, 58–64, 118–132.

10. Tejel, *Syria's Kurds*, 48–49.

11. For more see Elie Podeh, *The Decline of Arab Unity, the Rise and Fall of the United Arab Republic*.

12. Tejel, *Syria's Kurds*, 49–52.

13. Michel ʿAflaq, *Fi Sabil al-Baʿth* [In the path of the Baʿth], 174–175.

14. Syrian Arab News Agency, February 9, 2011. See also Jawad Mella, *The Colonial Policy of the Baath Party in Western Kurdistan*, 60–62.

15. Muhammad Hilal Talib, *Al-Bahth fi al-Jawanib al-Qawmiyya wal-Siyasiyya*

wal-Ijtimaʿiyya li-Iqlim al-Jazira [A Study of the al-Jazira region from the ethnic, social, and political aspects]. An English translation can be found in Mella, *Colonial Policy of the Baath Party*, 63–227.

16. Mella, *Colonial Policy of the Baath Party*, 220–227.

17. See Moubayed, *Steel and Silk*, 83; see also Zisser, *Asad's Legacy*, 25–30.

18. Tejel, *Syria's Kurds*, 62–68; see also Middle East Watch, *Syria Unmasked: The Suppression of Human Rights by the Asad Regime*, 89–108.

19. Robert Olson, *Turkey's Relation with Iran, Syria, Israel and Russia, 1991–2000, The Kurdish and Islamist Questions*, 105–124. See also Eberhard Kienle, *Baʿth v Baʿth: The Conflict between Syria and Iraq, 1968–1989*.

20. Zisser, *Asad's Legacy*, 87–94; Eyal Zisser, *Commanding Syria: Bashar al-Asad and the First Years in Power*, 94–96.

21. Tejel, *Syria's Kurds*, 49–52.

22. Ibid., 68–107.

23. Zisser, *Commanding Syria*, 96–98.

24. *Al-Hayat* (London), December 12, 2002, June 26, 2003.

25. Zisser, *Commanding Syria*, 96–98; see also Tejel, *Syria's Kurds*, 114–132.

26. *Al-Jazira TV*, March 20, 2011; *al-Sharq al-Awsat*, March 23, 2011.

27. Syrian TV, June 21, 2011. See also Syrian Arab News Agency, June 21, 2011.

28. *Al-Sharq al-Awsat*, August 27, 2011.

29. *Al-Jazira TV*, July 16, October 6, 9, 2011; *al-Hayat* (London), July 19, 2011.

30. See *al-Sharq al-Awsat* (London), July 20, 2012, and March 3, 2013.

31. See, for example, *al-Safir* (Beirut), August 3 and September 19, 2013; *All4syria*, July 30 and August 2, 2013.

32. Tejel, *Syria's Kurds*, 9.

Toward a Generational Rupture within the Kurdish Movement in Syria?

This chapter was written in early 2012. Since then, new factors such as the Syrian civil war and the creation of militias in the north have altered the dynamics analyzed in this work.

1. On the cross-border and transnational character of the Kurdish issue, see Hamit Bozarslan, "La régionalisation du problème kurde"; Bozarslan, *La question kurde. États et minorités au Moyen-Orient*; and Bozarslan, "Le Kurdistan d'Irak aujourd'hui."

2. Reinhart Koselleck, "Préface," in *L'Expérience de l'histoire*, ed. Michael Werner.

3. For examples, see "Rage, Rap and Evolution: Inside the Arab Youth Quake," *Time*, February 17, 2011; "Bullets Stall Youthful Push for Arab Spring," *New York Times*, March 17, 2011.

4. World Bank, *Unlocking the Employment Potential in the Middle East and North Africa: Toward a New Social Contract*.

5. On this debate, see Leyla Neyzi, "Object or Subject? The Paradox of Youth in Turkey."

6. Emin Alper, "1968: Global or Local?" Arif Dirlik developed this argument in "The Third World in 1968." Ahmad Abdalla, *The Student Movement and National Politics in Egypt, 1923–1973*; Halim Barakat, *Lebanon in Strife, Student Preludes to the Civil War*.

7. Paulo Pinto, "Les Kurdes de Syrie," 259.

8. Although there are no official statistics relating to the Kurdish population, we estimate that around 600,000 Kurds out of a total of 1.5 million live in either Damascus or Aleppo.

9. The Khoybun League (1927–1944) embodied a sort of "unnatural marriage" between a Westernized intelligentsia and representatives of the traditional Kurdish world. Having sought exile in Syria and Lebanon, some intellectuals, former officers, landlords, and tribal leaders came together within the Khoybun to work out a new, common, nationalist syntax in order to oppose the Turkish regime. See Jordi Tejel Gorgas, *Le mouvement kurde en exil. Continuités et discontinuités du nationalisme kurde sous le mandat français en Syrie et au Liban, 1925–1946*.

10. Christian More, *Les Kurdes aujourd'hui. Mouvement national et partis politiques*, 205.

11. Jordi Tejel, *Syria's Kurds: History, Politics and Society*, 88–95.

12. In the 1980s, external pressure compelled Hafiz al-Asad to take an interest in the Kurdish nationalist movement in Turkey. Turkey and Syria were involved in a territorial dispute regarding sovereignty over the former Sanjak of Alexandretta, handed by France to Turkey in 1939. In addition, the Turkish dams on the Euphrates also threatened Syria's water supply. Al-Asad responded by inviting dozens of different guerrilla factions—among them the PKK—from Turkey to set up their headquarters in Damascus and later on in Lebanon.

13. Paul J. White, *Primitive Rebels or Revolutionary Modernizers? The Kurdish National Movement in Turkey*, 162–174.

14. Hamit Bozarslan, "Le nationalisme kurde, de la violence politique au suicide sacrificiel," 111.

15. Julie Gauthier, "Syrie: le facteur kurde," 227.

16. Jordi Tejel Gorgas, "Les Kurdes de Syrie, de la dissimulation à la visibilité?"; Jordi Tejel Gorgas, "Jeunesse kurde: entre rupture et engagement militant."

17. John Breuilly, *Nationalism and the State*, 260.

18. Bozarslan, *États et minorités*, 174–180.

19. Catherine Dupret-Schepens, "Les populations syriennes sont-elles homogènes?," 190.

20. Cha'ban Abboud, "Les quartiers informels de Damas: une ceinture de misère," 175.

21. Robert Lowe, "The Syrian Kurds: A People Discovered," 6.

22. See Tejel, *Syria's Kurds*, 108–133.

23. See ibid., 131–132.

24. *The Syria Report*, June 16, 2005.

25. At the beginning of 2007, twelve youths, three of them minors, were condemned to prison for two and a half years for having thrown Molotov cocktails at security forces in 2005. *AFP*, February 4, 2007.

26. The Syrian government issued Decree 49 on September 10, 2008. The decree amended Statute 41 of October 26, 2004, which regulated the ownership,

sale, and lease of land in border regions. In Kurdish circles, the decree was perceived as a strategy to stop the economic and social development of the Kurdish
areas situated across the Turkish-Syrian border. See Kurd Watch, "Decree 49—
Dispossession of the Kurdish Population? Commentary on the Political Implications and Economic Consequences of a Decree."

27. The draft of the National Council's political program stated that the ethnic
rights of the Kurdish people are to be anchored in the constitution. Moreover, it
also stated that the Kurdish question in Syria must be resolved democratically and
justly, but within the framework of the unity of the Syrian state. Although the
Kurds would receive the same civic rights and duties as all other citizens, some
declarations made by members of the SNC raised some concerns among Kurds.
Thus, for example, the president of the National Council, Burhan Ghalioun, compared Syrian Kurds to immigrants in France during an interview for German TV.
http://www.mesop.de/2011/10/29/kurds-are-genuin-migrants-kurden-sind-wie
-geborene-immigranten/ (accessed on November 25, 2011).

28. "Les Frères musulmans syriens accepteraient une intervention turque en
Syrie," *Le Monde*, November 17, 2011.

29. "Concern for Syrian Kurds as Violent Crackdown Continues," *Rudaw*,
February 18, 2012, accessed February 22, 2012, http://www.rudaw.net/english
/news/syria/4435.html.

30. "Political Parties Divide Syria's Kurdish Youth," *Rudaw*, July 1, 2011, accessed July 4, 2011, http://rudaw.net/english/news/syria/3789.html.

31. "Internet Post Claim Syrian Kurds Are Taking Up Arms," *Rudaw*, October
10, 2011, accessed October 10, 2011, http://rudaw.net/english/news/syria/4043
.html.

32. Ibid.

33. "Turkey's Henchmen in Syrian Kurdistan Are Responsible for the Unrest
Here," interview with Salih Muslim Muhammad, accessed November 27, 2011,
http://www.kurdwatch.org/html/en/interview6.html.

34. Political and security pressure affect not only the PKK but also the Kurdish
political movement at large. Leaders of the Peace and Democracy Party (BDP) say
that close to five thousand Kurdish political activists were arrested by the Turkish
police over a period of three years, the majority of them in 2011. "Decline in Public Protests by Turkey's Kurds," *Rudaw*, December 25, 2011, accessed December
26, 2011, http://www.rudaw.net/english/news/turkey/4260.html.

The Kurds in Iran: The Quest for Identity

1. For further information, see, for example, Walker Connor, *Ethnonational-
ism: The Quest for Understanding*; Walker Connor, "The Politics of Ethnonation-
alism"; Ernest Gellner, *Nations and Nationalism*; Dov Ronen, *The Quest for Self-
Determination*; Anthony D. Smith, *The Ethnic Origins of Nations*; Anthony D.
Smith, *National Identity*; Crawford Young, "The Dialectics of Cultural Pluralism:
Concept and Reality"; Hugh Seton-Watson, *Nation and States: An Inquiry into the
Origins of Nations and the Politics of Nationalism*; Joseph Rothchild, *Ethnopolitics:
A Conceptual Framework*; E. J. Hobsbawm, *Nations and Nationalism since 1780*;

Donald Horowitz, *Ethnic Groups in Conflict*; and Benedict Anderson, *Imagined Communities: Reflections on the Origin and Spread of Nationalism*. See also Chimene Keitner, "National Self-Determination in Historical Perspective: The Legacy of the French Revolution for Today's Debate"; David Brown, "Ethnic Revival: Perspectives on State and Society."

2. Seton-Watson, *Nation and States*, 5.

3. Anderson, *Imagined Communities*, 15.

4. See Firoozeh Kashani-Sabet, *Frontier Fictions: Shaping the Iranian Nation, 1804–1946*, 4–9.

5. Ibid., 5.

6. Mostafa Vaziri, *Iran as Imagined Nation: The Construction of National Identity*.

7. For details, see Nader Entessar, *Kurdish Ethnonationalism*, 11–14; and Nader Entessar, *Kurdish Politics in the Middle East*, chap. 2.

8. For details of the Mahabad Republic and its aftermath, see Entessar, *Kurdish Politics in the Middle East*, 14–23; Archie Roosevelt, Jr., "The Kurdish Republic of Mahabad"; and Abdul Rahman Ghassemlou, *Kurdistan and the Kurds*. For an excellent study of the rise and fall of the Autonomous Government of Azerbaijan, see Touraj Atabaki, *Azerbaijan: Ethnicity and the Struggle for Power in Iran* (London: I. B. Tauris, 2000), especially pp. 129–178. For an interesting firsthand account of the campaign against the Azerbaijan uprising, see Ali Akbar Derakhshani, *Khaterat-e Sartip Ali Akbar Derakhshani* [The Memoirs of Ali Akbar Derakhshani], 19–50 and 313–360.

9. Hassan Arfa, *The Kurds: An Historical and Political Study*, 102–103.

10. For an analysis of the role of language in Kurdish nationalism, see Amir Hassanpour, *Nationalism and Language in Kurdistan: 1918–1985*, 1–48 and 102–147. For a conceptual analysis of dissimilative and assimilative ethnic factors in the Middle East, see Nader Entessar, "Ethnicity and Ethnic Challenges in the Middle East."

11. A. R. Ghassemlou, "Kurdistan in Iran," 122.

12. Ibid., 124.

13. The most detailed account of the shah's dealing with Barzani and other Kurdish leaders has been offered by Col. Issa Pjeman, who was an intelligence officer and chief liaison between the shah's government and the Iraqi Kurds. See Erfan Q. Fard, *Tondbad-e Havades: Goftogo ba Issa Pejman* [The Storm of Events: An Interview with Issa Pejman].

14. Ghassemlou, "Kurdistan in Iran," 124.

15. Ibid., 125; Fard, *Storm of Events*, 153–206.

16. *Matn-e Kamel-e Qanoon-e Assasi-e Jomhoori-e Eslami Iran* [The Complete Text of the Constitution of the Islamic Republic of Iran] (Tehran: Hamid Publications, 1983), 28.

17. Shaul Bakhash, *The Reign of the Ayatollahs: Iran and the Islamic Revolution* (New York: Basic Books, 1984), 73.

18. Ayatollah Hossein Ali Montazeri, *Matn-e Kamel-e Khaterat-e Ayatollah Hossein Ali Montazeri* [The Complete Text of the Memoirs of Ayatollah Hossein Ali Montazeri] (Essen, Germany: Union of Iranian Editors in Europe, 2001), 252.

19. Ibid., 252–253.

20. Ayatollah Haj Sheikh Sadeq Khalkhali, *Khaterat-e Ayatollah Khalkhali, Avalin Hakem-e Shar'-e Dadgahaye Enqelab* [Memoirs of Ayatollah Khalkhali, the First Religious Judge of the Revolutionary Courts] (Tehran: Sayeh Publications, 2001), 293–294.

21. For the complete text of Ayatollah Khomeini's November 16, 1979, letter to the Kurds, see *Ettelaat*, November 17, 1979.

22. Nasser Mohajer, "Ensheab dar Hezb-e Demokrat-e Kordestan-e Iran" [A Division within the Kurdistan Democratic Party of Iran], 25–29.

23. Ibid., 27.

24. For a complete account of the Mykonos verdict and documents related to this case, see Mehran Payandeh, Abbas Khodagholi, and Hamid Nozari, *Hanooz dar Berlin Qazi Hast: Terror va Dadgah-e Mykonos* [There Is Still a Judge in Berlin: Terror and the Mykonos Court]; and Parviz Dastmalchi, *Mykonos: Matn-e Ra'ye Dadgah* [Mykonos: The Court's Verdict].

25. For details, see "Jonbesh-e Moqavemat-e Khalq-e Kord va Komala" [The Resistance Movement of the Kurdish Masses and the Komala].

26. Mohammad Khatami, *Islam, Liberty and Development* (Binghamton, NY: Institute of Global Cultural Studies, 1998), 4.

27. For a selection of Khatami's speeches on this and similar topics, see Seyyed Mohammad Khatami, *Tose'-e Siyasi, Tose'-e Eqtesadi va Amniyat* [Political development, economic development and security] (Tehran: Tarh-e No, 2000), 55–97.

28. Islamic Republic News Agency (IRNA), April 9, 2001.

29. *Asr-e Azadegan*, March 6, 2000. Also, see Hamid Reza Jalaipour, *Kordistan: Elat-e Tadavom-e Bohran-e An Pas Az Enghelab-e Eslami* [Kurdistan: Causes for the perpetuation of its crisis following the Islamic Revolution]. For a critical analysis of the role of the Kurds in Mohammad Khatami's reform movement, see Khaled Tavakkoli, "Kurdistan va Vaqa'ye Dovom-e Khordad" [Kurdistan and the events of the Second of Khordad).

30. Mohammad Ali Zakariaee, ed., *Konferans-e Berlin: Khedmat ya Khiyanat* [The Berlin Conference: Service or Treason], 211; and Nader Entessar, "The Impact of the Iraq War on the Future of the Kurds in Iran," 182–184.

31. *Emrouz*, April 13, 2005, http://www.emrouz.info/ShowItem.aspx?ID=12 26&p=1; and Ataollah Mohajerani, "Entekhab-e Talabani" [Talabani's Election], *Emrouz*, April 7, 2005, http://www.emrouz.info/ShowItem.aspx?ID=1117&p=1.

32. Kasra Naji, *Ahmadinejad: The Secret History of Iran's Radical Leader* (Berkeley: University of California Press, 2008), 29–31.

33. "Final Results of the Ninth Presidential Election," Interior Ministry, The Islamic Republic of Iran, June 25, 2005, http://www.mo.gov.ir/news.aspx?id =12593.

34. Interior Ministry, The Islamic Republic of Iran, June 22, 2005, http://www.mo.gov.ir/news.aspx?id=123888.

35. See, for example, *Sirwan*, July 25, 2005, and Fars News Agency, August 13, 2005. See also Nader Entessar, "The Kurdish National Movement in Iran since the Islamic Revolution of 1979," 270–275.

36. Phil Sands, "Kurds Prepare for Guerrilla War in Iran," *Gulf News Online*, April 14, 2005, http://gulfnews.com/news/region/iraq/kurds-prepare-for-guer

rilla-war-in-iran-1.284387. For a brief discussion of possible future paths for the Iranian Kurds, see Kerim Yildiz and Tanyel B. Taysi, *The Kurds in Iran: The Past, Present and Future*, 107–117.

37. Quoted in *Baztab*, August 18, 2005, http://www.baztab.com/news/278 67.php.

38. For background details, see Khosrow Kordpour's interview in *Mihan* 89 (July–August 2005), http://www.mihan.net/89/mihan-89-06.htm.

39. *Payamner*, July 24, 2005, http://www.peyamner.com/article.php?id=172 49&lang=farsi.

40. *Rooz*, August 4, 2005, http://www.roozonline.com.

41. *Rooz*, July 22, 2008, http://www.roozonline.com/archives/2008/07/post _8443.php. For a succinct overview of recent cases of human rights abuses of the Kurds by the Iranian authorities, see Amnesty International, *Iran: Human Rights Abuses against the Kurdish Minority*, 36–41.

42. *Iran*, March 17, 2009, and *Kayhan*, March 18, 2009.

43. For details, see the Province of Kurdistan, Ministry of Interior, Islamic Republic of Iran, "Implementing Regulations of the Foreign Investment Promotion and Protection Act," May 22, 2009, http://en.ostan-d.ir/Default.aspx?TabID=56.

44. For a general overview of the Green Movements, see Danny Postel and Nader Hashemi, eds., *The People Reloaded: The Green Movement and the Struggle for Iran's Future* (New York: Melville House, 2011); and Hamid Dabashi, *Iran, the Green Movement and the USA: The Fox and the Paradox* (London: Zed Books, 2010).

45. *Manshoor-e Jonbesh-e Sabz* [The Manifesto of the Green Movement], revised version, February 22, 2011. Also, see Mir Hussein Moussavi's Announcement 18, June 15, 2010, http://www.rahesabz.net/story/17494.

46. Shahabedin Sheikhi, "The Green Movement and Iranian Ethnicities," *Gozaar*, July 13, 2010, http://www.gozaar.org/english/articles-en/The-Green-Move ment-and-Iranian-Ethnicities.html.

47. Ibid.

48. "Karroubi to 'Right Some Wrongs,' 'Better Policies.'" *Press TV*, May 17, 2009, http://edition.presstv.ir/detail/95082.html.

49. *Jonbesh-e Rah-e Sabz*, February 19, 2011, http://www.rahesabz.net/story /32812.

50. See, for example, the statement of the Coordinating Council of Kurdish Reforms published in *Emrouz*, November 20, 2011, http://www.emruznews .com/2011/11/post-8172.php.

51. Mehdi Tajik, "Goftogo ba Mohammad Ali Tofighi: Federalism va Democracy rahe Hall-e Moshkel-e Aghvam," [A conversation with Mohammad Ali Tofighi: Federalism and democracy are solutions to the ethnic problem], *Rah-e Sabz*, August 9, 2011, http://www.rahesabz.net/story/40946/.

52. Shayan Ghajar, "Iran's Minorities Look to Greens for Equal Rights," March 16, 2010, http://www.insideiran.org/critical-comments/iran%E2%80% 99s-minorities-look-to-greens-for-equal-rights/.

53. Ibid.

54. See Adbdul Rahman Ghassemlou's interview in *MERIP Report* 98 (July–August 1982): 17. Also, see "Asnad-e Kongereh-e Dahom-e Hezb-e Demokrat-e

Kordestan-e Iran" [The documents of the Tenth Congress of the Kurdistan Democratic Party of Iran], April 1995.

55. Jalaipour, *Kordestan*, 164–165.

The Nostalgic Republic: The Kurdish Republic of 1946 and Its Effect on Kurdish Identity and Nation Building in Iran

1. David McDowall, *A Modern History of the Kurds*, 221.

2. Hassan Arfa, *The Kurds: An Historical and Political Study*, 58.

3. Abdurrahman Qasimlo, *Kurdistan and Kurds*.

4. The Kurdish Republic of 1946 is also known as the Kurdish Republic of Mahabad because it was established in the town of Mahabad. Its authority did not go beyond Mahabad and a few surrounding towns. Nevertheless, it aimed at self-determination for all the Kurds in Iran. Therefore, the Kurdish Republic of 1946 is the more appropriate term.

5. Muhammad Abbasi, "Introduction to Sharaf-nameh," 98.

6. Book review of Wilhelm Gernot, *The Hurrians*, trans. Jennifer Barnes (Warminster, UK: Aris and Philip Ltd., 1989), in *International Journal of Kurdish Studies* 7, nos. 1 & 2 (1994): 112–113.

7. See Kirzioğlu M. Fahrettin, *Kürtlerin Kökü* [The origin of the Kurds]. The author, a history teacher, tries to prove that the Kurds are of Turkish origin.

8. Kendal Nezan, "The Kurds under the Ottoman Empire," 68.

9. Austin H. Layard, *Discoveries among the Ruins of Nineveh and Babylon*, 323.

10. Taufiq Wahby, "The Origins of the Kurds and Their Language." Lecture delivered to the KSSE, UK branch conference on December 22, 1964. This is an offprint from the magazine *Kurdistan* of the Kurdish Student Society in Europe (KSSE), nos. 9 and 10, p. 2, reprinted in Sweden in 1982.

11. Fahrettin, *Kürtlerin Kökü*, 5.

12. Martin van Bruinessen, "Kurdish Society, Ethnicity, Nationalism and Refugee Problems," 49.

13. Nezan, "The Kurds under the Ottoman Empire," 24–25.

14. Fereshteh Koohi-Kamali, "The Development of Nationalism in Iranian Kurdistan," 172–175.

15. Ibid., 172.

16. Ibid., 173.

17. Louise L'Estrange Fawcett, *Iran and the Cold War: The Azerbaijan Crisis of 1946*, 1.

18. Borhanedin Yassin, "A History of the Republic of Kurdistan," 128.

19. Sayyid Muhammad Samadi, *J. K Çibu, Çi Dewist ve Çi be ser hat?* [What was J. K., what did it want and what happened to it?], 11.

20. Jalil Gadani, *Pencah Sal Xebat: Kurteyek li Mijoyi Hizbi Dimokrati Kurdistani Iran* [Fifty years of struggle: A short history of the Kurdistan Democratic Party of Iran], 21.

21. John Bulloch and Harvey Morris, *No Friends but the Mountains: The Tragic History of the Kurds*, 106.

22. Dana/Muhammad Biha'addin Mella Sahib, *Qazi Muhemmed u Kumari Mahabad* [Qazi Muhammad and the Kurdish Republic of Mahabad], 29.

23. Susan Meiselas, *Kurdistan: In the Shadow of History*, 2nd ed. (Chicago: University of Chicago Press, 2008).

24. Archie Roosevelt Jr., "The Kurdish Republic of Mahabad," 135, 142.

25. Arfa, *The Kurds*, 86.

26. A. R. Ghassemlou, "Kurdistan in Iran," 118.

27. Meiselas, *Kurdistan*, 182.

28. Abbas Vali, *Kurds and the State in Iran: The Making of Kurdish Identity*, 98.

29. Sahib, *Qazi Muhemmed u Kumari Mahabad*, 45.

30. Edgar O'Ballance, *The Kurdish Struggle 1920–94*, 32.

31. Sahib, *Qazi Muhemmed u Kumari Mahabad*, 32–36; Qasimlo, *Kurdistan and Kurds*, 95.

32. Samadi, *J. K Çibu, Çi Dewist ve Çi be ser hat?*, 15.

33. Roosevelt, "The Kurdish Republic of Mahabad," 141.

34. Ghassemlou, "Kurdistan in Iran," 120.

35. Ali Ahmadi Rawshani, *Kurdistan in the Mirror of History*, 200.

36. Kemal Kirisci and Gareth M. Winrow, *The Kurdish Question and Turkey: An Example of a Trans-State Ethnic Conflict*, 12.

37. "An Important Historical Document," *Peyam Newspaper* (Kurdish), March 6, 1998, 1, 2.

38. Roosevelt, "The Kurdish Republic of Mahabad," 149.

39. Mostafa Hejri, *Kurdistan*, January 19, 2001, 2.

40. Peyamner News Agency, February 19, 2012.

41. Hemin Khoshnaw, "Disunity in Focus at Anniversary of the Kurdistan Republic of Mahabad."

42. Ako Muhammed, "Kurdish Leaders Insist on Peaceful Struggle."

43. Ibid.

44. For a while both factions called themselves the KDPI. As tension grew over the name, the Hassanzadah faction changed its name to the KDP, but in essence both sides are identical in their goals. Here the KDPI is used to avoid confusion with the Iraqi KDP.

45. Khoshnaw, "Disunity."

46. Although the Kurdistan Workers' Party, the PKK, has accepted the national anthem, it still has not recognized the republic's flag but has instead created a flag of its own.

47. *Agri*, August 5, 2012, p. 7.

48. McDowall, *A Modern History of the Kurds*, 249.

49. Modern Iran only includes a small part of Kurdistan. Nearly two-thirds of Kurdistan is located in Turkey, Iraq, and Syria.

50. Shrikant G. Talageri, *The Aryan Invasion Theory: A Reappraisal*, 317–318. See also Mehrdad R. Izady, *The Kurds: A Concise Handbook*, 32, 34.

51. Percy Sykes, *A History of Persia*, vol. 1, 2–3.

52. This author, who was born and brought up in Kurdistan, has not seen or heard of any Zoroastrian Kurds, nor did he meet anyone else who has.

53. The Kurds of the Ēzidî faith and other Kurds call it "Ēzidî." Outside Kurdistan and in writing it is often called Yazidi, but this is sometimes mistaken for the

supporters of Yazid bin Mu'awiya, who was an Arab and the second Umayyad caliph. There is no relation between ĕzidî and Yazid.

54. Wahby, "The Origins of the Kurds and Their Language," 2.

55. Ibid., 5.

56. American chargé d'affaires (Merriam) to the secretary of state (USA), Tehran, May 1, 1936, cited in Lokman I. Meho, *The Kurdish Question in U.S. Foreign Policy: A Documentary Sourcebook*, 409–410.

57. Ted Robert Gurr and Barbara Harff, *Ethnic Conflict in World Politics*, 39.

58. Nikki Keddie, "Iran: Understanding the Enigma: a Historical View," 3.

59. Denise Natali, *The Kurds and the State: Evolving National Identity in Iraq, Turkey, and Iran*, 122.

60. Ibid., 134.

61. The majority of the Iraqi population are Shi'is; there are also significant numbers of Shi'is in Lebanon and other parts of the Middle East. Nevertheless, Iran is considered the birthplace and center of Shi'ism and still has considerable influence on non-Iranian Shi'is.

62. Keddie, "Iran: Understanding the Enigma," 5.

63. Nader Entessar, *Kurdish Ethnonationalism*, 29–30.

64. David McDowall, *The Kurds: A Nation Denied*, 76.

65. Brenda Shaffer, "Iran's Volatile Ethnic Mix," *International Herald Tribune*, June 2, 2006.

66. Barry Rubin, "Regime Change in Iran: A Reassessment," 3–4.

67. Maurice Danby Copithorne, *Report on the Situation of Human Rights in the Islamic Republic of Iran, January 16, 2002*, 15.

68. *Reaction to the Events of Kurdistan in Persian Publications*, compiled and published by the KDPI, no. 7, June 1993, 31.

69. *Kurdistan*, Organ of the Central Committee of Democratic Party of Iranian Kurdistan no. 189 (September 1992): 4.

70. Natali, *The Kurds and the State*, 153.

71. "A Brief Review of the Struggle of Kurdish Masses from the Kurdish Republic of Kurdistan to the Present," 13.

72. "Party's Constitution," PJAK website, http://pjak.org/pers.php?id=1147.

73. Ibid.

74. This author has had several conversations with the KDPI leadership in which they rejected the PJAK as an Iranian Kurdish political party. They therefore refused to join them in a Kurdish front.

75. Natali, *The Kurds and the State*, 155–156.

76. Nader Entessar, "Competing National Identities: The Kurdish Conundrum in Iran," in *Kurdish Identity Human Rights and Political Status*, ed. Charles G. MacDonald and Carole A. O'Leary (Florida: University Press of Florida, 2007), 199.

77. Martin van Bruinessen, "The Kurds between Iran and Iraq," 23.

78. An exception to this could be a change in the Iranian state structure, as happened in Iraq, which might create a political space for the Kurds of Iran to achieve some form of autonomy. If the Islamic Republic of Iran continues with its current policies, then such a change is quite possible.

Conclusion: The Kurdish Momentum

1. See Ofra Bengio, *The Kurds of Iraq: Building a State within a State*, 5–10.

2. Simla Yerlikaya, *Yeni Komşumuz Kürdistan*.

3. For the impact of these two pacts on the Kurds, see Wadie Jwaideh, *The Kurdish National Movement: Its Origins and Development*, 123–124, 270–271.

4. *Nefel*, March 23, 2013, http://www.nefel.com/articles/article_detail.asp?RubricNr=1&ArticleNr=7494. This report, which appeared in the Kurdish outlet, did not get much publicity in the Turkish press.

5. In October 1998, Turkey and Syria signed the Adana agreement, according to which Syria recognized the PKK as a terrorist organization and agreed to expel all PKK members from its territory, including Öcalan. Many of the PKK members found their way to the KRG. On the agreement, see Mustafa Cosar Unal, *Counterterrorism in Turkey*, 70–74. After these relations collapsed, it transpired that Damascus did not share the PKK archives with Turkey. Tulin Daloglu, *Al-Monitor*, April 7, 2013.

6. Martin van Bruinessen, "The Kurds in Movement: Migrations, Mobilisations, Communications and the Globalisation of the Kurdish Question."

7. For a discussion of the complicated relationship between the nation-state and ethnonationalism, see Nader Entessar, *Kurdish Politics in the Middle East*, 2, 217–219.

8. The upheavals in the region may be considered as an expression of participatory democracy. The Internet too may be considered as such.

9. In fact, after World War I the Kurds were divided into five states, the fifth being the Soviet Union, where Kurds also resided, especially in Azerbaijan and Armenia. This volume does not include this fifth part. However, two points should be mentioned regarding Kurds in the Soviet Union. First, since the Soviet Union was initially tolerant toward Kurdish cultural activities, it was there that free cultural activity was initiated. For example, the first newspaper in the Kurdish dialect Kurmanji—the *Ria Taza* (the new way)—was published in 1930 in Armenia. Second, Azerbaijan adopted the same repressive policies against the Kurds as Turkey, including forced assimilation and repressing the use of the Kurdish language. For a discussion of the Kurds in the Soviet Union, see Ismet Cheriff Vanly, "The Kurds in the Soviet Union." Vanly estimated the number of Kurds in 1990 at 450,000; see p. 164. However, according to statistical data for 1989, the total population of Kurds in the Soviet Union was 152,717; see http://www.encyclopedia.com/topic/Kurds.aspx.

10. The second half of the 1960s was characterized by the evolution of Kurdish activism toward a more organized form. The reinvigoration of the Kurdish national movement in Iraq has had a direct bearing on this development. Cengiz Gunes, *The Kurdish National Movement in Turkey: From Protest to Resistance*, 57.

11. For the negative impact of such localism, see Jwaideh, *The Kurdish National Movement*, 293.

12. For a discussion of the public space in Diyarbakır, see Muna Güvenç, "Constructing Narratives of Kurdish Nationalism in the Urban Space of Diyarbakır, Turkey."

13. On Mursi's dictatorial moves, see Raymond Stock, "On Mistaking Mohamed Mursi for His Mask."

14. Gunes, *The Kurdish National Movement in Turkey*, 136.

15. Interestingly enough, in Turkey, for example, some suggested that the "Kurds have in fact been the medium through which more democracy is demanded all over the country." Yılmaz Ensaroğlu and Dilek Kurban, *How Legitimate Are the Kurds' Demands? The Kurdish Question through the Lens of Turkey's West*, 18.

16. For an analysis of the change, see Gunes, *The Kurdish National Movement in Turkey*, 124–151.

17. http://setimes.com/cocoon/setimes/xhtml/en_GB/features/setimes/features/2011/07/20/feature-02. On the articulation of the democratic discourse, see Abdullah Öcalan, *The Road Map to Negotiations*.

18. *Fair Observer*, January 7, 2013. On the Islamization of Egypt under Mursi, see Stock, "On Mistaking Mohamed Mursi." An Egyptian commentator maintained that the Islamists in Egypt "know nothing about democracy, and have no interest in it; they simply use it to strengthen Egypt as an Islamic state." Mohamed Nosseir, *Ahramonline*, January 7, 2013, http://english.ahram.org.eg/NewsContentP/4/61771/Opinion/Democracy-and-Islam-deteriorated-after-the-Egyptia.aspx.

19. UNAMI FOCUS, News Bulletin no. 35. It should be pointed out, however, that one of the Islamist lists was in conjunction with that of a socialist party, so that the actual percentage of the Islamists may be only 12 percent.

20. *Rudaw*, August 21, 2012, http://www.rudaw.net/english/news/turkey/5114.html.

21. *Radio France Internationale*, December 25, 2012, http://www.english.rfi.fr/middle-east/20121225-christians-iraq-celebrate-christmas-kurdistan.

22. According to Eibner, after the fall of Saddam Hussein in 2003, over 40 percent of all Iraqi refugees were Christians, even though they represented less than 4 percent of the population. This means that close to half of the approximately one million Christians living in Iraq in 2003 fled the country at the very time when the United States conducted "Operation Freedom—Iraq." John Eibner, "The Plight of Christians in Iraq," http://www.aina.org/reports/CSIIraqFieldMission2007.pdf.

23. For the plight of Christians in the post-Mubarak regime, see Frontpagemag.com, December 12, 2011, http://frontpagemag.com/2011/jamie-glazov/congress-hears-of-the-plight-of-egypt%E2%80%99s-christians/.

24. Reuters, March 3, 2012.

25. "The Kurdistan Region, Invest in the Future," http://belkib.com/women-in-kurdistan.html.

26. Gunes, *The Kurdish National Movement in Turkey*, 119.

27. *New York Times*, January 11, 2013.

28. *Sendika.Org*, December 30, 2012, http://www.sendika.org/yazi.php?yazi_no=50509&ref=bm.

29. Maxime Azadi, January 8, 2013, http://www.actukurde.fr/actualites/401/les-kurdes-syriens-redigent-les-principes-et-les-lois-de-leur-autonomie.html.

30. http://www.firathaberajansi.org/haberayrinti.php?id=17836.

31. Can Mutlu, *Kurds in Cyberspace*, http://web.uvic.ca/~onpol/spring2007/3 -Mutlu.pdf, p. 30.

32. For a discussion of such categorization of states, see Nina Caspersen and Gareth Stansfield, eds., *Unrecognized States in the International System*.

33. South Korea was registered as having an embassy in Erbil. Erbillifestyle, http://erbillifestyle.com/erbil/embassies-in-erbil. For further details, see Foreign Relations Department, Kurdistan Regional Government, http://dfr.krg.org/p/p .aspx?p=37&l=12&s=020100&r=363.

34. *Nefel*, April 2, 2013, http://www.nefel.com/articles/article_detail.asp?Ru bricNr=1&ArticleNr=7505.

35. One of the pioneering studies of the Syrian Kurds is by Jordi Tejel, *Syria's Kurds: History, Politics and Society*.

36. *Sada*, February 5, 2013, http://carnegieendowment.org/2013/02/05/%D 8%B5%D8%B9%D9%88%D8%AF-%D8%A7%D9%84%D8%A3%D9%83 %D8%B1%D8%A7%D8%AF-%D9%81%D9%8A-%D8%B3%D9%88 %D8%B1%D9%8A%D8%A7/fa8e.

37. Maxime Azadi, January 8, 2013, http://www.actukurde.fr/actualites/401 /les-kurdes-syriens-redigent-les-principes-et-les-lois-de-leur-autonomie.html.

38. http://www.actukurde.fr/actualites/415/les-kurdes-syriens-prennent-le -contrle-d-une-zone-petroliere.html.

39. Gunes, *The Kurdish National Movement in Turkey*, 173–174.

40. There were other political causes, which are beyond the scope of this book.

41. See Entessar, *Kurdish Politics in the Middle East*, 15–59.

42. Interview with a Kurdish activist, February 2012.

43. David McDowall, "The Kurdish Question: A Historical Review," in Kreyenbroek and Sperl, *The Kurds: A Contemporary Overview*, 24.

44. Munir Morad, "The Situation of Kurds in Iraq and Turkey: Current Trends and Prospects," in Kreyenbroek and Sperl, *The Kurds: A Contemporary Overview*, 96.

45. For such prospects, see *The Economist*, April 20, 2013.

46. Ismail Beşikçi, interview to *Rudaw*, September 27, 2012, http://www.mal press.com/english/politics/710-ismail-beikci-this-is-the-century-of-the-kurds .html.

Bibliography

Books and Articles

Abbasi, Muhammad. "Introduction to Sharaf-nameh." In *Amir Sharaf-Khan-e-Bidlisi Sharafnameh*. Tehran: Elmi, 1994.

Abboud, Cha'ban. "Les quartiers informels de Damas: une ceinture de misère." In *La Syrie au présent. Reflets d'une société*, edited by Baudouin Dupret et al., 169–176. Paris: Actes Sud, 2007.

Abdalla, Ahmad. *The Student Movement and National Politics in Egypt, 1923–1973*. London: Saqi Books, 1985.

Ahmadzade, Hashim. *Nation and Novel: A Study of Kurdish and Persian Narrative Discourse*. Uppsala, Sweden: Acta Universitatis Uppsaliensis, 2003.

Ahmed, Mohammad M. A. "Laying the Foundation for a Kurdistani State." In *The Evolution of Kurdish Nationalism*, edited by Mohammed M. A. Ahmed and Michael Gunter, 149–187. Costa Mesa, CA: Mazda Publishers, 2007.

———, and Michael Gunter, eds. *The Evolution of Kurdish Nationalism*. Costa Mesa, CA: Mazda Publishers, 2007.

Ainsworth, W. F. *Travels and Researches in Asia Minor, Mesopotamia, Chaldea and Armenia*. Vol. 1. London: John Parker, West Strand, 1842.

Al-Istrabadi, Feisal Amin Rasoul. "Rebuilding a Nation: Myths, Realities, and Solutions in Iraq." *Harvard International Review* 29, no. 1 (2007): 14–19.

Allawi, Ali A. *The Occupation of Iraq: Winning the War, Losing the Peace*. New Haven, CT: Yale University Press, 2007.

"Al-Maliki's Description of Iraq as Arab Country rankles Kurds." TREND News Agency. http://news-en.trend.az/world/wnews/1447629.html.

Alper, Emin. "1968: Global or Local?" *Red Thread* 2 (2010). http://www.red-thread.org/en/article.asp?a=38.

Alter, Peter. *Nationalism*. London: E. Arnold, 1989.

Amedroz, H. F. "The Marwanid Dynasty at Mayyafariqin in the Tenth and Eleventh Centuries A.D." *Journal of the Royal Asiatic Society* (January 1903): 123–154.

Amnesty International. *Iran: Human Rights Abuses against the Kurdish Minority*. London: Amnesty International, 2008.

———. *Syria: Kurds in the Syrian Arab Republic One Year after the March 2004 Events*. http://web.amnesty.org/library/print/ENG-MDE240022005.

Anderson, Benedict R. *Imagined Communities: Reflections on the Origin and Spread of Nationalism*. London, New York: Verso, 1991.

Antonius, George. *The Arab Awakening*. New York: Capricorn, 1965 [1946].

Arato, Andrew. *Constitution Making under Occupation: The Politics of Imposed Revolution in Iraq*. New York: Columbia University Press, 2009.

Arfa, Hassan. *The Kurds: An Historical and Political Study*. London: Oxford University Press, 1966.

Argue, Steven. "Kurdish Culture, Repression, Women's Rights, and Resistance." June 12, 2007. http://www.indybay.org/newsitems/2007/06/12/18426957.php.

Arjomand, Said. "Constitutions and the Struggle for Political Order: A Study in the Modernization of Political Traditions." *European Journal of Sociology* 3, no. 1 (1992): 39–82.

Aslan, Senem. "Incoherent State: Controversy over Kurdish Naming in Turkey." *European Journal of Turkish Studies* 10 (2009). http://ejts.revues.org/index4142.html.

Aslan, Sulayman Asad. "Clashes of Agencies Formation and Failure of Early Kurdish Nationalism 1918–1922." Ph.D. diss., University of London, 2002.

Aytürk, İlker. "Turkish Linguists against the West: The Origins of Linguistic Nationalism in Ataturk's Turkey." *Middle Eastern Studies* 40, no. 6 (November 2004): 1–25.

Badem, Candan. *The Ottoman Crimean War (1853–1856)*. Leiden, Netherlands, and Boston: E. J. Brill, 2010.

Bal, İhsan. "The Democratic Initiative Knocked over the KCK." *Journal of Turkish Weekly*, December 2009. http://www.turkishweekly.net/columnist/3260/the-democratic-initiative-knocked-over-the-kck.html.

Barakat, Halim. *Lebanon in Strife: Student Preludes to the Civil War*. Austin and London: University of Texas Press, 1977.

Baram, Amatzia. *Culture, History and Ideology in the Formation of Ba'thist Iraq, 1968–89*. New York: St. Martin's Press, 1991.

Barkey, Henri J., and Graham E. Fuller. *Turkey's Kurdish Question*. Lanham, MD: Rowman & Littlefield, 1998.

Barrès, Maurice. *Scènes et doctrines du nationalisme*. Paris: Plon, 1925 [1902].

Batatu, Hanna. *The Old Social Classes and the Revolutionary Movements of Iraq*. Princeton, NJ: Princeton University Press, 1982.

———. *Syria's Peasantry, the Descendants of Its Lesser Rural Notables, and their Politics*. Princeton, NJ: Princeton University Press, 1999.

Bell, Gertrude. *Review of the Civil Administration of Mesopotamia*. London: His Majesty's Stationery Office, 1920.

Ben Israel, Hedva. *In the Name of the Nation: Studies in Nationalism and Zionism*. Ben Gurion Research Institute for the Study of Israel and Zionism, Ben Gurion University of the Negev Press [Hebrew], 2004.

Bengio, Ofra. "Autonomy in Kurdistan in Historical Perspective." In *The Future of Kurdistan in Iraq*, edited by Brendan O'Leary, John McGarry, and Khaled Salih, 173–185. Philadelphia: University of Pennsylvania Press, 2005.

———. "Iraqi Kurds: Hour of Power?" *Middle East Quarterly* 10, no. 3 (Summer 2003): 39–48.

———. "A Kurdish Call for Self-Determination: Crossing the Rubicon?" *Tel Aviv Notes* 4, no. 18 (December 26, 2010).

———. *The Kurds of Iraq: Building a State within a State*. Boulder, CO: Lynne Rienner Publishers, 2012.

———. "The Muses Do Not Remain Silent: A Love Story in the Service of Kurdish Nation-Building." *Tel-Aviv Notes*, November 4, 2008.

———. "Nation Building in Multiethnic Societies: The Case of Iraq." In *Minorities and the State in the Arab World*, edited by Ofra Bengio and Gabriel Ben-Dor, 149–169. Boulder, CO: Lynne Rienner Publishers, 1999.

———. *Saddam's Iraq: Political Discourse and the Language of Power*. Tel Aviv: Dayan Center, 1996.

———. *Saddam's Word: Political Discourse in Iraq*. Oxford: Oxford University Press, 1998.

Benomar, Jamal. "Constitution-Making after Conflict: Lessons for Iraq." *Journal of Democracy* 15, no. 2 (April 2004): 81–95.

Bernhardsson, Magnus Thorkell. *Reclaiming a Plundered Past: Archaeology and Nation-Building in Modern Iraq*. Austin: University of Texas Press, 2005.

Bidlisi, Prince Sharaf al-Din. *The Sharafnama or the History of the Kurdish Nation*. Translated by M. R. Izady. Costa Mesa, CA: Mazda Publishers, 2005.

Bodley, John H. *Cultural Anthropology, Tribes, States, and the Global System*. Mountain View, CA: Mayfield Publishing, 1994.

Bozarslan, Hamit. "Le Kurdistan d'Irak aujourd'hui." *Critique internationale* 29 (2006): 25–36.

———. "Le nationalisme kurde, de la violence politique au suicide sacrificial." *Critique internationale* 21 (2003): 93–115.

———. *La question kurde. États et minorités au Moyen-Orient*. Paris: Presses de Sciences Po, 1997.

———. "La régionalisation du problème kurde." In *La nouvelle dynamique au Moyen-Orient. Les relations entre l'Orient arabe et la Turquie*, edited by Elizabeth Picard, 155–161. Paris: L'Harmattan, 1993.

———. "Tribal Asabiyya and Kurdish Politics: A Socio-Historical Perspective." In *The Kurds: Nationalism and Politics*, edited by Faleh A. Jabbar and Hosham Dawod, 130–147. London: Saqi Books, 2006.

Breuilly, John. *Nationalism and the State*. Manchester, UK: Manchester University Press, 1993.

Brown, David. "Ethnic Revival: Perspectives on State and Society." *Third World Quarterly* 11, no. 4 (October 1989): 1–16.

Brown, Nathan. *Constitutions in a Nonconstitutional World: Arab Basic Laws and the Prospects for Accountable Government*. Albany: State University of New York Press, 2002.

———. "The Final Draft of the Iraqi Constitution." Analysis and Commentary. Carnegie Endowment for International Peace, September 16, 2005.

Brown, Paula. *Highland Peoples of New Guinea*. Cambridge: Cambridge University Press, 1978.

Buchanan, Allen E. *Secession: The Morality of Political Divorce from Fort Sumter to Lithuania and Quebec*. Boulder, CO: Westview Press, 1991.

Buchheit, Lee C. *Secession: The Legitimacy of Self-Determination*. New Haven, CT: Yale University Press, 1978.

Bulloch, John, and Harvey Morris. *No Friends but the Mountains: The Tragic History of the Kurds*. London: Viking, 1992.

Burns, Ross. *Damascus: A History*. New York: Routledge, 2005.

Byman, Daniel L., and Kenneth M. Pollack. "Democracy in Iraq?" *Washington Quarterly* 26, no. 3 (2003): 119–136.

Cahen, Claude. *Der Islam I: vom Ursprung bis zu den Anfängen des Osmanenreiches*. Frankfurt am Main: Fischer Weltgeschichte Band 14, Fischer Taschenbuch Verlag, 1968.

Çarkoğlu, Ali, and William Hale, eds. *The Politics of Modern Turkey*. Abingdon, UK: Routledge, 2008.

Caspersen, Nina, and Gareth Stansfield, eds. *Unrecognized States in the International System*. London: Routledge, 2011.

Çelik, Ayşe Betûl. "Transnationalization of Human Rights Norms and Its Impact on Internally Displaced Kurds." *Human Rights Quarterly* 27 (2005): 969–997.

Çolak, Yılmaz. "Language Policy and Official Ideology in Early Republican Turkey." *Middle Eastern Studies* 40, no. 6 (November 2004): 67–91.

Comaroff, John L., and Paul C. Stern, eds. *Perspectives on Nationalism and War*. Amsterdam: Gordon and Breach, 1995.

Connor, Walker. *Ethnonationalism: The Quest for Understanding*. Princeton, NJ: Princeton University Press, 1994.

———. "The Politics of Ethnonationalism." *Journal of International Affairs* 27, no. 1 (1973): 1–21.

Conversi, Daniele, ed. *Ethnonationalism in the Contemporary World: Walker Connor and the Study of Nationalism*. London: Routledge, 2002.

Copithorne, Maurice Danby. *Report on the Situation of Human Rights in the Islamic Republic of Iran, 16 January 2002*. Special Representative of the Commission on Human Rights (UN).

Cosar Unal, Mustafa. *Counterterrorism in Turkey*. London: Routledge, 2012.

Crone, Patricia. "The Tribe and the State." In *States in History*, edited by J. A. Hall, 48–77. New York: Basil Blackwell, 1986.

Cunningham, A. B., ed. *The Early Correspondence of Richard Wood, 1831–1841*. London: Royal Historical Society, 1966.

Damon, Arwa. "Female Fighters: We Won't Stand for Male Dominance." *CNN.com/world*, October 6, 2008. http://edition.cnn.com/2008/WORLD/meast/10/06/iraq.pkk/.

Daugherty, William. *Executive Secrets: Covert Action and the Presidency*. Lexington: University Press of Kentucky, 2006.

Davis, Eric. "Democracy's Prospects in Iraq." *American Diplomacy* 9, no. 3 (2004).

Deeks, Ashley S., and Matthew D. Burton. "Iraq's Constitution: A Drafting History." *Cornell International Law Journal* 40, no. 1 (2007): 1–87.

Delanty, Gerard, and Krishnan Kumar, eds. *The Sage Handbook of Nations and Nationalism*. London: Sage, 2006.

Dirlik, Arif. "The Third World in 1968." In *1968: The World Transformed*, edited by Carole Fink, Philipp Gassert, and Detlef Junker, 295–317. Cambridge: Cambridge University Press, 1999.

Douwes, Dick. *The Ottomans in Syria: A History of Justice and Oppression*. London: I. B. Tauris, 2000.

Dupret-Schepens, Catherine. "Les populations syriennes sont-elles homogènes?" In Baudouin Dupret et al., *La Syrie au présent. Reflets d'une société*, 215–224. Paris: Actes Sud, 2007.

Eagleton, William. *The Kurdish Republic of 1946*. London: Oxford University Press, 1963.

Edmonds, C. J. "Kurdish Nationalism." *Journal of Contemporary History* 6, no. 1 (1971): 87–107.

———. *Kurds, Turks and Arabs*. London: Oxford University Press, 1957.

Ensaroğlu, Yılmaz, and Dilek Kurban. *How Legitimate Are the Kurds' Demands? The Kurdish Question through the Lens of Turkey's West*. TESEV Yayınları, 2011.

Entessar, Nader. "Competing National Identities: The Kurdish Conundrum in Iran." In *Kurdish Identity: Human Rights and Political Status*, edited by Charles G. MacDonald and Carole A. O'Leary, 188–200. Gainesville: University Press of Florida, 2007.

———. "Ethnicity and Ethnic Challenges in the Middle East." In *Ethnicity and Governance in the Third World*, edited by J. M. Mbaku, P. O. Agbese, and M. S. Kimenyi, 149–164. London and Burlington, VT: Ashgate Publishing, 2001.

———. "The Impact of the Iraq War on the Future of the Kurds in Iran." In *The Kurdish Question and the 2003 Iraqi War*, edited by Mohammed M. A. Ahmed and Michael M. Gunter, 182–184. Costa Mesa, CA: Mazda Publishers, 2005.

———. *Kurdish Ethnonationalism*. Boulder, CO, and London: Lynne Rienner Publishers, 1992.

———. "The Kurdish National Movement in Iran since the Islamic Revolution of 1979." In *The Evolution of Kurdish Nationalism*, edited by Mohammed M. A. Ahmed and Michael M. Gunter, 270–275. Costa Mesa, CA: Mazda Publishers, 2007.

———. *Kurdish Politics in the Middle East*. Lanham, MD: Lexington Books, 2010.

Eppel, Michael. "The Demise of the Kurdish Emirates: The Impact of Ottoman Reforms and International Relations on Kurdistan during the First Half of the Nineteenth Century." *Middle Eastern Studies* 44 (2008): 237–258.

Eskander, Saad B. "The Fayli Kurds of Baghdad and the Baath Regime." In *The Kurds: Nationalism and Politics*, edited by Faleh A. Jabar and Hosham Dawod, 180–206. London: Saqi Books, 2006.

Esman, Milton. *Ethnic Politics*. Ithaca, NY: Cornell University Press, 1994.

———. *An Introduction to Ethnic Conflict*. Cambridge, UK: Polity Press, 2004.

Fawcett, Louise L'Estrange. *Iran and the Cold War: The Azerbaijan Crisis of 1946*. Cambridge: Cambridge University Press, 1992.

Fraser, James Bailie. *Travels in Koordistan, Mesopotamia and Including an Account of Parts of Those Countries Hitherto Unvisited by Europeans: With Sketches of the*

Character and Manners of the Koordish and Arab Tribes. Vol. 1. London: Richard Bentley, 1840.

Gause, Gregory. "Can Democracy Stop Terrorism?" *Foreign Affairs* 84 (September–October 2005): 62–76.

Gauthier, Julie. "Syrie: le facteur kurde." *Outre-Terre. Revue française de géopolitique* 14 (2006): 217–230.

Geertz, Clifford. "The Integrative Revolution: Primordial Sentiments and Civil Politics in the New States." In *Old Societies and New States: The Quest for Modernity in Asia and Africa*, edited by Clifford Geertz, 105–157. New York: Free Press, 1963.

———, ed. *Old Societies and New States.* New York: The Free Press, 1963.

Gellner, Ernest. "Adam's Navel: 'Primordialists' versus 'Modernists.'" In *People, Nation and State: The Meaning of Ethnicity and Nationalism*, edited by E. Mortimer and R. Fine, 31–35. London: I. B. Tauris, 1999.

———. *Muslim Society.* Cambridge: Cambridge University Press, 1982.

———. "Nationalism and Modernization." In *Nationalism*, edited by John Hutchinson and Anthony D. Smith, 55–63. Oxford: Oxford University Press, 1994.

———. *Nations and Nationalism.* Oxford: Blackwell, 1983.

———. "Tribalism and the State in the Middle East." In *Tribes and State Formation in the Middle East*, edited by Philip Khoury and Joseph Kostiner, 109–126. London: I. B. Tauris, 1991.

Gettleman, Marvin E., and Stuart Schaar. *The Middle East and Islamic World Reader.* New York: Grove Press, 2003.

Ghareeb, Edmund. *The Kurdish Question in Iraq.* Syracuse, NY: Syracuse University Press, 1981.

———, and Beth Dougherty. *Historical Dictionary of Iraq.* Lanham, MD, and Oxford: Scarecrow Press, 2004.

Ghassemlou, Abdul Rahman. *Kurdistan and the Kurds.* Prague: Publishing House of the Czechoslovak Academy of Sciences, 1965.

———. "Kurdistan in Iran." In *People without a Country: The Kurds and Kurdistan*, translated by Michael Pallis, edited by Gerard Chaliand, 107–134. London: Zed Press, 1980.

Gonzalez-Perez, Margaret. *Women and Terrorism: Female Activity in Domestic and International Terror Groups.* New York: Routledge, 2008.

Guibernau, Montserrat. "Anthony D. Smith on Nations and National Identity: A Critical Assessment." *Nations and Nationalism* 10, no. 1/2 (2004): 125–141.

Gunes, Cengiz. *The Kurdish National Movement in Turkey: From Protest to Resistance.* London: Routledge, 2012.

Gunter, Michael M. "The Changing Kurdish Problem in Turkey." *Conflict Studies 270*, Institute for the Study of Conflict and Terrorism RISCT (May 1994).

———. "Federalism and the Kurds of Iraq: The Solution or the Problem?" In *The Kurds: Nationalism and Politics*, edited by Faleh A. Jabar and Hosham Dawod, 231–257. London: Saqi Books, 2006.

———. *Historical Dictionary of the Kurds.* Lanham, MD: Scarecrow Press, 2004.

———. *The Kurds of Iraq: Tragedy and Hope.* New York: St. Martin's Press, 1992.

————. *The Kurds in Turkey: A Political Dilemma*. Boulder, CO: Westview Press, 1990.

Gurr, Ted Robert, and Barbara Harff. *Ethnic Conflict in World Politics*. Boulder, CO: Westview Press, 1994.

Güvenç, Muna. "Constructing Narratives of Kurdish Nationalism in the Urban Space of Diyarbakır, Turkey." *TDSR* 23, no. 1 (2011).

Haig, Geoffrey. "The Invisibilisation of Kurdish: The Other Side of Language Planning in Turkey." In *Die Kurden: Studien zu ihrer Sprache, Geschichte und Kultur*, edited by Stephan Conermann and Geoffrey Haig, 121–150. Schenefeld: EB-Verlag, 2003.

Halas, Elzbieta. "Constructing the Identity of a Nation-State: Symbolic Conflict over the Preamble to the Constitution of the Third Republic of Poland." *Polish Sociological Review* 1, no. 1 (2005): 49–67.

Hale, William. *Turkish Foreign Policy 1774–2000*. London: Frank Cass Publishers, 2000.

Hallward, Maia. "Who Is Iraqi? The Changing Boundaries of Identity in Contemporary Iraq." Paper presented at the Annual Meeting of the International Studies Association's 49th Annual Convention, Bridging Multiple Divides, San Francisco.

Hamoudi, Haider Ala. "Notes in Defense of the Iraq Constitution." *University of Pennsylvania Journal of International Law and Social Change* 14 (2011): 1277–1300.

————. "Ornamental Repugnancy: Identitarian Islam and the Iraqi Constitution." *Legal Studies Research Paper Series*, Working Paper no. 2010–35 (October 2010): 1–25.

Hamoudi, Humam. "My Perceptions on the Iraqi Constitutional Process." *Stanford Law Review* 59, no. 5 (2007): 1315–1320.

Hassanpour, Amir. "The Making of Kurdish Identity: Pre-20th Century Historical and Literary Discourses." In *Essays on the Origins of Kurdish Nationalism*, edited by Abbas Vali, 106–162. Costa Mesa, CA: Mazda Publishers, 2003.

————. *Nationalism and Language in Kurdistan: 1918–1985*. San Francisco: Mellen Research University Press, 1992.

Haviland, William A. *Cultural Anthropology*. New York: Harcourt Brace, 1975.

Hayes, Carlton. *Historical Evolution of Modern Nationalism*. New York: McMillan, 1948.

Hechter, Michael, Tuna Kuyucu, and Audrey Sacks. "Nationalism and Direct Rule." In *The Sage Handbook of Nations and Nationalism*, edited by Gerard Delanty and Krishnan Kumar, 84–93. London: Sage, 2006.

Henry, Jules. *Jungle People, a Kaingang Tribe of the Highlands of Brazil*. New York: Vintage Books, 1964.

Heper, Metin. *The State and Kurds in Turkey: The Question of Assimilation*. New York: Palgrave Macmillan, 2007.

Herder, Johann Gottfried von. Ideen zur Philosophie der Geschichte der Menschheit. München: C. Hanser, 2002 [1784].

Hiltermann, Joost R. "Kirkuk as a Peace-Building Test Case." In *Iraq: Preventing a New Generation of Conflict*, edited by Markus E. Bouillon, David M. Malone, and Ben Roswell, 125–142. Boulder, CO: Lynne Reinner Publishers, 2007.

Hobsbawm, Eric J. "The Nation as Invented Tradition." In *Nationalism*, edited by John Hutchinson and Anthony D. Smith, 76–83. Oxford: Oxford University Press, 1994.

———. *Nations and Nationalism since 1780*. Cambridge: Cambridge University Press, 1990.

Horowitz, Donald L. "Constitution Making: A Process Filled with Constraint." *Review of Constitutional Studies* 12, no. 1 (2006): 1–17.

———. *Ethnic Groups in Conflict*. Berkeley: University of California Press, 1985.

Human Rights Foundation Turkey. Democratic Turkey Forum, October 2010.

Hutchinson, John. "Ethnicity and Modern Nations." *Ethnic and Racial Studies* 23, no. 4 (2000): 651–669.

Ibn al-Athir, ʿIzz al-Din. *The Annals of the Saljuq Turks: Selections from al-kamil fi al-taʾrikh of ʿIzz al-Din bin al-Athir*. Translated and annotated by D. S. Richards. London and New York: Routledge Curzon, 2002.

———. *The Chronicle of Ibn al-Athir for the Crusading Period from al-kamil fi al-taʾrikh. Part 1: The Years 491–541/1097–1146, The Coming of the Franks and the Muslim Response*. Translated by D. S. Richards. Aldershot and Burlington, UK: Ashgate Publishing Co., 2006.

International Free Women's Foundation. *Psychological Consequences of Trauma Experiences on the Development of Migrated Kurdish Women in the European Union: Final Results and Background of a Survey in Five European Countries and Turkey*. Rotterdam: International Free Women's Foundation, 2007.

Iraq Body Count 2010. *Documented Civilian Deaths from Violence*. http://www.iraqbodycount.org/database/.

Ismael, Tareq Y., and Jacqueline S. Ismael. *The Communist Movement in Syria and Lebanon*. Gainesville: University Press of Florida, 1998.

Izady, Mehrdad. Book review of Wilhelm Gernot, *The Hurrians*, translated by Jennifer Barnes (Warminster, UK: Aris and Philip Ltd, 1989.) *International Journal of Kurdish Studies* 7, nos. 1 & 2 (1994).

———. *The Kurds: A Concise Handbook*. Washington, DC: Taylor & Francis, 1992.

Jawad, Saad. *Iraq and the Kurdish Question, 1958–1970*. London: Ithaca, 1981.

Joseph, John. *The Nestorians and Their Neighbors*. Princeton, NJ: Princeton University Press, 1961.

Jwaideh, Wadie. *The Kurdish National Movement: Its Origins and Development*. New York: Syracuse University Press, 2006.

Karaveli, Halil M. "Reconciling Statism with Freedom: Turkey's Kurdish Opening." Silk Road Paper (October 2010). www.silkroadstudies.org/new/docs/silkroadpapers/1010Karaveli.pdf.

Kashani-Sabet, Firoozeh. *Frontier Fictions: Shaping the Iranian Nation, 1804–1946*. Princeton, NJ: Princeton University Press, 1999.

Katzman, Kenneth. "The Kurds in Post-Saddam Iraq." *Congressional Research Service Report for Congress*, April 2009, 1–10.

Keddie, Nikki. "Iran: Understanding the Enigma: A Historian's View." *Middle East Review of International Affairs Journal* 2, no. 3 (September 1998): 1–10.

Kedourie, Elie. *Nationalism*. London: Hutchinson & Co. Ltd., 1960.

Keesing, Roger M. *Cultural Anthropology*. London: Holt, 1975.

Keitner, Chimene. "National Self-Determination in Historical Perspective: The Legacy of the French Revolution for Today's Debate." *International Studies Review* 2, no. 3 (Fall 2000): 3–26.

Kelly, Michael J. "The Kurdish Regional Constitution within the Framework of the Iraqi Federal Constitution: A Struggle for Sovereignty, Oil, Ethnic Identity, and the Prospects for a Reverse Supremacy Clause." *Penn State Law Review* 114, no. 3 (2010): 707–808.

Khoury, Philip S. *Syria and the French Mandate: The Politics of Arab Nationalism 1920–1945*. Princeton, NJ: Princeton University Press, 1988.

Khoury, Philip S. *Urban Notables and Arab Nationalism: The Politics of Damascus, 1860–1929*. Cambridge: Cambridge University Press, 1983.

Kienle, Eberhard. *Ba'th v Ba'th: The Conflict between Syria and Iraq, 1968–1989*. London: I. B. Tauris, 1990.

Kirisci, Kemal, and Gareth Winrow. *The Kurdish Question and Turkey*. London: Frank Cass Publishers, 2003.

Kirmanj, Sherko. "The Construction of the Iraqi State and the Question of National Identity." Ph.D. diss., University of South Australia, Adelaide, 2010.

———. "Identity and Nation in Iraq." Boulder, CO: Lynne Rienner Publishers, 2013.

Kohn, Hans. *Prelude to Nation-States: The French and German Experience, 1789–1815*. Princeton, NJ: D. Van Nostrand Company, 1967.

———. "Western and Eastern Nationalisms." In *Nationalism*, edited by Anthony D. Smith and John Hutchinson, 162–165. Oxford: Oxford University Press, 1994.

Koohi-Kamali, Fereshteh. "The Development of Nationalism in Iranian Kurdistan." In *The Kurds: A Contemporary Overview*, edited by Philip G. Kreyenbroek and Stefan Sperl, 171–192. London: Routledge, 1992.

Koselleck, Reinhart. *L'Expérience de l'histoire*. Edited by Michael Werner. Paris: Gallimard et Le Seuil, 1997.

Kostiner, Joseph. "Transforming Dualities: Tribes and State Formation in Saudi Arabia." In *Tribes and State Formation in the Middle East*, edited by Philip Khoury and Joseph Kostiner, 226–251. London: I. B. Tauris, 1991.

Kreyenbroek, Philip G., and Stefan Sperl, eds. *The Kurds: A Contemporary Survey*. London: Routledge, 1992.

Kurd Watch. "Decree 49—Dispossession of the Kurdish Population? Commentary on the Political Implications and Economic Consequences of a Decree." http://www.kurdwatch.org/index.php?cid=186.

Kurdo, J. [pseud.]. *Kurdistan: The Origins of Kurdish Civilization*. Stockholm: Sarah Distribution, 1988.

Kutschera, Chris. *The Kurds in the 19th and 20th Centuries*. Tehran: Sadaf, 1990.

———. "Mad Dreams of Independence: The Kurds of Turkey and the PKK." *Middle East Report* 189, *The Kurdish Experience*, July–August 1994.

———. "A Silent Scream." *The Middle East* 227 (October 1993): 33–35.

Layard, Sir Austen Henry. *Discoveries among the Ruins of Nineveh and Babylon: With Travels in Armenia and Kurdistan, and the Desert*. New York: Harper and Brothers, 1853.

———. *Nineveh and Its Remains*. Vol. 1. London: John Murray, 1854.

———. *Popular Account of Discoveries at Nineveh*. London: John Murray, 1851.

Lewis, Bernard. *The Emergence of Modern Turkey*. 2nd ed. London: Oxford University Press, 1969.

Longrigg, Stephen. *Iraq, 1900 to 1950*. London: Oxford University Press, 1953.

Lowe, Robert. "The Syrian Kurds: A People Discovered." *Middle East Programme Briefing Paper* 6, no. 1 (2006): 1–7.

Lukitz, Liora. *Iraq: The Search for National Identity*. London: F. Cass, 1995.

———. "Nationalism in Post-Imperial Iraq: The Complexities of Collective Identity." *Critical Review* 21, no. 1 (2009): 5–20.

MacDonald, Charles, and Carole O'Leary, eds. *Kurdish Identity: Human Rights and Political Status*. Gainesville: University Press of Florida, 2007.

Mallat, Chibli. "Legal Developments and Constitutional Structures in Iraq." Address to the International Law Section of the State Bar of Michigan, Dearborn, September 19, 2008.

Marcus, Aliza. *Blood and Belief: The PKK and the Kurdish Fight for Independence*. New York and London: New York University Press, 2007.

Marr, Phebe. *The Modern History of Iraq*. Boulder, CO: Westview Press, 2004.

May, Stephen. "Language Policy and Minority Rights." In *An Introduction to Language Policy: Theory and Method*, edited by Thomas Ricento, 255–272. Victoria, AU: Blackwell Publishing, 2006.

McDowall, David. *The Kurds: A Nation Denied*. London: Minority Rights Group, 1992.

———. *A Modern History of the Kurds*. London and New York: I. B. Tauris, 2005.

McKiernan, Kevin. *The Kurds: A People in Search of Their Homeland*. New York: St. Martin's Press, 2006.

Meho, Lokman I. *The Kurdish Question in U.S. Foreign Policy: A Documentary Sourcebook*. London: Praeger, 2004.

Meiselas, Susan. *Kurdistan: In the Shadow of History*. 2nd ed. Chicago: University of Chicago Press, 2008.

Mella, Jawad. *The Colonial Policy of the Baath Party in Western Kurdistan*. London: Western Kurdistan Association, 2006.

———. *Kurdistan and the Kurds: A Divided Homeland and a Nation without State*. London: Western Kurdistan Association Publications, 2005.

Melson, Robert, and Howard Wolpe. "Modernization and the Politics of Communalism." *American Political Science Review* 64, no. 4 (1970): 1012–1030.

Middle East Watch. *Syria Unmasked: The Suppression of Human Rights by the Asad Regime*. New Haven, CT: Yale University Press, 1991.

Minorsky, Vladimir. "Annazids." *EI*, New Edition (Leiden, Netherlands: E. J. Brill, 1954–2003), vol. 1, 512–513.

———. *Studies in Caucasian History*. London: Taylor's Foreign Press, 1953.

Mojab, Shahrzad. "Nationalism and Feminism: The Case of Kurdistan." In *Institute Simone de Beauvoir Bulletin*, 65–73. Montreal: Concordia University Press, 1995.

———, ed. *Women of a Non-State Nation: The Kurds*. Costa Mesa, CA: Mazda Publishers, 2001.

More, Christian. *Les Kurdes aujourd'hui. Mouvement national et partis politiques.* Paris: L'Harmattan, 1984.

Mortimer, Edward, and Robert Fine, eds. *People, Nation and State: The Meaning of Ethnicity and Nationalism.* London: I. B. Tauris, 1999.

Moubayed, Sami. *Steel and Silk: Men and Women Who Shaped Syria, 1900–2000.* Seattle: Cune Press, 2004.

Natali, Denise. "The Kirkuk Conundrum." *Ethnopolitics* 7, no. 4 (2008): 433–443.

———. *The Kurdish Quasi-State: Development and Dependency in Post-Gulf War Iraq.* Syracuse, NY: Syracuse University Press, 2010.

———. *The Kurds and the State: Evolving National Identity in Iraq, Turkey, and Iran.* Syracuse, NY: Syracuse University Press, 2005.

———. "Manufacturing Identity and Managing Kurds in Iraq, Turkey, and Iran: A Study in the Evolution of Nationalism." Ph.D. diss., University of Pennsylvania, 2000.

Nebez, Jemal. *The Kurds: History and Culture.* London: Western Kurdistan Association, 2004.

Neyzi, Leyla. "Object or Subject? The Paradox of Youth in Turkey." *International Journal of Middle East Studies* 33, no. 3 (2001): 411–432.

Nezan, Kendal. "The Kurds under the Ottoman Empire." In *A People without Country: Kurds and Kurdistan,* edited by G. Chaliand, 11–37. London: Zed Books, 1993.

Nieuwenhuis, Tom. *Politics and Society in Early Modern Iraq: Mamluk Pashas, Tribal Shayks and Local Rule between 1802–1831.* The Hague and Boston: M. Nijhoff, 1982.

Northedge, Alastair. "Al-Iraq al-Arabi: Iraq's Greatest Region in the Pre-Modern Period." In *An Iraq of Its Regions: Cornerstones of a Federal Democracy?,* edited by R. Visser and G. Stansfield, 151–166. New York: Columbia University Press, 2007.

O'Ballance, Edgar. *The Kurdish Revolt 1961–1970.* London: Faber and Faber Ltd., 1973.

———. *The Kurdish Struggle 1920–94.* London: MacMillan Press Ltd., 1996.

Öcalan, Abdullah. *The Road Map to Negotiations.* Cologne, Germany: International Initiative Edition, 2012.

O'Leary, Brendan. *How to Get Out of Iraq with Integrity.* Philadelphia: University of Pennsylvania Press, 2009.

Olson, Robert. *The Emergence of Kurdish Nationalism and the Sheikh Said Rebellion, 1880–1925.* Austin: University of Texas Press, 1989.

———. *The Goat and the Butcher: Nationalism and State Formation in Kurdistan-Iraq since the Iraqi War.* Costa Mesa, CA: Mazda Publishers, 2005.

———. *Turkey's Relation with Iran, Syria, Israel and Russia, 1991–2000: The Kurdish and Islamist Questions.* Costa Mesa, CA: Mazda Publishers, 2001.

O'Neil, Mary Lou. "Linguistic Human Rights and the Rights of the Kurds." In *Human Rights in Turkey,* edited by Zehra F. Kabasakal Arat, 72–86. Philadelphia: University of Pennsylvania Press, 2007.

Özcan, Ali Kemal. "PKK Recruitment of Female Operatives." *Terrorism Focus* 4, Issue 28 (September 11, 2007). http://www.jamestown.org/single/?no_cache=1&tx_ttnews[tt_news]=4394.

———. *Turkey's Kurds: A Theoretical Analysis of the PKK and Abdullah Öcalan*. London and New York: Routledge, Taylor & Francis Group, 2006.

Ozoglu, Hakan. *Kurdish Notables and the Ottoman State: Evolving Identities, Competing Loyalties and Shifting Boundaries*. New York: State University of New York Press, 2004.

———. "State-Tribe Relations: Kurdish Tribalism in the 16th and 17th Century Ottoman Empire." *British Journal of Middle Eastern Studies* 23 (1996): 8–11.

Pinto, Paulo. "Les Kurdes de Syrie." In *La Syrie au présent. Reflets d'une société*, edited by Baudouin Dupret et al., 259–267. Paris: Actes Sud, 2007.

Podeh, Elie. *The Decline of Arab Unity, the Rise and Fall of the United Arab Republic*. Brighton, UK: Sussex Academic Press, 1999.

Pollack, Kenneth M. "The Seven Deadly Sins of Failure in Iraq: A Retrospective Analysis of the Reconstruction." *Middle East Review of International Affairs* 10, no. 4 (2006): 1–20.

Qasimlou, Abdurrahman. *Kurdistan and the Kurds*. Spanga, Sweden: APEC, 1996.

Rawlison, H. C. "Notes on a Journey from Tabriz, through Persian Kurdistan, to the Ruins of Takhti-Soleiman." *Journal of the Royal Geographical Society* 10 (1841): 1–64.

Rawshani, Ali Ahmadi. *Kurdistan in the Mirror of History*. N.p., 1998.

Renan, Ernest. *Qu'est-ce Qu'une nation? Et autres écrits politiques*. Paris: Éditions Mille et Une Nuits, 1997.

Rich, Claudius J. *Narrative of a Residence in Koordistan*. Vol. 1. London: James Duncan, 1836; repr., Farnborough, UK: Gregg International Publishers, 1972.

Ricks, Thomas E. *Fiasco: The American Military Adventure in Iraq*. New York: Penguin Press, 2006.

Romano, David. *The Kurdish Nationalist Movement: Opportunity, Mobilization, and Identity*. Cambridge: Cambridge University Press, 2006.

———. "Turkey Addresses PKK Challenge with Kurdish Language Reforms." *Terrorism Focus* 6, no. 1 (January 15, 2009).

Ronen, Dov. *The Quest for Self-Determination*. New Haven, CT: Yale University Press, 1979.

Roosevelt, Archie Jr. "The Kurdish Republic of Mahabad." In *People without a Country: The Kurds and Kurdistan*, translated by Michael Pallis, edited by Gerard Chaliand, 135–152. London: Zed Press, 1980.

Rothschild, Joseph. *Ethnopolitics: A Conceptual Framework*. New York: Columbia University Press, 1981.

Rubin, Barry. "Regime Change in Iran: A Reassessment." *Middle East Review of International Affairs Journal* 7, no. 2 (June 2003): 68–78.

Safran, William. "Ethnic Conflict and Third-Party Intervention." In *Ethnonationalism in the Contemporary World: Walker Connor and the Study of Nationalism*, edited by Daniele Conversi, 184–205. London: Routledge, 2002.

Salibi, Kamal, and Yusuf K. Khoury, eds. *The Missionary Herald: Reports from Northern Iraq 1833–1847*. Vol. 1. Amman: Royal Institute for Interfaith Studies, 2002.

Sandwith, Humphrey. *A Narrative: The Siege of Kars*. London: John Murray, 1856.

Savelsberg, Eva, and Siamend Hajö. "Ten Years of Bashar Al-Asad and No Compromise with the Kurds." *Syrian Studies Association Newsletter* 16, no. 1 (2011).

Seale, Patrick. *The Struggle for Power for Syria: A Study of Post-War Arab Politics, 1945–1958*. New Haven, CT: Yale University Press, 1965.

Secor, Anna. "'There Is an Istanbul That Belongs to Me': Citizenship, Space and Identity in the City." *Annals of the Association of American Geographers* 94, no. 2 (June 2004): 352–368.

Seton-Watson, Hugh. *Nation and States: An Inquiry into the Origins of Nations and the Politics of Nationalism*. Boulder, CO: Westview Press, 1977.

Shafer, Boyd C. *Faces of Nationalism: New Realities and Old Myths*. New York: Harcourt Brace and Jovanovich, 1972.

———. *Nationalism: Myth and Reality*. New York: Harcourt Brace and World, 1955.

Shakely, Ferhad. *Kurdish Nationalism in* Mam u Zin *of Ahmad-I Khani*. Brussels: Kurdish Institute of Brussels, 1992.

Skutnabb-Kangas, Tove. "Language Policy and Linguistic Human Rights." In *An Introduction to Language Policy: Theory and Method*, edited by Thomas Ricento, 273–291. Victoria, AU: Blackwell Publishing, 2006.

Sluglett, Peter. "Is Democracy the Problem?" Carnegie Endowment (2006). http://carnegieendowment.org/publications/?fa=view&id=20640.

Smith, Anthony D. *The Ethnic Origins of Nations*. Oxford, UK: Blackwell, 1987.

———. *Ethnosymbolism and Nationalism: A Cultural Approach*. New York: Routledge, 2009.

———. "The Nation: Real or Imagined." In *People, Nation and State: The Meaning of Ethnicity and Nationalism*, edited by E. Mortimer and R. Fine, 36–42. London: I. B. Tauris, 1999.

———. *National Identity*. London: Penguin, 1991.

———. *Theories of Nationalism*. New York: Harper & Row, 1972.

———. "When Is a Nation?" *Geopolitics* 7, no. 2 (2002): 5–32.

Soane, E. B. *To Mesopotamia and Kurdistan in Disguise*. 2nd ed. London: John Murray, 1926.

Speer, Robert. *The Foreign Doctor*. New York: Fleming H. Revell, 1911.

Spencer, Philip, and Howard Wollman. *Nationalism: A Critical Introduction*. London: Sage, 2002.

Stansfield, Gareth. *Iraqi Kurdistan: Political Development and Emergent Democracy*. New York: Routledge Curzon, 2003.

Stilt, Kristen A. "Islamic Law and the Making and Remaking of the Iraqi Legal System." *George Washington International Law Review* 36 (2004): 695–756.

Stock, Raymond. "On Mistaking Mohamed Mursi for His Mask." *Foreign Policy Institute*, February 2013.

Strohmeier, Martin. *Crucial Images in the Presentation of a Kurdish National Identity: Heroes and Patriots, Traitors and Foes*. Leiden, Netherlands: E. J. Brill, 2003.

Sykes, Percy. *A History of Persia*. London: McMillan and Co. Ltd., 1930.

Tabari. *History of Tabari (Ta'rikh al-Rusul wal-Muluk)*. Vol. 14, *The Conquest of Iran*. Translated by G. Rex Smith. Albany: State University of New York Press, 1994.

————. *History of Tabari (Ta'rikh al-Rusul wal-Muluk)*. Vol. 15, *The Crisis of the Early Caliphate*. Translated by R. Stephen Humphreys. Albany: State University of New York Press, 1990.

Tahiri, Hussein. *The Structure of Kurdish Society and the Struggle for a Kurdish State*. Costa Mesa, CA: Mazda Publishers, 2007.

Talageri, Shrikant G. *The Aryan Invasion Theory: A Reappraisal*. New Delhi: Aditya Prakashau, 1993.

Taşpınar, Ömer. *Kurdish Nationalism and Political Islam in Turkey*. New York: Routledge, 2005.

Taylor, Gordon. *Fever and Thirst: Dr. Grant and the Christian Tribes of Kurdistan*. Chicago: Academy Chicago Publishers, 2005.

Tejel Gorgas, Jordi. "Jeunesse kurde: entre rupture et engagement militant." In *La Syrie au présent. Reflets d'une société*, edited by Baudouin Dupret et al., 269–276. Paris: Actes Sud, 2007.

————. "Les Kurdes de Syrie, de la dissimulation à la visibilité?" *Revue des mondes musulmans et de la Méditerranée* 115–116 (2006): 117–133.

————. *Le mouvement kurde en exil. Continuités et discontinuités du nationalisme kurde sous le mandat français en Syrie et au Liban, 1925–1946*. Bern: Peter Lang, 2007.

————. *Syria's Kurds: History, Politics and Society*. London: Routledge, 2009.

Tibi, Bassam. *Arab Nationalism: A Critical Enquiry*. Translated by Marion Farouk-Sluglett and Peter Sluglett. 2nd ed. New York: St. Martin's Press, 1990.

————. "The Simultaneity of the Unsimultaneous: Old Tribes and Imposed Nation-States in the Modern Middle East." In *Tribes and State Formation in the Middle East*, edited by Philip Khoury and Joseph Kostiner, 137–143. London: I. B. Tauris, 1991.

Tilly, Charles. "States and Nationalism in Europe 1492–1992." In *Perspectives on Nationalism and War*, edited by John L. Comaroff and Paul C. Stern, 187–205. Amsterdam: Gordon and Breach, 1995.

Toprak, Binnaz. "The State, Politics, and Religion in Turkey." In *State, Democracy and Military: Turkey in the 1980s*, edited by Metin Heper and Ahmet Evin, 119–135. New York: Walter de Gruyter, 1988.

Trial Records Öcalan. Preamble, May 31, 1999–November 25, 1999. İmralı Island, Mudanya, Turkey.

Tripp, Charles. *A History of Iraq*. Cambridge: Cambridge University Press, 2002.

Uçarlar, Nesrin. *Between Majority Power and Minority Resistance: Kurdish Linguistic Rights in Turkey*. Lund, Sweden: Lund University, 2009.

Vali, Abbas. "The Kurds and Their 'Others': Fragmented Identity and Fragmented Politics." In *The Kurds: Nationalism and Politics*, edited by Faleh A. Jabar and Hosham Dawod, 49–78. London: Saqi Books, 2006.

————. *Kurds and the State in Iran: The Making of Kurdish Identity*. London: I. B. Tauris, 2011.

————, ed. *Essays on the Origins of Kurdish Nationalism*. Costa Mesa, CA: Mazda Publishers, 2003.

Van Bruinessen, Martin. *Agha, Shaikh and State: The Social and Political Structures of Kurdistan*. London: Zed Books, 1992.

————. "Between Guerilla War and Political Murder: The Workers' Party of Kurdistan." *Middle East Report* 153, *Islam and the State* (July–August 1988).

————. "Ehmedi Xani's *Mam U Zin* and Its Role in the Emergence of Kurdish National Awareness." In *Essays on the Origins of Kurdish Nationalism*, edited by Abbas Vali, 40–57. Costa Mesa, CA: Mazda Publishers, 2003.

————. "Kurdish Society and the Modern State: Ethnic Nationalism versus Nation-Building." In *Kurdistan in Search of Ethnic Identity*, edited by Turaj Atabaki and Margreet Dorleijn, 24–51. Utrecht, Netherlands: Department of Oriental Studies, 1991.

————. "Kurdish Society, Ethnicity, Nationalism and Refugee Problems." In *The Kurds: A Contemporary Overview*, edited by Philip G. Kreyenbroek and Stefan Sperl, 26–52. New York: Routledge, 1992.

————. "Kurdish Tribes and the State of Iran: The Case of Simko's Revolt." In *Kurdish Ethno-Nationalism versus Nation-Building States*, edited by Martin van Bruinessen, 125–155. Istanbul: ISIS, 2000.

————. "Kurdistan in the Sixteenth and Seventeenth Centuries as Reflected in Evliya Celebi's *Seyahatname*." *Journal of Kurdish Studies* 3 (2000): 1–11.

————. "The Kurds between Iran and Iraq." *MERIP Reports* 121 (February 1984): 6–12.

————. "The Kurds between Iran and Iraq." *Middle East Report*, July–August 1986.

————. "The Kurds in Movement: Migrations, Mobilisations, Communications and the Globalisation of the Kurdish Question." Working Paper no. 14, Islamic Area Studies Project. Tokyo, Japan, 1999.

————. "The Kurds in Turkey." *MERIP Reports* 121 (February 1984): 6–12.

————. "The Sadate Nerhi or Gilanizade of Central Kurdistan." *Journal for the History of Sufism* 1 (2000): 3–5.

————, and Hendrik Boeschoten, eds. *Evliya Celebi in Diyarbekir: The Relevant Section of the Seyahatname*. Leiden, Netherlands: E. J. Brill, 1988.

Vanly, Ismet Cheriff. "The Kurds in the Soviet Union." In *The Kurds: A Contemporary Overview*, edited by Philip G. Kreyenbroek and Stefan Sperl, 152–172. New York: Routledge, 1992.

————. "The Kurds in Syria and Lebanon." In *The Kurds: A Contemporary Overview*, edited by Philip G. Kreyenbroek and Stefan Sperl, 163–164. New York: Routledge, 1992.

Varennes, Fernand de. *Language, Minorities, and Human Rights*. The Hague: Martinus Nijhoff Publishers, 1996.

Vaziri, Mostafa. *Iran as Imagined Nation: The Construction of National Identity*. New York: Paragon House, 1993.

Visser, Reidar, and Gareth R. V. Stansfield. *An Iraq of Its Regions: Cornerstones of a Federal Democracy?* New York: Columbia University Press, 2007.

Watts, Nicole F. "Allies and Enemies: Pro-Kurdish Parties in Turkish Politics, 1990–1994." *International Journal of Middle East Studies* 31, no. 4 (November 1999): 631–656.

White, Paul. *Primitive Rebels or Revolutionary Modernizers? The Kurdish National Movement in Turkey*. London: Zed Books, 2000.

Wilson, Arnold. *Loyalties: Mesopotamia 1917–1920*. Oxford: Oxford University Press, 1931.

Woods, John E. *The Aqqoyunlu Clan, Confederation, Empire*. Minneapolis and Chicago: Bibliotheca Islamica, 1976.

Yapp, M. E. *The Making of the Modern Near East 1792–1923*. London and New York: Longman Group UK Ltd., 1987.

Yassin, Borhanedin. "A History of the Republic of Kurdistan." *International Journal of Kurdish Studies* 11, nos. 1–2 (1997): 115–240.

Yavuz, M. Hakan. "Five Stages of the Construction of Kurdish Nationalism in Turkey." *Nationalism and Ethnic Politics* 7, no. 3 (Autmn 2001).

———. "A Preamble to the Kurdish Question: The Politics of Kurdish Identity." *Journal of Muslim Minority Affairs* 18, no. 1 (1998): 9–18.

Yeğen, Mesut. "Banditry to Disloyalty: The Kurdish Question in Turkey." *SETA* (2008). http://www.setav.org/public/BilgiBelge.aspx?Dil=tr.

———. "Turkish Nationalism and the Kurdish Question." *Ethnic and Racial Studies* 30, no. 1 (2007): 119–151.

Yildiz, Kerim. *The Kurds in Turkey: EU Accession and Human Rights*. London: Pluto Press, 2005.

———, and Tanyel B. Taysi. *The Kurds in Iran: The Past, Present and Future*. London: Pluto Press, 2007.

Young, Crawford. "The Dialectics of Cultural Pluralism: Concept and Reality." In *The Rising Tide of Cultural Pluralism: The Nation-State at Bay?*, edited by Crawford Young, 3–35. Madison: University of Wisconsin Press, 1993.

Yüksel, Metin. "The Encounter of Kurdish Women with Nationalism in Turkey." *Middle Eastern Studies* 42, no. 5 (September 2006): 777–802.

Zana, Leyla. *Writings from Prison*. Watertown, MA: Blue Crane Books, 1999.

Zeidel, Ronen. "The Iraqi Novel and the Kurds." *Review of Middle East Studies* 45, no. 1 (Summer 2011): 19–35.

———. "A Question of Language and Audience: On the Possibility of 'Iraqi Novels' in Hebrew." *Hebrew Studies* 50 (2009): 229–243.

Zisser, Eyal. *Asad's Legacy: Syria in Transition*. New York: New York University Press, 2000.

———. *Commanding Syria: Bashar al-Asad and the First Years in Power*. London: I. B. Tauris, 2007.

Other Languages

'Aflaq, Michel. *Fi Sabil al-Baʿth*. Beirut: Dar al-Taliʿa, 1970.

Ahmad, Kamal Mudhir. *Kirkuk wa Tawabiʿuha: Hukm al-Taʾrikh wa al-Damir: Dirasa Wathaiʾqiyya ʿan al-Qadiyya al-Kurdiyya fi al-ʿIraq*. Vol. 1. Sulaymaniyya: Matbaʿat Renwen, 2004.

Akdemir, Erhan. "Avrupa Parlamentosu Türkiye Raporu'un Değerlendirilmesi." *Günlük Dğerlendirmeler, ASAM*, May 23, 2008.

'Ala al-Din, Abdul Khaliq, ed. *Dildar: Shaʿiri Shorshgeri Kurd*. Baghdad: Directorate of Culture and Youth, 1983.

Al-ʿAlawi, Hasan. *Al-Shiʿa wa al-Dawla al-Qawmiyya fi al-ʿIraq 1914–1990*. Qum: Dar al-Thaqafa Liltibaʿa wa al-Nashr, 1990.

Al-Ayyubi, Azad. *Efin . . . Wa Intizar al-Fajr*. ʿAmman: al-Ahliyya, 2004.

al-Baladhuri, Ahmad bin Yahya bin Jabbar. *Futuh al-Buldan*. Beirut: Dar al-Nashr lil-Jamaʿin, 1985.

Al-Bayyati, ʿAbd al- Rahman Idris. *Shaykh Mahmud al-Hafid wa al-Nufudh al-Britani fi Kurdistan al-ʿIraq hatta ʿam 1925*. London: Dar al-Hikma, 2005.

Al-Bitlisi, Al-Amir Sharaf Khan. *Sharafnama*. Translated by Muhammad Jamil Al-Rojbayani. 2nd ed. Erbil: Dazgay Mukiryani, 2001.

Al-Dahoodi, Zuhdi. *Tahawwulat*. Beirut: al-Muʾassasa al-ʿArabiya, 2007.

Al-Dujaili, Hasan, and Maskuni Yousuf. *Taʾrikh Biladik wa Ummatik fi Bidʾihi lil-Saff al-Ra biʿ al-Ibtidaʾi*. 3rd ed. Baghdad: Ministry of Education—I, 1951.

Al-Durra, Mahmud. *Al-Qad iyya al-Kurdiyya*. Beirut: Dar al-Taliʿa, 1966.

Al-Ghamrawi, Sami. *Qissat al-Akrad fi Shimal al-ʿIraq*. Cairo: Dar al-Nahda al-ʿArabiyya, 1967.

Al-Ghita, ʿAli Kashif. *Saʿd Salih wa Mawaqifihi al-Wataniyya 1920–1950*. Baghdad: Al-Raya Press, 1989.

Al-Jazaʾiri, Zuhayr. *Harb al-ʿAjiz*. Beirut: al-Saqi, 2009.

———. *Mudun Fadhila*. Damascus: al-Ahali, 1992.

Al-Kash, ʿAli. *Al-Dawr al-Takhribi al-Irani fi al-ʿIraq: Intifada Shaʿbaniyya am Safhat al-Ghadr wa al-Khiyana*. Watan, 2008. Accessed August 8, 2009. http://www.watan.com/feature-more/2716-2008-07-16-12-57-33.html.

Al-Khatib, Burhan. *Shaqqa fi Shariʿ Abi Nuwwas*. Beirut: al-ʿAwda, 1972.

Al-Takarli, Fuʾad. *Al-Masarrat wal Awjaʿ*. Damascus: al-Mada, 1998.

Amin, Haval. *Al-Bum wal-Miqass*. Beirut: al-Saqi, 2008.

Amin, Muhammad Zaki. *Khulasat taʾrikh al-Kurd wa Kurdistan min aqdam al-ʿusur hatta al-ʾan*. Cairo: Al-Saʿada Press, 1939.

———. *Khulasat taʾrikh al-Kurd wa Kurdistan, Taʾrikh al-duwal wa al-imarat al-Kurdiyya fi al-ʿahd al-Islami*. Translated from Kurdish to Arabic by Mohammad ʿAli ʿAwni. Vol. 2. Cairo, 1948; repr., London: Kurdish Students Aid Committee, 1986.

Amin, Nawshirwan Mustafa. *Mirayati Baban la newan Bardashi Rom u Ajamda*. Berlin: Awadani, 1998.

"Anadili Türkce Olan Nüfus ile Kürtçe Olan Nüfus Arası Eğitim Uçurumu Var." BETAM Araştırma Notu 9, no. 49 (October 13, 2009). http://betam.bah cesehir.edu.tr/tr/wp-content/uploads/2009/10/ArastirmaNotu049.pdf.

Averyanov, L. I. *Kurdi w woynakh Rosii c Perciej i Turcej w teczenie 19 ctoletia. Tifilic Tiblisi: Tipografia sztaba Kawkazkiego woennego okruga*. Tiblisi: The Press of the Military Staff of the Caucasus Region, 1900. Russian.

Baban, Jamal. *Handek Dadwari Banawbang*. Baghdad: Kori Zanyari, 1981.

Bekas, Sherko. *Diwani Sherko Bekas Bargi Seyam 1971–1993*. Vol. 3. Kurdistan: n.p., 2006.

Bengio, Ofra. *Mered Ha-Kurdim Be-Iraq*. Tel Aviv: Hakibbutz Hammeuhad, 1989.

Bidlisi, Sharaf al-Din Khan. *Sharafnameh, Fi Taʾrikh al-Duwal wal-Imarat al-Kurdiyya*. 2 vols. Translated into Arabic by Muhammad ʿAli ʿAwni, edited by Yahya al-Khashab. Damascus: Dar al-zaman liltiba'a wal-nashr wal-tawzi', 2006.

Biha'addin Mella Sahib, Dana/Muhammad. *Qazi Muhemmed u Kumari Mahabad*. Sulaymaniyya: Raperin Publications, 1970. Kurdish.

Çaylak, Adem, and Adem Çelik. "Osmanlı ve Cumhuriyet Modernleş(tir)mesinde tarih din ve etnisite algısı." In *Osmanlı'dan İkibinli Yıllara Türkiye'nin Politik Tarihi*, edited by Adem Çaylak, Cihat Göktepe, Mehmet Dikkaya, and Hüsnü Kapu, 93–133. Ankara: Savaş Yayınevi, 2009.

Ceyhan, Müge Ayan, and Dilara Koçbaş. *Çift Dillilik ve Eğitim*. Istanbul: Sabancı Üniversitesi, Kasım 2009.

Coşkun, Vahap, M. Şerif Derince, and Nesrin Uçarlar. *Dil Yarası: Türkiye'de Eğitimde Anadilinin Kullanılamaması Sorunu ve Kürt Öğrencilerin Deneyimleri*. Diyarbakır: Disa Yayınları, 2010.

Dankoff, Robert, ed. *Evliya Celebi in Bitlis*. Leiden, Netherlands: E. J. Brill, 1990.

Dastmalchi, Parviz. *Mykonos: Matn-e Ra'ye Dadgah*. Los Angeles: Dehkhoda Bookstore, 2001.

Derakhshani, Ali Akbar. *Khaterat-e Sartip Ali Akbar Derakhshani*. N.p., 1994.

Djalil, Djalile. *Kurdi Ocmanskoi Imperii Pervoy Polovine 19 Beka*. Moscow: Nauka, 1970. Russian.

Evren, Gürbüz. *Avrupa Birliği Sürecinde Kürtçülük*. Istanbul: Truva, 2007.

Fahrettin, Kirzioğlu M. *Kürtlerin Kökü*. Ankara: Ayyildiz Matbaas, 1963.

Fard, Erfan Q. *Tondbad-e Havades: Goftogo ba Issa Pejman*. Tehran: Elm Publishers, 2012.

Gadani, Jalil. *Pencah Sal Xebat: Kurteyek li Mijoyi Hizbi Dimokrati Kurdistani Iran*. Iraqi Kurdistan: Ministry of Education's Publication, 1987.

Gökalp, Ziya. *Türkçülüğün Esasları*. Ankara: Elips, 2006.

Gökşen, Fatoş, Zeynep Cemalcılar, and Can Fuat Gürlesel. "Türkiye'de İlköğretim Okullarında Okulu Terk ve İzlenmesi ile Önlenmesine Yönelik Politikalar." Eğitim Reformu Girişimi (Haziran 2008). http://erg.sabanciuniv.edu/sites/erg.sabanciuniv.edu/files/AÇEV_Okulu%20Terk%20Raporu.pdf.

HaIslam miLedato vead Tehilat HaImperia HaOthmanit. Tel Aviv: Dvir, 1995.

Hamdi, Walid. *Al-Kurd wa Kurdistan fi al-Watha'iq al-Britaniyya*. London: Matabi' Sijil al-'Arab, 1991.

Hilmi, Rafiq. *Yaddasht*. Sulaymaniyya: Dazgay Sardam, 2003.

Husayn, Fadil. *Mushkilat al-Mosul*. Baghdad: Matba'at Eshbiliya, 1977.

Hamdi, Walid. *Al-Kurd wa Kurdistan fi al-Watha'iq al-Britaniyya*. London: n.p.

Ibn al-Athir, 'Izz al-Din. *Al-kamil fi al-ta'rikh*. Vols. 9 and 10. Beirut: Dar Beirut lil-Tiba'a wal-Nashr, 1966.

Ibn Khaldun. *Ta'rikh al-'alamat*. 4 vols. Beirut: Dar al-Katib al-Lubnani, 1958.

"Important Historical Document." *Peyam Newspaper*, March 6, 1998, 1, 2 (Kurdish).

Jalaipour, Hamid Reza. *Kordistan: Elat-e Tadavom-e Bohran-e An Pas Az Enghelab-e Eslami*. Tehran: Foreign Ministry Press, 1993.

Khani, Ahmedi. *Mem u Zin*. 3rd ed. Erbil: Chapkhaney Hewler, 1968.

Kızılkaya, Muhsin. *Bir Dil Niye Kanar?* Istanbul: İletişim Yayınları, 2010.

Matabi' Sijill al'Arab, 1991. N.p.

Matar, Salim. *Al-dhat al-Jariha*. Beirut: al-Mu'assasa al-'Arabiya Lil Dirasat wa al-Nashr, 2000.

———. *Jadal al-Hawiyyat*. New Edition. Beirut: al-Mu'assasa al-'Arabiya Lil Dirasat wa al-Nashr, 2003.

Mina, Amin Qadir. *Amni Stratiji Iraq w Sekuchkay Ba'siyan: Tarhil, Ta'rib, Tab'ith*. 2nd ed. Sulaymaniyya: Kurdistan Centre for Strategic Studies, 1999.

Mohajer, Nasser. "Ensheab dar Hezb-e Demokrat-e Kordestan-e Iran." *Aghazi 7* (Summer 1988): 25–29.

Mukiryani, Giwi, ed. *Diwani Haji Qadiri Koyi*. 3rd ed. Hawler: Chapkhanay Hawler, 1969.

Mutlu Sefa. "PKK'da Yeni Açılımlar." *ASAM, Günlük Değerlendirmeler* (April 30, 2009).

Nuri Pasha, Ihsan. *Mejuy Rishay Nazhadi Kurd*. Erbil: Aras Publisher, 2003.

Ölmez, A. Osman. *Türkiye Siyasetinde DEP Depremi*. Ankara: Doruk, 1995.

Payandeh, Mehran, Abbas Khodagholi, and Hamid Nozari. *Hanooz dar Berlin Qazi Hast: Terror va Dadgah-e Mykonos*. Essen, Germany: Nima Verlag, 2000.

Pirim, Oktay, and Süha Örtülü. *PKK'nın 20 Yıllık Öyküsü*. Istanbul: Boyut, 2000.

Sabir, Rafiq. *Iraq: Dimokratizakirdin yan Halwashandinawa*. Sulaymaniyya: Bureau of Thought and Consciousness (PUK), 2005.

Salihpaşaoğlu, Yaşar. "Türkiye'nin Dil Politikaları ve TRT 6." Gazi Üniversitesi Hukuk Fakültesi Dergisi C. 11, nos. 1–2 (2007): 1033–1048.

Saloom, Sa'd. *"Burhan Shawi bil-Ahmar wal-Aswad."* Electronic copy.

Samadi, Sayyid Muhammad. *J. K. Çibu, Çi Dewist ve Çi be ser hat?* Mahabad, 1981. Kurdish.

"Seçim Analizi." Konda, June 2011. Accessed November 4, 2013. http://www.konda.com.tr/tr/raporlar.php.

Shawi, Burhan. *Al-Jahim al-Muqaddas*. Baghdad: Dar al-Asda', 2008.

Siwayli, Rebwar. *Ktebi Nali*. Erbil: Mukiryani, 2001.

Siyasi Partiler Kanunu [Law on Political Parties], Decree: 2820, April 22, 1983.

Talib, Muhammad Hilal. *Al-Bahth fi al-Jawanib al-Qawmiyya wal-Siyasiyya wal-Ijtima'iyya li-Iqlim al-Jazira*. London: Western Kurdistan Association, 2006.

Tavakkoli, Khaled. "Kurdistan va Vaqa'ye Dovom-e Khordad." *Got-O-Gu* 40 (August–September 2004): 35–44.

Türkiye'nin Demokratikleşmesi ve Kürt Sorununda Çözüme Dair Siyasi Tutum Belgesi. Accessed March 30, 2011. www.bdp.org.tr/yayinlarimiz/demokratik-ozerklik/demokratik-ozerklik.html.

Wifaq. *Aladhi yahsul al-Aan fi al'-Iraq min Tahmish wa Tamyiz Mu'lim jiddan*. Iraqi National Accord, 2008. http://www.wifaq.com/pnews/new685.htm.

Yayman, Hüseyin. *Şark Meselesinden Demokratik Açılıma Türkiye'nin Kürt Sorunu Hafızası*. Ankara: SETA Yayınları, 2011.

Yeğen, Mesut. *Müstakbel Türk'ten Sözde Vatandaşa: Cumhuriyet ve Kürtler*. Istanbul: İletişim Yayınları, 2006.

———. *Son Kürt İsyanı*. Istanbul: İletişim Yayınları, 2011.

Yerlikaya, Simla. *Yeni Komşumuz Kürdistan*. Istanbul: Timaş Yayınları, 2013.

Zakariaee, Mohammad Ali, ed. *Konferans-e Berlin: Khedmat ya Khiyanat*. Tehran: Tarh-e No, 2000.

Zangana, Abdullah, ed. *Roji Kurd: Govari Jivati Hevi Qutabiyani Kurd 1913— Astamul*. Sulaymaniyya: Binkai Zhin, 2005.

Newspapers and Online Articles—English and French

"Abdullah Öcalan, A Short Biography." Partiya Parkeren Kurdistan (PKK). http://www.pkkonline.com/en/index.php?sys=article&artID=22.

"About." Kurdish Women against Honour Killing (KWAHK). http://www.kwrw.org/kwahk/.

"About." Kurdish Women's Rights Watch (KWRW). http://www.kwrw.org/.

"About Us." *Roj Women: Kurdish and Turkish Women's Rights*. http://rojwomn.com/about/.

Ako, Muhammed. "Kurdish Leaders Insist on Peaceful Struggle." *Kurdish Globe*, February 25, 2012. http://www.kurdishglobe.net/display-article.html?id=9A641E8CD512A9E95AF6BFFDCC6C6344.

Al-Jaafari, Ibrahim. "A New Marshall Plan for Iraq." *Times* (London), June 27, 2005.

Bagikhani, Nazand. "Kurdish Women and National Identity." *KurdishMedia.com*, November 8, 2003. http://kwahk.org/articles.asp?id=37.

Barzani, Mas'ud. "Kurdistan Is a Model for Iraq." *Wall Street Journal*, November 12, 2008.

"Civil Disobedience Call for Kurdish Issue." *Hürriyet Daily News*, March 23, 2011. http://www.hurriyetdailynews.com/n.php?n=turkey8217s-leading-kurdish-platforms-declare-civil-disobedence-actions-2011-03-23.

"Conditions for Enlargement." European Commission. http://ec.europa.eu/enlargement/the-policy/conditions-for-enlargement/index_en.htm.

Fadel, Leila, and Hussein Kadhim. "Some Sunni Muslims Won't Salute Iraq's New Flag." *McClatchy Newspapers*, January 25, 2008. http://www.mcclatchydc.com/2008/01/25/25471/some-sunni-muslims-wont-salute.html.

Hassanpour, Amir. "Ferment and Fetters in the Study of Kurdish Nationalism." *Monthly Review*, November 24, 2008. http://mrzine.monthlyreview.org/2008/hassanpour241108.html.

Haynes, Deborah. "The Kurdish Women Rebels Who Are Ready to Fight and Die for the Kurdish Cause." *KurdNet*, October 24, 2007. http://www.ekurd.net/mismas/articles/misc2007/10/turkeykurdistan1455.htm.

Human Rights Watch. "He Loves You, He Beats You: Family Violence in Turkey and Access to Protection." *Human Rights Watch*, May 4, 2011. http://www.hrw.org/en/reports/2011/05/04/he-loves-you-he-beats-you.

Jenkins, Gareth. "DTP Presents Final Defense in Closure Case." *Eurasia Daily Monitor*, September 16, 2008.

"Judicial Reform Index for Iraq: Kurdistan Supplement." *Iraq Legal Development Project*. Washington, DC: American Bar Association, 2006.

Kalnoky, Boris. "Feminists and Terrorists? Women and the PKK." *Women in Focus*, April 14, 2010. http://www.sofeminine.co.uk/key-debates/women-and-the-pkk-d12319.html.

Khoshnaw, Hemin. "Disunity in Focus at Anniversary of the Kurdistan Republic of Mahabad." *Rudaw*, March 2, 2012. http://www.rudaw.net/english/kurds/4483.html.

"Kurdish Women Fight for Rights of Both Groups, Istanbul Deputy Says." *Hürriyet Daily News*, June 30, 2010. www.hurriyetdailynews.com/n.php?n=kurdish-women-fight-for-woman-rights-deputy-says-2010-06-30.

"Kurdish Women in Southeast Turkey Grow Strong Support Networks." Originally printed in *Hürriyet Daily News*, December 10, 2010. http://www.peacewomen.org/news_article.php?id=2589&type=news.

"Labor, Democracy and Freedom Block Elections Manifesto." *Fırat News Agency*, May 10, 2011. http://en.firatnews.com/index.php?rupel=article&nuceID=2161.

"Leyla Zana: No Freedom without Women's Freedom." *Roj.women*, March 12, 2011. http://rojwomen.com/2011/03/12/zana-no-freedom-without-womens-freedom/.

"Opened with a Flourish, Turkey's Kurdish-Language Schools Fold." *Christian Science Monitor*, October 5, 2005. http://www.csmonitor.com/2005/1005/p07s02-woeu.html.

"Patriarchy—The Enslavement of Women." From "All Articles" on the Partiya Karkerên Kurdistan (PKK) website, in English. http://www.pkkonline.com/en/index.php?sys=article&artID=56.

Pirbal, Ferhad. "When Did the Word Kurdistan Appear?" *Kurdish Globe*, August 14, 2008, 14.

S., Eda. "We Can Change . . ." Finalist in WLPS Youth Essay Contest Group 2: 18–25 years. January 16, 2011. http://wwwlearningpartnership.org/blog/2010/turkey-kurdish-women/.

Schemm, Paul. "Kurdish Fighters Offer Guerilla Feminism." *AFP*, November 28, 2006. Found on Kurdish Aspect—Kurdish News and Points of View. http://www.kurdishaspect.com/Kurdishfightersofferguerrillafeminism.html.

"Second Democratic Solution Tent in Istanbul." Dicle News Agency, March 26, 2011. http://diclenews.com/2/22/1/viewNews/248522.

"72 Women Killed in the Past Year in South East Turkey." *Rojwomen.com*, March 12, 2011. Translated by Berna Özgencil. http://rojwomen.com/2011/03/12/72-women-killed-in-the-past-year-in-the-south-east/.

Shaffer, Brenda. "Iran's Volatile Ethnic Mix." *International Herald Tribune*, June 2, 2006.

Shakely, Ferhad. "Haji Qadir Koyi." *Kurdish Globe* (Irbil-Hewler), February 7, 2010.

"Soruları ve Cevaplarıyla Demokratik Açılım Süreci: Milli Birlik ve Kardeşlik Projesi." AK Parti Tanıtım ve Medya Başkanlığı, Ocak 2010. www.akparti.org.tr/acilim220110.pdf.

"Turkey's Kurds Protest for Religious Rights Ahead of Elections." *Ekurd*, June 9, 2011. http://www.ekurd.net/mismas/articles/misc2011/6/turkey3243.htm.

"Turnout for Iraq Election Solid at 62 pct." Reuters, March 8, 2010. http://www.alertnet.org/thenews/newsdesk/LDE6270X9.html.

Uslu, Emrullah. "Turkey's Kurdish Question: Irony within Irony." *Eurasia Daily Monitor* 6, no. 37 (February 25, 2009).

Other Languages

Agri, August 5, 2012, p. 7. Fortnightly publication of KDPI. Kurdish.

"Anadil İçin Kalem Kırıldı." *Diyarbakır Haber*, January 4, 2011. http://www.diyar bakirhaber.gen.tr/haber-459-Anadil-Icin-Kalem-Kirildi.html.

"BDP Eşbaşkan Vekillleri 15 Mayıs Kürt Dil Bayramı Nedeniyle Bir Kutlama Mesajı Yayımladı." *İnternet Haber*, May 14, 2011. http://www.internethaber .com/bdpden-kurt-dil-bayrami-kutlamasi—346911h.htm#ixzz1V0p2Nv6E.

"BDP Lideri Demirtaş: AK Parti İmamlar Ordusu Kuruyor." *Milliyet*, April 6, 2011. http://www.milliyet.com.tr/bdp-lideri-demirtas-ak-parti-imamlar-ordusu -kuruyor/siyaset/sondakikaarsiv/06.04.2011/1374112/default.htm.

"BDP's Civil Disobedience Campaign Followed by Adhan in Kurdish." *Today's Zaman*, June 7, 2011. http://www.todayszaman.com/newsDetail.action;jses sionid=1UamwV2FbiDyOhsvcitqAQhJ?newsId=246518&columnistId=0.

"Belediyeden İki Dilli Levhalar." *Ergani Gündem*, December 28, 2010. http:// www.erganigundem.com/news_detail.php?id=1142.

"Brief Review of the Struggle of Kurdish Masses from the Kurdish Republic of Kurdistan to the Present." *Komala's Newsletter* 154 (January 18, 1982). Kurdish.

Çağaptay, Soner. "Women 'Appear' in Turkey's Parliament." *Hürriyet Daily News and Economic Review*, July 17, 2011. http://www.hurriyetdailynews.com/n.php ?n=women-8216appear8217-in-turkey8217s-parliament-2011-07-17.

"Diyarbakır'da Yol Levhaları Artık Kürtçe." *Radikal*, November 26, 2009. http:// www.radikal.com.tr/Radikal.aspx?aType=RadikalHaberDetayV3&ArticleID =966251&Date=13.08.2010&CategoryID=98.

"Eğitimde Anadilinin Kullanımı ve Çiftdilli Eğitim: Halkın Tutum ve Görüşleri, Türkiye Taraması 2010." *Eğitim-Sen*, February 21, 2011. http://www.egitim sen.org.tr/down/ANADIL-ANA%20RAPOR.pdf.

"Erdoğan: Kürtçe TV Başka Adımlara da Vesile Olacak." *Radikal*, January 2, 2009. http://www.radikal.com.tr/ Radikal.aspxaType=RadikalHaberDetayV 3&ArticleID=915164&Date=02.01.2009&CategoryID=98.

İmset, İsmet. *PKK Ayrılıkçı Şiddetin 20 Yılı (1973–1992)*. Ankara: Turkish Daily News Yayınları, 1993.

"KCK Davasında 'Bilinmeyen Dil' Krizi." *Radikal*, November 4, 2010. http:// www.radikal.com.tr/Radikal.aspx? aType=RadikalDetayV3&ArticleID=102 7417&CategoryID=77.

"KCK'ye Avukatlardan Boykot." *Birgün*, April 27, 2011. http://www.birgun.net /actuel_index.php?news_code=1303917357&year=2011&month=04&day =27.

"Kürtçe Serbest Mumu Seçime Kadar Yandı." Özgür Gündem, July 2, 2011. http://www.ozgur-gundem.com/.

"Kürtçe Siyasi Propagandaya 'Sözde' Serbestlik Geliyor." *Bianet*, March 26, 2010. http://bianet.org/kadin/siyaset/120910-kurtce-siyasi-propagandaya-sozde -serbestlik-geliyor.

Lutfi, Khalid ʿAbd al-Majid. *"Fi al-Dhikra al-Miʾawiyya limiladihi . . . al-Adib wal-Mufakkir al-ʿIraqi al-Kurdi ʿAbd al-Majid Lutfi."* Accessed April 12, 2011. www.aliraqi.org/forums/archive/index.

Masifi, Anwar. *Awan dallen wlatek niya ba nawi Kurdistan*. Kurdistan net. http://kurdistannet.info/indexkon.php?id=6540.

Peyamner News Agency, February 19, 2012. Accessed August 2, 2012. http://www.peyamner.com/english/PNAnews.aspx?ID=267299.

"TRT'nin Kürtçe Kanalı TRT 6 Yayına Başladı." *Zaman*, January 1, 2009. http://www.zaman.com.tr/haber.do?haberno=790806.

"12 Haziran'da seçilen kadın milletvekilleri 'rekor' kırdı." *BBC Turkey*, June 13, 2011. http://www.bbc.co.uk/turkce/haberler/2011/06/110613_turkish_electi ons_women_minorities.shtml.

"Üniversitede Kürt Dili ve Edebiyatı Bölümüne YÖK'ten Onay Çıktı." *Radikal*, March 1, 2011. http://*www.radikal.com.tr/Radikal.aspxaType=RadikalDetayV3 &ArticleID=1041536&Date=01.03.2011&CategoryID=77*.

"YÖK'ten Kürtçe Lisans Bölümüne Onay Çıktı." *Radikal*, September 23, 2011. http://www.radikal.com.tr/Radikal.aspx?aType=RadikalDetayV3&ArticleI D=1064226&Date=23.09.2011&CategoryID=77. http://www.defense.go /home/features/Iraq_Reports/Index.html.

Official Documents and Publications

Kurdistan. Organ of the Central Committee of Democratic Party of Iranian Kurdistan no. 189 (September 1992).

"Lausanne Treaty: Part 1." *HRI*. www.hri.org/docs/lausanne/part1.html.

"Party's Constitution." *PJAK website*, http://pjak.org/pers.php?id=1147.

Reaction to the Events of Kurdistan in Persian Publications. Compiled and published by the KDPI, No. 7, June 1993.

U.S. Department of Defense. *Measuring Stability and Security in Iraq: March 2009 Report to Congress*. Washington, DC. Accessed May 20, 2009. http://www.de fense.gov/home/features/Iraq_Reports/Index.html.

———. *Measuring Stability and Security in Iraq: September 2009 Report to Congress*. Washington, DC. Accessed December 15, 2009. http://www.defense .gov/home/features/Iraq_Reports/Index.html.

World Bank. *Unlocking the Employment Potential in the Middle East and North Africa: Toward a New Social Contract*. Washington, DC: World Bank Publications, 2004.

Other Languages

Constitution of the Iraqi Kurdistan Region, 2002 Draft. Accessed from the official website of Unrepresented Nations and Peoples Organization. http://www .unpo.org/article/538.

Constitution of the Iraqi Kurdistan Region, 2008 Draft. Translated by U.S. Department of State Office of Language Services Translating, August 19, 2008. Accessed from http://gjpi.org/2009/06/24/draft-kurdish-constitution/.

Constitution of the Iraqi Kurdistan Region, 2009 Draft. Accessed from the official website of Max Planck Institute for Comparative Public Law and International Law: http://www.mpil.de/ww/en/pub/research/details/know_transfer/iraq/legal_documents/constitution.cfm.

Drafts of the Constitution. Official 2009 Draft accessed from the KRG website, http://www.krg.org/uploads/documents/Draft_constitution_Kurdistan_2009_06_22_h12m34s53.pdf.

KRG-ME, Kurdistan Regional Government—Ministry of Education. *Mejuy Sharistaniyakan Poli Chwarami Wejayi*. Lebanon: Al-Mustaqbal Press, 2006.

———. *Babaten Komalayati Pola Penje Saratayi*. Erbil: Ministry of Education, 2004.

———. *Mejuy Nwe w Hawcharkh Poli Dwazdahami Amadayi Wejayi*. 4th ed. Lebanon: Al-Mustaqbal Press, 2008.

Kurdish Democratic Party of Iran (KDPI). "Asnad-e Kongereh-e Dahom-e Hezb-e Demokrat-e Kordestan-e Iran." April 1995.

Kurdistan Institute for Political Issues (KIPI). *Rapirsi lasar Pirsi Ziman u Nasnama la Kurdistan*. Accessed June 20, 2008. http://www.rojev.org/index.php.

———. *La Hawlatiyawa bo Dasalat*. Erbil: Mukiryan, 2007.

RI-ME, Republic of Iraq—Ministry of Education. *Al-Mujaz fi al-Jugrafiya wa al-Ta'rikh hasab Manhaj al-Sufuf al-Sadisa al-Ibtida'iyya*. Baghdad: Ministry of Education, 1961.

———. *Al-Ta'rikh al-ʿArabi al-Islami lil-Saf al-Thani al-Mutawassit*. Baghdad: Ministry of Education, 2003.

———. *Al-Ta'rikh al-Hadith lil-Watan al-ʿArabi lil-Saf al-Sadis al-Ibtida'i*. 3rd ed. Baghdad: Ministry of Education, 1980.

———. *Al-Ta'rikh al-Hadith wa al-Muʿasir lil-Watan al-ʿArabi lil-Saf al-Sadis al-Adabi*. 18th ed. Baghdad: Ministry of Education, 2001.

———. *Al-Ta'rikh al-Hadith wa al-Muʿasir lil-Watan al-ʿArabi lil-Saf al-Thalith al-Mutawassit*. 18th ed. Baghdad: Ministry of Education, 2009.

———. *Al-Ta'rikh al-Hadith wa al-Muʿasir lil-Watan al-ʿArabi lil-Saf al-Sadis al-Adabi*. 25th ed. Baghdad: Ministry of Education, 2009.

———. *Al-Ta'rikh al-Qadim lil-Watan al-ʿArabi lil-Saf al-Awwal al-Mutawassit*. 12th ed. Baghdad: Ministry of Education, 2000.

Contributors

ELI AMARILYO holds a PhD in Middle Eastern Studies from Tel-Aviv University (2008). He is a researcher and lecturer at the Interdisciplinary Center in Herzliya and specializes in the modern history of Iraq. His doctoral thesis was on tribalism, ethnicity, and sectarianism in Iraq between 1920 and 1958. The thesis was published as a book by the Moshe Dayan Center at Tel-Aviv University in 2011. The English version is forthcoming.

DUYGU ATLAS is a native of Izmir, Turkey. She completed her BA degree at Ege University in Izmir and her MA degree in Middle Eastern History at Tel-Aviv University. She is currently a PhD candidate at Tel-Aviv University, School of History and a junior researcher at the Moshe Dayan Center for Middle Eastern and African Studies. She is the program coordinator of the Süleyman Demirel Program for Contemporary Turkish Studies. She is also on the editorial board of the Middle East News Brief and is the cofounder of the center's new audiovisual library. In her research, she focuses on the cultural and social history of Turkey, minorities in Turkey, and contemporary Turkish politics. Her published articles include "Turkey: A Conservative Road" (*Tel-Aviv Notes* 6, no. 13 [July 10, 2012]) and "Turkey's Elections: Erdoğan's Partial Mandate" (*Tel-Aviv Notes* 5, no. 12 [June 26, 2011]).

HEIDI BASCH-HAROD holds an MA degree from Tel-Aviv University and is a research assistant at the Moshe Dayan Center for Middle Eastern and African Studies at Tel-Aviv University. Her research interests include the Israeli-Palestinian conflict and the status of women in the Middle East and North Africa.

OFRA BENGIO is professor emeritus of Middle East History and a senior research fellow at the Moshe Dayan Center for Middle Eastern and African Studies, Tel-Aviv University. Her fields of specialization are contemporary Middle Eastern history, the modern and contemporary politics of Iraq, and the Arabic language. She is the author of *The Turkish-Israeli Relationship: Changing Ties of Middle Eastern Outsiders* (2004, in Hebrew); *Türkiye İsrail: Hayalet İttifaktan Stratejik İşbirliğine* (2009, in Turkish); and *The Kurds of Iraq: Building a State within a State* (2012). She edited, with Gabriel Ben-Dor, *Minorities and the State in the Arab World* (1999) and *Women in the Middle East: Between Tradition and Change* (1999, in Hebrew), and, with Meir Litvak, *The Sunna and Shiʿa in History: Division and Ecumenism in the Muslim Middle East* (2012). She translated *The Love and Wine Poems of Abu Nuwas* (1999, Hebrew) and, with Shmuel Regolant, *Mahmoud Darwish: Like Almond Flowers or Further* (2008); *Nazim Hikmet: Blue-Eyed Giant* (Tel-Aviv: Hakibbutz Hameuhad, 2009); *Kurdish Revolt in Iraq* (1989, Hebrew) and *Saddam Speaks on the Gulf Crisis, A Collection of Documents* (1991); and *Saddam's Word* (1998).

NADER ENTESSAR is professor and chair of the Department of Political Science and Criminal Justice at the University of South Alabama. His research focuses on ethnonationalism in the Middle East and Iranian domestic and foreign policy. He is the author and/or editor of several books and articles. His most recent book is *Kurdish Politics in the Middle East* (Lexington Books, 2010).

MICHAEL EPPEL holds a PhD from Tel-Aviv University. He is associate professor in the Department of Middle Eastern History at the University of Haifa and in the Oranim College of Education. He was head of the Department of Middle Eastern History, University of Haifa (2008–2011) and visiting professor in the Department of History at the University of Minnesota, Minneapolis (2007–2008). He is the author of *The Palestine Conflict in the History of Modern Iraq* (Frank Cass, 1994) and *Iraq from Monarchy to Tyranny: From Hashemites to the Rise of Saddam* (University Press of Florida, 2004). He has written numerous articles about inter-Arab and international relations, society and politics in the Arab states, the Arab-Israeli conflict, the social conditions of the political arena in Arab states, the history of Iraq, Syrian-Iraqi relations, the involvement of Russia and China in the Middle East, and Kurdistan and the Kurds in Iraq since Saddam Husayn. He has been interviewed by the

Israeli, Swedish, American, Polish, German, Italian, Brazilian, Chinese, and Kurdish Iraqi press and electronic media.

RACHEL KANTZ FEDER is a PhD candidate at Tel-Aviv University, School of History. She was awarded the international Dan David Prize for her doctoral work on revivalism and modernization in Shiʻism and the evolution of Muhammad Baqir al-Sadr's intellectual project. Her most recent article is "Fatima's Revolutionary Image in *Fadak fi al-Taʼrikh*: The Inception of Muhammad Baqir al-Sadr's Intellectual and Political Activism," *British Journal of Middle Eastern Studies*, Special Issue: Intellectuals in the Modern Middle East, January 2014.

She is also a lecturer at Tel-Aviv University and a junior researcher at the Moshe Dayan Center for Middle Eastern and African Studies, where she focuses on Iraqi history and politics, modern Shiʻi history, political Islam, and legal history.

SHERKO KIRMANJ earned his PhD in international studies at the University of South Australia. He is currently a visiting senior lecturer at the University of Utara Malaysia (2013–). He was visiting academic at the University of South Australia serving also as a post-doctoral research fellow, Ministry of Higher Education, Kurdistan Regional Government, Iraq (2012–2013). He lectured at the College of Law and Politics at the University of Salahaddin, Erbil, Kurdistan (2010–2011). He is the author of *Identity and Nation in Iraq* (Lynne Rienner, 2013) and *Politicisation of Islam: The Phenomenon of Islamism* (Sardam House for Publishing, 2005). He has published widely in Kurdish newspapers and has been interviewed broadly by the Kurdish press and electronic media.

BENYAMIN NEUBERGER is professor emeritus of political science at the Open University of Israel. He holds BA and MA degrees in political science, economics, and African studies from the Hebrew University of Jerusalem, and a PhD degree in political science from Columbia University in New York. As a visiting professor he also taught at the University of Pennsylvania, Haverford College, the University of Cape Town, and the University of Swaziland. From 2003 to 2005 he was senior associate member at St Antony's College at Oxford University and a visiting scholar at Oxford's Yarnton Centre for Jewish and Hebrew Studies. In 2011 he was a visiting scholar at Brandeis University. He has published widely on nationalism, ethnicity, religion and state, and democracy in Africa, the Middle East, and Israel.

HUSSEIN TAHIRI has completed his PhD in political science at the University of Melbourne, Australia. He has worked as a lecturer, teaching Middle East politics. He is the author of *The Structure of Kurdish Society and the Struggle for a Kurdish State* (Mazda Publishers, 2007). He has co-edited a book, contributed chapters to other books, and written numerous academic and commentary articles. He is a commentator on Kurdish and Middle East affairs in the Australian and international media. He is currently an adjunct associate professor with the Centre for Cultural Diversity and Well-Being at Victoria University, Melbourne, Australia.

JORDI TEJEL is research professor at the International History Department of the Graduate Institute of International and Development Studies in Geneva, Switzerland. His most recent books include *Irak: chronique d'un chaos annoncé* (Lavauzelle, 2006), *Le mouvement kurde de Turquie en exile. Continuités et discontinuités du nationalisme kurde sous le mandat français en Syrie et au Liban (1925–1946)* (Peter Lang, 2007), *Syria's Kurds: History, Politics and Society* (Routledge, 2009), and *Writing the Modern History of Iraq: Historiographical and Political Challenges*, edited by Jordi Tejel, Peter Sluglett, Riccardo Bocco, and Hamit Bozarslan (World Scientific, 2012).

HAY EYTAN COHEN YANAROCAK holds an MA from Tel-Aviv University. He is a junior researcher at the Moshe Dayan Center for Middle Eastern and African Studies and a doctoral candidate in Tel-Aviv University's School of History. As an academic who is a native Turkish speaker he has written several academic articles and op-eds that analyze the fundamentals of contemporary Turkish politics, Turkish foreign policy, Turkey's national security, and Turkish society. He has been interviewed by the Turkish, Israeli, American, Dutch, and Kurdish Iraqi press and electronic media.

RONEN ZEIDEL is deputy head of the Center for Iraq Studies at the University of Haifa. His research, which is based on Iraqi novels, focuses on culture, society, and identity in modern Iraq. He teaches at the universities of Haifa, Jerusalem, and Tel-Aviv. He has published dozens of articles in leading journals in America, Europe, Israel, and Iraq (in Arabic).

EYAL ZISSER is the dean of the Faculty of Humanities at Tel-Aviv University. He was the director of the Moshe Dayan Center for Middle

Eastern and African Studies from 2007 to 2010 and was head of the Department of Middle Eastern and African History. He has written extensively on the history and modern politics of Syria and Lebanon and on the Arab-Israeli conflict. Among his books are *Assad's Syria at a Crossroads* (Tel-Aviv, 1999); *Asad's Legacy: Syria in Transition* (New York, 2000); *Lebanon: The Challenge of Independence* (London, 2000); *Faces of Syria* (Tel-Aviv, 2003); *Commanding Syria: Bashar al-Asad's First Years in Power* (London, 2006); and *The Bleeding Cedar* (Tel-Aviv, 2009).

Index

Index **357**

Bagikhani, Nazan, 184
Bahçeli, Devlet, 146, 153
Bahdinan, 53, 110
Bahrain, 207
Bakdash, Khalid, 18, 196
Baktashiyya, 48
Ballisan, 110
Baluba, 16, 31
Baluchis, 15, 234, 265
Baneh, 73, 244, 247
Barres, Maurice, 19
Barzani, 61, 67, 75–78, 88, 109, 114,
    116, 220, 238, 253, 258, 259, 260,
    272
Barzani, Mas'ud, 8, 101, 108, 109, 114,
    116, 204, 207, 260, 270
Barzani, Mulla Mustafa, 26, 33,
    75–78, 161, 204, 207, 220, 238,
    258, 259, 261, 272, 279
Barzani, Neçirvan, 270
Barzinja, 66
Barzinji, Mahmud, [Shaykh Mahmud;
    Sheikh Mahmud], 70, 77, 88, 93,
    253
Basra, 46, 50, 52
Ba'th, 97, 98, 103, 108, 120, 122, 127,
    130, 218, 223, 237, 238; coup of
    March 1963, 199, 201–203
Batman, 167, 169
Battle of Chaldiran, 46
Battle of Malazgird, 43
Bazargan, Mehdi, 240, 241
Bedir Khan, Ali, 67
Bedouins, 52, 126
Beg, Tughril, 43
Begzadeh, 68
Bekaa Valley, 144
Berbers, 15, 16, 22, 26, 31, 65
Berlin Conference, 245
Beşikçi, Ismail, 281
Bey, 'Ali, 53
Biafra, 29, 30, 31, 32, 34
Biafran War, 32
Bidlis, 46, 48, 49, 59
Bidlisi, Mevlana Idris, 45
Bilad al-Sham, 194, 195
Bismil, 169

Black Sea, 55, 58
Black September, 86
Board of Higher Education (YÖK),
    165
Botan, 53, 55, 57, 58
Bozlak, Murat, 144
Bradost, 53, 66, 67, 68, 72, 76
British-Iraqi Treaty, 86
Bucak, Faik, 162
Bucak, Mustafa Remzi, 161
Bukan, 247
Burkay, Kemal, 151
Bush, George, 207
Butimar, Hiwa, 247
Buwayhid, 42, 43
Byzantine Empire, 39, 40, 43

calendar, Kurdish, 87
Caliph 'Uthman, 40
Caucasus, 42, 43, 44, 51, 58, 234
Chagatay, 20
Chaldeans, 110
Chamran, Mustafa, 250
Chelebi, Evliya, 48, 177
Christians, 30, 40, 45, 51, 55, 56, 57,
    203, 209, 224, 234, 265
Chwar Chira Square, 259
Çiftkuran, Zahit, 168
Circassians, 153, 198
civil disobedience, 149–150, 167, 278
Cizre, 59,168
CNN Türk, 147, 151
Committee for the Independence of
    Kurdistan, 20
Conference for National Salvation,
    210
Constitutional Court of Turkey, 143,
    144, 145, 146, 148
Copenhagen criteria, 163
Cote Française des Somalis, 16
Council of Guardians, 244
coup d'état of 1971, 140, 162
coup d'état of 1980, 141, 162
Çubuk, 140

Damascus, 24, 126, 127, 169, 196,
    197, 200, 204, 206, 207, 213, 219,